PRAISE FOR
BUSINESS EDUCATION AND
THE NOBLE PURPOSE OF THE MARKET

"Offers profound and transformational ways for business schools to catch up to 21st century corporate realities. This is the intellectual foundation for the next generation of business leaders. Society needs it, industry is ready for it, and students are demanding it."

> **—PAUL POLMAN**, former CEO of Unilever; coauthor of *Net Positive: How Courageous Companies Thrive by Giving More Than They Take*

"Professor Hoffman is bringing one of capitalism's core tenets, creative destruction, to business schools. He is offering a curriculum that the next generation of students need and demand."

> **—CAROLINE CHISHOLM**, MBA 2023; Senior Consultant, EY-Parthenon

"How do we transform a market system that is responsible for the climate crisis and social injustice? Andrew Hoffman's recommendations for business education are both radical and pragmatic. While warning about the inefficiency of small peripheral changes, he does not advocate for a tabula rasa. Instead, acknowledging the versatility of capitalism, he advocates for a move beyond shareholder capitalism and urges business schools to place nature and social justice at the heart of their curriculum. His book is a tremendous source of inspiration for any academic and business leader, teacher, or student passionate about transforming business schools and driving meaningful change in the business world."

> **—LAURENT MUZELLEC**, Dean of the Trinity Business School, Trinity College Dublin

"Rigorous, accessible, and full of good ideas. With clear moral urgency, Hoffman outlines how unfettered capitalism is risking the future of life on this planet, notably through environmental collapse and political unrest borne of gross economic disparities. This book shows why business schools have failed to address these facts, and how we can fix that. I'd recommend this to any business student or business leader. A new capitalism, outlined here, might reacquaint managers with the social purpose of our work. It might also give us a future."

—**JOHN BENJAMIN**, MBA 2018; Startup Operator and Business
Writer for *Time*, *The New Republic*, and *Barron's*

"Makes a compelling case for rethinking the core principles taught in business schools to address the pressing challenges of our planet. A call to action for educators, policymakers, and business leaders, this book is a blueprint for creating a more equitable and resilient future."

—**ANDRÉ HOFFMANN**, Vice-Chair of Roche; coauthor of *The New
Nature of Business: The Path to Prosperity and Sustainability*

"As an MBA student coming from a military and nonprofit background, I feared I might have to compromise my values to succeed in business. However, Professor Andrew Hoffman's work is a beacon of hope in what sometimes seems like a bleak tomorrow."

—**AKBAR ARSIWALA**, MBA 2024; Navy Veteran;
Senior Marketing Associate, Nike

"Andy Hoffman is one of the world's most thoughtful and impactful critics of higher education in business and management. There is as much in this work with which I disagree – sometimes strongly – as there is with which I agree. I predict it will move your priors, as it did mine. This conversation must be had and now."

—**ANDREW KAROLYI**, Dean and Professor, SC Johnson
College of Business, Cornell University; Board Chair,
Responsible Research in Business & Management

"A piercing wake-up call for business education to cultivate a new type of leader; one who creates both prosperity and purpose, serving shareholders and society alike. To read it as a business student is to discover a renewed vision of capitalism as a powerful force for good."

—**ELI FORRESTER**, MBA 2024; cofounder and COO, Volta

"I would highly recommend this book to all academic leaders wanting to understand the disconnect between the curricula of leading business schools and the major societal and environmental challenges the world and businesses face. Hoffman argues that most business schools have merely dropped an elective or two as a saddlebag onto the problematic traditional curriculum. As a business school Dean for the past over 18 years, I can confidently state that the barriers as stated in the book can be overcome by courage and leadership."

—**SANJAY SHARMA**, Dean of the Grossman School of Business, University of Vermont

"If you're enrolled in business school, or already have an MBA, you should read this book. It questions the role that business schools play in training and influencing future generations of leaders. Will we idly stand by and hope that today's business school programs, curriculums and cultures will equip students to wrangle complex problems around climate change and capitalism's 'externalities?' Or can we harness and redirect the ambition of business school education? Hoffman's book gives us this vision."

—**AMELIA BRINKERHOFF**, MBA 2022; Senior Associate, Sustainability & Climate Transformation Consulting, PwC

"While my business school education helped prepare me for the market that we've known for decades, I found it difficult to challenge the status quo with any sort of critical questions. This is the book we all need to have the larger discussion of our economic systems, the way business and society interacts, and how to create a sustainable world for future generations."

—**COLTON BABLADELIS**, MBA 2022; Project Manager, Positive Scenarios Consulting

"Business has the potential to be one of our most powerful levers for change, but it requires a transformative shift, addressing the urgent systemic challenges of climate change and income inequality. This book prepares students to make a positive impact."

—LEXX MILLS, MBA 2022; cofounder and CEO, Revvl

"Hoffman offers a refreshing vision for business programs that imbue students with a sense of moral duty and a concern for societal good. As someone who came to business school to learn how the private sector could better address climate change, Hoffman's reimagined vision of the MBA is one that I wish I had access to. This book is an antidote to cynicism and an indispensable resource for educators, students, and business leaders committed to meaningful change."

—KATHERINE CUNNINGHAM, MBA 2021; Senior Associate, Climate Tech Policy and Sales Consulting, The Ad Hoc Group

"If the recommended actions Professor Hoffman outlines to correct the failures of shareholder capitalism and update business education are implemented, every industry and every person will be changed for the better. Only since graduating from business school have I come to understand the consequences of misaligned incentives on our healthcare and food systems specifically, and this devil's bargain is why Americans are getting sicker, fatter, and more infertile every year. This is the book I wish I had read before getting my MBA and should be required reading for any leader."

—SONJA MANNING, MBA 2021; Health & Wellness Entrepreneur, Sonja Manning LLC

"*Business School and the Noble Purpose of the Market* argues that to turn the market to a force for good, we need business leaders who push beyond 'making the business case' and bravely ask the harder questions that can move us beyond shareholder capitalism. Drawing on years of experience teaching in leading business schools, Professor Hoffman lays out a call to action for students, professors, and administrators to demand and drive this much-needed reformation."

—IAN MAKOWSKE, MBA 2016; Finance, Rivian

"This may be the most consequential decade for business leaders to figure out how to thrive amid the economic transformation caused by climate change. Business schools urgently need to update their curricula to prepare graduates for this upheaval. By challenging the outdated doctrines of short-term shareholder capitalism, *Business School and the Noble Purpose of the Market* offers a blueprint for doing just that. I hope business leaders and faculty alike will take this call to action seriously, so that we can grow the business leaders we need to accelerate the transition and drive prosperity for all."

—**ALEXIS HAASS**, MBA 2007; former Chief Sustainability Officer, Arcadis

"Recent decades have shown that addressing social and environmental challenges while still clinging to 'shareholder primacy' is not going to drive the systemic change we need. This book is a must read for students and future business leaders who want to find market-driven solutions to today's challenges."

—**EMILY HANNING**, MBA 2005; Vice President,
Food & Nutrition, Lifelong: Health for All

"Very few of us have purely monetary incentives in life, so why should money be the sole focus of a business school education? The ideas in this book have dramatically influenced how I view my role as a leader within my organization and the values I want to embody as my career grows."

—**TOM KRAEUTLER**, MBA 2023; Supplier Decarbonization
Manager, Thermo Fisher Scientific

BUSINESS SCHOOL AND
THE NOBLE PURPOSE OF THE MARKET

BUSINESS SCHOOL
and the
NOBLE PURPOSE
of the
MARKET

Correcting the Systemic Failures
of Shareholder Capitalism

ANDREW J. HOFFMAN

STANFORD BUSINESS BOOKS

AN IMPRINT OF STANFORD UNIVERSITY PRESS • STANFORD, CALIFORNIA

Stanford University Press
Stanford, California

Special discounts for bulk quantities of Stanford Business Books are available to corporations, professional associations, and other organizations. For details and discount information, contact the special sales department of Stanford University Press by emailing sales@www.sup.org.

Library of Congress Cataloging-in-Publication Data
Names: Hoffman, Andrew J., 1961- author.
Title: Business school and the noble purpose of the market : correcting the systemic failures of shareholder capitalism / Andrew J. Hoffman.
Description: Stanford, California : Stanford Business Books, an imprint of Stanford University Press, 2025. | Includes bibliographical references and index.
Identifiers: LCCN 2024038052 (print) | LCCN 2024038053 (ebook) | ISBN 9781503642461 (cloth) | ISBN 9781503642478 (ebook)
Subjects: LCSH: Industrial management—Study and teaching—United States. | Business education—Moral and ethical aspects—United States. | Business ethics—Study and teaching—United States. | Social responsibility of business—United States. | Capitalism—Moral and ethical aspects—United States.
Classification: LCC HD30.42.U6 H64 2025 (print) | LCC HD30.42.U6 (ebook) | DDC 650.071/173—dc23/eng/20240924
LC record available at https://lccn.loc.gov/2024038052
LC ebook record available at https://lccn.loc.gov/2024038053

Cover design: Martyn Schmoll

Contents

Illustrations and Tables

FIGURES

TABLES

Why I Am Writing This Book Now

"Speak the truth and all nature and all spirits help you with unexpected furtherance. Speak the truth, and all things alive or brute are vouchers, and the very roots of the grass underground there, do seem to stir and move to bear you witness."

—RALPH WALDO EMERSON

This book is a provocation and a call to arms. It comes at a time when business education, as I have experienced it, is at a crossroads. Systemic failures of shareholder capitalism, notably (but not only) climate change and income inequality, pose threats to the stability of the natural and social worlds on which we depend and must coexist. And yet, while many, both inside and outside the market system, call for change, business schools have been slow to respond, continuing to teach the same curriculum that feeds those systemic problems within capitalism. It is time for a fundamental rethink of business school education and research.

I come to this conclusion after having spent the last thirty years in business schools focusing on environmental protection and sustainability. In the early 1990s, the simple choice to study these issues in a business school was viewed as radical, or perhaps misguided. More recently, the topic has gained acceptance but only insofar as it is adapted to fit within the market's existing norms and structures, framing issues like climate change and species extinction as market concerns and ways to increase profits. I employed this approach early in my career, thinking it would appeal to business leaders who could address these issues as business problems to be solved without delving into their underlying implications. Over time I came to see that this approach has two significant drawbacks.

First, it oversimplifies complex issues, ignoring their moral aspects. As journalist Anand Giridharadas has argued, "When [the market] becomes the only language . . . it leaves us with a very impoverished sense of how to live together. It's good for creating wealth and creating things and building things, but it's not . . . a useful vocabulary for living together."[1] Instead of making the business case to address climate change, for example, author Duane Elgin asks, "When will humanity express its moral outrage that it is wrong to devastate an entire planet for countless generations to come, just to satisfy the consumer desires of a fraction of humanity for a single lifetime?"[2] As business schools continue to fixate on the business case to justify any action our students can take as business leaders, we are leaving them impoverished for addressing many of the serious challenges they will face.

Second, I came to realize that we must shift from fitting sustainability into existing capitalist systems to reshaping these systems around sustainability. Climate change is not, in its truest sense, an environmental issue; it is a systems breakdown. By the same token, wealth and income inequality—another focus of this book—is not just a simple problem that requires a band-aid fix. While some conveniently call these problems "externalities" or "unintended consequences," they are actually embedded in our economic systems. We are creating them by misguided design. Therefore, the solutions must go far deeper. To fix these systemic failures, we must fix the systems that caused them. Those systems are business, the market, and capitalism.

So, in recent years, I've revamped my teaching approach, developing new courses that address the deeper questions that face capitalism today, focusing on the intersection of the market, business, public policy, and society. In one course, "Business in Democracy: Advocacy, Lobbying and the Public Interest," I bring together business and public policy students in a cross-listed format to examine the issue of responsible lobbying and ways in which business and government can work together. In another, "Reexamining Capitalism," I teach business students to be stewards of the economy by exposing them to the foundational thinking of capitalism (both analysis and critique from Adam Smith, Karl Marx, and more), how it is viewed today from both the left and right ends of the political spectrum, the many forms that exist around the world and ways that it can be amended. In a third course, "Management as a Calling," I guide students through exercises to discern their vocation in business to serve society. This last course challenged me to adopt a different mode as professor, acting less as a knowledge source and more as a guide, placing students into a context in which they can discern their own path and purpose for themselves.

I am proud of these courses, and all of this new teaching informs the contents of this book. But they are still not enough. Offering individual electives in a broader curriculum that remains fixated on stale notions of shareholder primacy and virtuous greed can only have limited effect. We need to rethink the structure, pedagogy, and purpose of business education. Just as we need systemic solutions within the market, we also need systemic solutions within business education.

That is where my attention now lies. At this point in my career, I am shifting my emphasis away from the extrinsic metrics by which college professors are judged—publishing only academic journal articles to amass endless citation counts—and more towards the intrinsic motivations for why I got into this profession in the first place—to make a difference in how business interacts with the natural environment and makes a better society. I am now in a position where my focus is not on elevating my own professional status but instead helping those who come after me and the institutions in which they are being developed.

So, with this book, I want to encourage others to do the same, whether they be students, faculty, administrators, alumni, recruiters; anyone who cares about business education and its role in creating a better future. The market is a place where we can—indeed we must—address the grand challenges of our day. I want to encourage all who read this book to follow essayist Ralph Waldo Emerson's admonishment to "speak the truth" and help transform business education. If you do, Emerson offers the encouraging news that "all spirits help you with unexpected furtherance."[3] Visionary business leaders are needed more than ever, and I want to motivate all who read this book to embrace the challenge of being a catalyst for constructive and aspirational change in a world that desperately needs it.

Andrew J. Hoffman

Ann Arbor, MI

Part I

RETHINKING THE PURPOSE
OF BUSINESS EDUCATION

ONE

Business Schools Are Broken

It's Time to Fix Them

"The time has come . . . to rejuvenate intellectually and morally the training of our future business leaders."
—RAKESH KHURANA, HARVARD UNIVERSITY

Today's business schools were designed for a world that no longer exists, one that elevated the primacy of shareholder profits above the interests of employees, the environment or broader society; viewed government more as an intrusion on the free market than an arbiter of its proper functioning; and promoted unlimited economic growth despite the obvious physical, environmental, and economic limitations on such a goal. Given this, (largely Western) business schools are not preparing future leaders with the skills, knowledge, and wisdom they will need to deal with planetary challenges such as climate change and social challenges at home such as widening income inequality. It is time to rejuvenate the business school curriculum to turn the power of business and the market towards a role that is more consistent with its place within society.

The market, comprising business, government, civil society, and others, is the most powerful set of organizing institutions on Earth, and business is the most powerful entity within it. In fact, the past 150 years of capitalism have been tremendously successful in addressing the problems of society. It can be credited with raising the standard of living for billions of people by increasing the world economy by a factor of 14, tripling the global per capita income, extending average life expectancy by almost two-thirds, and decreasing the number of people living in extreme poverty from 56 percent in 1920 to 10 percent today.[1] This advance in prosperity is due in large part to advances in medicine, shelter, food production, and other amenities brought about by the market.

Businesses will continue to play a role in addressing humanity's challenges—but it's not clear whether it will be a positive one. To be sure, businesses hold enormous powers of ideation, production, and distribution to provide solutions to society's problems at the scale we need them. They also hold the potential to multiply the effects of the darkest of human impulses and result in exploitation, materialism, and greed.[2] To tip the scale in the right direction, there is an urgent need to nurture a new breed of business leaders who view business not only as a means to profitability but also as a vehicle to serve society. As Hubert Joly, former CEO of Best Buy, writes in his book *The Heart of Business*, it is time to reconnect with the noble purpose of business and bring about the "next era of capitalism."[3] Crucially, leaders that take this path should be acutely aware of the current shortcomings and ethical dilemmas inherent in today's capitalism. And they should see it as their duty to guide this system towards a more equitable model that better responds to the complexities and challenges of the twenty-first century. As I will argue later, business schools are currently not producing enough of these leaders.

The Market's Failures in Our Natural and Social Environments

Today's version of capitalism is encountering critical issues that it isn't equipped to tackle. Humanity stands at a pivotal juncture, facing numerous profound challenges requiring immediate action. Key concerns include the perils (and opportunities) of advanced artificial intelligence, the continued use of forced labor, gender and racial inequality, persistent global poverty, conflict and hunger, the lingering threat of nuclear weapons, and increasing worries about future global pandemics, to name just a few. However, this book narrows its focus to climate change and wealth inequality. That is because these challenges feel particularly grave, and because there is no greater indictment of our current economic system than the looming specter of systemic failures in both our natural and social environments.

The Market's Failure in Our Natural Environment

At this point, the arithmetic of climate change is both well-known and ter-rifying. Scientists have established 350 ppm as the safe limit for atmospheric CO_2 to preserve our stable environment. However, human activities since the Industrial Revolution have raised this level to 421 ppm in 2022, leading to a 1°C (1.8°F) rise in global temperatures.[4] This temperature rise is already causing more frequent and intense natural disasters such as wildfires, droughts, and hurricanes, along with sea-level rise, disease spread, species extinction, and more.

Some scientists warn that if we don't reverse current rises in CO_2 levels by 2030, damage to the global climate will be irreversible.[5] If we reach a rise of 3°C (5.4°F), risks of crossing irreversible "tipping points" increase dramatically.[6] On our current trajectory, temperature rise could exceed 4°C (7.2°F) by the of the century.[7] If we allow the trends to go that far, we will not be able to simply adapt or innovate our way out of the problem. For example, human life cannot survive at so-called "wet bulb" temperatures above 35°C (95°F) which, taking into account both temperature and humidity, corresponds to a temperature of 35°C (95°F) at 100 percent humidity, 46°C (115°F) at 50 percent humidity, or 50°C (122°F) at 35 percent humidity. Beyond these thresholds the human body can no longer cool itself by evaporating sweat to maintain a stable body core temperature. These thresholds have already been crossed in some regions around the world. In 2017, India recorded its highest temperature of 51°C (124°F), and in 2023, China recorded its highest temperature of 52.2°C (126°F). These temperatures were experienced in populated regions that, according to experts, tested "the limits of human survivability."[8]

Some estimates of the potential global economic damage from climate change reach a present-discounted value of $22.5 trillion by 2100 in lost labor productivity, declining crop yields, food shortages, early deaths, property damage, breakdown of infrastructure networks, water shortages, air pollu-tion, flooding, fires, and more.[9] The Bank for International Settlements, an umbrella organization for the world's central banks, warned in 2020 that cli-mate change could be one of the largest economic dislocations in history.[10] Beyond the direct economic costs to the economy, climate change will dis-place millions of people around the world, stressing the supply of humanitar-ian aid and causing massive climate migrations that will have an impact on national borders. In 2023, UNICEF reported that at least forty-three million children alone were displaced by extreme weather events, most notably floods and storms, over the prior six years.[11] Unfettered capitalism is causing these problems to happen; unfettered capitalism can't fix them.

The Market's Failure in Our Social Environment

Our society is becoming dangerously unequal as disparities in economic wealth and opportunity grow to levels not seen in the United States since the Gilded Age in the 1870s–1890s. Figure 1.1 shows that the share of national income earned by the top 1 percent doubled between 1980 and 2016 while the share for the bottom 50 percent was cut nearly in half. That has led to a vast concentration of wealth over time. By 2014 in the United States, "the top 1% of households possessed 38.6% of the nation's wealth, compared with – 0.1% (that's right) for the bottom 50%."[12] By 2017, the country's three richest individuals—Bill Gates, Warren Buffett, and Jeff Bezos—collectively held more wealth than the bottom 50 percent of the domestic population, a total of 160 million people, and roughly one fifth of Americans had "zero or negative net worth."[13] According to the Rand Corporation, between 1975 and 2020, $50 trillion was transferred from the bottom 90 percent of US wage earners to the top 1 percent.[14] By 2023, the twenty-six richest billionaires had more money than the US Treasury,[15] and 76 percent of the total wealth in the United States was owned by the top 10 percent of earners while the lowest 50 percent of earners only owned 1 percent.[16] A result of this inequality has been a hollowing out of the middle class (see Figure 1.2), whose share of aggregate income fell from 62 percent in 1970 to 43 percent in 2018, compared to an increase for upper-income households from 29 percent to 48 percent and a decrease for lower-income households from 10 percent to 9 percent. Overall, the share of American adults who live in middle-income households decreased steadily from 61 percent in 1971 to 51 percent in 2019.[17]

With statistics like that, it should be no surprise that the United States's Gini coefficient (a measure of an economy's equality wherein a score of 0 correlates with perfect equality and everyone has an equal share in everything and a score of 1 correlates with complete inequality and one person owns everything) rose from 0.35 in 1980 to 0.49 in 2021, which ranks it as more unequal than many countries, including India, Kenya, and Russia.

And this has been happening around the world (see Figure 1.3) as, accord-

FIGURE 1.1

Income Share of the Top 1% and Bottom 50% in the US, 1980–2016

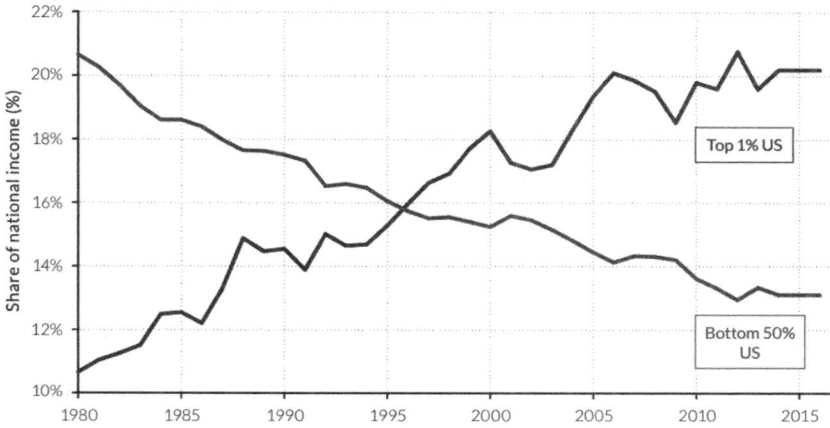

FIGURE 1.2

The Decline of the Middle Class in the US, 1970–2018

The gaps in wealth between upper-income and middle- and lower-income families are rising, and the share held by middle-income families is falling

Median family wealth, in 2018 dollars, and share of U.S. aggregate family wealth, by income tier

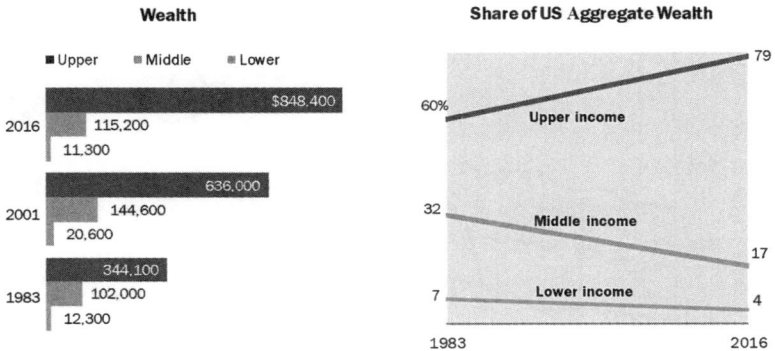

Note: Households are assigned to income tiers based on their size-adjusted income. Incomes are scaled to reflect a three-person household.

ing to one astute economic observer, "most economies are failing to provide the conditions in which their citizens can thrive, often by a large margin."[18] By 2019, the twenty-six richest billionaires mentioned above owned as many assets as the 4.6 billion people who make up the poorest 60 percent of the planet's population.[19] And that wealth kept growing. Between 2020 and 2023, the wealth of the world's five richest men more than doubled, growing three times faster than the rate of inflation, while the world's poorest 60 percent— almost 5 billion people—had actually lost money.[20] According to Oxfam, the richest 1 percent acquired nearly two-thirds of all new wealth (worth $42 trillion) created between 2020 and 2023, almost twice as much money as the bottom 99 percent of the world's population.[21]

The implications of such inequality are multiple and dangerous. One is that the wealthy become socially disconnected from the broader realities faced by the struggling majority. This detachment can lead them to exert their disproportionate influence on politics in ways that do not address or improve the living and working conditions for most people, exacerbating societal dispari-

FIGURE 1.3

Income Share of the Wealthiest 10% Around the World, 1980–2016

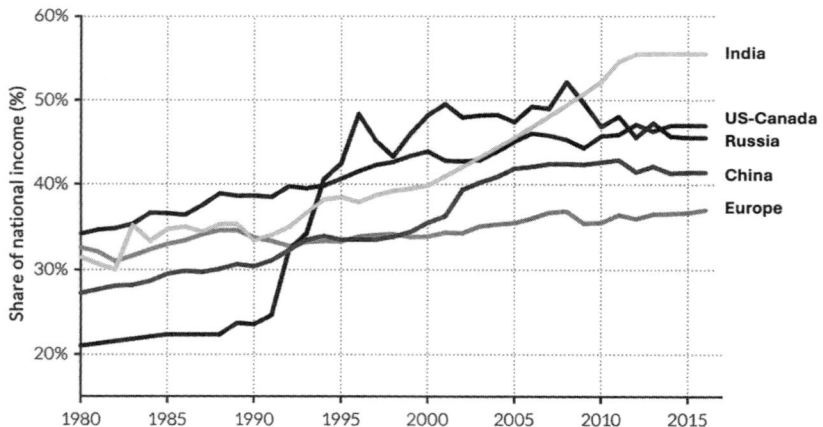

Note: In 2016, 47% of national income was received by the top 10% in US-Canada, compared to 34% in 1980.

Source: F. Alvaredo, L. Chancel, T. Piketty, E. Saez, and G. Zucman, *World Inequality Report,* 2018, https://wir2018.wid.world/ (accessed December 10, 2023). CC BY 4.0.

ties. Another danger is that large portions of the population become cynically disconnected from a political and economic system that seems unresponsive to their needs.[22] As a result, they may have no compunctions about breaking those systems, whether in the voting booth through the support of populist demagogues or in the street through increased conflict and "revolution of one sort or another."[23]

Unfortunately, warns Columbia University economist Joseph Stiglitz, these dangers of inequality are interconnected, forming a destructive cycle: increasing economic inequality leads to more political inequality in a system heavily influenced by money, which in turn leads to deregulation and weaker rules, further deepening economic disparities, and raising the risk of social unrest.[24] One need look no further than the tax code to see this cycle playing out. In 1960, the country's richest families paid 56 percent of their income in taxes, helping to fund the creation of social safety nets like Medicare, Medicaid, and food stamps; by 2018, while their share of the national income grew, their tax rate fell to only 23 percent.[25] According to a report from Oxfam, US billionaires became 46 percent richer between 2020 and 2024, yet they paid an effective average federal income tax rate of 8.2 percent compared to the average American income tax rate of 13 percent.[26] We can't count on the market to fix this as it is presently structured.

The Market Can Be Corrected to Fix These Failures

The problems described in the previous section have been caused by today's version of unfettered capitalism. Inequality and climate change are systemic failures that are the result of choices in how the market is presently structured by those in power who benefit.[27] But collectively, we can amend today's rules of capitalism so that it can be unleashed to tackle these and other mega challenges. It's easy to forget that capitalism is not an immutable law of nature. It is a system of human rules and institutions, designed in the service of humans and able to evolve when those interests are no longer served. Its nature is neither static nor uniform, and it has shown flexibility in responding to various challenges. Historical examples such as the emergence and regulation of monopoly power, the successful tackling of ozone layer depletion, the reduction of water pollution, and the mitigation of acid rain demonstrate this adaptability. The pressing question now is how capitalism will be reformed to meet the challenges of climate change and inequality in this century, particularly by those who will hold positions of power.

The reform will need to be significant. Specifically, the present system of shareholder capitalism—what is alternatively referred to as market fundamentalism or the neoliberal doctrine—must be amended into a new form of capitalism, one in which the corporation seeks to provide value to society and not just to enrich the few. New guardrails in the market will be needed to cease the endless pursuit of economic growth, the view of nature as a limitless source for materials and sink for wastes, and the mindless consumption that drives it all.[28]

For that to happen, we need a new kind of business leader, one focused on mastering the domains of commerce while also recognizing that they have an interest and responsibility in maintaining the integrity, stability, and equity of the system in which they practice that craft. Rather than exploit a broken market or political system for personal gain, future business leaders must take ownership for fixing the market.[29] As Stiglitz argues, their emphasis will need to move away from "wealth extraction . . . trying to steal a larger fraction of the economic pie" and towards "wealth creation . . . a recognition of the true sources of wealth of a country and . . . the ability to get wealthy by creating wealth and contributing to society."[30]

This is where business education enters the picture—or doesn't.

Business Education Is not Rising to the Challenge

In recent years, many business schools in the United States,[31] Europe,[32] and elsewhere have added climate change to their curriculum. But the guiding motivation behind this new focus is the business opportunity that climate change presents in the form of new products, services, and practices that address the climate challenge.[33] Selling climate solutions is an important first step, but it will not be enough. It will only slow the velocity at which we are heading towards inevitable system collapse; it will not reverse course.[34] Simply adding electives while the curriculum remains focused primarily on profits for the shareholder will fail to address the scope and scale of the challenge.

Indeed, business schools have largely focused on simplistic notions of "expanding the pie" or "win-win" solutions to address climate change—for example, teaching students how more efficient agricultural practices can also increase crop yields and thus profits. However, such solutions rely heavily on depleting groundwater and topsoil, employing excessive amounts of chemical pesticides, herbicides, and fertilizers, putting small-scale farmers out of business, making larger-scale farmers into serfs for multinational corporations, destroying rural economies, and often providing unhealthy foods that contribute to epidemics of obesity, diabetes, and cancer.[35] They ignore the more difficult (and more interesting) "win-lose" scenarios that will be necessary in a future for which deeper systemic solutions are required.[36]

How, for example, can we bring about an orderly and just transition to a carbon- and fossil-fuel-free economy?[37] It is not sufficient to hope that new energy sources and new forms of carbon capture technology will emerge to make the transition frictionless. The most likely scenario is a transition that will be painful for businesses and consumers. For instance, switching to renewables will require up-front investments. While the costs will likely be borne by utilities, they will be passed on to consumers. If the average consumer wants to take matters into their own hands, installing a new HVAC system like heat pumps will require an up-front refit of their home. Buying an electric car will require not only the up-front cost of the vehicle, but the installation of a charging station or the availability of one nearby.[38] Politicians are hesitant to call out these costs; business schools are missing an opportunity to force their students to tackle these challenging truths head on.

The reason for this failure is that business education has ossified into outdated ideas and models about the world, society, the market, business, and the people within them. The MBA in particular has become a "product" that has been packaged for students in its present and unvaried form for decades. It is fixated on fifty-year-old notions of shareholder primacy[39] and a variant of the "greed is good" mentality.[40] Business education teaches students ways to make "the business case" and gain market advantage when addressing climate change, while giving very limited attention to the pragmatic reality that we are talking about an existential threat to life on Earth or the moral reality that it is the people of the rich countries that are primarily responsible for climate change and the people of the poor countries who will feel its effects first and hardest.[41] Making only a business case around climate change is not just absurd, it's sociopathic (as Figure 1.4 humorously points out).

Indeed, corporate attorney James Gamble warns that the business case

FIGURE 1.4.

"Somehow we need to monetise this - and quickly"

Source: Cartoon by Jonesy. Originally published in *Prospect* magazine (September 2021). https://www.jonesycartoons.com/.

emphasis compels business leaders "to act like sociopaths," running their companies as "textbook case[s] of antisocial personality disorder" in which the company "is obligated to care only about itself and to define what is good as what makes it more money."[42] He may be on to something. In an era of record fossil-fuel extraction and record climate change impacts, what else can explain oil industry executives using the resources of their companies to spread misinformation about climate change to confuse the public and stall regulatory action to boost share price,[43] or a fossil-fuel industry trade group launching an eight-figure media campaign to increase the use of oil and, in the words of an industry leader, "dismantle policy threats" to the sector?[44] What can explain a multinational pharmaceutical company increasing profits by aggressively promoting a product that has killed over 450,000 people and addicted countless more?[45] What can explain a leading management consulting firm earning massive profits by not only helping that pharmaceutical company in its misinformation campaign[46] but also helping authoritarian regimes repress people in their own countries?[47] Why might a social media company adopt a slogan of "company over country" and pursue massive profits by promoting misinformation and disinformation?[48] And what can explain a former hedge fund manager acquiring the rights to a sixty-two-year-old drug and then raising the price from $13 to $750 per tablet because people need it to treat a life-threatening parasitic infection and have no choice but to pay or risk death?[49] The answer lies in a thirst for profits and money over any kind of responsibility to society.

Business journalist and writer Duff McDonald excoriates business schools for fostering such thinking, writing that the business curriculum is devoid of normative viewpoints, "has always cared less about moral leadership than career advancement and financial performance," and as a result, creates "a generation of corporate monsters" who lack "a functioning moral compass."[50] This is harsh, but I think even the most committed B-school faculty would wince in a moment of self-recognition at McDonald's description. The reality is that business schools are stuck, unable to change, even though many within them know there is a problem. What stands in the way?

How Did Business Schools Lose Their Way?

The first collegiate business school in the United States was the Wharton School at the University of Pennsylvania, founded in 1881. The Tuck School of Business at Dartmouth College was founded as the first graduate school of management in 1900, and the Harvard Graduate School of Business Administration offered the first MBA in 1908. Harvard professor Rakesh Khurana writes that these early business schools were "originally founded to train a professional class of managers in the mold of doctors and lawyers to seek the higher aims of commerce in service to society." In 1927, for example, the second dean of the Harvard Business School, Wallace B. Donham, stated in an address to the American Association of Collegiate Schools of Business that "I have reached the conclusion that the greatest need of a civilization such as ours, if it is to progress in an orderly evolution, is for socially minded business men. I am convinced that this social need is the sole basis which justifies our ancient university . . . in entering upon business training."[51] In the 1940s, the

third dean of the Harvard Business School, Donald David, repeated that ambition, declaring that there are "three important qualities of a business leader.
The first of these is competence in the management of his business activity.
The second is the development and application of social skill so as to make his
business enterprise a 'good society.' The third is the willingness to participate
constructively in the broader affairs of the community and nation."[52]

But, Khurana writes, business schools have "effectively retreated" from
these higher goals, "leaving a gaping moral hole at the center of business education and perhaps in management itself."[53] Many point to the late 1950s and
early 1960s as the beginning of that retreat, when seminal reports funded by
the Carnegie Corporation and the Ford Foundation[54] appraised the state of
business education in the United States and described it "as a collection of
trade schools lacking a strong scientific background."[55] The influential political scientist Herbert Simon called business education a "wasteland of voca-
tionalism."[56] These kinds of assessments galvanized a transformation of the
American business school from a practice orientation to the more "academically and discipline-based orientation" we have today.[57]

What Have Business Schools Become?

While the transformation of business schools may have been an important
corrective for its time, the pendulum has swung too far, with the teaching mission being overtaken by the research agenda and, more important, research
focused primarily on questions of theoretical, not empirical, relevance. Management professors Warren Bennis and James O'Toole wrote twenty years ago
that business schools have adopted an "inappropriate—and ultimately self-
defeating—model of academic excellence. Instead of measuring themselves
in terms of the competence of their graduates, or by how well their faculties
understand important drivers of business performance, they measure themselves almost solely by the rigor of their scientific research."[58] Not much has
changed since. And as this research has become disconnected from real-world
issues for both business and society, the teaching mission has followed close
behind. Business schools have become professional schools that have lost interest and connection to the profession they profess to serve. One can observe
this in the faculty, many of whom have never worked in business or even engaged with business in any real sense. It is a strange irony that many business
schools will not admit a student into their MBA program without four to five

years of working experience, while many of those same schools will admit students into their PhD program without any business experience at all, and they will become teachers of those MBAs. Further to the point, much of the doctoral education for business professors lacks any real attention to the art and craft of teaching. As academic scholars, many risk retaining views of the business enterprise that are largely theoretical. That is because, at the end of the day, most business school professors see themselves as academic researchers first and teachers of business practice second.

There have been some attempts at change, such as alternative delivery formats for MBAs, compressed degree programs, specialized masters, and undergraduate business degrees. But according to a 2016 book by a group of academics, these changes have amounted largely to "tinkering at the margins."[59] Business schools, to a large extent, have become critical sources of billions of dollars in revenue,[60] where the market demand is based more on perceived status than deep rigorous education and training.[61] Even efforts at reform reinforce this reality, where the threat to future enrollment and therefore revenues is the chief motivation for change and the search for solutions maintains an insular view by looking only at the top business schools,[62] ignoring plentiful business research that powerful incumbents are not usually the source of new ideas.

Stanford Business School professor Jeff Pfeffer argues that the primary value of business education is access to networks for salary enhancement and points out that the rigor of the degree ranks far below other disciplines while the party atmosphere exceeds them.[63] He adds that there are questions about the effectiveness of this product when "neither possessing an MBA degree nor grades earned in courses correlate with career success."[64] Some have noted that classroom learning has become less important to MBA students than attending recruiting events, planning club activities, and finding a job. One dean noted, "The focus has shifted from learning to earning."[65] If we know there is a problem, why can't we respond?

What Keeps Business Schools Stuck?

My focus in this book will be on ideas—specifically, how to change the structure, focus, and overall orientation of the business school curriculum and pedagogy. Before such an examination, it is important to understand the organizational reasons why business schools have all drifted towards homogeneity in recent decades, and why they have been so resistant to innovation. Three constraints are mostly to blame.

Academic Reward Systems. Today, the prevalent criteria for faculty advancement, including promotion and tenure, heavily emphasize publishing in prestigious academic journals. These publications often cater to specialized theoretical communities, prioritizing their interests over matters directly relevant to students, businesses, and the broader society.[66] Historian Russell Jacoby writes that the goal of academic research "registers not the needs of truth but academic-empire building."[67] To build that empire, faculty use their research to talk to narrow academic audiences, using a language that even well-educated readers struggle to understand, publishing in journals that non-academics don't read, and asking questions for which the public has little concern. How many businesspeople have heard of, much less read, the top academic journals in management, such as *Administrative Science Quarterly*, *Academy of Management Journal*, *The Journal of Marketing*, *Academy of Management Review*, and *Strategic Management Journal*? I am willing to bet very few. How many have read a synthesis of the results of such research in easily accessible formats? Again, I am willing to bet very few. That is because the intended audience for this work is not businesspeople; it is other scholars. The goal is to garner citations, thereby enhancing the author's academic reputation and contributing to the metrics used in the tenure and promotion process.[68]

Whether this work could create real-world change is a question rarely, if ever, asked.[69] Taken to the extreme, some view any engagement with the general public as a distraction from the scholarly "real" work or as an anti-intellectual waste of time, what is commonly referred to as the "Carl Sagan effect" in reference to celebrity scientist Carl Sagan's denial of admission to the National Academy of Sciences for being seen as a "popularizer" of science.[70] American journalist and political commentator Nicholas Kristof argues that academia is in thrall to a "culture of exclusivity" that "glorifies arcane unintelligibility while disdaining impact and audience," concluding that "to be a scholar is, often, to be irrelevant."[71]

In this reality, teaching is a distant second in the list of priorities. Many devalue teaching, seeing it as a burden and calling it a "teaching load." As a result, the curriculum remains ossified in large part because the incentives to develop new and innovative courses are low, if not negative, as such time spent on developing new courses is time taken away from producing more research. Capturing the absurdity of students learning from instructors who place a low value on teaching, Sydney Finkelstein of the Tuck School of Business delivered a sharply worded rebuke at the Association to Advance Collegiate Schools of Business 2022 Deans Conference, asking "Are business schools a scam?"[72] In a speech that critiqued a culture-and-reward system that produces narrowly focused studies that rarely challenge the status quo, he said, "If we're not publishing work that managers care about, what are we doing? If we're not publishing work that's addressing the big issues in society, then who are we talking to?"[73]

Academic Rankings. Business school rankings, primarily from prominent publications such as *US News & World Report, Bloomberg, Financial Times*, and *Fortune*, often have the perverse effect of inhibiting innovation and reform, forcing a homogenization of programs as institutions vie for higher positions based on a common set of criteria.[74] In this environment, business schools converge towards a monoculture, aligning their models and metrics with what is deemed as ideal by these influential rankings.

The consequence is an education system resistant to innovative reforms; put simply, if a business school dean were to pursue radical reforms that resulted in a drop in the rankings, they would find themselves out of a job. A notable example of the extreme influence and pressure of the rankings system was the case of Moshe Porat, former dean of Temple University's Richard J. Fox School of Business and Management, who was sentenced to fourteen months in prison, three years of supervised release, and a $250,000 fine after being convicted of fraud for artificially inflating the school's program rankings.[75]

While there are signs of change, with some institutions, like Columbia University, opting out of the general rankings, this movement is still in its infancy, particularly within the business school sector. Currently, opting out is predominantly an option for elite schools with established reputations and resources, leaving most institutions bound to the status quo dictated by these influential rankings.

Institutional Challenge. Finally, a profound transformation of business education is an institutional challenge, one that requires a coordinated shift in the entire ecosystem—school accreditation, corporate recruiting, faculty hiring, journal review, faculty reward criteria, school rankings, student admissions, curriculum design, and more. That means that it would be very hard, if not impossible, for one school to do all this alone. In academia, which operates as a competitive marketplace, faculty members often function as autonomous agents, adhering to universally recognized norms of research and teaching. If one school were to establish idiosyncratic measures for academic advancement or teaching pedagogy that were at variance with those at other schools, faculty members would be reluctant to conform. Junior faculty may be ill-advised to follow them unless guaranteed tenure. For if their tenure packet were to be denied, they would need to have a marketable publication record on the open job market. And if the pursuit of a different set of metrics diminished that record, they will have done serious damage to their career and future within academia. Senior faculty may be unwilling to follow if changes in research expectations diminish their stature in the field or if the considerable effort required to change the curriculum is not sure to result in adoption.

Despite all these forces for stasis, business schools must still try to change the curriculum. And if they don't, students must still find ways to get the education they need in a flawed system.

It's Time to Rejuvenate Business Education

Business education teaches valuable tools of management, the *how* of business found in "the core" curriculum of strategy, accounting, finance, operations, and organizational behavior. To bring its content into line with twenty-first-century realties, however, this core curriculum must now be augmented to focus on *why* one will deploy those tools and how to fit them together with the realities of a changing world. That augmentation begins with an acknowledgment of the elevated power that business leaders possess in today's world to shape and guide society and to instill the sense of responsibility that comes with that power. Students are taught the rational skills of profit maximization, but schools must also attend to pride of craft, developing valuable products and services that their customers want and need without harming society and the environment in the process. This involves teaching to their entire self, cultivating the virtues of wisdom, character, and purpose. In the words of Rakesh Khurana, "The time has come . . . to rejuvenate intellectually and morally the training of our future business leaders."[76]

The rest of this book will argue how to do that. It is meant as a springboard, offering a series of chapters that explore some core topics of a twenty-first-century business education that are currently either poorly addressed or not addressed at all. While this book does not delve into exhaustive detail—avoiding the pitfalls of becoming an overwhelming and narrowly prescriptive volume—it is intended as a roadmap for how to enhance business education. My hope is that—in avoiding being overly prescriptive—the book will encourage readers to foster diverse methodologies tailored to the unique resources of individual institutions.

The remaining chapters in Part I constitute a brief examination of what this book means for students, faculty, and administrators, with the following chapters clustered into three additional parts. Part II will explore the nature of business, the market, and capitalism. Part III will envision a new role for government in helping the market serve society. And Part IV will propose how to reconfigure the business school's pedagogy and purpose to fulfil its role in bringing about a just and sustainable world.

Part I: Rethinking the Purpose of Business Education

Chapter 2—The Implications for Students. Today's students are different from those of earlier eras, with growing numbers wanting to challenge the norms of business and business education. But until business schools are changed to serve their needs, students must shed the notion that they are a "customer" and that the school provides them with a "product." Instead, they must think of themselves as being dropped into a resource-rich environment from which they can draw what they want and need. They should not simply just take the curriculum as given, but instead build the program they seek through both course and noncourse activities that the entire university makes possible.

Chapter 3—The Role of Faculty and Administrators. Every professor knows that the primary metrics for academic success are publications in academic journals. It is time for more to shift their mindset towards one that connects business education more tightly to the needs of society. To do this, faculty can create new courses and new pedagogy. Going further, some faculty can adopt the role of "elder," focusing less on elevating their professional status and more on helping those who come after them and the institutions in which they are being developed. This means pushing for institutional change in the areas of rewards, training, engagement, selection, and more to bring a new spirit and sensibility to the business school.

Part II: Capitalism, Business, and the Market:
The Old Paradigm and the New

Chapter 4—The Coming End of Shareholder Capitalism. Most business school students and faculty today are familiar only with shareholder capitalism. But other variants of capitalism existed before it and other variants will follow it. In fact, evidence suggests that the era of shareholder capitalism is coming to an end, having not lived up to its promises in recent years as evidenced by dangerous environmental damage, significant income inequality, and even poor market performance as measured by stock market growth, productivity, return on assets, and federal investment in public goods. This chapter explores the myriad failings of capitalism as practiced in its present form.

Chapter 5—Bringing Adam Smith into the Present: Reexamining the Fundamentals of Capitalism. Where the prior chapter makes a critique of the present variant of capitalism, this chapter explores the fundamentals for amending it. It begins with a simple question—What is capitalism? This would seem to be a logical question for any education in business, yet it gets surprisingly little coverage in the curriculum. Capitalism, frequently assumed as a natural law like gravity, is in fact a robust human-created system, crafted to serve societal needs. Recognizing its imperfections and historical evolution is crucial. Contemporary capitalism has inherent issues, and business education must prepare students to be market stewards. They should understand capitalism's core principles, strengths, weaknesses, and the potential for transformation.

Chapter 6—Alternative Capitalisms Around the World. The United States has the world's highest gross domestic product (GDP) but lags in other human well-being measures such as wealth distribution and standard of living. This isn't a flaw of capitalism itself, but of the specific version practiced in the US and other Western economies since the 1970s. By studying different global capitalism models, future business leaders can learn to improve our market system and adapt to various international contexts.

Chapter 7—The Purpose of the Firm: It's Not to Make Shareholders Rich, It's to Serve Customers and Society. The purpose of the firm is not to make money for the shareholder. Firms should aim to also serve both their customers and society. Although shareholder primacy offers a simple metric for corporate performance, it fosters harmful practices including short-termism and problematic CEO compensation, undermining long-term firm health. This narrow focus restricts the vision and judgment of future business leaders, preventing them from addressing societal issues and adhering to their values. With some beginning to question corporate purpose, it's crucial for business schools to join this dialogue.

Part III: The Crucial Role of Government in the Marketplace:
Corporate Political Responsibility, Constructive
Lobbying, and a New Role for Government

Chapter 8—How Money Corrupts Healthy Government and Democracy: Why the Corporation Is Not a "Natural Person." Between chapters on the purpose of the firm and the roles of government and the market, we need to make a stop on the question of whether the corporation is a "natural person," imbued with the same rights as people under the US Constitution. Currently, courts recognize these rights, especially regarding the First Amendment's free speech clause, which is now interpreted to include political spending. This interpretation significantly broadens corporate influence in politics and policymaking. With expanding rights, such as the First Amendment's freedom of religion now extended to corporations, it's time to examine if this trend has crossed a line, empowering corporations in ways that America's founders feared.

Chapter 9—The Necessary and Constructive Role of Business in Policymaking . . . and the Need for Guardrails. Business leadership crucially shapes capitalism's future through government engagement, especially via lobbying—a fundamental aspect of democratic politics which is often viewed as an unofficial branch of government, guiding market rules and reforms. Surprisingly, few business schools teach about lobbying, particularly its responsible form that serves the public interest beyond mere competitive gain. Many students are unaware of lobbying's once illegal status in the United States and its evolution into a recognized profession. As corporate roles in social and political issues grow, there's a pressing need for checks on business influence on government. With corporations increasingly drawn into sociopolitical debates, business education must provide future leaders with the political acumen to effectively navigate these complexities.

Chapter 10—The Necessary and Constructive Role of the Government in the Market: Not More or Less Government, the Right Level of Government. From the 1930s to the 1970s, Keynesian economics, which argued that economies do not self-correct and necessitate significant government intervention, was predominant. However, from the 1970s onwards, neoclassical economics, advocating for a self-correcting economy with minimal government interference, gained prominence. This approach is currently facing criticism due to its inability to address escalating income inequality and climate change. Some experts are now exploring emerging alternatives such as "supply-side progressivism," "the abundance agenda," or simply "industrial policy," which revolve around leveraging government influence to strategically stimulate economic growth and sectoral development. This chapter will show how the focus needs to shift from the binary debate of more or less government intervention and spending to defining a constructive and collaborative role between government and industry.

Part IV: Business School Built on a Balanced Curriculum

Chapter 11—Outdated Business School Principles and Concepts: Efficiency, Value, Prosperity, and Metrics. This chapter begins by questioning the overriding and unrealistic belief within business education that technological change will solve all of our problems. Then it challenges business schools to take a closer look at the ways that the present curriculum steers business in the wrong direction in three areas. First, we need to rethink what we teach about what business strives for, focusing on our conceptions of efficiency, value, prosperity, and metrics. Second, we need to reimagine how business provides benefit through the market, focusing on a reimagining of competition and trade. Third, we need to reintroduce a sensible discussion of limits on economic growth and unbridled consumption. The chapter concludes by advocating for curriculum redesign to encourage systems thinking, both breaking down silos within business schools and fostering interdisciplinary collaboration across the university.

Chapter 12—The Noble Calling of Business and Business Education. Research has shown that students who apply to business school typically score higher on the traits of narcissism, psychopathy, and Machiavellianism. Research also shows that a business school education amplifies those traits. But there is also evidence that today's students are more willing to challenge these trends and are demanding an education that equips them to solve society's challenges through commerce. The challenge for business schools is to help them along this path by guiding them to consider *management as a calling* in a spirit similar to that with which we train doctors—a move away from the simple pursuit of a career for private personal gain and towards a *vocation* that is based on a higher professional and moral purpose.

Education That Is Both Business-Centric and Market-Centric

The time is right for a transformation of business education. The host of problems facing the business world are clarifying the need for change. Whether those problems are climate change, species extinction, habitat destruction, inequality (in all its forms, including economic, gender, racial, and sexual orientation), forced labor, global poverty, war and conflict, pandemics, or so many more, people are turning to business to step up and help solve them. But the only way that business and the market can fully respond is to shift their orientation from wealth extraction to wealth creation at a very deep and systemic level. As Stiglitz writes, "The neoliberal fantasy that unfettered markets will deliver prosperity to everyone should be put to rest."[77]

There are signs that business is at least trying to respond. The Business Roundtable[78] and World Economic Forum[79] have both tried to redefine corporate purpose to think beyond shareholders and include all stakeholders in society. Former Unilever CEO Paul Polman and Andrew Winston are calling on businesses leaders to be "net positive," a term they use to describe a business venture that "improves well-being for everyone it impacts."[80] BlackRock CEO Larry Fink has stated that the effort to adjust investing in this direction "is not about politics. It is not 'woke.' It is capitalism."[81] The backlash to Fink's position highlights the extent to which some may see these efforts as an attack on capitalism. But they are quite the opposite. They are efforts to amend and reform capitalism, to bring it back in line with the needs of society that have evolved greatly since the 1970s when our present variant emerged and took hold.

It is now time for business schools to step up to the challenge; to engage in these debates and help bring about an evolved form of capitalism that serves society's needs in the twenty-first century. To do this, we need to recognize that we are still working on a model that is no longer relevant and to fundamentally alter our teaching pedagogy and research focus accordingly. There are glimpses of that change occurring, from alterations in faculty reward systems to encourage more socially relevant research[82] to course innovations that speak to the challenges our students will face. Whether it be "Reimagining Capitalism" at the Harvard Business School, "Economic Inequality" at Virginia's Darden School of Business, "Alternative Economic Models" at the Audencia Business School, or "The End of Globalization" at Yale's School of Management,[83] programmatic change on the social and environmental dimensions of business activities can be found in a growing number of business programs.[84] Business education needs more such content in conjunction with a deep redesign of the overall curriculum.

The book advocates for a pivotal shift in business education from guiding students on how to manage businesses for personal gain to educating them on how to manage both prosocial businesses and a market in which they will operate—activities which will incidentally result in personal gain. The proposals in this book are transformational, not incremental, as transformation is what is needed. But it also recognizes that transformation invites resistance, rigidity, and obstruction. That is to be expected and welcomed. It is time to begin.

TWO

The Implications for Students

"I have never let schooling interfere with my education."
—MARK TWAIN, AMERICAN ESSAYIST

The challenge of transforming business education is a complex institutional task, one that requires a coordinated shift in the entire ecosystem, from deans to faculty, students, accrediting bodies, recruiters, journal editors, donors, magazine rankings, and more. As a result, this book is written for all who care about the future of business education, business leadership, and its profound impact on the world around us. But two audiences are of particular importance in this transformation. This chapter is addressed to students. The next chapter will focus on faculty and administrators, those who design and deliver their education.

Today's Students Are Different

Students: You are the reason that business education exists. Whether you are thinking about, applying to, accepted at, enrolled in, or already graduated from a business school, this book is a challenge for you to think carefully about what you are learning (or learned), what is missing from that education, what values are embedded within the curriculum, and what type of degree and education you ultimately seek. To take the message in this book to heart, you cannot take the curriculum as given, but must instead take control over what you are learning and have an influence on what future students will learn.

My generation was the first to learn about climate change and to watch income inequality reach extraordinary levels, but we failed to take the actions necessary to address these systemic problems. That task now falls to the next generation, the first to grow up with climate change and inequality as a part of their everyday reality and to be saddled with the real challenge to do something about them.

The silver lining of an entire generation facing systemic, global challenges such as climate change is that they affect everyone, which means you likely won't be alone in your desire to address them. Today's business students are asking new and important questions of the market and business. Whereas thirty years ago, students who wanted to make a difference in the world gravitated towards schools of government or nonprofit management, increasing numbers today are turning to schools of business. They arrive with a fresh perspective, keen to explore and redefine the economic, social, and environmental roles of corporations, as well as their own roles as future leaders. Contemporary business school students still want to learn the essentials of running successful businesses, but many are also concerned about the mounting threats of climate change, inequality, health care, living wages, and more. Increasing numbers are bringing with them a desire to make a difference in the world and see business as a place to do it.

One survey shows that 60 percent of Gen Zers and Millennials are alarmed or concerned about climate change;[1] another survey shows that more than 70 percent of the Gen-Z business school cohort want content that responds to such concerns.[2] This emerging activism extends into students' plans postgraduation. One survey found that 67 percent of business students want to incorporate environmental sustainability considerations into whatever job they choose;[3] another found that 88 percent of business school students think that learning about social and environmental issues in business is a priority, and 83 percent state they are willing to take a salary cut for a job that makes a social or environmental difference in the world.[4] In 2019, business ethics entered the top five most popular subjects at business school for the first time.[5]

The growing numbers of students who are willing to direct their business studies and their careers towards the great challenges of our day suggest a movement that should provide momentum for anyone who wishes to join it. But it is not enough. I hear too many professors glibly look to the next generation as their source of hope; that they will be the ones to solve the great societal challenges we face today. However, business schools often fail to take the critical next step of equipping these students with the necessary tools to achieve such ambitious goals. This book argues that this deficiency must be addressed. But until such changes are implemented, students should proactively seek out the resources they need beyond the traditional curriculum—exploring other academic departments and engaging in extracurricular learning opportunities across the university. Fortunately, accessing these additional resources is more feasible than it might initially appear.

Get the Most Out of Your Education Today

The central messages for students in this book are threefold. First, business school is broken, as the chapters in this book elaborate. Second, students should go to business school anyway. A business degree is still an essential credential to convince hiring managers, investors, and other societal gatekeepers of your value. Your ability to have an influence on the world through business is enormous—but first you must be given entry into business's upper ranks. The actions of corporations, and more important the individuals that exercise authority in them, decide how we will live and adapt in a world that climate change, income inequality, and other social and environmental issues are altering.

Third, don't just sit back and be spoonfed an incomplete educational diet. Take control of your learning; expand it and augment it. Following Mark Twain's remark—"I have never let schooling interfere with my education"— recognize that business education and a business degree are two related but different things. To have the most personally rewarding career, today's students must shed the notion that they are a "customer" and that the school provides them with a "product." Instead, students must think of themselves as being given an opportunity to be dropped into a resource-rich environment from which they can draw and build what they want and need. From that empowered position, students should not simply just take the curriculum as given. They should look deeply at what they are being taught, not with a license to simply pick and choose what to accept, but to question, debate, and understand its deeper foundations as they relate to the world that they will live and work in.

To initiate this critical inquiry, the chapters of this book are crafted to highlight the key areas where current business education falls short in preparing students for the challenges of the future. They are meant to offer context and counterpoint to what today's business students are likely to encounter. They are also meant as a springboard, since many of the answers to society's great challenges are not yet known. But the search for answers requires a re-examination of some of the foundational issues in business education—What is capitalism? What is the future of shareholder capitalism? What is the role of government in the market? Can an economy based on consumption be truly sustainable? These are just some of the challenging questions of our day, and they will not be covered in enough depth (or at all) in today's business curriculum. But they may be answered by piecing together an education (not schooling) with courses at the business school and within the broader university of which it is a part.

The key point is to personalize and create your own education. Each student enters the business school with a different aptitude, ambition, and set of aspirations. It is your degree, and it is here to prepare you for your life; make the most of it. If you are a passive student, you will get an education designed for someone else or, worse, little education at all. I am always surprised when students do not step beyond the narrow confines of their coursework and customize their education with content from the social and natural sciences, public policy, political science, engineering, ecology, social work, and so on. Students cannot be bound by the disciplinary silos of today's university; I can assure you that the challenges in the world are not.

So, for example, students can learn from the business school about how to structure a business deal around a windfarm or solar array; bring in the necessary financing, line up the array of supply-chain partners, and work with potential customers to execute the deal. But they can also learn from the public-policy school about the tax structures that make it work now and may make it work better in the future. From the schools of sociology or community engagement, they can learn why some local communities are opposed to renewable energy development, and how they can understand their concerns. From engineering, they can learn what technological hurdles are on the horizon that could make these technologies more economical and effective, and what needs to happen for them to be realized. From schools for the environment, biology, or ecology, they can learn how these developments affect the local environment and wildlife. From schools of economics or political science, they can learn how they can provide benefits to the local community, local farmers, and local landowners. There is such an array of questions to be asked and issues to be addressed that if you are only approaching these kinds of issues "as a businessperson" you will find your vision limited and stunted. Today's education should expand your vision and allow you to tailor it to your goals and aspirations.

Beyond coursework, much of the value of education lies outside the classroom. The list above does not mean that you must take classes in all the schools mentioned, though you can if you wish. But there are experts among these faculty, seminars and lectures scheduled throughout the year, student clubs, and peers that can open your eyes to new ways of viewing these challenges. To find those opportunities, the first step can be to simply ask for office hours with a professor or staff member to explore what is possible. If the desired resources are not immediately available, they can often be found or even made. There are resources available to create all kinds of activities on campus. I encourage students to organize a student club, a conference, a panel discussion of experts, or an invited speaker. They can do an independent study or become a research assistant. They can make connections and learn from people within the business school, across the university, and even outside the university. If you contact professionals in the area of their interest to be part of an event on campus, you are far more likely to get a response than if you contact those same people upon graduation for an informational interview about a job. Many professionals like speaking to students and helping them understand the part of the world they know well. If there is a professional conference you want to attend but can't afford, contact the organizers and offer free labor in exchange for admission. The opportunities for improvising the education process are limited only by your imagination, initiative, and finding the right staff and faculty to help you achieve what you seek.

Bring Your Whole Self to Business Education

My students often ask me where they should take their careers in order to have the most impact. I am quick to reply, "Wrong question, try again." I could tell them that their greatest impact would come from working for a large resource-extraction company and from the perspective of carbon-accounting and environmental protection, and that may be true. But if they don't like finance and do not want to work in a large multinational company, they will not thrive. In fact, they will likely die inside and not be able to make any impact at all. The better question is one that only they can answer for themselves: "What were you meant to do with your life?"[6]

Mark Twain once said, "The two most important days in your life are the day you are born and the day you find out why." You had no choice in that first day; your parents chose it for you. But you have everything to do with that second day. You need to find it. During your years in college, you take classes and learn about running a business. But the key to the second awakening that Twain describes is not just what you learn in class; it's also what you develop in the "in-between" time. Be sure to put yourself in experiences and the company of others who think and feel deeply about the same things that you do. This gives you a supportive community and culture as you lay the foundation for your future work and purpose. But you will also need to put yourself in experiences and the company of those who think differently than you; they will test and help to clarify your beliefs. Finally, you need to find time for yourself. It is by taking time for reflection that you will discern what you truly believe.

The conviction of your beliefs is what will get you out of bed every morning and what will get you through the tough times. And you will have tough times. There are days when I turn off the radio when I hear another news story about climate change. There are days when I get discouraged that reform is just too hard—when a US Senator brings a snowball to the Senate floor to "prove" that global warming is not real, for example, or the government of Florida bans state officials from using the words "climate change," or the newly elected president makes it his first priority to withdraw from the Paris Agreement on climate change. If I was doing this just for money, I would likely quit. But I get out of bed and keep working because I believe I must; it is my purpose, and it is my calling.

In my faith tradition it is said, "For of those to whom much is given, much is required." I look at myself and I look at my students, and I see people to whom much is given: intelligence, opportunity, passion, wisdom, and vision. My belief that we have a responsibility to put those gifts to good use gives me persistence, especially when I get discouraged or tired. It forces me to look deep inside myself and muster the strength to keep trudging forward. To quote T. S. Eliot's poem *The Dry Salvages*, "We are only undefeated because we have gone on trying."[7]

This endurance is easier to maintain when the world is viewed from an unorthodox—at times lonely—angle. As an example, over the past years the stock market has been reaching new heights. Is that the world you see? Or do you also recognize that income inequality is widening? Do you see that sustainability is going mainstream, as evidenced by the proliferation of annual sustainability reports, chief sustainability officers, sustainability strategies, and sustainable products? Or do you also recognize that many of the sustainability concerns that these efforts are supposed to resolve continue to get worse? Carbon dioxide levels are rising past critical thresholds. Man-made chemicals permeate our environment. What kind of a world do you see?

From there, your unorthodox angle should compel you to ask what kind of world you want to help create. I would hope that in seeing clearly the challenges of our present reality, you will not stop at lamenting the current environmental and social imbalances. We have no shortage of cynics in today's world; that is not a resource that we need more of. In their essay *The Death of Environmentalism*, Michael Shellenberger and Ted Nordhaus argue that environmentalists tend to focus too much on the negative, and that the negative does not motivate people to follow a leader.[8] They point out that Martin Luther King Jr., did not give a speech called "I Have a Nightmare," but rather "I Have a Dream." So, the challenge for you as a student is to use the gift of your educational opportunity to look beyond the problems of the world to focus on solutions that lead to a future that is optimistic and attractive, one that includes a life of meaning, security, prosperity, and happiness for ourselves, our children, all of humankind, and all of nature. That is bold work. But as the Welsh writer Raymond Williams once wrote, "To be truly radical is to make hope possible, not despair convincing."[9] Leaders inspire people to action by creating a vision of a desirable future, not by scaring them with warnings that the end is near. What future do you see? I want you to think about that and think about it hard. It will be the goal of your life's work.[10]

Advocate for Tomorrow's Students

The last thing I want to impress upon today's business students is to think about the next generation of business students that will follow you. By taking control of your education, you can lead by example and encourage others along the same path. But you can also actively act as a mentor, teaching and encouraging others to realize the potential that they seek. Going even further, you can lobby school administrators and faculty to make changes in programming to make this path easier for you and for others that follow you. In short, you can be a "positive deviant" in your education, a subversive who will change the world of business education through thoughtful, engaged, and determined actions.

That is what I am trying to do in this book. My goal is to help you to see business education's strengths, its weaknesses, where it serves you, where it doesn't, and how you can make it what it needs to be. Today's students—who will be tomorrow's business leaders—have a role to play in changing business education and then business. We need visionary leaders, and this book is intended to inspire you to accept the challenge to be a force for constructive and aspirational change in a world that needs that force more than ever. To equip you to be better prepared for tomorrow's realities, I want to provide you with a clear view of what you are getting in business education today and empower you to demand more. Are you ready to take on that challenge? This book is to help you along your journey to fulfill that hope.

THREE

The Role of Faculty and Administrators

"Teaching is more difficult than learning because what teaching calls for is this: to let learn. The real teacher, in fact, lets nothing else be learned than learning."

—MARTIN HEIDEGGER, GERMAN PHILOSOPHER

In the wake of the 2008 financial crisis, when it became clear that MBA-trained financial professionals had contributed to the near collapse of the global economy, many top business schools underwent some degree of introspection. A 2010 report from the Harvard Business School noted that the "industry" of business education was "wrestling with basic questions of purpose, positioning and program design" as companies in fields traditionally favored by graduates (investment banking, private equity, and hedge funds) were "starting to shift their hiring away from MBAs."[1] A 2011 report from a group of European business scholars lamented that "European business schools make a mistake in blindly following their North American cousins" and have entered a "business school bubble" that is disconnected from real-world issues.[2] A 2016 report from Boston University noted that "business schools . . . remain stuck in approaches to business education that have changed very little for more than half a century."[3]

Some critics went further, lamenting not just business education's drift from relevance, but a negative influence on business practice through its teaching. A 2016 article in *The Journal of Open Innovation* argues, "Let's not mince words: Our MBA graduates marched out and destroyed the world financial system. Few in academe have stepped up to take responsibility" for what "has become a race to the bottom."[4] That scathing critique came nearly a decade after Sumantra Ghoshal of the London Business School and founding dean of the Indian School of Business in Hyderabad wrote that "by propagating ideologically inspired amoral theories, business schools have actively freed their students from any sense of moral responsibility."[5]

After much handwringing, however, not much was done to actually reform business school practices in the wake of Ghoshal's critique or even the financial crisis. This seems to be a trend—a corporate scandal emerges (be it Enron's fraudulent accounting in the late 1990s or the creation of toxic financial instruments in the run-up to the 2008 crisis), prominent voices urge reform at the business schools that trained some of the culprits, the public's attention moves on, and nothing happens beyond some minor tinkering around the margins. This time has to be different. This book is not a post-mortem, after all, it is a pre-mortem—it is written in the emerging shadow of an existential calamity that awaits humanity if we do not prepare the next generation of leaders to rise up to the challenges we are facing. That's where faculty and administrators come in.

Recommit to the Reasons Why You Chose to Enter Academia

Members of the faculty: Why did you choose to become a professor? When I feel myself losing track of the purpose or meaning behind my work, I return to this simple question. And my answer is equally simple—I want my research, teaching, and outreach to have a positive imprint on the world. That is my choice and my direction. And yet, I, like most other professors, come to a point in life when we ask, "What is my legacy? What did I accomplish?" The answers to these questions, for me, will not be my citation counts, A-level publications, and h-index. When I come to the end of my days, those will not be the metrics for how I will measure the worth of my career. It will be measured instead by the difference I made in students' lives and how I influenced the profession in the way people think and act.[6]

Yet every professor is keenly aware that this is not the primary metric for advancement in academia; it is research, and in particular research published in academic journals, the ones considered to have "impact." Every university, school, and department has a list of such journals, those it considers to be the most prestigious in their fields. And the rankers of institutions have similar lists, like those designated as important by the *Financial Times*.[7] With such lists as a guide, academics establish their credentials by publishing in these journals, and universities grant tenure and promotion on the basis of these credentials. Various institutions even pay their professors a bonus for publishing in select journals. But this narrow focus gets in the way of a vital responsibility of business professors, and that is to teach the next generation of business leaders. Now, more than ever, we need changes within the business school curriculum, and we need professors to do this work even if the explicit rewards of our field do not encourage us to move in this direction. Not every academic must take on this role. Some great scholars produce valuable research that others can make accessible in the classroom or take into the world beyond. But some do take on this role, and many others want to but do not. The obstacles vary and are different for each level of the professoriate.

As junior faculty, we need to wrestle with the tensions of satisfying the metrics by which we are judged and the personal direction we originally set out to follow, asking how to remain true to ourselves while also satisfying the gatekeepers of the institutions. Approaching this dilemma with an open mind can alleviate the daunting pressures associated with achieving tenure—after all, what value does the proverbial brass ring hold if you've had to sacrifice your identity and beliefs to capture it? This refreshed perspective empowers faculty to pursue their true passions in tackling real-world problems and in teaching the next generation to do the same. But it requires a dynamic tension between pursuing these personal goals and also recognizing the rules of academia for achieving tenure, becoming what Stanford professor Deb Meyerson calls a "tempered radical." In this role, Meyerson argues, people "walk the tightrope between conformity and rebellion" and "stick to their values, assert their agendas, and provoke learning and change without jeopardizing hard-won careers."[8]

As senior faculty, we have a responsibility to act with courage to help these junior scholars along their path by innovating the kinds of research questions we pose, the projects we undertake, the audiences we seek to reach, and the kind of organizational culture and school policies we create or shape. As the primary decision makers in the schools at which we work, we have the obligation to craft, articulate, and model an ethos that celebrates an engaged and enlightened approach to research and teaching. And we have an obligation to change the institutional rules so as to support young scholars coming up the ranks who seek to undertake meaningful work with social impact.[9] In the words of former University of Michigan president Mark Schlissel:

> We forget the privilege it is to have lifelong security of employment at a spectacular university. And I don't think we use it for its intended purpose. I think that faculty on average through the generations are becoming a bit careerist and staying inside our comfort zones. If we're perceived as being an ivory tower and talking to one another and being proud of our discoveries and our awards and our accomplishments and the letters after our name, I think in the long run the enterprise is going to suffer in society's eyes, and our potential for impact will diminish. The willingness of society to support us will decrease."[10]

As professors we have an opportunity, indeed an obligation, to make our teaching and research more relevant to the world. To do that, we must broaden the tent of what it means to be a professor and allow for more research, teaching, and engagement that connects with real-world issues and real-world practitioners. We can do this by rethinking both what and how we teach.

Innovate in the Curriculum. The first way you can begin the process of changing the curriculum is to change your own teaching portfolio. Revising business school courses to reflect today's realities—notably, climate change and inequality—requires us to teach a new sensibility in business. To do this, new courses can

- Help students develop a critical understanding of how multiple capitalisms are structured, the underlying models on which they are based, and the importance of their using this knowledge to become stewards of the market

- Explain how these systems have evolved into the form of shareholder capitalism we know today, what is wrong with that variant, and what form it might take in the future

- Reimagine the purpose of the firm to consider how customers, employees, the environment, or broader society fit into the priorities of the twenty-first-century firm

- Offer more coverage of the role of government in setting and enforcing the rules of the market

- Offer corollary content in the constructive role for business in policy-making, one that serves society

- Stop teaching metrics and models for business calculations that are based on outmoded, even discredited ideas; instead, add new models that provide the tools and vocabulary for addressing what are conveniently called "externalities" or "unintended consequences" but are actually embedded in our economic systems

- Expose the underlying assumptions and implications of consumption, planned obsolescence, perpetual economic growth, and an overriding belief in cutthroat competition as the only form of market strategy

- Integrate more physical, social, and political sciences into the curriculum to help students see the impact of their future business decisions on the world around them

- Cover topics that are of relevance to the world that is to come, such as artificial intelligence, poverty, inequality, and environmental degradation

- Acknowledge that the problems of the twenty-first-century do not fit into neat disciplinary silos and introduce more systems thinking to help students make sense of the larger social, economic, political, and environmental systems of which business is a part

Innovate in the Pedagogy. Beyond developing new courses, faculty can go further and change the pedagogy, moving away from the standard modes of teaching (such as strict lecture formats or a heavy reliance on the case study method) and teach in new and innovate formats—the flipped classroom, co-learning, peer coaching, collaborative design, action-based learning, real-world projects, and more. We can move to construct environments wherein we engage the whole student, creating the context that allows students to find their own way in business and, if necessary, get out of the way. As German philosopher Martin Heidegger writes,

> Teaching is more difficult than learning because what teaching calls for is this: to let learn. The real teacher, in fact, lets nothing else be learned than learning. His conduct, therefore, often produces the impression that we properly learn nothing from him, if by "learning" we now suddenly understand merely the procurement of useful information. . . . The teacher is far less assured of his ground than those who learn are of theirs. If the relation between the teacher and the taught is genuine, therefore, there is never a place in it for the authority of the know-it-all or the authoritative sway of the official. It is still an exalted matter, then, to become a teacher—which is something else entirely than becoming a famous professor.[11]

Heidegger challenges professors to practice more humility, and his approach requires us to abandon the current "deficit model" of teaching, in which we are the experts who pour our knowledge into students' brains so that they will think like us and make good decisions.[12] Instead, we must aim to touch students' hearts, not just their heads—inspire them, not just inform them. Whereas we have traditionally seen the classroom as a place in which we impart knowledge, we must also see it as a place where we guide students in developing character, wisdom, judgment, and purpose. I admit, such an approach poses a great challenge to who we are as professors. For some, this will be an unfamiliar and even terrifying role, and they might be unprepared and even unwilling to take it on. But it is a role that we can grow into, developing more skills and confidence as we advance in the profession. To help faculty along this path, we need to change the institutions of academia. And that challenge may be better suited to senior professors, those who take on a new role as academics.

Become an "Elder"

Who can take on the responsibility of revising an ossified curriculum? I believe it is a job for faculty who have already earned an exalted professional status that allows them to stop focusing on their own careers and start looking to the next generation, moving to what David Brooks calls "the second mountain"—a place where they are not self-focused, but other-focused.[13] Rather than seeking extrinsic recognition, they can begin looking within themselves for their deeper measures of meaning, purpose, connection, and legacy. They can begin to adopt the role of "elders."[14]

Elders must be the ones to push for curriculum and institutional reform, not only because they have developed the vision after years of teaching, but also because they have less to lose. Under our current academic system, the incentives for innovating the overall curriculum are low, if not negative, as it takes time away from the standard metrics of research production. But elders can defy those rules, speaking truth to power without suffering career-limiting consequences. Unfortunately, not enough senior professors seem willing to advocate for change, despite the security their tenure and reputation provides. A colleague once quipped that "we have too many senior professors thinking and acting like junior professors," chasing the same kinds of academic publications, amassing ever more citation counts, and seeking the affirmation of peers. These pursuits become a never-ending quest. Instead, we can channel that energy into considering how to remake the institutions and culture of the business school, to steer it more towards an emphasis on teaching that serves students and society on the issues of the twenty-first century. How can we do that?

Formal and informal incentives would be a likely first place to start that task, encouraging faculty to focus on more teaching and research that addresses critical issues in society and the future of capitalism.[15] This could include changes in performance criteria and tenure review to include more attention to innovative teaching, as well as support for research that has more applied outputs, is published in outlets that reach the community of practice, and is tracked using metrics to determine broader public impact. Some schools have included impact-based metrics (such as Altmetric, Plum Analytics, and Sage Policy Profiles) to the annual review process. Others have offered reduced teaching obligations as a reward for innovations that bring more contemporarily relevant content into the curriculum. Still others offer public affirmation through awards and honors.

From there, one may focus on training at all ranks, from doctoral students to junior faculty to senior faculty, on the grand challenges before us and the ways that capitalism can be brought to bear, both in its present state and in an amended state. I know that many of my colleagues are hesitant to engage classroom discussions around climate change and inequality because they are concerned that their students know more than they do. They are often correct, but this is no reason to avoid the necessary engagement students need. To overcome this deficiency, some schools have offered seminars from experts around campus to teach the basics of these issues, and then created weekly newsletters, often curated by students, that keep faculty up to date on the latest developments on these issues. Some schools offer enhanced programming in the art of teaching (from PhD level through senior faculty), as well as skills in media engagement, government testimony, engaging with the public sector, and communicating with general audiences through print and social media. Beyond the individual institution, a growing array of external formal training platforms is becoming available that can help faculty become more connected to real-world issues and bring them into the classroom.

Ongoing support for what these rewards and training encourage can include funding for new products that fit within the existing formats for teaching (such as new case study development) and that foster new teaching pedagogy in the classroom. This support must be accompanied by a refocus of curriculum committees that select and approve course content, and the kinds of teaching support that faculty receive. Some schools choose to refocus school and departmental resources to support a shift in teaching and research emphasis. Some have repurposed communications specialists and media relations staff away from image management in support of school development and admissions efforts and towards new mandates for faculty impact, by helping to prepare media releases, write editorials, and place articles that increase the visibility of faculty research. This kind of effort aligns the present interests of faculty research with the future interests of teaching innovation.

All of these efforts at changing the ways that content is developed through research and taught in the classroom can be accelerated by changing the kinds of people that are selected to be a part of that process. Student acceptance criteria can be expanded to include more attention to prosocial interests and behavior, sorting for people who wish to use their careers in business to serve society more than their own financial interests. Doctoral student acceptance criteria can be amended to include more real-world experience and an interest in engaging with the issues that are relevant to today's societal challenges.

Faculty hiring can emphasize the need for more professors who focus on topical issues of practical relevance, possess an interest in external engagement with communities of practice, and have a deep desire for excellent teaching. Finally, the selection of deans and their staff of administrators can focus more on those who have a vision for changing the rules, norms, and culture of the schools they will lead. By changing those who are members of the community, it can be easier to change the culture of that community.

Beyond the individual school, there are efforts under way to change broader academic institutions. Some are pressing the academic journals to shift their review criteria to encourage more research that serves the public good (such as pursuing the UN's Sustainable Development Goals as a guide).[16] There are also pressures to change the accreditation process to value teaching and public engagement. For example, the Association to Advance Collegiate Schools of Business, the organization that grants accreditation to business schools in the United States and increasingly around the world, uses its accreditation criteria to encourage societal impact of business school teaching, research, and outreach. Even some magazines and newspapers, notably the *Financial Times*, have sought to promote more relevance in business schools through their powerful rankings. The overarching objective of all these efforts is to promote the idea that business schools should have a positive impact on society and that business itself can become a force for good.

On all these efforts, the "elder" has the roles of both changing the institutions of the academy and also directly helping the next generation of professors to continue this work while also succeeding within the academic system as it presently exists. Senior faculty need to guide junior faculty through long-term visions of the arc of their careers and show them what opportunities exist to achieve their aspirations, not only in terms of the profession as it is but also in terms of what the profession might become. They can help faculty give more thought to not only *what* they're teaching, but *whom* they're teaching. Our greatest impact is through the students at the university. But we can also reach businesspeople, government officials, nonprofits, the general public, and others.

In sum, these are some of the pieces of the changing mosaic of the academic environment. As more experiments take hold, more innovation will continue, and adoption will accelerate the broad cultural change within academia. The future lies in the diffusion of these kinds of innovations to create a shift in the entire ecosystem of academia. All of this may seem to be a massive and risky undertaking. Yet it is not as daunting as it may seem, as there is a ready market awaiting. Today's students are anxious for this content and many are feeling underserved.

The Time Is Now: Students Are Ready and Waiting

In many ways, today's business students are already ahead of business schools, questioning basic assumptions about the market and bringing new attitudes about the economic, social, and environmental purpose of corporations. Numerous surveys show that increasing numbers of today's generation of business students—who will be tomorrow's generation of business leaders—are concerned about the mounting threats of climate change, inequality, health care, living wages, and the world they are inheriting and want to take action to solve them. Chapter 2 listed survey data to show that business students are looking for change. There is also survey data to show that they are frustrated at the lack of change and feeling underserved.

The *Financial Times* notes that "[f]or business schools, there may never have been a more demanding cohort than . . . Generation Z, born between the late 1990s and the early 2010s." Seventy percent of this demographic wants "course content that really reflects the changes going on in society, from diversity and inclusion to sustainability and poverty."[17] Putting voice to this concern in the *New Republic*, MIT Sloan School MBA student John Benjamin wrote (while he was still in business school) that the business curriculum stifles discussion of the common good while emphasizing the overriding objective of profit maximization as unquestioned. Rather than cultivating open-minded stewards of the economy, he argued, they are taught to "ignore shareholder capitalism's obvious ethical lapses" and avoid any kind of systemic analyses of it.[18] In a 2019 *American Affairs* essay, Harvard Business School graduate Sam Long described an educational system that produces "a business elite dominated by financiers and their squires, presiding over a disordered economy gutted of both its productive energy and the ability to generate mass prosperity."[19]

The incoming generation of business students are interested in taking ownership of the world they are inheriting and want to apply their careers in business to do that. But some students report that they are going into internships or jobs and finding that they are the expert in the room on issues like climate change and social responsibility even though their formal education offered limited coverage on the topics.[20] This should not be the norm, and business schools cannot let these students down. We, as professors, can admit that we do not have all the answers and do not fully know what that future will look like, and can work with students to discover and create it. Conveniently, they possess an energy that can be tapped to help us make business education better together.

Part II

CAPITALISM, BUSINESS, AND THE MARKET

The Old Paradigm and the New

FOUR

The Coming End of Shareholder Capitalism

**"Now that we have four decades of this experiment, I
think we can declare it unambiguously a failure."**

—JOSEPH STIGLITZ, COLUMBIA UNIVERSITY

Our current variant of capitalism has become entrenched in our political and
social discourse. Most people cannot even imagine another way to structure
the economy than the incarnation of so-called "shareholder capitalism" that
we have now. As Fredric Jameson once noted, "It is easier to imagine the end
to the world than the end of capitalism."[1] In the business curriculum, the history of capitalism and its various incarnations over time receives little attention. Its form and function are taken as a given. This is a major oversight.

In fact, the variant of capitalism dominant in Western economies today
emerged only in the 1970s. This "shareholder capitalism" was a response to a
particular time, marked by increased foreign competition, high budget deficits, the OPEC oil embargo, high inflation, and uneven economic growth. It is
now showing signs of strain, with many questioning whether it is still suited
to the challenges we face.[2] The evidence is fairly compelling that shareholder
capitalism has not lived up to its promise, feeding inequality and environmental damage on a breathtaking scale. To properly prepare tomorrow's leaders,
business education needs to provide training on the history of capitalism, how
it has evolved into the form we know today, where it has failed, what form it
might take in the future, and how we may guide it into what it needs to be.[3]

A Short History of American Capitalism

From its founding, capitalism has grappled with two persistent friction points: fear of excessive corporate power and the debate over the government's role in the market. These concerns have not only influenced economic policies but also sparked questions about the nature of democracy, challenging citizens to consider whether they live under a government of, by, and for the people or the corporation.[4] As these debates continue into the present, it's crucial for business leaders to understand their origins and evolution. To better structure this complex history, this chapter divides the evolution of capitalism into six distinct eras, starting from the seventeenth century with the rise of the first American corporations.[5]

State Charters: 1600s–1840s. The first corporations were chartered through individual acts of incorporation, called "special acts," provided by state legislatures and tailored to specific purposes for specific amounts of time. These were not the kinds of corporations we think of today, formed to create a product or service that the owners wished to create. Instead, corporations were formed to address a particular public need, such as building roads; making rivers navigable; and operating universities, banks, and insurance firms (and later building railroads).[6] In this role, they were often granted special monopoly rights over their enterprise. The primary advantage of these early corporations was their capacity to amass and manage substantial capital for capital-intensive projects, a feat beyond the reach of government capabilities at the time. The chartered corporations also addressed numerous contracting problems such as the protection of individual investors from personal liability.[7]

One of the first US corporations was the Harvard Corporation (or the President and Fellows of Harvard College), chartered in 1636 by the Massachusetts Bay Colony. The first chartered business corporation was the New London Society for Trade and Commerce, a Connecticut land bank chartered in 1732 by the Connecticut General Assembly. While Harvard still exists, the charter for the New London Society was revoked the year after it was formed when the General Assembly decided that the notes it was issuing lacked adequate backing. Such instability was typical in this era, leading to the relative scarcity of corporations until the late eighteenth century.

Until the US Continental Congress in 1774, most corporations had legal tie-ins with colonial European powers. But an early success of a wholly owned US corporation was the Potomac Company, chartered in 1785 by the Virginia Legislature to improve the navigability of the Potomac, James, and Ohio Rivers via a network of roads, canals, and locks in order to expedite the transportation of produce and people between the east and the west.[8] While this corporate form proved successful, only about three hundred companies were incorporated by state governments between 1776 and 1800, with the majority (about 60 percent) chartered in New England.[9]

A comprehensive understanding of American capitalism requires the inclusion of the role of slavery and the tensions between the agrarian southern states and the industrialized northern states. Between 1800 and 1840, per capita income grew at a solid 2.1 percent per year in New England and 1.45 percent per year in the Middle Atlantic, but only 0.43 percent in the South Atlantic.[10] This difference was due, in part, to the extent to which the northern states were becoming industrialized and urbanized while the South remained largely rural, dependent on the North for capital and manufactured goods and on slavery for labor.

While slaves constituted nearly 12 percent of the entire population of the fledging United States in 1776, almost 50 percent of the population of South Carolina and Georgia and some parts of North Carolina was enslaved people.[11] Most of these slaves were used to help grow and harvest cotton. At first a small-scale crop, cotton boomed after the 1793 invention of the cotton gin, which separated raw cotton from seeds and other waste and made the crop far more profitable. US cotton exports grew by over 1,200 percent between 1772 and 1804.[12] Planters in the South then began to consolidate, buying land from small farmers and forming large plantations which, supported by slave labor, made some families extremely wealthy.

This consolidation had broader implications for white workers as well, leading to their disenfranchisement. The abolitionist Frederick Douglass sought to unite white laborers and enslaved people against wealthy plantation owners by highlighting how the influx of inexpensive black labor created by slavery was competing with and often displacing the employment opportunities of less affluent white workers.[13] Born the same year as Karl Marx (1818), Douglass called out themes similar to those of his German counterpart, arguing that the wealthy's "unbridled accumulation" is part of the "mighty machine" of capitalism, which results in the accumulation of wealth for some and leads to poverty for others. He did not see this as an unchangeable outcome, but rather, the "consequence of wealth unduly accumulated."[14]

By 1840, the South was growing 60 percent of the world's cotton.[15] Meanwhile, the Northern states continued to industrialize. Overall, the country was still largely agrarian, but the numbers of farm workers were declining. In 1776, 85 percent of the US population worked in agriculture; by 1840, that number had dropped to 63 percent as more people moved to cities and worked in the country's growing industrial base, primarily in the North.

General Laws of Incorporation: 1840s–1870s. The period of the 1840s and 1850s was marked by strong economic growth in the North. As demand for charters increased, the process of state legislature approval on a case-by-case basis grew cumbersome and slow. To accelerate the process, some states began to establish General Laws of Incorporation to allow corporations to be formed without a charter. New York was the first to enact a corporate statute in 1811, allowing for free incorporation with limited liability, but only for manufacturing businesses. Others followed: New Jersey in 1816; Connecticut in 1837. These early laws were restrictive in design, often with the intention of preventing corporations from gaining too much wealth and power by articulating specific purposes to which they were required to comply.[16]

During this time as well, the US economy underwent a major and differentiated seismic shift as a result of the US Civil War from 1861 to 1865. Before the war, from 1839 to 1859, the South's wealth was increasing through the expanded exploitation of slave labor, whose numbers had reached nearly four million by 1860.[17] By some estimates, increased output per enslaved worker was responsible for between 123 percent and nearly 300 percent of the growth in commodity output per capita for the Southern United States between 1839 and 1859.[18] The Northern victory in the US Civil War in 1865 marked an abrupt end to the slave-labor system, severely damaged the economic prospects of the large Southern cotton plantations. It stripped them of their means of production and their slave "assets," which were a significant part of their wealth. In 1860, the total value of these assets was estimated to be between $2.7 and $3.7 billion, making it one of the largest capital assets in the US at the time,[19] roughly equivalent to the total value of all farmland and farm buildings in the

South.[20] In contrast, the North's industry experienced rapid expansion due to the demands of the war, a growth that continued post-conflict. This surge in industrial activity significantly increased the wealth and power of corporate owners, enabling them to exert considerable influence in various facets of the nation's social and political affairs.[21]

Between 1790 and 1860, just over twenty-two thousand corporations were chartered in the United States under special legislative acts while seven thousand to eight thousand more were formed under general incorporation laws, mostly in the 1840s and 1850s. But this growth in corporations stirred concerns among the American public. The fear that these "artificial entities" with "perpetual life" could eventually dominate the social landscape was articulated throughout early American history by statesmen such as James Madison, Andrew Jackson, and Abraham Lincoln.[22] Others feared that they could corrupt public life by opening state legislatures to the temptation of bribes and crony capitalism.[23] These fears came to the fore in the late nineteenth and early twentieth centuries as smaller companies were driven out of business by larger corporations called trusts that consolidated wealth to levels that were previously unimaginable. Many Americans felt threatened by the power of this new class of corporation and the ultra-wealthy men that owned them.

The Trusts: 1870s–1920s. As demand to form corporations grew, state governments began to adopt more permissive corporate laws—called Enabling Laws—with fewer mandatory features to draw more businesses (and tax dollars) to their states. New Jersey was the first in 1896. Delaware followed later that year. But when New Jersey repealed its laws in 1913, many corporations relocated to Delaware, making it the leading corporate state, a status it has held ever since. Its courts continue to have a dominant influence on American corporate law today. By 1910, there were roughly 450,000 corporations in the world, and 60 percent of them (roughly 270,000) were in the United States.[24] This burgeoning form of capitalism helped the country make the transition into an industrial powerhouse, as machines replaced humans in most areas of the economy, leading some to refer to the United States as the first "corporation nation."[25]

Over the same period, mergers and consolidation in many industries put the power of much of the country's industrial base in the hands of around fifty organizations. Large trusts came to dominate the economic landscape with monopoly or cartel powers, including US Steel, Standard Oil, General Electric, American Cotton, National Biscuit, American Tobacco, International Harvester, and more. These trusts were structured as collective groups of companies that were directed by one board. For example, Standard Oil was a federation of forty companies that operated from one headquarters in New York and controlled 90 percent of oil production and distribution in the United States. The American Sugar Refining Company, structured similarly, controlled 98 percent of the sugar industry.

With limited controls, corporations and trusts grew unrestrained, creating what Mark Twain dubbed "the Gilded Age" to describe a period that he saw as glittering on the surface but corrupt underneath. The age produced extraordinary wealth inequality, with the richest four thousand families in the United States (representing less than 1 percent of the population) owning roughly the same amount of wealth as the other twelve million families combined, eleven million of whom lived below the poverty line.[26] Of particular note was a class of very wealthy business tycoons, called "Captains of Industry" by some and "Robber Barons" by others. They included Andrew Carnegie, John D. Rockefeller, Cornelius Vanderbilt, James J. Hill, and J. P. Morgan.

These tycoons attained unrivaled economic and political power to dominate markets, squelch competition, and heavily influence the government. They saw themselves as providing benefit to society by rationalizing industries and stabilizing the extreme swings in prices common to their era. At times, they rivaled the government in their power. J. P. Morgan, for example, saved the country from financial collapse during the panic of 1907 by organizing a consortium to make necessary loans to the US government when it had not yet created a central bank to perform that function.

Many tycoons justified their business dominance and extreme wealth through the social theories of Herbert Spencer, an English philosopher who applied Charles Darwin's ideas of natural selection in biology to human society. Spencer coined the term "survival of the fittest," advocating that businesses be allowed to fight for survival in an early version of *laissez faire* capitalism that was free from government intrusion.[27] Spencer's ideas introduced an early version of "lifeboat ethics," which holds that a superior class of human should be allowed to rise to the top.[28] When Andrew Carnegie first encountered Spencer's ideas he exclaimed, "Light came in as a flood, and all was clear." John D. Rockefeller compared *laissez faire* capitalism to the breeding of an American Beauty rose "by sacrificing the early buds which grew around it. This is not an evil tendency in business. It is merely the working out of a law of nature and a law of God."[29]

The tycoons' conspicuous wealth amidst widespread poverty, coupled with instances of cronyism and corruption of government officials, created a growing public backlash against the trusts. Nineteenth-century diplomat Charles Francis Adams wrote that society had "created a class of artificial beings who bid fair soon to be masters of their creator . . . they are already establishing despotisms which no spasmodic popular effort will be able to shake off."[30] In his 1901 State of the Union Address, President Teddy Roosevelt pledged to take action and launched a campaign to break the trusts, arguing that "[g]reat corporations exist only because they are created and safeguarded by our institutions; and it is therefore our right and our duty to see that they work in harmony with those institutions. . . . [This view is] based upon sincere conviction that combination and concentration should be, not prohibited, but supervised and within reasonable limits controlled."[31]

In 1911, the US Supreme Court ruled that the Standard Oil Trust was to be dissolved under the Sherman Antitrust Act, which was passed in 1890 in response to price-fixing abuses and was the first measure passed by the US Congress to outlaw monopolistic business practices. Rockefeller's trust was split into thirty-four companies, creating the forerunners of Exxon, Amoco, Mobil, and Chevron. Over the succeeding years, other breakups followed, such as J. P. Morgan's railroad conglomerate, the Northern Securities Company, American Tobacco Company, and more. In 1914, the Sherman Act was strengthened by the Clayton Act[32] to continue reigning in monopolistic power by prohibiting certain kinds of interlocking directorships, tie-in sales, and certain mergers and acquisitions if they were deemed to lessen competition in a market. Even with the decline of the trusts, the US economy continued to boom, producing 36 percent of world industrial output in the early part of the twentieth century, compared to 16 percent from Germany and 14 percent from the United Kingdom.[33]

The Great Depression and the New Deal, 1929–1930s. All of this economic prosperity came to an end with the Great Depression, the most severe economic downturn in US history, marked by a drop in industrial production between 1929 and 1933 of nearly 47 percent, a decline in gross domestic product (GDP) of 30 percent, a fall in wages of 42 percent and an unemployment rate that reached as high as 25 percent.[34] It was triggered by a series of escalating events, starting with an unprecedented expansion of the stock market in the 1920s when many perceived stock investing as a simple path to financial gain, frequently resorting to borrowing funds to invest in stocks. But during the stock market crash between September and November of 1929, stock prices fell 33 percent, causing a panic as people rushed to sell their holdings, accelerating further stock declines and causing even more panic. This created a deep loss of confidence in the economy and a steep cut in consumer spending, which in turn reduced industrial output and increased job losses. A run on banks ensued as large numbers of bank customers, fearful of their bank's solvency, simultaneously attempted to withdraw their deposits in cash. Between 1930 and 1932 the United States experienced four extended banking panics, with one-fifth of the banks in existence in 1930 having failed by 1933.

In the midst of the Depression, British economist John Maynard Keynes pioneered the use of macroeconomics to support the idea that government intervention can stabilize the economy. His most famous work, *The General Theory of Employment, Interest and Money*, was published in 1936 and advocated for increased government expenditures and lower taxes to stimulate demand and pull the global economy out of the Depression.[35] What came to be termed "Keynesian economics" caught on first in Europe and later in America when it found its way into the administration of President Franklin D. Roosevelt.

FDR passed a set of laws called the "New Deal" to reflect a new relationship between the American people and their government with the creation of an expanded list of agencies to control the market: the Agricultural Adjustment Administration to raise farm prices; the Civilian Conservation Corps to give jobs to unemployed youths to improve the environment; the Federal Emergency Relief Administration to give jobs to unemployed workers in other industries; the Tennessee Valley Authority to provide electricity to those who never had it before; the National Recovery Administration to revitalize industry and legalize the workers' right to unionize; the Farm Security Administration to resettle the rural poor and improve working conditions for migrant laborers; and the Social Security system to provide unemployment insurance.

Other important developments included the Glass-Steagall Act of 1933, which barred commercial banks from investment banking activities to protect depositors from potential losses through stock speculation; a series of securities acts (1933, 1934, and 1940) that required publicly traded corporations to disclose more information to their stockholders and the public; the Federal Deposit Insurance Corporation (FDIC) in 1933, which insured banks, thus reducing the risk of future bank runs; and the Social Security Act of 1935, which created a social insurance program designed to pay retirement benefits to workers.

Unsurprisingly, given its extreme expansion of government into the economy, the New Deal was highly controversial. For many Americans it represented a slide towards socialism, a concern that continues today for many Americans over government-provided "entitlements" like Medicaid, Medicare, Social Security, unemployment insurance, and welfare programs.

Managerial Capitalism, 1930s–1970s. As the economy began to come out of the Depression, a new incarnation of capitalism emerged, one that created more stability in the way corporations were organized. This shift was largely influenced by Adolf Berle and Gardiner Means's 1932 seminal work *The Modern Corporation and Private Property*, in which the duo argued that ownership and control of corporations should be separated to maintain effective operations. Once it caught on, this organizing structure brought the era of CEO owners like John D. Rockefeller, Andrew Mellon, Andrew Carnegie, and J.P. Morgan to an end, and ushered in a new class of professional CEOs who, in theory at least, were more dependable and less volatile in the management of large corporations.[36]

This era of "managerial capitalism" saw a shift in public opinion about business. In the early 1900s, a career in business was often scorned by intellectuals—with one commentator describing it as a "despicable way of life, pursued only by the stupid and unimaginative."[37] However, this perception changed as the business sector became more professionalized and gained respect. The transformation was particularly evident during the country's engagement in World War II from 1941 to 1945. Corporations played a crucial role in the war effort, regaining much of their lost prestige by efficiently producing airplanes, ships, tanks, and other armaments, thereby demonstrating their societal and economic value.

Historian Alfred Chandler observed that Adam Smith's famous "invisible hand" of the market was replaced by the "visible hand" of management as the most efficient way to organize business activity, and the multifunctional enterprise administered by salaried managers became "the most powerful institution in the American economy."[38] In the decades following the war, particularly the 1950s and 1960s, US businesses flourished, benefiting from minimal foreign competition as other countries focused on rebuilding after the war's devastation. In addition, the relative lack of domestic competition, owing to oligopolistic market structures dominated by very large corporations, further fueled their growth.[39] However, this expansion and consolidation of corporate power did not go unchecked. Economist John Kenneth Galbraith observed that "countervailing forces" from both government and big labor unions played a critical role in balancing corporate influence.[40]

While American society during this period of "managerialism" still contained enormous economic injustice—particularly for women and minorities—it was, overall, a period of shared prosperity for many Americans. The period from the 1950s to the 1970s marked a distinct phase in American corporate history, when major companies such as General Motors, US Steel, General Electric, and Chrysler not only pursued profits but also balanced the interests of various stakeholders and equitably shared the wealth created. These corporations, among the biggest employers in America at the time, fostered close government relationships, invested significantly in their communities, and were characterized by strong unionization. They offered their employees middle-class salaries, lifetime employment, and robust pension programs, epitomizing a commitment to the broader societal and employee welfare.[41] Summing up this sense of corporate responsibility, Frank Abrams, chairman of Standard Oil of New Jersey, wrote in 1951 that "the job of management is to maintain an equitable and working balance among the claims of the various directly interested groups . . . stockholders, employees, customers and the public at large."[42] GM CEO Charles Wilson put it even more simply when he defended his ownership of company shares during confirmation hearings to become US Secretary of Defense, stating that "what was good for our country was good for General Motors, and vice versa."[43]

This period also spawned critics. A conservative, homogenous corporate culture created a class of "company men" who relished life at the office and pursued growth up the corporate ladder and the status it conferred. In 1950, the book *The Lonely Crowd* noted that far too many corporate executives were "other directed" and more concerned with the good opinion of others in the office rather than "inner directed" with their own inner compass.[44] William Whyte, in his 1956 critique *The Organization Man*, wrote that most Americans came to believe that organizations could make better decisions than individuals, so serving an organization became preferable to advancing one's individual creativity.[45]

During this era, despite being largely excluded from mainstream economic opportunities, a "golden age" of black businesses and business thinkers also emerged. Management professors Leon Prieto and Simone Phipps have highlighted that many black business pioneers constructed their enterprises in ways that bolstered and empowered those around them—employees, customers, and local communities. This approach wasn't just altruistic; it was strategic and reciprocal. Successful black businesses often enjoyed robust support from the African American community, which eagerly patronized organizations that demonstrated care and commitment to its members' welfare.[46]

One notable figure from this period was Charles Clinton Spaulding, who led the North Carolina Mutual Life Insurance Company from 1900 to 1952, making it the largest black-owned business in the country. Spaulding's management style was intentionally inclusive, benefiting a wide range of stakeholders and earning him the nickname "Mr. Cooperation." Through his firm, he supported numerous local black-owned businesses and promoted economic development, gaining Durham the nickname of "the Black Wall Street." He fostered employment opportunities for both men and women, contributing significantly to the growth of a black middle class. It is worth noting that Spaulding's inclusive businesses—as inspiring as they were—were a necessary response to the US government's lamentable failure to ensure equal rights and the resulting disproportionate unemployment and underemployment among black citizens.

By the 1960s, the relatively widely distributed growth that the US economy had enjoyed in the 1940s and 1950s had begun to come to an end. Other world economies were now beginning to regain their competitive strength following the postwar rebuilding effort, often rebuilding with the latest technologies to present a powerful challenge to US corporations. By the 1970s, the US economy was starting to show the effects of this increased competition. As a result, managerialism came to be seen within some investment circles as emblematic of immovable executives who were running bloated businesses.[47]

Shareholder Capitalism, 1970s–Present. The late 1960s and early 1970s witnessed high domestic unemployment and inflation (combining stagnation and inflation, the term "stagflation" was invented). Keynesian technocrats seemed unable to fix the slumping market, and shareholders grew impatient that companies were not providing the same level of returns as the post–World War II economy. At the same time, corporations began to come under fire for seeming to put profits above the interests of society. Ralph Nader's 1965 exposé *Unsafe at Any Speed* put a focus on the auto industry in general, and GM in particular, for putting profit ahead of safety.[48] The book helped trigger an American consumer movement against corporations. Such criticisms precipitated a vigorous response, first from academia and then by the corporate sector.

During the 1960s, the Chicago School of Economics, led by economists Friedrich August von Hayek, George Stigler, and Milton Friedman, challenged Keynesian government policies. Instead, they advocated for a new classical macroeconomics approach that favored limited government intervention, relying primarily on manipulating the money supply to influence economic growth, as opposed to the more intrusive methods of the Keynesian-inspired New Deal. Friedman's book *Capitalism and Freedom* was published in 1962 and advocated for a reduced role for government in the market, relying instead on free markets to help society achieve prosperity by allowing individuals the freedom to pursue their own rational interests. Where economists like Adam Smith were considered classical economists, this new breed were dubbed neoclassical economists. By another telling, the name was coined as a form of scorn by opponents of, what were at the time, classical economists that blended *laissez-faire* approaches to political economy with new forms of marginal analysis.[49]

Friedman's views received a boost in 1971 when lawyer and jurist Lewis Powell was commissioned by the US Chamber of Commerce to write a memorandum defending the free enterprise system. Titled "Attack on the American Free Enterprise System," it was an anti-Communist and anti–New Deal blueprint for conservative business interests in America.[50] Dubbed the "Powell Memorandum" or simply the "Powell Memo," it decried a shift in American consumer sentiments away from corporations and argued that this shift not only undermined the power of private business but was leading the country towards socialism. Powell's views built on his prior experience as a corporate lawyer and board member of Philip Morris at a time when the tobacco industry was facing growing backlash because of scientific evidence linking smoking to cancer deaths.

The Powell Memorandum encouraged wealthy Americans to use their private charitable foundations to pursue a vision of a pro-business, antisocialist, minimally regulated America. The goal was to return the country to what Powell saw as the heyday of early American industrialism before the Great Depression and the New Deal. Powell's call was heeded. A rise of conservative philanthropy led to a powerful conservative intellectual movement of right-leaning think tanks and lobbying organizations that embraced neoliberal policies, including a reinvigorated American Enterprise Institute (founded in 1938) and the newly formed Heritage Foundation and American Legislative Exchange Council (both founded in 1973). Their rising influence coincided with a weakening of the countervailing forces of government and organized labor. As a result, mainstream political discourse began to shift away from a focus on business serving many stakeholders within society towards a focus on business serving primarily only one—the shareholder.

In 1976, a formative article by economists Michael Jensen and William Meckling called "Theory of the Firm: Managerial Behavior, Agency Costs, and Ownership Structure," ushered out the era of "managerial capitalism"; in its place, Jensen and Meckling proposed the ideas of agency theory and shareholder capitalism.[51] The duo argued that professional managers often prioritized their own interests and financial gain at the expense of business owners (shareholders). They proposed that CEOs should focus on "maximizing shareholder value," and that corporate boards should ensure the alignment of senior management's interests with those of shareholders through mechanisms like stock-based compensation schemes. The duo also took aim at government intervention to regulate business. "The corporation is neither the creature of the state nor the object of special privileges extended by the state," they wrote. "The corporation did not draw its first breath of life from either a minister of state or civil servant. More importantly, the corporation requires for its existence only freedom of contract."[52]

In the 1980s, Milton Friedman became an advisor to US president Ronald Reagan and British prime minister Margaret Thatcher. Both leaders' policies came to reflect Friedman's ideas about monetary policy, taxation, privatization, and deregulation. The shift from Keynesian economic models to Friedman's supply-side economics—often referred to as Reaganomics or trickle-down economics—was complete. As the Soviet Union fell and capitalist nations pronounced victory over communist economies, the prevailing belief came to be that the loosening of regulatory controls on the market would allow the economy to be liberated and create more jobs, increase prosperity, and improve the lives of millions of people. Not restricted to the United States, neoliberal policies—what to some came to be known as the "Washington Consensus"—formed the standard reform package for helping developing countries in crisis by Washington, D.C.–based institutions like the International Monetary Fund (IMF) and the World Bank. The Washington Consensus focused on free-market policies such as trade and finance liberalization, privatization, and fiscal and monetary policies intended to minimize fiscal deficits and inflation. Friedman's variant of capitalism remains largely in place in the United States and other Western economies—but is now the subject of increasing scrutiny and pressure to change.

The Failures of Shareholder Capitalism

For some critics, the questions today are whether shareholder capitalism is fit for purpose, and, more specifically, whether it continues to work in the interests of society. For some, the answer is a very definitive no. According to economist Joseph Stiglitz, "Now that we have four decades of this experiment [of Reaganomics], I think we can declare it unambiguously a failure."[53] For Stiglitz and others, the problems with the current, dominant incarnation of shareholder capitalism are four-fold.

Shareholder capitalism has depleted finite natural resources and degraded the environment. In 2005, the UN Millennium Ecosystem Assessment concluded that between 1953 and 2003, "humans have changed ecosystems more rapidly and extensively than in any comparable period of time in human history."[54] Climate change is just one marker (what are called "planetary boundaries," shown in Figure 4.1)[55] of a broader shift to what some scientists have called the Anthropocene,[56]—the Age of Humans—in which the human population has grown to such numbers and our technology to such power that we are now altering the planet's systems.[57] Some have suggested that the proper term should be the "Capitalocene" to call out capitalism, and particularly the Western economy, as the cause.[58]

We are causing the "sixth mass extinction," in which roughly 70 percent of mammals, birds, and reptiles have declined between 1970 and 2016 and as much as 30 percent of all present species could be extinct by 2100.[59] We have released unprecedented amounts of nitrogen and phosphorous into our rivers and oceans through fertilizer runoff that is severely threatening marine life. We are converting natural habitat, in the form of forests, grasslands, and wetlands, into agricultural use at unsustainable rates. Freshwater availability is

FIGURE 4.1

Planetary Boundaries

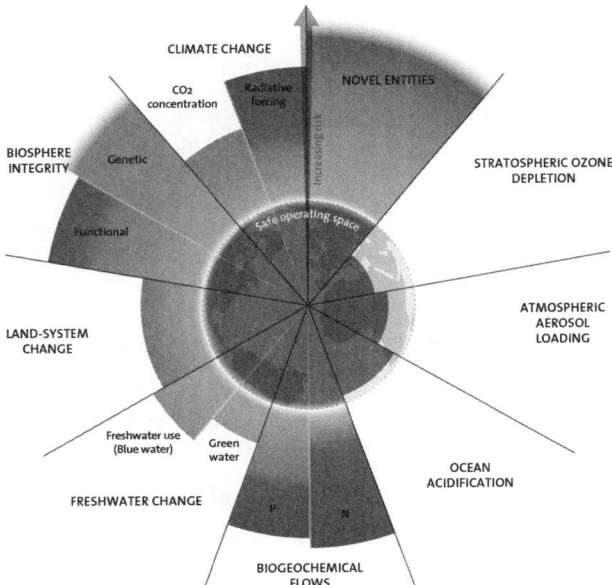

Source: Stockholm Resilience Center, *Planetary Boundaries*, "Azote for Stockholm Resilience Centre, based on analysis in Richardson et al 2023," 2023, https://www.stockholmresilience.org/research/planetary-boundaries.html (accessed October 31, 2023). CC BY-NC-ND 3.0.

decreasing rapidly, such that almost a half a billion people could experience water scarcity by 2050. Other markers that scientists are watching include ocean acidification and the release of atmospheric aerosols.[60] Naturalist and writer David Attenborough warned business leaders in Davos in 2019 that "[g]lobal businesses, international co-operation and the striving for higher ideals, these are all possible because for millennia, on a global scale, nature has largely been predictable and stable. Now in the space of one human lifetime— indeed in the space of *my* lifetime all that has changed. . . . The Garden of Eden is no more."[61]

Shareholder capitalism has led to record inequality. Alongside its significant impact on the natural environment, the market has also exploited people, resulting in increasing economic disparity, both in the United States and globally. The current situation is drawing comparisons to a new Gilded Age, marked by stark contrasts in wealth and economic conditions. Indeed, the wealthiest 20 percent consume 77 percent of all the world's goods and services while the poorest 20 percent consume just 1.5 percent,[62] leading to a concentration of wealth, through which the world's wealthiest 10 percent own 76 percent of global net wealth while the poorest 50 percent own just 2 percent.[63] This extraordinary income gap is being paralleled by a similarly alarming "climate divide"[64] under which the poorest of the world are least responsible for climate change and are most at risk, while the affluent of the world are most to blame but have the resources to adapt to its impacts (at least in the short term). People in New York may be able to afford to build sea walls but people in Bangladesh cannot. Other variants of inequality that remain rife are gender inequality, under which women are paid 82 percent of that which men are paid; racial inequality, under which the median net worth of white households is ten times higher than that of black households and eight times higher than Latinx households;[65] and geographic inequality, under which two-thirds of all US job growth between 2007 and 2019 was concentrated on twenty-five cities and dynamic hubs, while low-growth and rural communities where seventy-seven million live had flat or falling employment.[66]

Shareholder capitalism has led to the concentration of power. In their book *The Captured Economy*, Brink Lindsey and Steven Teles write that wealthy special interests have captured the policymaking process for their own benefit by creating regressive regulations that stifle competition, entrepreneurship, and innovation for the benefit of wealthy individuals.[67] Large companies have also squashed competition through so-called "catch and kill" acquisitions and other merger-and-acquisition tactics. In the 2010s, Amazon, Apple, Facebook, Google, and Microsoft made a combined four hundred acquisitions globally, which tamed upstart competition.[68] In the world of politics, a 2014 study supports this thesis, concluding that economic elites and narrow interest groups were very influential in the establishment and form of federal policy between 1981 and 2002 while the views of ordinary citizens had virtually no independent effect at all, concluding that "the preferences of the average American appear to have only a minuscule near-zero, statistically non-significant impact upon public policy."[69] While some disagree, suggesting that the poor, middle class, and rich agree on a great number of policies and that many Americans just aren't politically engaged and don't want to be politically engaged,[70] many point to disengagement as one more outcome from a system in which power and influence are not fully shared.

Shareholder capitalism has been a poor engine for value creation. If there is one stakeholder or constituent that you'd expect to benefit from free-market capitalism it would be shareholders, but that may not even be the case. In the period of managerial capitalism from 1932 to 1976, total real compound annual return on stocks of the S&P 500 was 7.6 percent; during shareholder capitalism from 1976 to 2011, it dropped to 6.4 percent. Former dean of the Rotman School of Business Roger Martin observes that by modifying the start and end dates of the two periods, performance numbers can be equalized, but they cannot be made to show that shareholders fared better in the era of shareholder capitalism.[71]

Going further, productivity (output per hours worked) was an average of 2.82 percent between 1920 and 1970 (a period that also includes the Great Depression) and fell to 1.62 percent between 1970 and 2014.[72] From 1948 to 1970, real incomes grew by 3 percent annually and gains were spread fairly evenly among all levels of society. But from 2005 to 2019, real incomes grew only 0.7 percent[73] and most of that gain was enjoyed by the top 1 percent. Firm performance as measured by return on assets for the US economy declined by three quarters between 1965 and 2012 (see Figure 4.2),[74] while at the same time, federal investment in public goods, such as education, infrastructure, and scientific research, declined from approximately 2.5 percent of GDP in

FIGURE 4.2

Return on Assets for the US Economy, 1965–2012

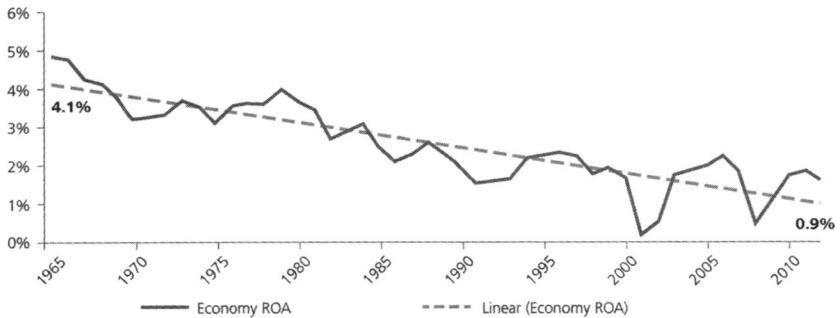

Source: J. Hagel, J. Seely Brown, T. Samoylova, and M. Lui, *Success or Struggle: ROA as a True Measure of Business Performance* (New York: Deloitte University Press, 2013).

1980 to less than 1.5 percent of GDP in 2020. Private-sector investments in public infrastructure, including public-private partnerships, also fell over the same period, declining at an even faster rate following the 2008 recession.[75]

The hallmark of shareholder capitalism is to align executive interests with shareholder interests through equity-based compensation, which rose from an average of 0 percent of the median executive's pay at *Fortune* 500 firms in the 1980s to roughly 60 percent in 2001[76] and 85 percent by 2020.[77] But the sought after alignment did not happen, as growth in executive compensation has not correlated with corporate performance.[78] When a category of people secure more value for themselves than they create it is called "rent-seeking." Here, the evidence is clear this is happening among CEOs. Between 1978 and 2020, CEO pay increased by 1,460 percent, but that growth was eight times more than that of corporate profits, 28 percent more than S&P stock market growth (of 1,063 percent), and more than productivity growth.[79] In 2021, CEOs at the top 350 firms in the United States were paid an average of $27.8 million, fueling the growth of top 1 percent and top 0.1 percent incomes, leaving fewer of the gains of economic growth for ordinary workers and widening the gap between very high earners and the bottom 90 percent. CEO pay rose more than six times more than the top 0.1 percent of wage earners between 1978 and 2021 and more than seventy-three times more than the growth of the typical worker's pay, which grew by just 18 percent. In 1965, the ratio of CEO-to-typical-worker compensation was 20-to-1; in 2021 it reached 399-to-1 (see Figure 4.3).[80] In other words, the average CEO earned in one year nearly nine times what the average person will earn over a lifetime.[81] By 2023, seven out of ten of the world's largest corporations had a billionaire as CEO or principal shareholder, despite stagnation in living standards for millions of workers around the world.[82]

Rent-seeking is occurring from entire industries in the economy too, which also contributes to shareholder capitalism's lackluster performance. In particular, the finance sector increasingly extracts "rent" from the market while contributing less actual value by helping the economy shift towards debt-fueled speculation, rather than productive lending to new businesses. Banks, hedge funds, mutual funds, insurance firms, and trading houses that

FIGURE 4.3

CEO-to-Worker Compensation Ratio, 1965–2021

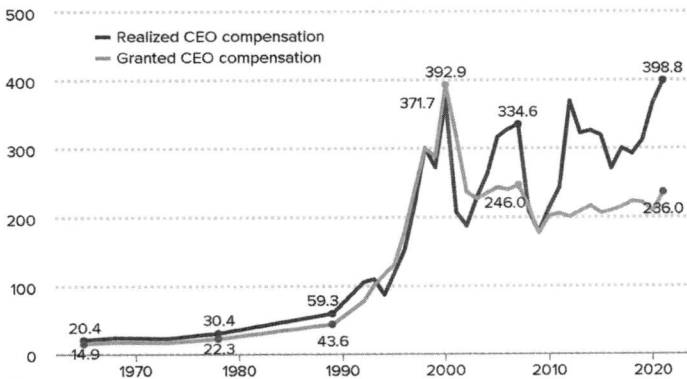

CEOs make 399 times as much as typical workers

Notes: Average annual compensation for CEOs at the top 250 US firms ranked by sales. "Typical worker" compensation is the average annual compensation (wages and benefits of a full-time, full-year worker) of production/nonsupervisory workers in the industries that the top 350 firms operate in.

Source: J. Bivens and J. Kandra, "CEO pay has skyrocketed 1,460% since 1978," *Economic Policy Institute,* October 4, 2022.

previously provided loans to business to increase productivity are increasingly lending against existing assets such as housing and stocks,[83] such that only 15 percent of the funds managed by the finance industry go to business in the real economy. Despite currently taking around 25 percent of all corporate profits, the financial sector creates a mere 4 percent of all jobs.[84]

Even big industrial corporations are shifting their core business from making material things to engineering financial products. Consider the evolution of GE from a primarily manufacturing-based company to one that produced nearly 60 percent of its profits from GE Capital, its financial arm, before selling it off in 2015.[85] Indeed, the finance sector's share of value in the economy doubled from 3.7 percent in 1960 to 8.4 percent in 2014, while manufacturing fell from 25 percent to 12 percent. In 1970, finance and insurance company profits amounted to 24 percent of the profits of all other sectors combined. By 2013, that percentage had grown to 37 percent.[86] According to *Financial Times* associate editor Rana Foroohar, this shift tends to "suck the economic air out of the room," leading the economy to gradually become "a zero-sum game between financial wealth holders and the rest of America."[87] This can be seen in an even higher strata of CEO salaries. While top financial executives earned the same as their peers in other industries in 1980, they were making a 250 percent premium by 2006.[88] In 1979, finance professionals made up 8 percent of the top 1 percent of wage earners; by 2005, their share grew to 14 percent.[89]

Some critics even question whether the seeming winners in this economy—namely, CEOs—are doing as well as chief executives in previous eras. To be sure, they are wealthier, but are their lives and careers more enriching? Paul Polman, former CEO of Unilever, suggests that the prevalent approach in corporate leadership is short term, self-serving, and meaningless. As he sees it, CEOs often focus on maximizing company performance in a brief period, usually three to five years, through aggressive tactics. Then they leave the company for their successors to deal with the aftermath, often involving restructuring and write-offs, while reaping significant personal financial rewards. Polman contrasts this with past eras when managers were more integrated into the communities they served, witnessing firsthand the value they created. He describes the life of today's CEOs as ultimately unfulfilling, with many retiring to affluent, warm-weather enclaves, disconnected from the broader societal issues. "They get themselves installed on these islands of prosperity in a sea of poverty, and they are oblivious to anything that's going on around them in the real world. It's a sad life, in my opinion."[90]

A New Capitalism Will Emerge from the Old

Over history, the benefits of capitalism cannot be overlooked. It has led to unprecedented economic growth and human prosperity over the last century, when the world population increased by a factor of four, the world economy increased by a factor of fourteen, global per capita income tripled, and average life expectancy increased by almost two thirds.[91] This is the product of the market's ability to provide the food, shelter, medical care, safety, and security that we need to thrive.

But today's variant of shareholder capitalism has lost its way and is now damaging society and the planet. Is that sustainable? Peter Georgescu, CEO of advertising firm Young & Rubicam, worries that capitalism "has been slowly committing suicide." He writes that "capitalism is a brilliant factory for prosperity. Brilliant. And yet the version of capitalism we have created here works for only a minority of people."[92] Georgescu, who was eighty-four years old in 2023, reflects that he was mentored by a post–World War II culture that fostered a sense of community over individuality, when corporate executives weren't paid such exorbitant salaries and workers enjoyed consistently rising wages. But while the capitalism that dominated before the 1970s "optimized the well-being of customers, employees, shareholders and the nation," the shareholder capitalism that replaced it allowed profits to soar at the expense of worker pay. The wealth of the median family as well as life expectancy have both declined in this transition. Warren Buffett remarked, "There's class warfare, all right, but it's my class, the rich class, that's making war, and we're winning."[93]

Currently, business schools are still teaching students the tenets of this flawed variant of capitalism and placing high status on high-salary jobs to boost rankings and place students in a bind. To succeed, they must ignore the system's flaws and exploit a bad system for personal gain. This leads to dissatisfied students or, worse, a student body composed of greedy, self-interested people who can happily opt in to exploiting a broken system. Rather than fostering what economist Joseph Stiglitz labels "exploitative" capitalism,[94] business schools should shift their focus towards developing a new variant of capitalism through research, teaching, and outreach—one that more effectively addresses and serves societal needs.

While some, such as Martin Parker, professor at the University of Bristol, think "we should call in the bulldozers and demand an entirely new way of thinking about management, business and markets,"[95] that is neither likely nor desirable. The process of social change makes the idea of wiping the capitalist slate clean and developing a new system unrealistic. Every set of institutions by which society is structured has evolved from some set of institutions that preceded it. The late Harvard paleontologist Stephen Jay Gould made the evolutionary case powerfully clear with his essay "The Creation Myths of Cooperstown," in which he pointed out that baseball was not invented by Abner Doubleday in Cooperstown, New York, in 1839.[96] In fact, "no one invented baseball at any moment or in any spot." It evolved from games that came before it. Similarly, Adam Smith did not invent capitalism in 1776 with his book *The Wealth of Nations*. Smith saw changes taking place in European economies in the eighteenth century, noted what he saw, and built upon it with innovations that he envisioned.

In the same way, we cannot simply invent a new system to replace capitalism (and no serious commentator would promote a centrally planned economy after the spectacular failures of Soviet economies and their imitators during the Cold War). Whatever form of commerce and interchange we adopt tomorrow must evolve out of the form we have today. Looking at history to set a baseline for what that form might be, we can see a steady back and forth in the balance of power between corporations on the one side and the countervailing forces of government and civil society (notably labor) on the other. The goal is to find a new balance. In 2020, Senator Elizabeth Warren proposed a return to the corporate charter idea with the Accountable Capitalism Act, which would have required that very large American corporations obtain a federal charter as a "United States Corporation," obligating them to serve society's interests.[97] If a US Corporation failed to meet this requirement, the federal government could revoke its charter. While the bill did not receive a vote, it offered one view for a correction.

Another corrective may lie in addressing the extreme levels of wealth that are being accumulated by a small number of individuals, for example, through a wealth tax. In retort, critics of a wealth tax turn to the oft-used Laffer Curve to argue that there is a level at which tax rates will decrease the interest in working and, as a result, decrease the amount of government tax revenue (see Figure 4.4). But at what level is this true?

Certainly, a tax rate of 100 percent will eliminate the desire to work. But is money the only reason that people work? It is an empirical fact that people still work even when they are rich. Mark Zuckerberg still goes to work, despite having amassed far more wealth than he will ever need. Steven Pearlstein puts a provocative question forward in his 2018 book *Can American Capitalism Survive?*: "Does anyone really think that the $1 billion a year earned by top hedge fund managers actually reflects their economic contribution? Are financial and labor markets so perfectly rational and competitive that we know there isn't someone every bit as brilliant, cunning and hardworking who would be willing to do it for $750 million? If they were paid a mere $500 million, would these masters of the universe decide to withhold their excellence and head for the bench? Somehow, I doubt it."[98]

These questions and more will animate much of the debate in the pages that follow, forming a baseline for a renewed understanding of capitalism and deeper examination of the variant that will work best for our twenty-first cen-

FIGURE 4.4

The Laffer Curve

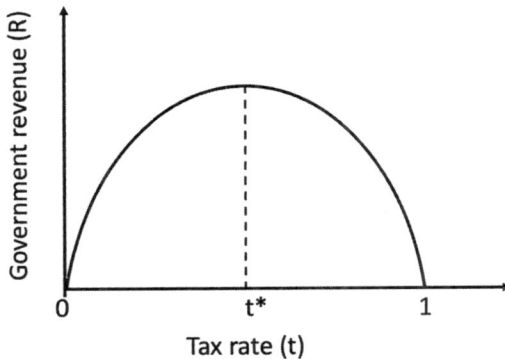

Source: Figure created by author.

tury challenges. University of Michigan professor Jerry Davis argues that "[i]n 20 years, we may look back at shareholder capitalism as a misguided 40-year experiment that was inevitably doomed to collapse, replaced (hopefully) by something more human-centric and less distorting of our common values. The tools to achieve this future are available now, if we can correct course and recover from the wrong turn we took."[99]

More to the point, can we help our students find this new replacement? While our present variant of capitalism has been mythologized and distorted in society, business schools must help future business leaders become educated on the deeper facets of how we organize our economy, to have an understanding of what capitalism once was and to be prepared to have a role in deciding what it will be. Some elements will remain, some will be amended, others will be eliminated, and new ones will be added. With this history as a foundation and a context for analyzing the state of capitalism in today's world, we can begin to consider more deeply the variant of capitalism that must replace it, and how we will get from the present to that future system.

FIVE

Bringing Adam Smith into the Present

Reexamining the Fundamentals of Capitalism

"One of the best-kept secrets in economics is that there is no case
for the invisible hand. After more than a century trying to prove the
opposite, economic theorists investigating the matter finally concluded
in the 1970s that there is no reason to believe markets are led, as if by
an invisible hand, to an optimal equilibrium—or any equilibrium at all."

—JONATHAN SCHLEFER, *THE ASSUMPTIONS ECONOMISTS MAKE*

When I ask my students to define capitalism, they often appear shocked, as if
I was asking, "What is gravity?" To them, it's one of those things that just "is,"
and always will be. They fumble some answers and get close in the end, but
only with some real prodding. This isn't a surprise. Defining capitalism should
be a logical place to start for a business education. Yet it gets surprisingly little
coverage in the curriculum. So, while young people sense something is wrong
with the way power and wealth are distributed in our economy, and how our
markets currently treat our natural resources,[1] business schools are not helping them understand the causes and how to fix them. To do that, students
must first understand the foundations of capitalism, how it has evolved and at
times deviated from serving its original purpose, and what tools are available
for amending it. In short, business schools should equip students with the
knowledge to become stewards of the market, to think critically about the
role of business in society, their role as a manager in guiding those businesses,
and how to maintain the overall system in which they will practice their craft.

The Foundations of Capitalism

In fairness to my tongue-tied students, defining capitalism is not an easy task. It can be seen first as an economic system. But it is also closely tied with the political and social institutions in which it operates. What follows is an intentionally brief overview of some central thinkers, books, and ideas that structure our notions of capitalism. It is not intended to be a deep immersion in the intricacies of political science or the history of capitalism's many facets. But it is intended to cover some basic facts about capitalism to help us identify areas where tensions exist between capitalism as it is practiced today and the real-world problems it is creating.

Capitalism Is First and Foremost an Economic System

Capitalism is a set of institutions focused on the creation of wealth through the private ownership of capital, production, and distribution. Humbolt University Fellow Jürgen Kocka names three central elements that form the foundation of those institutions. First, the root term, "capital," is a central feature that allows for present investment in expectation of higher future gains and the accumulation of profit as an overriding goal. Second, individuals and organizations have private property rights that extend to the resources and tools used for producing goods and services. This enables them to make their own decisions regarding the use, development, and distribution of these resources. In other words, they control the "means of production." Third, a market (or the economy) is the main mechanism for the allocation of goods, services, and wealth.[2]

These three elements provide the core foundations of capitalism and cannot be removed if the system is to still be called capitalism. But that just scratches the surface. There are many dynamics that are inherent to capitalism, including competition, change (economic competitors and technologies will rise and fall), and growth (economies will reap the rewards of greater productivity). An entire society benefits from these dynamics, but the benefits are not evenly distributed—and that's to be expected. Those who effectively manage their capital build wealth, whereas others may not achieve similar financial success. Within this framework of institutions, there exists an ideal of capitalism, one free from the inherent complications and confusion of real-world social dynamics. But when we consider how capitalism has deviated in the real world, we can begin to outline some areas for improvement.

The first major work that treated economics as a comprehensive system was Adam Smith's 1776 book *The Wealth of Nations* (or if you prefer the full name, *An Inquiry into the Nature and Causes of the Wealth of Nations*). It is worth noting that Smith does not mention capitalism in his book, but instead refers to "commercial society" to describe the domain of economic life that has come to form classical free-market economic theory. His work is a subject of much debate as well as much misunderstanding. But his ideas permeate our understanding of capitalism as we know it today; many of these ideas we now take for granted but should examine as we consider amending shareholder capitalism.

To begin, Adam Smith was a moral philosopher, as were John Stuart Mill and John Locke. This distinction is crucial in understanding that the field of economics, often perceived as solely focused on scientific analysis, has its roots in a deeper moral discourse. Smith believed that human beings are fundamentally self-interested, but driven by a desire for approval, attention, praise, and recognition, and he hoped that commercial society would lead them to be more virtuous.

For Smith, self-interest and selfishness are two very different things. In Smith's first book, *The Theory of Moral Sentiments* (1759), he sought to understand how one might develop one's ability for moral judgment, which he saw as beginning with feeling, or sentiment, and not with reason. Of all the sentiments, he saw mutual sympathy as especially important. Smith writes, "Sympathy . . . cannot, in any sense, be regarded as a selfish principle."[3] People are selfish if they act purely to gain for themselves by taking more than their "fair share." People act with self-interest when they include the interests of other people as well as their own. For Smith, individuals are inherently aware of their own needs, but under appropriate societal conditions, they can fulfill these needs while simultaneously creating an environment where others can also meet their own needs, harmoniously balancing self-interest with mutual benefit.

A social order, therefore, can encourage self-interest and self-restraint, persuading people to develop the virtues that will help them fulfill their obligations to others in a just society. This social order can be imposed not by the monarch or aristocracy, but by what he called the "impartial spectator." He argued that "gradually we learn what emotions and actions seem proper to others. We try to temper them to the point where an impartial spectator would fully share our sentiments and regard them as appropriate. Indeed, we are prompted to go further and show real concern for others, because we know that an impartial spectator would approve, and we take pleasure from that."[4] Under this scrutiny, we develop certain habits and behaviors which evolve to form our conscience, guiding our moral and ethical decisions.[5] This is similar to Warren Buffett's "newspaper test" some two hundred and fifty years later: if you have any doubt about whether a particular decision or action is right or wrong, imagine how you would feel if it was reported in the newspaper and is read by family, friends, and neighbors.[6]

This idea animates much of Smith's thinking in *The Wealth of Nations*, in which he saw the market as a powerful tool of discipline, helping (not forcing) people to desire frugality and self-restraint, which in turn would lead to the ultimate goal, as he saw it, of greater prosperity for all of society. Indeed, for Smith, material prosperity and wealth were essential to happiness and a good society—but only insofar as they liberated people to move from self-preservation to more prosocial pursuits. So, for Smith, a nation is wealthy when consumer items are inexpensive and a comfortable life is within reach.[7] He writes that "before we can feel much for others, we must in some measure be at ease ourselves; if our own misery pinches us very severely, we have no leisure to attend to that of our neighbor."[8] In a well-functioning society, then, our sentimental tendencies to self-regard can become inclinations to sympathy and decency to others. But Smith acknowledged that a well-functioning society takes work; it requires social institutions designed to channel the sentiments towards this kind of moral formation. Those institutions, taking the form of markets, were Smith's life-long obsession.

Smith saw capitalism as based on free trade and competition. He was a strong voice in the Scottish Enlightenment and a strong critic of mercantilism, which had dominated economic affairs until his time in history. Mercantilism (or bullionism) was based on the idea that production, consumption, and profit were all geared towards and guided by the sovereign. The wealth of a nation was based on the amount of bullion (usually gold) it possessed. Since the predominate view was that the world's wealth remained fairly constant and that a state could increase its wealth primarily at the expense of another state through conquest or beneficial trade, the sovereign forbade the export of gold and severely limited the import of finished goods. In this system, people's lives were ruled by their station in life, and their interests were subordinated to the interests of the sovereign. Smith challenged these notions and argued that an individual could, through hard work, improve their lot in life. The goal was to set the system in place that allowed that to happen. Once the proper incentives are established, Smith believed, markets can run with limited control from governments or aristocrats.

However, Smith was not an advocate of a *laissez faire* market, recognizing the important functions played by government and civil society in establishing the guardrails by which that market would be structured.[9] He believed that the rules of the market are not self-legislating nor are they naturally obvious. Rather, he saw the market as a public institution that requires rules imposed upon it.[10] But with those guardrails in place, the power of the "invisible hand" could arrange the two most important components of a capitalist exchange: the buyer and the seller. He writes, "By directing that industry in such a manner as its produce may be of greatest value, [the business owner] intends only his own gain, and he is in this, as in many other cases, led by an invisible hand to promote an end which was no part his intention."[11] He elaborates on a more altruistic version of the invisible hand in *The Theory of Moral Sentiments*, where he writes that the rich "consume little more than the poor, and in spite of their natural selfishness and rapacity, they divide with the poor the produce of all their improvements. They are led by an invisible hand to make nearly the same distribution of the necessities of life which would have been made had the earth been divided into equal portions among all its inhabitants."[12] In this way, Smith felt that our inclinations would be restrained by our moral sentiments, which could be guided by the invisible hand of the market under the constraints set by the government.

Out of this idea came one of his oft-quoted lines to describe how one's pursuit of their own interests, guided by the market, would benefit others: "It is not from the benevolence of the butcher, the brewer, or the baker that we expect our dinner, but from their regard for their own interest. We address ourselves not to their humanity but to their self-love, and never talk to them of our own necessities but of their advantages. Nobody but a beggar chooses to depend chiefly upon the benevolence of his fellow citizens."[13] This passage is often read as a description of selfishness, but Corey Robin, Distinguished Professor of Political Science at Brooklyn College, argues that Smith actually meant it as an injunction to empathy, to change our perspective from looking at only our own interests to look at the exchange through the other's eyes. "If we fail at that task," he writes, "we will fail to get what we want out of the market. Thus does the market impose on us the rule of empathy."[14]

Smith's invisible hand is not an actual entity or power; it is the sum of many phenomena that occur naturally when consumers and producers engage in commerce. But for this to work properly, it presumes "free and fair" competition through what may be called the "holy trinity" of self-interest, rational expectations, and efficient markets.

When capitalism is working efficiently to meet supply and demand, the nature of work changes. Specifically, workers become more productive and more specialized. In capitalism's early years, productivity gains came from divisions of labor. Smith used the analogy of a pin factory (what he concedes was a "a very trifling manufacture") to describe the ways in which ten workers could produce forty-eight thousand pins per day with a division of labor, where a single worker could possibly make only one. "One man draws out the wire, another straights it, a third cuts it, a fourth points it, a fifth grinds it at the top for receiving the head; to make the head requires two or three distinct operations; to put it on, is a peculiar business, to whiten the pins is another; it is even a trade by itself to put them into the paper; and the important business of making a pin is, in this manner, divided into about eighteen distinct operations, which, in some manufactories, are all performed by distinct hands."[15]

With these (and other) key elements of the structure of capitalism and the market laid out by Adam Smith, one of its most powerful features becomes clear; it never stops changing. There are countless additions to Smith's understanding of capitalism, but Joseph Schumpeter added a critical element in his 1942 book *Capitalism, Socialism and Democracy.* As he observed the steady progression of technology over time, he noted that capitalism can never be stationary and is in a constant state of "creative destruction." "The opening up of new markets, foreign or domestic, and the organizational development from the craft shop and factory to such concerns as U.S. Steel," Schumpeter writes, "illustrate the same process of industrial mutation—if I may use that biological term—that incessantly revolutionizes the economic structure from within, incessantly destroying the old one, incessantly creating a new one. This process of creative destruction is the essential fact about capitalism. The fundamental impulse that sets and keeps the capitalist engine in motion comes from the new consumers' goods, the new methods of production or transportation, the new markets, the new forms of industrial organization that capitalist enterprise creates."[16] This, to Schumpeter and many others, is the genius of the capitalist system; its ability to constantly lead to the creation of new and (usually, but not always) better products and services.

Capitalism Is Also a Political and Social System

Capitalism is described above as a self-regulating machine in constant motion that makes society continuously more economically productive and thus wealthier. But capitalism has never been merely an economic system—it requires a political decision to organize one's society around its principles, and it embodies a set of values that guide human behavior. In his 1905 book *The Protestant Ethic and the Spirit of Capitalism*, Max Weber puzzled over the question of why capitalism gained traction within certain populations at a certain time and place. What he concluded was that capitalism aligned with the Protestant doctrines of faith that encouraged planning, hard work, and self-denial in the pursuit of a calling. Where the Roman Catholic Church assured salvation to individuals who accepted the church's sacraments and submitted to clerical authority, the Protestant (particularly Calvinist) ethic encouraged people to engage in work in the secular world as blessed by God, as much as any "sacred" calling. While there were certainly successful Catholic entrepreneurs in Weber's time, Protestants enjoyed a greater degree of freedom to strive systematically for profit for its own sake and to view worldly success as a sign that they were saved. A "vocation" from God was no longer limited to the clergy or church but applied to any occupation or trade.[17] In other words, the Protestant work ethic was an important force behind the unplanned and uncoordinated emergence of modern capitalism.[18]

In his 1944 book *The Great Transformation*, the Hungarian anthropologist Karl Polanyi drew the links between capitalism and human social relations and community. As Fordham University Gabelli Fellow Anthony Annett points out, Polanyi argued that markets cannot solely be understood as economic domains and instead, one must think of the market economy as "embedded in social institutions and given shape by law and governments"[19] in what he called the "market society." Economist Mariana Mazzucato draws from Polanyi that this "renders meaningless the usual static juxtaposition of state vs. market."[20] In essence, he believed that a self-regulating market could not happen without the intervention of state control, which he observed had grown with the advent of industrialization. Polanyi writes that "the road to the free market was opened and kept open by an enormous increase in continuous, centrally organized and controlled intervention."[21] As the Omidyar Network notes more recently, to build more inclusive and equitable societies, we must see that "markets are not 'naturally' occurring. They are not inherently free; they are built. They are deliberately shaped by ideas, norms, values, culture, capital, politics, laws, and of course, power and people. The balance between markets and government in any society is always contested and evolving."[22]

Enduring Critiques of Capitalism

Within these elements of the economic, political, and social dimensions of capitalism lie the building blocks for a new variant of capitalism to amend shareholder capitalism. To tease them out, we turn to the ongoing criticism and unease towards capitalist activities that have been a part of Western civilization for centuries, evident even in biblical times when Jesus expelled merchants and lenders from a Jerusalem temple for defiling it with commerce.

What may be considered the first organized resistance specifically targeting modern capitalism can be traced to the Luddite Revolution from 1811 to 1816, which was carried out by British weavers and textile workers who rebelled against the rise of mechanized looms, or the "dark satanic mills" of the industrial revolution as the poet William Blake described them. Most of these workers were trained artisans who had spent years perfecting their craft, and they were angered that unskilled (and underpaid) machine operators were robbing them of their way of life and their social standing. Cheap competition of early textile factories was particularly threatening to the artisans, and a few desperate weavers began breaking into factories and smashing textile machines. The movement was said to be named after Ned Ludd, an apprentice who allegedly smashed two stocking frames in 1779 and whose name had become emblematic of machine destroyers. But Ned Ludd was fictional and used as a way to suggest an organized movement. In any case, the Luddite movement was brought to an end when Parliament made "machine breaking" a capital crime and military force was used to capture, try, and punish accused and convicted Luddites, often with penal transportation or execution.[23] Luddites fought against the rush of capitalism and industrialization that was destroying their way of life. Their concerns continue today and form one of the primary friction points between capitalism and the interests of society.

Capitalism can be unfairly dehumanizing and oppressive for some and not others. The themes of the Luddite Revolution were evident in the writings of Karl Marx, who recognized capitalism as a social system as much as an economic one thirty years after the Luddites. And more important, he saw the system as a form of oppression and the division of labor as a form of evil that commodified workers, making them into cogs in a machine—somebody else's machine—that deprived them of the product of their work. That somebody else was the capitalist or the bourgeois, which, to Marx, exerted a form of oppression that was no different from that of a sovereign. As he writes in the 1848 *Communist Manifesto,* "The modern bourgeois society that has sprouted from the ruins of feudal society has not done away with class antagonisms. It has but established new classes, new conditions of oppression, new forms of struggle in place of the old ones."[24] He warned that the gap between rich and poor would grow in a capitalist system, with the end state being that of monopoly or oligarchy. To counter this outcome, he argued that "the theory of communists may be summed up in the single sentence: Abolition of private property." He writes that "communism is for us not a state of affairs which is to be established, [but] an ideal to which reality [will] have to adjust itself. We call communism the real movement which abolishes the present state of things. The conditions of this movement result from the premises now in existence," adding that "only in community with others has each individual the means of cultivating his gifts in all directions; only in the community, therefore, is personal freedom possible."[25] Marx believed that capitalism would be destroyed by the proletariat, whom capitalism had exploited, and he relished the prospect, concluding *The Communist Manifesto* with the words "Workers of the world, unite! You have nothing to lose but your chains!"[26]

What is interesting about Marx's critiques is that they were not completely foreign to the ideas of some of the writers that supported capitalism. As a moral philosopher whose ultimate aim was a more prosperous society, Adam Smith believed that extreme inequality was not something to be desired nor even possible if the market system was properly structured with profits kept in check and labor wages maintained. To Smith, legislation in favor of the worker was "always just and equitable," land should be distributed widely and evenly, and inheritance laws should partition fortunes.[27] He also warned against the moral dangers of the division of labor that he championed, writing that "the man whose whole life is spent in performing a few simple operations . . . becomes as stupid and ignorant as it is possible for a human creature to become."[28]

This warning presaged developments just over a hundred years later as Frederick Taylor, an engineer and one of the first management consultants, pioneered scientific management through time and motion studies for orchestrating human activity in industrial processes.[29] Taylor's system rationalized the workplace so that it could be staffed by interchangeable workers who performed simple individual tasks. American management consultant and expert in organizational behavior Mary Parker Follett saw this practice as having a dehumanizing effect upon employees. An influential contemporary of Taylor, she was the originator of the term "transformational leadership," and described management as "the art of getting things done through people." She championed the idea that neither "working for someone nor paying someone's wages ought to give you power over them"[30] and offered a view of the organization wherein both managers and workers strive towards the same common purpose and that "the most essential work of the leader is to create more leaders."[31] These tensions lie at the heart of many of the labor disputes today and reflect deeper clashes over the values in capitalism being at odds with the values in broader society.

The values embodied in capitalism can displace and degrade the values of broader society. Some writers of capitalism worried about its darker side. Max Weber lamented that the religious underpinnings to capitalism's spirit were largely gone from society and had led to a kind of involuntary servitude to mechanized industry. He introduced the idea of the "iron cage," which traps people in systems that are driven by efficiency, rational calculation, and control. He wondered if capitalism was becoming compulsive and meaning-less, and imperiling freedom, spontaneity and humanity; an unstoppable ero-sive force replacing morals with contracts, community with society, and social ties with market calculation.[32]

Polanyi also worried that the development of market society was under-mining and replacing prior modes of human interaction, which were based on relationships. Prior to industrialization, markets played a very minor role in human affairs. But after industrialization, the notion of human nature's ten-dency towards rational free trade became widely accepted. His analysis was at times a lament, arguing that "[t]o allow the market mechanism to be sole director of the fate of human beings and their natural environment, indeed, even of the amount and use of purchasing power, would result in the demoli-tion of society. . . . The idea of a self-adjusting market implied a stark utopia. Such an institution could not exist for any length of time without annihi-lating the human and natural substance of society; it would have physically destroyed man and transformed his surroundings into a wilderness."[33]

Echoing concerns about the dark values embedded in capitalism, econo-mist John Maynard Keynes opined in 1930 that "assuming no important wars and no important increase in population, the economic problem [the problem of subsistence] may be solved or be at least within sight of solution." But then he wondered, "Will this be a benefit? If one believes at all in the real values of life, the prospect at least opens up the possibility of benefit. Yet I think with dread of the readjustment of the habits and instincts of the ordinary man, bred into him for countless generations, which he may be asked to discard within a few decades. . . . we have been trained too long to strive and not to enjoy." An answer, as he saw it, was a resurgence of the religious values in society that both he and Weber saw as disappearing and a rejection of the values embedded in the market. "I see us free, therefore, to return to some of the most sure and certain principles of religion and traditional virtue—that avarice is a vice, that the exaction of usury is a misdemeanor, and the love of money is detestable, that those walk most truly in the paths of virtue and sane wisdom who take least thought for [tomorrow]. We shall once more value ends above means and prefer the good to the useful." How long would it take for us to reach this point? His answer was that we must continue with the falsities of the market that Weber lamented for "at least another hundred years [in which] we must pretend to ourselves and to everyone that fair is foul and foul is fair; for foul is useful and fair is not. Avarice and usury and precaution must be our gods for a little longer still. For only they can lead us out of the tunnel of economic necessity into daylight."[34]

Support and Critique of Capitalism in the Twenty-First Century

Present-day incarnations of capitalism have introduced new notions of what capitalism is, the values it promotes, and the new friction points it creates. Notably, Milton Friedman elevated capitalism to an ideal that created the context for finding one's noble purpose in life. In his 1962 book *Capitalism and Freedom*, he wrote that capitalism supports the personal freedom to pursue one's dreams and goals, start a business, fail, and try again. Where he saw capitalism and freedom as intimately linked, he saw socialism and subjugation similarly linked.[35] His overriding message was that "the role of competitive capitalism—the organization of the bulk of economic activity through private enterprise operating in a free market—is a system of economic freedom and a necessary condition for political freedom."[36] To Friedman, one threat to that freedom was the government, which he felt should be limited as much as possible,[37] writing "that is why the operation of the free market is so essential. Not only to promote productive efficiency, but even more to foster harmony and peace among the peoples of the world."[38] Elevating the interests of the individual and the importance of freedom, he writes that "[t]o the free man, the country is the collection of individuals who compose it, not something over and above them. . . . [He] will ask neither what his country can do for him nor what he can do for his country. He will ask rather 'What can I and my compatriots do through government' to help us discharge our individual responsibilities, to achieve our several purposes, and above all, to protect our freedom?"[39]

Building on the theme of personal freedom within capitalism, Russian-born American writer and public philosopher Ayn Rand also championed the value of individualism in a capitalist society, presenting a more extreme perspective on its social and cultural benefits, including a bold defense of self-ishness as a virtue. Her writing spoke often of the individual as a heroic entity who is liberated by the free market to pursue deeper aspirations, unchained from the constraints of others—notably the government—who drain their energies and creativity. Her belief that the highest ideal to which one could strive was largely to focus on our own interests helped her to develop followers as diverse as Alan Greenspan, Ronald Reagan, and Paul Ryan. Ayn Rand's philosophy of Objectivism celebrates the pursuit of personal happiness as the ultimate moral goal[40] and emphasizes the importance of productive achievement, rational thinking, and independence. Rejecting inherent societal or divine obligations, Rand advocated for living life guided by one's own values and desires and viewed altruism as destructive. "Don't try to be your brother's keeper or to force him to be yours. Live independently." She underscored the importance of wealth and production, viewing money as a key enabler of modern advancements and standards of living. According to Rand, "Money is your means of survival. The verdict you pronounce upon the source of your livelihood is the verdict you pronounce upon your life."[41] But with these as core values, what has capitalism become in the twenty-first century?

Today's capitalist values have become ugly and, at times, dangerous. As Ayn Rand and Milton Friedman make explicit in their writing, today's capitalism elevates the importance of greed and ego while treating markets as promoting freedom but they both ignore many of its faults and flaws. Naomi Oreskes and Erik Conway point out that many of Friedman's themes in *Capitalism and Freedom* were less about economic theory and more about promoting an ideological opinion that "valorizes individual freedom above all else."[42] At the time of *Capitalism and Freedom*'s release, one reviewer saw the book as "jammed with arguments that might make sense in principle but fail in practice, dismissing the realities of inequality, discrimination, and unequal access to resources and opportunity, and hanging on easily refutable historical claims."[43] A review of the book in *Business History Review* writes that "the tie between theory and actuality has practically disappeared," while a review for the journal *Ethics* found the book to be such "an unremitting catalogue of political errors that one wonders how we have managed to survive."[44] And yet, Friedman was a highly visible public intellectual who ardently and vigorously promoted a deregulated neoliberal order and the "magic" of the market to achieve our national objectives. His success in this effort is evident in the extent to which these views continue to dominate our view of the market.[45]

The tragedy of these views of the market, writes corporate attorney James

Gamble, is that they "have for a great many people taken on the power to transform selfishness into a virtue. If everyone acts in her rational self-interest, the market scripture goes, an invisible hand will cause the sum total of selfish acts to serve the common good. Faith in the invisible hand is the seed from which the maximize rule springs. The maximize rule in turn revises the faith."[46] John Maynard Keynes put it more succinctly: "Capitalism is the astonishing belief that the nastiest motives of the nastiest men somehow or other work for the best results in the best of all possible worlds."[47]

University of Michigan professor Jerry Davis points out additional dangers of today's capitalist values, asking, "Is shareholder capitalism a suicide pact?"[48] Because most American families are invested in the stock market either actively or passively through company 401k plans, he argues, social change will be severely limited, as "the well-being of most American households is tied to the performance of the stock market." People will be conflicted on policies that may be in society's best interests but that also restrict their investment performance. And to make sure that the latter stays top of mind, social media, phone apps, and TVs in subway stations, elevators, and restaurants bombard us with the latest stock fluctuations related to recent events. "Large scale participation in the stock market has become the political equivalent of an invisible dog fence," he writes, one "that gives your pet a mild electric shock if it tries to go outside a delimited boundary. Public policies that will lower the value of the S&P 500 are doomed in the court of public opinion, from winding down the petroleum industry to taxing Big Sugar to reining in Big Tech. All of us with a retirement fund are complicit. . . . As long as the (perceived) well-being of most American households is tied to the performance of the stock market, our willingness to veer from our current course is limited."[49]

There is an urgent need for meritocracy in capitalism and a control on corporate power. For many, the flaws in capitalism are more immediate and direct than through the stock market. Thomas Piketty's 2013 book *Capital in the Twenty-First Century* strikes chords similar to those of Marx, even alluding to the title of Marx's book, *Das Kapital* or *Capital*, but updates them for the twenty-first century. Piketty's main thesis is that capitalism results in inequality by the way it is designed. "When the rate of return on capital exceeds the rate of growth of output and income, as it did in the nineteenth century and seems quite likely to do again in the twenty-first, capitalism automatically generates arbitrary and unsustainable inequalities that radically undermine the meritocratic values on which democratic societies are based."[50] Without some kind of government intervention (such as a wealth tax), the democratic order will be threatened because much of the economy will be dominated by inherited wealth, and as political power grows with economic wealth, our society will lead to oligarchy. "What was the good of industrial development, what was the good of all the technological innovations, toil, and population movements if, after half a century of industrial growth, the condition of the masses was still just as miserable as before, and all lawmakers could do was prohibit factory labor by children under the age of eight?" he writes.[51]

Proponents of capitalism believe that gaps in income between rich and poor can be explained by differences in productivity. Marx, on the other hand, believed the gaps are due to exploitation—what economist Jeffrey Sachs described as "Marx's most deadly legacy."[52] But in recent years, the data seem to suggest Marx was on to something. How else can we explain the stagnating minimum wage, which has been stuck at $7.25 since 2009 in real terms (unadjusted for inflation). But the nominal rate (adjusted for inflation) was its highest in 1970 at $13 and has been in steady decline since. Workers today enjoy half the earning power they did in 1970 (see Figure 5.1). More recently, some states and municipalities have increased their local minimum wage above the federal rate. For example, Hawaii has increased to $14 and Washington, DC, has increased to $17.50. Yet these rates are still below the calculated living wage, which reaches $19.43 in Hawaii and $20.49 in Washington, DC.[53] To make matters worse, Figure 5.2 shows how productivity in the US economy quadrupled between 1948 and 2014 while the average real wage of workers kept pace with productivity only until 1973, after which it remained flat while productivity continued to grow.[54] This has left a large group of Americans—as many as 6.4 million people—falling behind their economic peers, unable to work their way out of poverty.[55]

Where Adam Smith believed that the market should allow people to improve their lot in life through hard work, the challenges of the working poor make them vulnerable to exploitation by the power that owners can exercise over them. University of Michigan professor Elizabeth Anderson argues in her 2017 book *Private Governments* that many corporations assert sweeping authoritarian power over their workers' lives, with one in four American

FIGURE 5.1

Nominal and Real Federal Minimum Wage in the US, 1938–2023

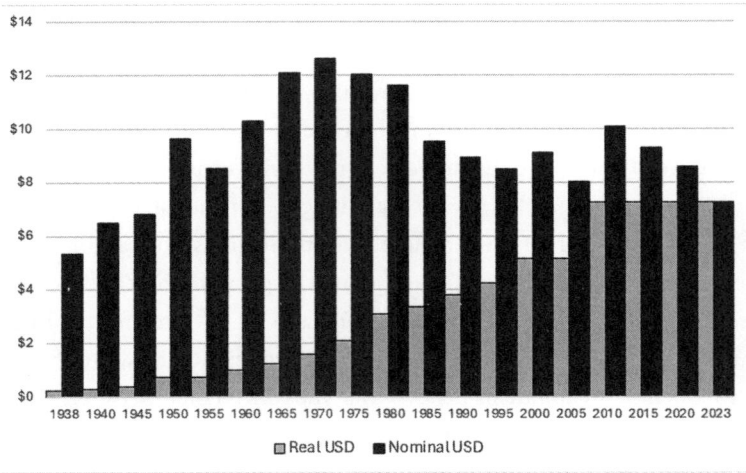

Source: Chart created by author using data from US Department of Labor, History of Federal Minimum Wage Rates Under the Fair Labor Standards Act, https://www.dol.gov/agencies/whd/minimum-wage/history/chart (accessed June 6, 2024).

FIGURE 5.2

Disconnect Between Productivity and a Typical Worker's Compensation, 1948–2014

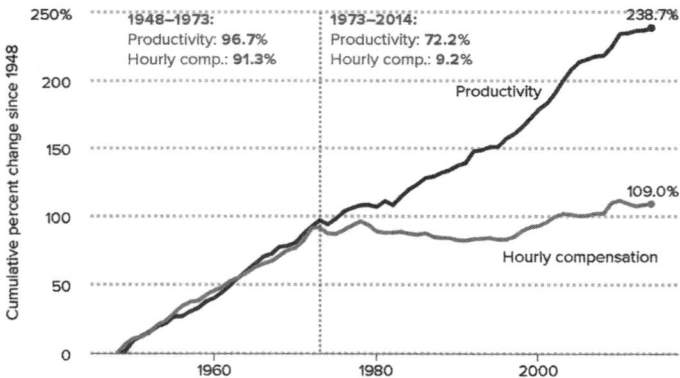

Note: Data are for average hourly compensation of production/nonsupervisory workers in the private sector and net productivity of the total economy. "Net productivity" is the growth of output of goods and services minus depreciation per hour worked.

Source: J. Bivens and L. Mishel, *Understanding the Historic Divergence Between Productivity and a Typical Worker's Pay: Why It Matters and Why It's Real,* Economic Policy Institute, Briefing Paper #406, September 2, 2015.

workers saying their workplace is a "dictatorship."[56] She documents how, for example, Amazon prohibits employees from exchanging casual remarks while on duty, calling this "time theft," and Apple inspects the personal belongings of its retail workers, some of whom lose up to a half-hour of unpaid time every day as they wait in line to be searched. She writes, "Workers can be fired for their political speech, recreational activities, diet, and almost anything else employers care to govern." And yet, she points out, "We continue to talk as if early advocates of market society—from John Locke and Adam Smith to Thomas Paine and Abraham Lincoln—were right when they argued that it would free workers from oppressive authorities. That dream was shattered by the Industrial Revolution, but the myth endures."[57]

Meritocracy is further degraded by creative destruction that is "creative" for some and "destructive" for others. Joseph Schumpeter marveled at the constant evolution of technology driving the economy. From the steam engine and textile mills dominating the manufacturing economy from about 1780 to 1830, to steel and railroads dominating the transportation economy from about 1830 to 1890, to electricity and chemicals dominating the energy and materials economy from about 1880 to 1930, to automobiles and oil dominating the mass mobility economy from 1930, upwards of 80 percent of all economic growth has been due to technological developments.[58] If he had lived to today, he would have witnessed information and communication technology dominating the digital economy since the 1990s.

But through the course of all these developments, the benefits often bypass workers and leave them behind. While new technology should lead to productivity gains that are spread through the economy, that is not always the case. Certainly, the massive growth of railroads, steel, and oil in the late nineteenth century largely benefited the monied classes of the Gilded Age, leading to massive wealth inequality. Today, there are similar questions being asked about the digital age. For example, despite enormous breakthroughs in cloud computing and internet technology, labor productivity has grown anemically since 2010, a phenomenon that has baffled experts.[59] And as robotics and artificial intelligence (AI) continue to ascend, many worry that these new technologies will amplify income inequality and the power imbalances between the rich and poor.

Certainly, robotics have been an ongoing concern for organized labor, displacing jobs by taking care of mundane repetitive tasks. But with the advent of AI, this concern grows even more pronounced as machines gain more nuanced capabilities that only humans could previously provide. In agriculture, AI is directing driverless combines to both plow fields and recognize and eradicate weeds. AI is helping robots acquire supplies for nurses and assist surgeons in directing their instruments more precisely.[60] AI is helping cars and trucks become autonomous, with the potential to displace a multitude of taxi and long-haul truck drivers. Even in education, AI is developing capabilities to replace the role of the professor with tools like ChatGPT becoming capable of answering student questions and grading papers.

A 2020 World Economic Forum report predicted that robotics and automation would displace eighty-five million jobs globally by 2025.[61] The report also predicted that the technologies would create ninety-seven million new jobs. But these jobs would require more skills and education. It is not clear who will provide this training or if workers' interests are even being considered in the creative destruction wreaked in the digital age.

It's Time to De-Mythologize the Free Market and the Invisible Hand

Returning to my students' shock at being asked to define capitalism, we have come to mythologize the free market and the invisible hand as unquestioned. It is time for that to end. For markets to work properly, Harvard professor Rebecca Henderson points out, "they must be genuinely free and genuinely fair."[62] Efficient markets typically require low transaction costs, perfect information, and minimal market power differences. This is a high hurdle to pass in the real world where people are not rational, transaction costs are ubiquitous, information is never perfect, market power is the norm, and most markets are not efficient. This becomes even more problematic in a world facing the collective existential threat of climate change where our knowledge is limited, spillovers are more common, and people are being marginalized.

In his book *Long Problems*, University of Oxford professor Thomas Hale points out that one of the great challenges of climate change is that it requires actions well in advance of outcomes. But while the costs of present action are known, the future benefits are uncertain and this leads to obstructionism, particularly from those who will bear the larger brunt of present costs.[63] A market cannot be efficient in such circumstances, nor will it be able to solve the climate challenge without some form of intervention and adjustment to replace the so-called invisible hand.

Jonathan Schlefer, author of *The Assumptions Economists Make*,[64] writes that "one of the best-kept secrets in economics is that there is no case for the invisible hand. After more than a century trying to prove the opposite, economic theorists investigating the matter finally concluded in the 1970s that there is no reason to believe markets are led, as if by an invisible hand, to an optimal equilibrium—or any equilibrium at all."[65] It is worth noting that Adam Smith made one and only one reference to the "invisible hand" in his book *The Wealth of Nations*. It was Milton Friedman who elevated the term as a central idea for his more contemporary model of an economy that would regulate itself with no coordination from government.[66] But economist Joseph Stiglitz writes that Milton Friedman "was wrong. . . . I remember long discussions with him on the consequences of imperfect information or incomplete risk markets; my own work and that of numerous colleagues had shown that in these conditions, markets typically didn't work well. Friedman simply couldn't or wouldn't grasp these results."[67] He adds, "Today, there is no respectable intellectual support for the proposition that markets, by themselves, lead to efficient, let alone equitable outcomes."[68] In the end, although the invisible hand and market equilibrium can exist in theory, they cannot exist in a competitive economy in the real world. With this as a starting point, several elements of capitalism as presently practiced and presently taught come open for discussion and debate.

It's time to reestablish the role of government in the market. Former labor secretary Robert Reich writes that "few ideas have more profoundly poisoned the minds of more people than the notion of a 'free market' existing somewhere in the universe, into which government 'intrudes.' According to this view, whatever we might do to reduce inequality or economic insecurity—to make the economy work for most of us—runs the risk of distorting the market and causing it to be less efficient, or of unintended consequences that may end up harming us."[69] The issue facing us today in moving beyond shareholder capitalism is not just the behavior of corporations but also, and perhaps more important, the role of the state.[70] Richard Posner of the University of Chicago Law School concludes, "Government has a duty to do more than prevent fraud, theft, and other infringements on property and contract rights, which is the only duty that libertarians believe government has. Without stronger financial regulation than that, the rational behavior of law-abiding financiers and consumers can precipitate an economic crisis. . . . [R]ational maximization by businessmen and consumers, all pursuing their self-interest more or less intelligently within a framework of property and contract rights, can set the stage for economic catastrophe."[71]

Market exchanges no longer boil down to just the buyer and the seller. Adam Smith's metaphor of "the benevolence of the butcher, the brewer, or the baker" who will provide our dinner without regard for "our own necessities but of their advantages" breaks down in an economy of multinational organizations wherein the corporate decision makers reside far from the actual transaction between the buyer and the seller and its consequences. Similarly, Smith's metaphor breaks down in an era of climate change when the link between action and outcome is separated because we do not experience the effects of climate change in a market exchange, or in any sense really. We cannot feel an increase in global mean temperature; we cannot see, smell, or taste greenhouse gases; and we cannot link an individual weather anomaly with global climate shifts. Instead, a real appreciation of the issue requires an understanding of large-scale systems through "big data" models, which in turn requires deep scientific knowledge about complex dynamic systems and the ways in which feedback loops, time delays, accumulations, and nonlinearities operate within the climate system. Or it requires trust in the scientists that analyze that data, something that seems to ebb in short supply today.

Private property creates a dilemma in an era of global environmental challenges. Private property is sacrosanct in capitalism. But the rights to use one's property cannot be absolute if we wish to protect the global environment. Milton Friedman writes that "if pollution arises from my use of my property, it is part of my property rights, and therefore I have an implicit right to pollute . . . if I own a factory, then my right to operate it as I see fit encompasses the right to pollute, and that right is 'extremely important' and has to be given 'considerable weight.'"[72] But the interconnected global environment in which we live requires more sophisticated notions of property use, particularly where it relates to resource use and pollution.

Under the lens of capitalism, nature is often seen primarily in terms of its economic value. This perspective can lead to a limited understanding of its true worth. For instance, if the decision to cut down an old-growth forest is left solely to its owner, crucial considerations like biodiversity and environmental stability may be overlooked. Recognizing a forest as more than just a private economic resource—such as a source of commercial lumber or even a sink for carbon—is essential. Viewing it merely as an economic asset implies that it is only valuable until a more profitable use is discovered. This approach neglects the broader significance of a forest's ecosystem, which encompasses a diverse range of life forms, their complex interactions and dependencies, and any deeper meanings or values beyond mere human utility.[73]

If you take the climate challenge seriously, there is a simple mathematical and pragmatic reality that oil companies cannot burn the 1.65 trillion barrels of proven oil reserves in their private possession if we expect to maintain temperatures below 2°C. According to the International Energy Agency, all new oil and gas exploration must stop immediately if we are to meet our climate targets.[74] In December 2023, the United Nations Conference of the Parties reached an agreement for "transitioning away from fossil fuels in energy systems, in a just, orderly and equitable manner . . . so as to achieve net zero by 2050 in keeping with the science."[75] But how does one do that in a market regime in which private property rights are sacrosanct? Those who stand to lose the most in such a transition will fight hard to protect their property rights: the oil majors, national oil companies, the Organization of the Petroleum Exporting Countries, as well US states including Texas, New Mexico, North Dakota, Alaska, and Wyoming that rely on oil for jobs and taxes.[76] Economically, an energy transition away from fossil fuels over the next three decades will cause massive dislocations for the nearly eight million jobs in the fossil-fuel industry,[77] as well as the investors who support a market capitalization of $3.3 trillion. A purely market response based on private property will not bring this complex economic system to an end. We need to develop processes that put a major industry like the fossil-fuel sector into "hospice."[78]

Inequality has dangerous consequences. Ray Dalio, the billionaire founder of the world's largest hedge fund, worries that increasing inequality in the United States could lead to conflict of one sort or another.[79] Peter Georgescu, chairman emeritus of Young & Rubicam, echoes this fear when he writes that he and other chief executives are "afraid where income inequality will lead. If inequality is not addressed, the income gap will most likely be resolved in one of two ways: by major social unrest or through oppressive taxes. . . . We are creating a caste system from which it's almost impossible to escape."[80] In his 2017 book *The Great Leveler,* Walter Scheidel writes that throughout history, the "Four Horsemen" of leveling have repeatedly destroyed the fortunes of the rich: (1) mass-mobilization warfare, (2) transformative revolutions, (3) state collapse, and (4) catastrophic plagues.[81] What form could these horsemen take today? While Scheidel feels that "the violence that reduced inequality in the past seems to have diminished," one might wonder if the US political chaos of the first quarter of the twenty-first century is a sign of this kind of kind of revolutionary adjustment. Research shows a strong correlation between income inequality and political polarization (see Figure 5.3). Is violence and a civil war between the upper and lower economic strata that Marx predicted possible?

FIGURE 5.3

Income Inequality and Political Polarization, 1947–2015

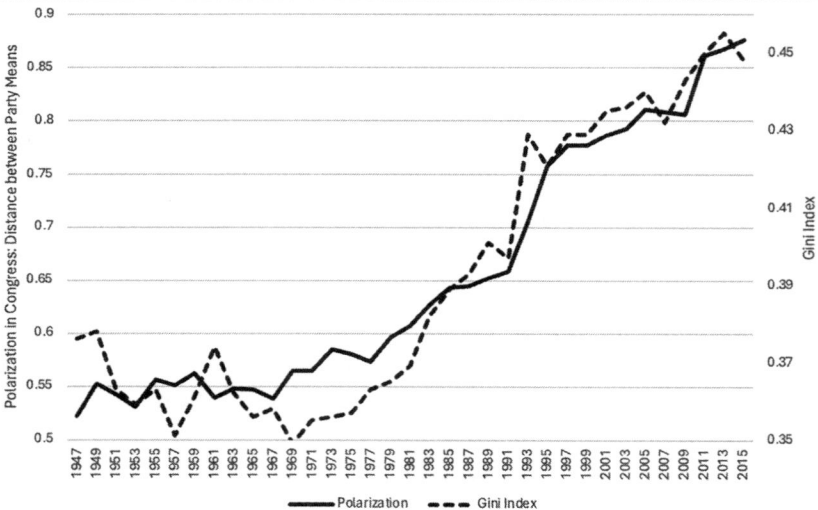

Source: Chart created by author using data from Vote View for Polarization in Congress Index, https://voteview.com/articles/party_polarization and US Census Bureau for Gini Index https://www.census.gov/topics/income-poverty/income-inequality/about/metrics/gini-index.html (both accessed June 12, 2024).

New values are needed for the Anthropocene Era. Adam Smith was both the product of and a central proponent of the Enlightenment, a cultural shift that brought about the "Age of Reason," exalted the human ability to understand and control the natural world around us, and formed the foundation of both our economic and democratic systems. But philosophers such as Bruno Latour, Mike Hulme, Dipesh Chakrabarty, and others have begun to question how the Anthropocene may challenge Enlightenment values, breaking down the age-old distinctions between nature and society, between natural history and human history, and giving rise to new approaches to issues of justice: "justice between generations, between small island-nations and the polluting countries (both past and prospective), between developed, industrialized nations (historically responsible for most emissions) and the newly industrialized ones."[82] With such new approaches comes the challenge and opportunity to recalibrate Enlightenment ideas such as "freedom, choice, morality, citizenship, difference, and rights."[83]

This may manifest itself, for example, in policies that compel a reduction in consumption, elevate the role of science in business and society, force an extension in corporate time horizons, and recognize that nature has value that goes beyond narrow human economic self-interest.[84] Already, we can see efforts to grant nature legally enforceable rights, as Ecuador established in 2008 by amending its constitution,[85] or granting specific ecosystems the legal status of personhood, as has been done in New Zealand, Canada, Pennsylvania, and Florida.[86] Overall, Ecuador, Bolivia, Uganda, the United States, Canada, Brazil, New Zealand, Mexico, and Northern Ireland have some recognition of the rights of nature in their constitutions, national laws, or local regulations, according to the Center for Democratic and Environmental Rights.[87] Going further, an effort is under way to draft laws for the legally enforceable crime of "ecocide" and criminalizing the destruction of the world's ecosystems.[88] These kinds of changes must be reflected in the capitalism that amends shareholder capitalism in the twenty-first century. To guide that outcome, business schools must become far more involved in the discussions over the state of capitalism and leverage points for stewarding it to a more productive and equitable form.

Train Business Leaders to Be Stewards of the Market

Joseph Schumpeter, a staunch defender of capitalism, opens the prologue to his 1942 book with the question "Can capitalism survive?" and his answer is "No, I do not think it can."[89] He worried that the enormous productivity of capitalism would eventually produce all the goods and services needed for daily life, freeing people to a life of leisure, one separated and removed from the actual process of entrepreneurship and production. As a result, they would no longer understand the roots of their own condition and turn against the economic system that made their lives possible, working to undermine the institutions of capitalism and entrepreneurship (which was the central focus of his work).[90]

Could we be seeing signs of this drift today? A 2019 report from Deloitte finds that young people are becoming disillusioned with capitalism, in large part because their financial circumstances are leaving them struggling.[91] When compared to other age demographics at the same point in their career, Millennials and Gen Zers have lower savings, are less likely to own a home, and carry increased debt which is directed primarily towards student loans.[92] Whereas 90 percent of children born in the 1940s grew up to earn more than their parents, only half of all children born in the 1980s have thus far been able to do the same.[93] In 2012, the median male in his twenties made 19 percent less (in real terms) than his father did at the same age.[94] As a result, a 2018 Gallup poll showed that decreasing numbers of Americans between the ages of eighteen and twenty-nine held a positive view of capitalism, while an increasing number held a positive view of socialism.[95] This is a cause for alarm among some.

But not all in this demographic have responded in this way. Other surveys show that some business students in this age demographic are asking hard questions of capitalism and business education and are willing to work hard to get both to change.[96] They see the problems with capitalism that cannot be ignored and are willing to roll up their sleeves and work with the system to improve it. They see what the United Nations Millennium Ecosystem Assessment sees, concluding that humans have changed the Earth's ecosystems over the second half of the twentieth century "more rapidly and extensively than in any comparable period of time in human history."[97] But while they may be attractive alternatives to some, communism and socialism have not shown a more constructive track record to avoid such change, as practiced in parts of the world. Public ownership of the "means of production," central economic planning, and a lack of market forces have not yielded the kind of prosperity that has been enjoyed in capitalist societies. Instead, they have been marked by cronyism, oligarchs, large wealth disparities, limited freedom, and rampant pollution.

That said, the debate between socialism and capitalism, and even the Gallup poll that shows young people's dissatisfaction with capitalism, presumes a binary distinction between the two. But, as Naomi Oreskes and Erik Conway point out, such a suggestion, "is a dangerous failure of vision" blinding us to the realities and possibilities before us.[98] In many parts of society, the mere mention of socialism leads to a breakdown in discourse. But socialist programs and policies can exist within a capitalist system, and there are varying shapes of grey across a spectrum from pure capitalism to pure socialism, with a caveat that pure forms of each may be impossible to arrange in reality, and each have their problems.

Even the US capitalist system is a hybrid of sorts. It is built on the importance of private ownership of assets and market rules guiding exchange. But the system also has public ownership of organizations (such as customer-owned COOPs and employee-owned ESOPs) as well as some highly regulated markets (such as insurance and electric utilities). The Chinese capitalist system is based on direct government influence over resource allocation, investment decisions, and the strategy of certain companies and industries. But since 1976, there has been an increase in the employment of capitalist practices such as market competition, stock market listings, and material incentives for corporate executives.[99] Whatever form of capitalism we adopt to amend shareholder capitalism must evolve out of the form we have today, but it can borrow, amend, and build upon many elements that are discussed in this chapter and explored in economic systems around the world. The pertinent exercise in business school is to focus on developing stewards of the market to guide it where it needs to go.

Harvard Business School professors Rebecca Henderson and Karthik Ramanna argue that when political processes are "thin"—managers have exclusive information, limited opposition, and restrained political engagement—

the opportunity to distort capitalism is strong and business leaders have a responsibility to correct the system. They should sacrifice easy profits from exploiting market flaws and support healthy institutions that are beneficial in the long run because they reinforce capitalism's legitimacy and the existence of a market society. Conversely, they argue, when political processes are thick—information is widely available, public interest is well represented, diverse opposing interests are engaged, and strong competition exists—lively debate will lead to institutions that support free and fair competition.[100] In today's context, political processes are thin and business schools should teach students to steward the future of capitalism.

In considering the future of that system, New York University Business School social psychologist Jonathan Haidt considers three possible outcomes, or three "stories" of capitalism that might guide our development of a revised variant.[101] The first is *capitalism as exploitation,* in which "capitalists developed ingenious techniques for squeezing wealth out of workers, and then sucked up all of societies' resources for themselves" by using its "wealth to buy political influence." This is obviously not a story we want to see. The second is *capitalism as savior,* in which "democratic institutions put checks on the exploitative power of the elites, which in turn allowed for the creation of economic institutions that rewarded hard work, risk-taking, and innovation. . . . In just a few centuries, poverty disappeared in these fortunate countries, and people got rights and dignity, safety, and longevity." While appealing, Haidt warns that this story leads some people to worship capitalism, preventing them from seeing any faults or flaws. The third and most compelling story is *capitalism as needing a fix,* which describes the situation we are in now.

> The long compression of income inequality, which had begun in the 1930s in many Western nations, ended. The gap between rich and poor within nations began to shoot upwards. Economic gains went mostly to the rich, who then used their money to buy legislators and laws. . . . And as market values expanded beyond the marketplace, and started taking over medicine, education, and other domains of life, many people lamented the crass and degrading materialism of modernity.

But Haidt argues,

This is our challenge for the 21st century: We celebrate the fact that the wide embrace of free markets has lifted more than a billion people out of poverty. Yet we know we can do better. If we can strip away the anger, the worship, and the ideology, we can examine capitalism and its ethical challenges more openly. We can see that the supply chains that keep our shelves stocked have their origins in the deadly sweatshops of Bangladesh. We can measure the polluted air and empty oceans we are bequeathing to our children. And we can have a more nuanced discussion of equal opportunity, particularly in America where schools are funded by local taxes and money buys your children a better starting line. So let us be grateful to the butcher, the brewer, and the baker for the bounty they bestow upon us, even when they are corporations. Let us look back in awe at the political and economic changes that brought us from the first story to the second. And then let us work together to write the third story, a story that must draw on insights from left and right, and from secular thinkers and religious leaders.[102]

SIX

Alternative Capitalisms Around the World

"I know that some people in the US associate the Nordic model with some sort of socialism. Therefore, I would like to make one thing clear. Denmark is far from a socialist planned economy. Denmark is a market economy."

—ANDERS FOGH RASMUSSEN, PRIME MINISTER OF DENMARK

The United States enjoys the highest gross domestic product (GDP) in the world at $23 trillion USD (in 2021). By this aggregate wealth metric, the US has the most productive form of capitalism. But by other metrics of human well-being such as wealth distribution, human development, standard of living, and natural capital stocks, the results are less impressive. The United States ranks eighth in GDP per capita, tenth in the OECD Better Life Index, twenty-first in the UN Human Development Index, twenty-fifth in the Social Progress Indicator, twenty-eighth in the UN Inclusive Wealth Index, and one hundred and seventh by Gini coefficient.

Economists Anne Case and Angus Deaton point out that America has witnessed rising rates of suicide, drug abuse, and alcoholic liver diseases since 1999. Drug overdose deaths alone have risen by almost five times since 1999 (see Figure 6.1). In their 2020 book *Deaths of Despair*, they identify one common feature among those three causes of death: great unhappiness with life among Americans.[1] The US surgeon general has also called attention to this feature of American life, issuing a warning in 2023 over the epidemic of loneliness and isolation in the United States.[2] Case and Deaton highlight that this despair is higher among those without a four-year college degree and the reduced "earnings premium" that education provides. And, while income is important, what is more important is the deterioration of opportunities for Americans without a college degree in basic areas of life, including marriage, participation in community and church activities, and, notably, access to affordable medical services in the increasingly expensive American health care system.

These outcomes are the product of a form of capitalism that is designed to optimize certain outcomes and incentivize certain behaviors. For example, in its quest for efficiency, shareholder capitalism has produced ever-expanding amounts of unhealthy food for the American consumer. Partly as a result, the percentage of Americas who are obese or severely obese has risen almost trifold since the mid-1970s (see Figure 6.2), while the Centers for Disease Control warns that the prevalence of diabetes has "significantly increased"

FIGURE 6.1

National Drug-Involved Overdose Deaths in the US, 1999–2020

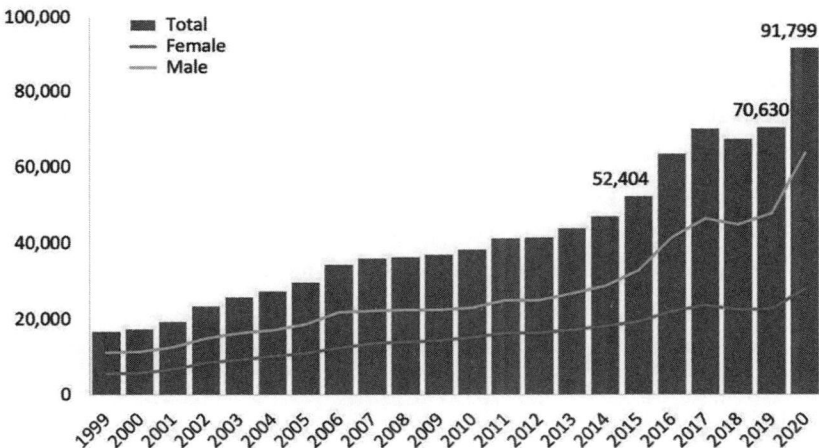

Note: Includes deaths with underlying causes of unintentional drug poisoning (X40–X44), suicide drug poisoning (X60–64), homicide drug poisoning (X85), or drug poisoning of undetermined intent (Y10–Y14), as coded in the International Classification of Diseases, 10th Revision.

Source: Centers for Disease Control and Prevention, *Multiple Cause of Death 1999-2020*, National Center for Health Statistics, 2021, CDC WONDER Online Database.

FIGURE 6.2

Age-Adjusted Trends in Overweight, Obesity, and Severe Obesity in the US, 1960–2018

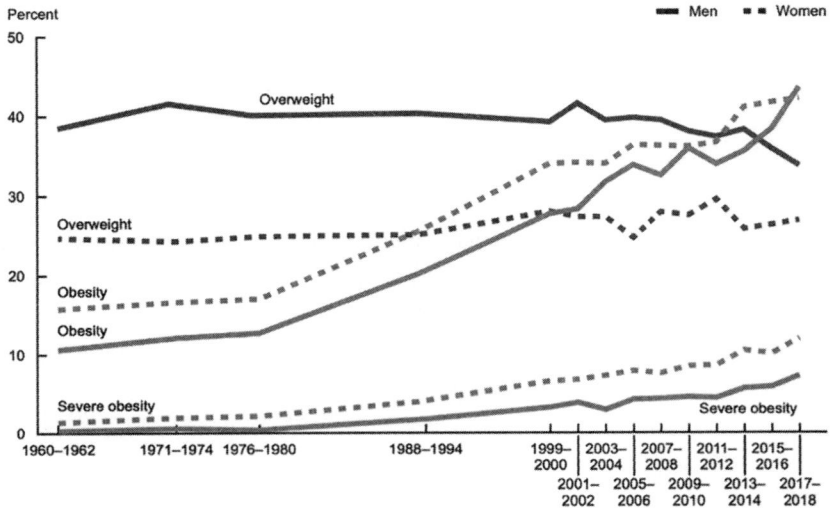

Source: 2017-2018 National Health and Nutrition Examination Survey (NHANES), US Centers for Disease Control, 2018.

between 2001 and 2020.[3] Political analyst Yuval Levin writes that capitalism today "empties social life of any higher meaning, and so leaves society morally bankrupt even as it grows materially wealthy. Is capitalism in fact just a means of replacing material poverty with spiritual poverty? Is the market a money-making machine that burns social capital for its fuel, leaving in its wake a society of opulent nihilists?"[4]

Levin's pessimism aside, there is no one form of capitalism. The variant of capitalism practiced in the United States is just one among many, each producing distinct social outcomes to reflect the interests and goals of different cultures. By studying these different variants, we can find valuable models and methods to refine and improve our own economic system.

Two Categories of Market Economies

Capitalism manifests differently around the world—the American model is drastically different from the Chinese or Nordic models, for example. To better understand these diverse forms, it is useful to categorize national economies into two primary types: liberal market economies (LME) and coordinated market economies (CME). This framework allows for a clearer analysis of the key characteristics and differences among the varied market economies around the world.[5]

Liberal Market Economies. Countries such as the United States, the United Kingdom, Canada, Australia, and Japan have competitive markets, arms-length relationships between government and business, and a reliance on prices to manage supply and demand. LMEs generally emphasize efficiency over equality and have higher rates of GDP growth and more radical innovation, but have lower social safety nets, greater income inequality, and higher unemployment. The United States is a prototypical liberal market economy that is market-driven with a focus on private ownership, shareholder value, competition, and a light regulatory approach. The economy has a significant wealth gap, a flexible labor market, at-will employment, weaker labor unions, and less governmental support for the unemployed than other developed countries. The US commits 22.7 percent of GDP to public social welfare spending, compared to 31.6 percent in France and other countries in the EU.[6] On a per-capita basis, the United States ranks tenth among OECD countries on social spending and has a limited public social safety net, with health care primarily provided through private insurance.[7] In theory, the distribution of income in the United States is meant to reflect an individual's contribution to the economy, operating under the premise that this system provides equal opportunities for success.[8] Any efforts to rebalance economic distribution are conducted through predistribution efforts, such as minimum wage and making it easier to form labor unions, as opposed to redistribution efforts, such as a wealth tax.

Coordinated Market Economies. Countries such as Sweden, Germany, Denmark, and Switzerland have deliberate coordination among firms and other stakeholders such as suppliers, unions, customers, and government, and place greater emphasis on trust-based relationships among these actors.

CMEs generally emphasize equality over efficiency, have lower rates of GDP growth and less radical innovation, but have higher social safety nets, lower income inequality, and lower unemployment.[9] Within the category of CMEs lie several variants.

Germany operates under a "social market economy,"[10] which blends the principles of free-market capitalism with a strong emphasis on social policies and regulations. The goal is to ensure fair competition while also providing substantial support for workers and welfare programs. In this system, the government plays a key role in coordinating economic activities and upholding social welfare, but it also recognizes and respects the self-regulating abilities of civil society.[11] Similarly, a "mixed economic system" such as that found in Scandinavia allows for private freedom, combined with centralized economic planning and government regulation that supports strong welfare programs. In Norway, for example, the government controls around 35 percent of the publicly listed companies on the Oslo stock exchange.[12] Sweden enjoys a competitive form of capitalism along with "state regulated cooperation between classes, values oriented toward collective solidarity and a high level of welfare services."[13]

The concept of a "networked market economy," particularly as it applies to Japan, refers to an economic system in which the production and distribution of goods and services are heavily influenced by intricate networks of relationships and alliances. In Japan, these networks often include various companies, suppliers, distributors, and even governmental entities. This model emphasizes the importance of social connections and collaborations in the business environment, in contrast to economies which are more transactional and less dependent on long-standing relationships. In Japan's networked market economy, these relationships and networks play a critical role in shaping business strategies and operations, leading to a unique blend of competition and cooperation among businesses, as well as a traditionally honored expectation among workers of life-time employment.

Among these different variants, we can analyze some of the choices that decide how an economy is and can be structured.

Differentiating Facets of Market Economies

Individual elements within each variant of capitalism may be appropriate in one context and not others. Around the world, the role of government in the market and the extent of services provided to citizens are key markers of the form of capitalism that a society adopts.

The Size of Government in the Economy. The size of the government in the economy can be measured both by the amount of money the government collects through taxes and the amount of money it spends as a percentage of GDP. The United States federal government imposes a 21 percent corporate rate and a 37 percent individual rate for the highest income brackets. This can reach as high as 47 percent when state income tax is included. Taxes raise $4.9 trillion, which is then fed back into the economy. But the US federal government spending as a percentage of GDP hovers around 20 to 25 percent, with portions of that going to health care (23 percent), social security (17 percent), education (19 percent), military (12 percent), welfare (7 percent) and interest on the national debt (6 percent). In 2022, the US spent $877 billion on defense spending, which amounts to around 3.26 percent of GDP. Government spending reaches as high as 55–60 percent of GDP in many European countries, such as France, Germany, and Finland, and as low as 20–30 percent in India, Ireland, and Costa Rica.[14] The percentage of that money spent on defense is significantly lower among European allies: Sweden (1.04 percent), Norway (1.62 percent), the United Kingdom (1.84 percent), France (2.26 percent), and Germany (1.18 percent).[15] This spending differential creates ancillary benefits to the US economy in technology development but also allows the allies—and has allowed them since World War II—to devote more resources to other priorities.

The level of US government spending is a cause for concern among some and a sign of government playing its proper role for others. The International Tax Competitiveness Index ranks the United States twenty-second for the extent to which its tax system promotes competitiveness, remains neutral, and controls government spending and debt. The index is based on the idea that the government's goal is to raise the most revenue with the fewest economic distortions, such as those created by targeted tax breaks for specific activities carried out by businesses or individuals. This will, in theory, keep marginal tax rates low and invite foreign direct investment.[16] But others see these "distortions" as representative of national priorities in delivering public goods and services and providing social protection.[17] These competing views on government spending levels and priorities form the core of the debate over the proper role of government in the market. A closely related debate is the extent to which government should control the market.

Government Controls in the Market. Markets are considered to be "free" if supply and demand regulate production with little to no government intervention. According to the Heritage Foundation's Index of Economic Freedom, the United States ranks as the twenty-fifth-freest economy. "Big government policies have eroded limits on government, public spending continues to rise and regulatory burden on business has increased," the report found.[18] The index ranks Singapore's economy as the freest, followed by Switzerland and Ireland. Singapore is praised for "strong protection of property rights and effective enforcement of anticorruption laws. Tax rates are competitive, and the regulatory environment is transparent. Openness to global commerce boosts productivity while facilitating the emergence of a more dynamic and competitive financial sector."[19] That said, critics point out that Singapore has an authoritarian government which supports a strong and open market but does not allow free and open political elections or complete freedom of speech.[20]

Again, these systems are deliberate choices about how to structure the economy and society. The decision to involve government in the market can be done for deliberate and desired outcomes. South Korea and Japan have used government intervention to develop their own markets and domestic industries, such as chip manufacturing, automobiles, and appliances. In Japan, government authorities (largely through the Ministry of Economy, Trade and Industry) cooperate very closely with the country's large private enterprises, the *zaibatsu*, and webs of interlocking businesses called the *keiretsu* (or *chaebol* in South Korea) to provide powerful support and direction to the development of specific industries, technology, and exports (such as cars and electronics),[21] directing the economy towards high productivity goals.

Coordination and Governance. Where American capitalism is focused primarily on the shareholder and fosters a relationship between labor and management that is more "arms-length" and contentious, capitalism in the European Union is more focused on a wider array of stakeholders, and labor has a more collaborative relationship with management. Germany, for example, has a system of laws called "codetermination" that allow workers to elect representatives for one-third to half of the supervisory board of directors in public and private companies. German workers also elect representatives to Works Councils at the local shop floor level that deal with day-to-day issues such as overtime pay, major layoffs, and monitoring and evaluation.[22] Japanese employers also develop long-term relationships with labor, at times prioritizing employees' interests over shareholders, avoiding layoffs, and favoring the sustainability of business over short-term growth maximization. As a result, Japan has some of the lowest unemployment rates in the world.[23] But one trade-off is that employees are expected to work long hours and have weak trade unions in exchange for security.[24]

Corruption and Cronyism. Increasing involvement of the government in the economy can open opportunities for corruption and cronyism. Around the world, the wealth of crony capitalists grew by 850 percent between 2000 and 2023 to $3 trillion, with Russia ranked as the most corrupt by the Crony-Capitalism Index. In the 1990s, the Russian economy made the transition to a market economy and began to privatize many of its state-run industries. Those with strong ties to the government were rewarded with majority ownership of these companies, leading to a burgeoning oligarchy and massive inequality. By 2023, billionaire wealth from crony sectors in Russia amounted to 19 percent of its GDP.[25] In the US, the wealth from the crony sector stood at around 2 percent of the country's GDP, with tech firms being the most cronyish for having "among the biggest lobbyists in Washington." China saw a decline in crony wealth after its "common prosperity" policy forced change in sectors such as technology, education, and entertainment. However, high-profile tycoons often moved their assets to Singapore, creating a boom in the city state for firms that manage individual assets, rising from just thirty-three firms in 1999 to seven hundred and fifty by the end of 2022.[26]

Scale of the Social Safety Net. In the United States, government support for public education, health care, and retirement are controversial topics. As in most liberal market economies, welfare spending is low. This is not so elsewhere. For example, seventy-two countries in the world now have universal health care, often with high levels of funding, well-trained health care professionals, and comprehensive coverage of health care services.[27] The Nordic countries, in particular, offer a stark contrast in the scale and scope of the safety net that can be provided to a country's citizenry. In fact, on many dimensions the Nordic Model stands out as a distinct form of capitalism worth a closer look.

The Nordic Model

The market economies of Nordic and Scandinavian countries including Sweden, Norway, and Denmark have received significant attention for their balance of capitalism and social welfare policies. But, representing the binary thinking of many in the United States, some have labeled these economies socialist. To correct these misperceptions, the Danish prime minister Anders Fogh Rasmussen declared in 2015, "I know that some people in the US associate the Nordic model with some sort of socialism. Therefore, I would like to make one thing clear. Denmark is far from a socialist planned economy. Denmark is a market economy. . . . The Nordic model is an expanded welfare state which provides a high level of security for its citizens, but it is also a successful market economy with much freedom to pursue your dreams and live your life as you wish."[28] In the Heritage Foundation's 2023 Index of Economic Freedom, Denmark, Sweden, and Norway are ranked as the ninth,- tenth,- and eleventh-freest markets, respectively. The US has historically been in the top ten freest or most capitalist countries, but now ranks twenty-fifth.[29]

Some economists refer to the Nordic Model as a more compassionate form of capitalism, contrasting with what is seen as more cut-throat capitalism in other Western countries. These are free-market capitalist countries, fully open to global trade, but are also strong welfare states. In the UN index of "happiest countries," all of the Scandinavian countries finished in the top ten. There is a generous social safety net, social security system, and public pension system with well-funded public services in a relatively high-tax economy. The Swedish government, for example, provides a high level of welfare services, including free health care and education; a pension; and subsidies on housing, child care, unemployment benefits, and job-training programs.[30] Seventy percent of the children of the poorest fifth of Swedes are enrolled in state sponsored child care.[31] Similarly, Denmark offers universal tax-funded health care, a strong child care system, generous parental leave time, and some of the highest educational spending in the OECD. In these economies, inequality and poverty are low, with Scandinavian countries boasting some of the highest levels of equality of opportunity.[32]

Despite an active role for government in their economies, the Nordics also offer an overall ease of doing business, underpinned by strong property rights, contract enforcement, and extremely low levels of corruption. In 2015, Norway, Sweden, Denmark, Finland, and Iceland were all in the top ten least corrupt states in the Corruption Perceptions Index. There is a high level of unionization—from 51 percent in Norway up to 88 percent in Iceland compared with the levels of 18 percent in Germany, 11 percent in the United States, and 8 percent in France.

One important factor that makes these systems work is trust between the government and the population. In a recent essay about Norway's economy, one commentator summed up the relationship: "The government trusts the people and gives them the freedom to do what they feel is right. In turn the people trust the government to act according to the national interest."[33] On the whole, Nordic companies also have a strong social partnership with their employees, using a collaborative approach to worker's rights. The government has established a framework for employers and unions to bargain on matters such as wages as well as lobby the government to come to an arrangement on legislation affecting employment in terms of conditions and regulation. One outcome is that there is no national minimum wage in Sweden, Denmark, or Norway.[34]

The government's role in the market is also noted in employment, with 30 percent of Norway's workers holding public-sector jobs, compared with 15 percent in the United States. Norway's government also owns 35 percent of its stock exchange and has full or partial ownership of "strategic" industries such as oil, banks, transportation, national defense, universities, and hospitals. This is all supported by a relatively high tax rate. In 2021, Denmark's overall tax-to-GDP ratio was 47 percent, and Norway's and Sweden's were 42 percent, compared to a ratio of 24 percent in the United States.[35] According to the Center for Political Studies, in addition to a tax on income, Danes pay a value-added tax (VAT) of 25 percent on the sale of every item. In Sweden, personal income tax is accompanied by a 38 percent social-security tax rate, of which 31 percent is employer covered and 7 percent covered by the employee.

Tax rates are generally flat, so all households pay relatively high levels of tax compared with most Western countries.[36]

Views of Capitalism Across the Political Spectrum

Can the United States shift some aspects of its economy to a more coordinated market economy as found in other parts of the world? The tensions in this question exist as far back as the New Deal (and earlier) and highlight today's partisan divide between liberal Democrats and conservative Republicans,[37] with the former leaning more towards a more coordinated market orientation and the latter leaning more towards a more liberal market orientation. This tension informs many debates around social welfare programs, with one's view of the proper role of government in dealing with these issues "sorted" by one's position on the political spectrum.

While the extreme stereotypes range from the "pro-market right ('greed is good, redistribution is theft and concern about inequality is nothing more than class envy')" and the "anti-market left ('all inequality is bad, the rich are just lucky and markets are morally corrupting')," [38] the divide between liberal and conservative is not so binary. At one time in this country, we had such identities as conservative Democrats and liberal Republicans, and the rise of the populist movement with Donald Trump has confused the traditional ways of viewing left and right even further. A first step to improving our current variant of capitalism lies not in reflexively resisting or supporting rigid positions, but in understanding the underlying values and interests that drive them. This approach allows us to adapt our economic system to meet the challenges and needs of today's world.[39]

On the *conservative right*, there are deep suspicions of government intrusion in the market, with fears this will lead to unfair competition and crony capitalism under which the government "picks winners and losers." Though they acknowledge that the market isn't perfect, conservatives view the market as the best method for serving society's needs and leading to positive ends.[40] Therefore, they tend to prefer smaller government, less regulation, and more services provided by the private sector in a free market, with a balanced budget being a high priority. They tend to see the world as more hierarchical and inequality as inevitable within a market system under which the outcome reflects the level of effort one puts into their work to improve their lot in life and that of their children.[41] Adam Smith's line that "[t]he wages of labor are the encouragement of industry, which, like every other human quality, improves in proportion to the encouragement it receives"[42] resonates strongly on this point. Charity should be provided more from people in the community than government programs. While not inherently opposed to aiding those in need, conservatives worry about a slippery slope along which such assistance extends beyond the most vulnerable populations, turning into entitlements for the elderly and middle class, irrespective of their actual need. Conservatives tend to believe that individuals should exercise personal responsibility and it is the government's role to hold them accountable even with severe penalties using laws that are enacted to reflect the best interest of the society as a whole. They are critical of managerial and administrative government, and fear the "welfare state," or what is dismissively called the "nanny state." Some research shows that "conservatives desire security, predictability and authority more than liberals do."[43] Conservatives believe in the importance of stability and promote law and order to protect private property. When it comes to the traditional forces of countervailing power to the corporate sector, 67 percent of Republicans versus 34 percent of Democrats say the federal government has too much power; 69 percent of Republicans versus 20 percent of Democrats say labor unions have too much power.[44] Some core principles of conservatism argue that

> [g]overnment often stands as the greatest obstacle to the progress and prosperity of free people. Free markets and free and fair-trade agreements allow for innovation, improvement and economic expansion as risk-takers, entrepreneurs and business owners are given the liberty to pursue the American dream and create more jobs and upward mobility for more people. We believe competition should be encouraged, and government intervention and regulation should be limited. The people are better qualified to make decisions about their own lives and finances than bureaucrats, and the private sector will outperform the public sector in virtually every scenario. The free enterprise system rewards hard work and self-sacrifice and is the basis and genius of the American economy.[45]

On the *liberal left*, there are deep suspicions of an unfettered market and unrestrained corporate power, which liberals see as necessitating government intervention. To that end, they see the problems with capitalism not just in its implementation, but also with its endemic nature. They believe that the very structure of capitalism inevitably results in significant inequality, with systemic barriers limiting equal access to opportunities for certain groups. As a result, they view government policies aimed at rectifying these inequities as both essential and fair. They are critical of market fundamentalism and the ability of unregulated *laissez-faire* or free-market capitalist policies to solve most economic and social problems. Liberals prefer more regulation and more services provided by the government to all citizens, such as universal health care, social security, and welfare. They are concerned with the growing inequality in the country, believe that many social services are human rights that should not be dependent upon one's financial resources, and support government intervention to sever that link. To this end, liberals tend to support increased tax rates on high-income earners to pay for government services that distribute wealth more equitably. Overall, they see a role for government in creating an economic and political system that is more fair and egalitarian, with laws that are enacted to protect every individual for an equal society, sometimes at the expense of economic freedom if necessary. Some research shows that "liberals are more comfortable with novelty, nuance and complexity" than conservatives.[46] Like conservatives, they are concerned about "government capture" but less for reasons of preserving free markets and competition and more for concerns that powerful corporations can set policies that do not serve the public interest. Some core principles of progressivism argue that

> [e]lected officials should be beholden to the people, not to wealthy donors and powerful CEOs. At the Progressive Caucus, we reject pay-to-play and revolving door politics and fight for a democracy where the power is in the hands of the people, not concentrated among the rich and well-connected. We reject the failed politics of the past that prioritized the deregulation of financial industries and big polluters and tax breaks for the wealthy and big corporations over the well-being of the public. And we support bold policies to close the gap between the rich and everyday Americans and ensure our government delivers essential services to every person in this country: Ensuring regulation of industry with strong

consumer protections, Strengthening oversight of financial institutions, Democratizing our society by getting money out of politics, eliminating political corruption, and protecting and expanding access to the ballot box, Ensuring that all of our economic and tax policies address or decrease income inequality, Protecting the federal government's role in delivering essential goods, taking on monopolies, and disciplining markets.[47]

Four Social Debates That Highlight Our Political Divide on Capitalism

Conservatives and liberals don't disagree on everything, of course. For example, a similar percentage of right- and left-leaning people see the extraordinary levels of wealth inequality in America as a problem,[48] with 77 percent of Democrats and 53 percent of Republicans agreeing that "the very rich should contribute an extra share of their total wealth each year to support public programs."[49] But very real policy disagreements persist—particularly related to four hot-button issues: gun control, climate change, national health care, and universal basic income.

Gun Control. Democrats are far more likely than Republicans to see gun violence as a "very big" national problem. But between 2021 and 2023, that percentage in each group has grown, with Republicans increasing from 19 percent to 38 percent and Democrats increasing from 70 percent to 81 percent. Both equally support preventing those with mental illnesses from purchasing guns and increasing the minimum age for buying guns to twenty-one years old.[50] But differences start to emerge when control measures begin to intrude on the market where the gun industry represents a substantial market sector and conservatives view attempts to regulate the sector as typical government overreach into the market. Republicans are also more likely to oppose steps that they see as infringements on the freedom of individuals, with 57 percent opposed to bans on assault-style weapons and high-capacity ammunition magazines, compared to 90 percent of Democrats who support these policies. Seventy-four percent of Republicans support teachers and school officials carrying guns in K–12 schools and 71 percent support allowing people to carry concealed guns in more places; such proposals are supported by just 27 percent and 19 percent of Democrats, respectively.[51]

Climate Change. Survey data from 2023 shows 78 percent of Democrats describe climate change as a major threat to the country's well-being, an increase from 58 percent in 2013. By contrast, only 23 percent of Republicans consider climate change a major threat, a share that's largely unchanged since 2013. Whereas 54 percent of American adults overall see climate change as a major threat, 73 percent of Germans and 81 percent of French adults describe it as such.[52] Many on the right are suspicious of climate science and climate policy as a covert way for the government to interfere in the economy, diminish personal freedom, and choose winners in the market.[53] For many, there is a belief that any response to climate change is inextricably tied to a liberal political ideology[54] and threatening to values they want to protect such as individual responsibility and the free-market economy.[55] Conservatives tend to show less trust in scientific findings that highlight the environmental and public health consequences of economic production, while displaying more confidence in scientific research that leads to innovations benefiting economic production.[56] This points to a dominant theme that conservatives fear what climate controls would do to the economy,[57] with multiple studies showing a strong correlation between support for free-market ideology and rejection of climate science.[58] Climate change challenges the great trust conservatives have that market forces will lead to positive ends.[59] For instance, many conservatives see renewable energy as only possible with large government subsidies and hold low regard for climate-action proponents' push for "green jobs" as just a way for "Greentech" firms to exploit governmental manipulation in the energy market.[60]

National Health Care. There is a social need to address health care costs in the United States. Sixty-six percent of all personal bankruptcies are due to medical bills,[61] a significant increase from only 8 percent in 1981 and significantly higher than in other countries like Canada (19 percent), Australia (10 percent), and the United Kingdom (8.2 percent).[62] Fifty-five percent of small business owners say the cost of providing health insurance to their employees is the biggest challenge they face, surpassing taxes and competition.[63] In 2022, the United States spent an estimated $4.5 trillion annually on health care expenses,[64] or $13,493 per person and 17.3 percent of the nation's GDP, more than any other industrialized country. Employers bear the highest burden of these health care costs. As a result, all this health care spending has led to reduced worker wages, higher consumer prices, and added costs to exports on global markets. General Motors, for instance, covers more than 1.1 million employees and former employees, and the company reports that it spends roughly $5 billion on health care expenses annually, which adds between $1,500 and $2,000 to the sticker price of every automobile it makes.[65] Yet 81 percent of Democrats and Democratic-leaning independents are in favor of health care coverage for all, while only 23 percent of Republicans and Republican-leaning Americans feel the same,[66] seeing national health care as a prime example of the government tampering in the market and trying to push through a socialist agenda.

Conservatives favor proposals that leverage the power of the market to solve the problem of rising health care costs. Rather than a government-run single payer or public option plan, groups like the Cato and Heartland Institutes view the most important element of health care reform as protecting the freedom to make one's own health care decisions as a "fundamental human right" and looks to government to protect that right and allow "innovation and competition [to] make health care more universal—better, more affordable, and more secure."[67] The underlying values supporting this position are a faith in the free market and a concern over the danger of placing "the dysfunctional federal government in charge of health care to improve access and reduce costs."[68]

Universal Basic Income (UBI). According to the Bureau of Labor Statistics, 6.4 million Americans were among the "working poor" in 2021, spending at least twenty-seven weeks in the labor force (that is, working or looking for work) but whose incomes still fell below the official poverty level.[69] But for decades, the idea of providing a stipend to Americans below a certain level of household income has stirred deep animus along party lines, with some on the right viewing it as a "capitalist road to communism" or a world free of work, while those on the left see it as a compassionate way to help people out of structural poverty in which wages do not cover living expenses. A 2021 poll found that around 66 percent of people in six European countries want governments to put in place a UBI, and a 2019 poll found that 55 percent of Americans were also in favor of UBI.[70] But while 70 percent of Democrats and Democratic leaners favor a UBI of $1,000 per person, only 20 percent of Republicans and Republican-leaning independents agree;[71] this despite the endorsement of UBI by some high-profile conservative voices, including Richard Nixon, Elon Musk, and even Milton Friedman, who reasoned that it would help to reduce poverty, increase employment, and grow the economy.

Described by economists as a negative income tax, one UBI proposal in 2021 outlined a basic income of $12,500 per year to all adults (plus an additional $4,500 per child), which would begin phasing out when household income (calculated for two-adult households) reaches $15,000 and would zero out at a household income of $70,000. The estimated cost was $876 billion per year, and studies have found that UBI made it easier for recipients to feed their children, pay their utility bills, invest in education, and pay the rent.[72]

One experiment in Vancouver found that those who received the UBI stipend spent more on necessities such as rent, food, and transit and not on "temptation goods" such as alcohol, drugs, and cigarettes, while also generating a net savings of $777 CAD per year by spending ninety-nine fewer days in shelters and fifty-five more days in stable housing.[73] Another experiment, in Stockton, California, found that UBI reduced unemployment by 4 percent during the program's first year, helped debtors pay off their creditors, improved the overall mental well-being of the recipients, and found that a majority of the basic income was spent on food, utilities, auto costs, and trips to Walmart or Dollar Stores. Less than 1 percent of the money went towards alcohol or tobacco.[74]

Despite these promising pilot programs, many Americans find it hard to get around the idea of paying people for not working and the opportunities this creates for fraud and cronyism with assistance reaching beyond the poor and needy. Views on UBI also fall on how one views the cause of poverty, whether it is the product of personal failings and inadequacies like laziness or lack of discipline or whether it is caused by structural or systemic barriers like the lack of quality jobs, adequate pay, affordable housing, and other issues. Research has supported the latter view, finding that systemic barriers carry more weight in engendering poverty than individual factors.[75]

Some Central Questions for Adopting a More Compassionate Capitalism
The challenges of overcoming the political differences in our views on the amendments to capitalism outlined earlier lie in Americans' ability to thread the needle between the conservative and liberal views, in effect finding the third way. One difficulty is that these policies typically require some form of up-front cost with the benefits coming later. The former are immediate and certain, the latter are projected in the future and uncertain. A second dif-

ficulty is bridging between an analytical view of the form of capitalism we seek and a values-based view that we need to build a meritocracy that rewards hard work without the government as arbiter of success. Three questions can help do that, each focusing on a different aspect of the tax revenue needed to support these initiatives.

Can social policies be developed that have a return on investment? In 2020, two Harvard economists studied 133 US social policies implemented during the last half-century and found that many such programs—especially those focused on children and young adults—made money for taxpayers, when all costs and benefits were considered. That's because they improved the health and education of enrollees and their families, who eventually earned more income, paid more taxes, and needed less government assistance overall.[76] Spending on services like Medicaid expansion, K–12 education, and college financial aid, they found, reduces long-term medical costs and makes children more likely to attend college, find high-paying work, and pay more in taxes as adults. "From a taxpayer perspective," the authors write, "these expenditures on children are investments, rather than just transfers,"[77] and the payoff for children's programs is so dramatic that it may not make sense to think of them as "spending" at all.[78] This kind of a long-term view is required when considering the full outcome of a social safety net. These policies will still require up-front costs to yield payouts later.

Can taxes be raised to support a social safety net? Raising income tax rates is seen as a third-rail issue in the United States. Yet most business students do not know a world in which the upper income tax rates were more than 30 percent. The reality is that before Ronald Reagan's presidency, those who fell into the highest tax bracket paid over half of their income in income tax, at times closer to 70 percent and even reaching over 90 percent during World War II and into the 1950s. After Reagan's policies in the 1980s, the rate dropped to 28 percent (see Figure 6.3). Tax cuts for the wealthy are often justified on the grounds that they will spur economic growth. For example, the Tax Foundation, a nonpartisan, conservative-leaning think tank, argued in its analysis of President Trump's 2016 campaign proposal that lowering the top income tax rate would lead to increased job opportunities.[79] But the Congressional Research Service published a report in 2012 that found no correlation between top tax rates and economic growth. *Politico* conducted a similar anal-

FIGURE 6.3

Historical Highest Marginal Income Tax Rates, 1913–2023

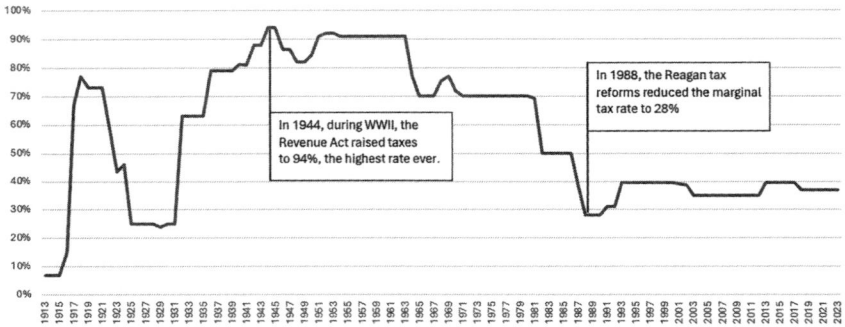

Source: Figure created by author using data from the Tax Policy Center, "Historical Highest Marginal Income Tax Rates," May 11, 2023, https://www.taxpolicycenter.org/statistics/historical -highest-marginal-income-tax-rates (accessed June 6, 2023).

ysis in 2017 and found that changing the top income tax rate does not have a predictable effect on economic growth.[80]

Can tax revenues to support social programs be maintained? There are hazards to committing to these levels of social support programs and being able to maintain support over the long term. All of this depends on the free market to generate the tax revenues that make an extensive welfare system possible over time. Some Nordic countries are facing a challenge as the post–World War II baby boom produced a large generation that's currently retiring or retired. This was also followed by a decline in the birth rate. The populations are still growing, but the percentage of people working and paying taxes is in decline. This is not unique to the Nordic countries—it's a problem that many other countries, such as Japan, are facing—but it hits them harder because of their heavy reliance on tax-paying citizens to support its generous social safety net.[81]

This relates to a second problem, as Nordic countries have experienced an influx of immigrants and a challenge for maintaining its system of strong welfare support. At first, Swedish leaders saw immigration as an opportunity to boost the labor force, expecting that the newcomers would learn Swedish, take jobs (such as caring for older Swedes), pay taxes, and help finance its extensive social welfare programs.[82] But instead, while the foreign-born population almost doubled to 20 percent of the population in 2020, many of these people were unable to learn to speak Swedish, lacked education, have not assimilated, and remained unemployed. The problem is exacerbated because the economy is centered on highly skilled, highly paid pursuits.[83] This has led to a backlash, with many Swedes seeing refugees as draining social welfare systems and an "assault on Swedish culture." As a corrective, the government has provided subsidies for home care employees, seeing low-wage service jobs (cleaning, taking care of children) as good for immigrants and good for the economy. But it also exposes vulnerabilities in the social democratic model of Nordic countries.

Our Current Problems Are Not Endemic to Capitalism

These models of capitalism around the world show that the problems faced in the United States are not endemic to capitalism, only to the form we have adopted. They are the result of the laws, rules, and norms of behavior that have been in place largely since the 1970s, although some were formed much earlier. But as Steven Pearlstein writes in his book *Can American Capitalism Survive?* the system of capitalism we presently have "offends the moral sensibilities even of people who are benefiting from it." The subtitle of his book highlights some deeper corrections that are needed—"greed is not good, opportunity is not equal, and fairness won't make us poor"[84]—from which Pearlstein argues that "capitalism doesn't have to reach the point of ruthlessness like it has here and other places."[85]

One proposed corrective in Congress would empower workers at United States corporations to elect at least 40 percent of board members, in a way similar to policies in place in Germany. It would also restrict the sales of company shares by the directors and officers, limiting the extent to which they can game share price to their own benefit.[86] It did not go up for a vote as it would not have received the level of support needed to pass. But, Pearlstein argues, political change is preceded by social change. When things get so unfair that trust becomes eroded, things have gone too far and the social fabric that holds society together starts to erode. That will lead to efforts to break the institutions of society. To avoid this, we need to build social capital, reestablish "the amount of trust that we all have in each other and in our institutions." In

Pearlstein's view, "We're at a tipping point now and things are about to change. You and I may disagree about what, exactly, we need to do, or how far we need to go, but I think there are enough positive signs in public opinion that suggest we're at a tipping point."[87]

One thing is for sure, business school students will play a role in determining what happens next.

SEVEN

The Purpose of the Firm

It's Not to Make Shareholders Rich,
It's to Serve Customers and Society

"Shareholder value ideology in fact is a relatively new development in the business culture. It is not supported by the traditional rules of American corporate law; is not consistent with the real economic structure of business corporations; and is not supported by the bulk of the empirical evidence on what makes corporations and economies work."

—LYNN STOUT, CORNELL LAW SCHOOL

What is the purpose of the firm? To many, the answer is obvious: the purpose of the firm is to make money for its shareholders. Thus the purpose of management is to maximize the firm's share price. I could ask just about anyone this question and I will likely get the same response. This idea is so common that most people take it for granted. But it turns out that maximizing shareholder profits isn't a legal requirement for American companies, and it doesn't even line up with how businesses and the economy really work.[1] So why do we believe this idea so strongly? Mainly, it's because it has been heavily promoted by a group of economists and organizations that favor the idea of free markets and small government.[2] If we look at things from a legal or business management perspective, we'll find that the purpose of a company is actually more complex. To begin this exploration, let's start with a basic question: What exactly is a firm?

The View of the Firm from Economics

Economics has played a major role in shaping how we think about the purpose of firms, and this shows up a lot in business education. If business students are taught anything at all about corporate purpose, their education is shaped by two ideas that dominate our views on the subject, even if they are not explicitly mentioned. In fact, I often find that business students are unaware of these bodies of literature. They are "transaction cost economics" and "agency theory."

Transaction Cost Economics. Our model of the corporation got its start with an economist named Ronald Coase. In 1937, he published a paper, "The Nature of the Firm,"[3] that introduced the concept of transaction costs for the first time. Beginning with a simple question—Why and under what conditions should we expect firms to emerge?—Coase hypothesized that, in theory, "production could be carried on without any organization at all" and that it could be more efficient to have a multitude of independent, self-employed people who contract with one another. But transaction costs are the hidden expenses that make it hard to do this. They can be the costs of searching for and gathering information, bargaining and contracting, and policing and enforcement of contracts, all of which add to the cost of procuring something from someone else. Figuring out the details, negotiating, and making sure everyone follows through take time and resources. Transaction cost economics analyzes ways to minimize those costs and create greater efficiencies in organizations.

As a result, Coase theorized, people will organize in firms when the transaction costs of coordinating production through the market are greater than the costs of coordination within the firm. That is to say, when it's cheaper to organize things within a single organization, people will form a business rather than work as independent contractors. The firm, then, is "a nexus for a set of contracting relationships" that brings together a collection of individuals and organizations—employees, investors, suppliers, customers, and so on—who contract with each other in the name of a "legal fiction" called the corporation to collaborate on something productive. With this work, Coase set the foundation for the transaction cost theory of the firm upon which other economists would build to examine the firm's purpose.

Starting with the foundational theories established by Coase, economist Milton Friedman expanded the discourse on the firm and capitalism with his own groundbreaking work. In his 1962 book *Capitalism and Freedom*, he argued that the growing pressure for corporations to be "socially responsible" and not just focus on profit was highly subversive to the capitalist system and can only lead towards totalitarianism, which would allow government bureaucrats to inhibit our freedom.[4] In 1970, he elaborated on these ideas in an article in the *New York Times Magazine* as a response to pressures from activists, notably Ralph Nader, who was campaigning against the auto sector for automobile safety issues and was gaining traction in fomenting an American consumer movement.[5] Friedman's argument followed the same reasoning of transaction cost economics that the firm was an artificial entity and also began to build the foundations for agency theory, the idea that managers are singularly responsible to shareholders, which would grow within economics through the 1970s. To explain corporate purpose, Friedman writes forcefully that

[t]he businessmen who believe that they are defending free enterprise when they declaim that business is not concerned "merely" with profit but also with promoting desirable "social" ends . . . are preaching pure and unadulterated socialism. Businessmen who talk this way are unwitting puppets of the intellectual forces that have been undermining the basis of a free society these past decades. . . . Only people can have responsibilities. A corporation is an artificial person and, in this sense, may have artificial responsibilities, but "business" as a whole cannot be said to have responsibilities, even in this vague sense. . . . In a free-enterprise, private-property system, a corporate executive is an employee of the owners of the business. He has direct responsibility to his employers. . . . the use of the cloak of social responsibility, and the nonsense spoken in its name by influential and prestigious businessmen, does clearly harm the foundations of a free society. . . . This may gain them kudos in the short run. But it helps to strengthen the already too prevalent view that the pursuit of profits is wicked and immoral and must be curbed and controlled by external forces. Once this view is adopted, the external forces that curb the market will not be the social consciences, however highly developed,

of the pontificating executives; it will be the iron fist of Government bureaucrats. . . . That is why, in my book "Capitalism and Freedom," I have called it a "fundamentally subversive doctrine" in a free society, and have said that in such a society, "there is one and only one social responsibility of business—to use its resources and engage in activities designed to increase its profits so long as it stays within the rules of the game, which is to say, engages in open and free competition without deception or fraud."[6]

Agency Theory. Economists Michael Jensen and William Meckling built on Coase's and Friedman's arguments with their 1976 paper "Theory of the Firm."[7] They agreed with Coase that a company is basically a "legal fiction"—a bundle of contracts held together to lower the costs of doing business. But Jensen and Meckling introduced a new wrinkle: the problem of "principal-agent costs."

Here's what that means. Imagine the company's owners as the "principals" and the managers as their "agents." Ideally, managers would always act in the best interests of the owners. But in the real world, sometimes managers might put their own interests first. This is called the "principal-agent problem," and agency theory analyzes these types of situations, seeking ways to align interests of both parties. The costs of correcting this misalignment come down to three components: (1) the costs of creating an agreement between the agent and principal to guarantee alignment of interests; (2) the principal's cost to monitor the agent and minimize misalignment; and (3) residual losses attributed to the divergence in principal-agent interests, even after monitoring and contracting costs are in place to minimize that divergence.[8] With this as a foundation for viewing the firm, Jensen and Meckling write using a forceful style and logic similar to Friedman to describe its purpose:

> The corporation is not an individual. It does not feel; it does not choose; it cannot bear the burden of taxes; it cannot bear the costs of regulation; it cannot benefit from tariffs or subsidies. All such actions, of course, can and generally do benefit or harm individuals who have some relationship with the corporation such as investors, employees or customers, but it is literal nonsense to say that the corporation is benefitted or is harmed. The viability and the prevalence of the corporation as an organizational form,

of course, depends on the cost of doing business as a corporation. Government policies which impose costs on firms who do business as a corporation will discourage the use of that organizational form. But those costs cannot be borne by the corporation, costs can only be borne by "real" as distinct from artificial beings. More to the point, the corporation cannot be socially (or otherwise) responsible! However, we end up defining it, the notion of "being responsible" is a normative concept strictly relevant only to human beings. A corporation can no more be responsible than can a lump of coal.[9]

This is the model of the nature and purpose of the firm that dominates business education today. It is built upon an idea that firms are merely collections of individuals who share nothing in common except their individual contractual arrangements with the fictional entity called the firm. There is no community, there is no culture, there is no common objective. In this view, managers within firms are fairly untrustworthy, are primarily motivated by money, and will pursue their own interests against the best interests of the firm if they are not properly incented and monitored. The firm's owners, and therefore the manager's boss, are considered to be the shareholders, and it naturally follows then that CEOs should focus on "maximizing shareholder value" and corporate boards should see their job as aligning the interests of management with shareholders through contractual agreements such as the use of stock-based compensation schemes. This creates a focus on share price as the singular metric of a corporation's health and long term prospects as well as the singular metric for that executive's performance. It also creates a convenient focus for economic analysis on "the simplicity of shareholder returns as the dependent variable for researchers."[10] In all these calculations, no other interests are relevant; not the community, the environment, the employees, or the customers (unless they add to the share price). Any kinds of legal or regulatory constraints or obligations on the activity of these managers or the firm are restraints on economic and therefore political freedom. This is the basis of shareholder capitalism. In theory, it might sound good. But in the real world it doesn't hold up. To understand why, we need to look at businesses through different lenses, like the law, sociology, and how companies are actually managed in practice.

The View of the Firm from Law

Our next, and perhaps most powerful, lens through which to understand corporate purpose is that of law. Through this lens, corporations are legally sanctioned entities with obligations to society, the communities they serve, the environment, and others in the market. They must operate and conform to the norms of society as codified in corporate law. These legal norms and obligations are the guardrails on the market that Adam Smith writes about. Here, a sports metaphor might be useful. Neoclassical economists believe the economy will play out fairly as long as the government doesn't interfere; they see legal rules as messing up the natural flow. Legal scholars however understand that without legal rules, the game won't be fair. They see the government's role as setting those rules, making sure everyone has an equal shot, creating a "level playing field," and stepping in to stop foul play.

For instance, corporate law scholar Lynn Stout argues that the notion that corporations are beholden primarily to the shareholder "can be hazardous to the health of investors, companies, and the public alike"[11] and that "Shareholder value ideology in fact is a relatively new development in the business culture. It is not supported by the traditional rules of American corporate law; is not consistent with the real economic structure of business corporations; and is not supported by the bulk of the empirical evidence on what makes corporations and economies work."[12]

Many people assume that US corporate law demands companies focus solely on making money for shareholders. However, as Stout argues, this isn't true. This common misconception often stems from a 1919 Michigan court case, *Dodge v. Ford Motor Company*.[13] In this case, Henry Ford, the majority owner of Ford, claimed he wanted to end special shareholder dividends in order to reinvest profits into the company—lowering car prices, hiring more people, and giving raises. Two minority shareholders, Horace and John Dodge, owned 10 percent of the company and wanted to use their dividends to start a new company. But Ford, by ending special dividends in favor of plant investments, was trying to starve them of capital to limit competition. In fact, Ford was so cavalier in his court testimony about his obligations to shareholders that some historians believe he was actually making it easy for the court to rule against him, thus requiring his company to pay the dividends. Ford lost, and in its decision, the court added a side note to its ruling stating that businesses exist mainly for stockholder profits. This editorial comment was added *mere dicta*, meaning that it wasn't related to the actual case and doesn't set a legal rule that courts have to follow, yet it's often misrepresented as the foundation of shareholder primacy.

In the words of Jonathan R. Macey, deputy dean and professor at the Yale Law School, "There are no cases other than Dodge v. Ford that actually operationalize the rule that corporations must maximize profits. The goal of profit maximization is to corporate law what observations about the weather are in ordinary conversation. Everybody talks about it, including judges, but with the lone exception of Dodge v. Ford, nobody actually does anything about it." He concludes that "[t]he rule of wealth maximization for shareholders is virtually impossible to enforce as a practical matter. The rule is aspirational, except in odd cases. As long as corporate directors and CEOs claim to be maximizing profits for shareholders, they will be taken at their word, because it is impossible to refute these corporate officials' self-serving assertions about their motives."[14] M. Todd Henderson from the University of Chicago Law School writes that "Dodge is often misread or mistaught as setting a legal rule of shareholder wealth maximization. This was not and is not the law. Shareholder wealth maximization is a standard of conduct for officers and directors, not a legal mandate. The business judgment rule [which was also upheld in this decision] protects many decisions that deviate from this standard."[15]

Shifting focus from these theoretical interpretations to practical legal advice for company owners and managers, the American Law Institute provides clear guidelines on directors' responsibilities and decision-making processes. In its *Principles of Corporate Governance*, Section 4.01, the Business Judgement Rule states that a court will not review a director's business decisions if they performed their duties

(1) In good faith; untainted by conflicts of interests and based on a reasonable attempt to be informed; (2) With loyalty; in a manner the directors reasonably believe to be in the best interests of the corporation; (3) Exercising due care; with the care that an ordinarily prudent person in a like position would exercise under similar circumstances.[16]

In a related statute defining the objective and conduct of the corporation, Section 2.01 states,

(1) A corporation should have as its objective the conduct of business activities with a view to enhancing corporate profit and shareholder gain. (2) Even if corporate profit and shareholder gain are not thereby enhanced, the corporation, in the conduct of its business: (a) Is obliged, to the same extent as a natural person, to act within the boundaries set by law; (b) May take into account ethical considerations that are reasonably regarded as appropriate to the responsible conduct of business; and (c) May devote a reasonable amount of resources to public welfare, humanitarian, educational, and philanthropic purposes.[17]

The corporate code of Delaware, where the majority of Fortune 500 businesses are incorporated, states that corporations can be formed for "any lawful purpose."[18] US Supreme Court Justice Samuel Alito argued a similar point in the 2014 *Burwell v. Hobby Lobby Stores, Inc.* case: "While it is certainly true that a central objective of for-profit corporations is to make money, modern corporate law does not require for-profit corporations to pursue profit at the expense of everything else, and many do not do so. For-profit corporations, with ownership approval, support a wide variety of charitable causes, and it is not at all uncommon for such corporations to further humanitarian and other altruistic objectives."[19] Many business students express stunned surprise when these facts are laid out before them. But there is more evidence to make the case for corporate purpose that goes beyond the shareholder.

The Practical View

Stout makes the argument that the principal-agent model that Jensen and Meckling developed "assumed without discussion the 'principals' in public corporations were the shareholders, and directors were the shareholders' 'agents.' Yet Jensen and Meckling were economists, not lawyers, and this assumption fundamentally mistakes the real economic and legal relationships among shareholders, executives, creditors, and directors in public corporations. . . . It's clearly incorrect, as a descriptive matter, to say the principal-agent model captures the reality of modern public corporations with thousands of shareholders, scores of executives, and a dozen or more directors."[20] She outlines three incorrect claims in the principal-agent model.

The first claim is that shareholders "own" the corporation. As a legal matter, they do not. "Corporations are independent legal entities that own themselves, holding property in their own names, entering their own contracts, and committing their own torts."[21] Shareholders own shares of stock, which are contracts between the shareholder and the corporation that give shareholders limited rights under limited circumstances, no different from bondholders, suppliers, and employees.

The second claim is that shareholders are the sole residual claimants in corporations and that other stakeholders like employees, customers, and creditors "are assumed to receive only the benefits their formal contracts and the law entitle them to (fixed salaries, interest, and so forth), while shareholders supposedly get all profits left over after the firm has met those fixed obligations." Again, this is incorrect. Shareholders are only treated as residual claimants when a company files for bankruptcy. In operating firms, shareholders only get money on the basis of their contractual relationship with the directors. "The corporation is its own residual claimant, and its board of directors decides which groups get what share of the corporation's residual," Stout writes.[22]

The third claim is that shareholders are principals and directors are agents. This is also wrong, according to Stout. "The shareholders as principals do not have the right to control the director's behavior as agents," she writes. "One of the most fundamental rules of corporate law is that corporations are controlled by boards of directors, not by shareholders. Although, in theory, shareholders have the right to elect and remove directors," in practice the costs of mounting a proxy battle would be very high and the case would be hard to win as the business judgment rule protects directors who may "place stakeholders' or society's interests above the shareholders' own."[23] In the end, the executives of a corporation are employees of the corporation, not the shareholders.[24]

The View of the Firm from Sociology and Management Practice

The next lens we must consider is that of the sociologist. Where neoclassical economists see the firm as the nexus of contracts and legal scholars see firms as entities bound by laws and norms, sociologists see firms as distinct social collectives that develop deep cultures around a common goal. As early as 1893, sociologist Emile Durkheim saw the social dimension of corporations and organizations in his book *The Division of Labor in Society*, arguing that the division of labor in capitalist society allocates and organizes people according to merit, skills, and aptitude, thereby creating social organizations.[25] These groupings develop a culture and collective purpose that coordinates and inspires its members to do great things, not merely with the carrot and stick of compensation and authority, but with the intrinsic rewards that come from being immersed in a community that is bound together by informal rules, transcendent values, and deep underlying beliefs.[26] This cultural lens sees managers as being able to supervise or manage large groups by facilitating these cultural structures. So, rather than being a "legal fiction" and "a nexus for a set of contracting relationships," companies are rich and thriving communities. Certainly, as companies strive to bring employees back to work after the Covid pandemic, it would suggest that most managers believe that the company is more than a group of individual contracts but a collective with group dynamics, culture, and value.

And this brings us to the final lens through which to the view the firm: that of actual practice. In the mid-twentieth century, management professor Peter Drucker also saw the firm as having a strong social dimension as well as an economic purpose, one that managers could and should work to shape.[27] Much of his work was based on personal observation gained by embedding himself in operating companies and studying their inner workings. In his 1946 book *Concept of the Corporation*, he studied the internal working of the General Motors Corporation and developed a deeper understanding of the human interactions within a company, and more specifically how power structures, political environments, information flows, decision making, and managerial autonomy contributed to success.[28] Like early twentieth-century management consultant Mary Parker Follett, Drucker saw workers as valuable resources rather than simply contractually arranged laborers and that managers should see their brains, and not their hands, as their most important asset.[29] To that end, he focused on decentralizing, democratizing, and breaking down hierarchy. He wanted to empower frontline workers with responsibilities and reward their initiative. His goal was to unite managers and their teams behind a shared purpose. Drucker placed a high value on problem solvers and creative thinkers. He wanted a culture in which everyone felt encouraged to contribute ideas, not just physical labor, and he strongly supported programs for workforce development for both managers and their team members.[30]

In 1973, Drucker made a sustained argument against shareholder value primacy in his book *Management*, wherein he argues that "there is only one valid definition of business purpose: to create a customer. . . . It is the customer who determines what a business is. It is the customer alone whose willingness to pay for a good or for a service converts economic resources into wealth, things into goods. . . . The customer is the foundation of a business and keeps it in existence."[31] Profits are one metric of how well the company performs this purpose but ultimately, he argues, "the business enterprise . . . exists for the sake of the contribution which it makes to the welfare of society as a whole."[32] For Drucker, this oriented the firm towards serving the customer through marketing and not just profits for the shareholder. He writes, "Because the purpose of business is to create a customer, the business enterprise has two— and only two—basic functions: marketing and innovation. Marketing and innovation produce results; all the rest are costs. Marketing is the distinguishing, unique function of the business."[33] When he referred to marketing, he envisioned an outward-facing function that sought to understand the interests of stakeholders in the external environment and respond to them. In this way, he saw businesses as existing as part of a larger social system; their decisions should reflect both their internal goals and their impact on the outside world. Above all, Drucker emphasized the value companies create for society by being profitable. This, he argued, allows them to create jobs and generate wealth, benefiting everyone.[34]

These ideas were mirrored by executives with experience within the market. Jamsetji Nusserwanji Tata, founder of the Indian conglomerate Tata Group, pronounced at the beginning of the twentieth century, "In a free enterprise, the community is not just another stakeholder in business, but is in fact the very purpose of its existence." Kenneth Mason, former president of Quaker Oats, wrote that Milton Friedman's ideas on corporate purpose were "a dreary and demeaning view of the role of business and business leaders in our society. . . . Making a profit is no more the purpose of a corporation than getting enough to eat is the purpose of life. Getting enough to eat is a requirement of life; life's purpose, one would hope, is somewhat broader and more challenging. Likewise with business and profit. . . . The moral imperative all of us share in this world is that of getting the best return we can on whatever assets we are privileged to employ. What American business leaders too often forget is that this means all the assets employed—not just the financial assets but also the brains employed, the labor employed, the materials employed, and the land, air, and water employed."[35] Even such a historic acolyte of shareholder value as former GE CEO Jack Welch turned against shareholder primacy, calling it "the dumbest idea in the world," and adding that "shareholder value is a result, not a strategy. . . . Your main constituencies are your employees, your customers and your products."[36]

As a corrective, former Unilever CEO Paul Polman and management expert Andrew Winston advocate that companies must be "net positive," playing an "active role in addressing our biggest shared challenges" that "improves well-being for everyone it impacts and at all scales—every product, every operation, every region and country, and for every stakeholder, including employees, suppliers, communities, customers, and even future generations and the planet itself."[37] In their radical view, such companies should be restorative and regenerative, take "responsibility for their total impact on the world, lead with transparency, and focus on the long term. They aim for cooperative leadership, not just competitive leadership, because the world's problems are so immense that it is beyond the scope and ability of a single company to fix them."[38] Mirroring Peter Drucker,[39] Polman argues that the role of the corporate leader is to embody and instill that purpose. "You cannot be a purpose-driven company if you're not purposeful yourself, finding your purpose, fighting for things that you believe in, be it our children or future generations. So, live what you preach."[40]

Why Is the View from Economics so Dominant?

Despite compelling arguments from legal experts, sociologists, management scholars, and even experienced professionals, the views of neoclassical economists continue to dominate. This is problematic, as economics is but one branch of the social sciences that is useful for understanding human society and social relationships. To help see its value in relation to the others, we can turn, of all places, to the Cuban Missile Crisis and an analysis by Harvard professor Graham Allison.

In October 1962, the Soviet Union placed offensive nuclear weapons on the island of Cuba, just over four hundred miles from the coast of Florida. This precipitated a thirteen-day stand-off between the United States and the Soviet Union, during which a blockade of the island was instituted by President John F. Kennedy and the Soviet premier Nikita Khrushchev eventually removed the missiles. One question that emerged was, how close did we come to a nuclear war? Allison, in his 1971 book *Essence of Decision*, answered that question using three different models to provide three different analyses.

Through the lens of the "rational actor model" (which is akin to neoclassical economics), his analysis suggests that "since nuclear war between the United States and Soviet Union would be mutual suicide, neither nation would choose nuclear war, and nuclear war [was] therefore not a serious possibility."[41]

However, through the lens of the "organizational process model," the story becomes more complex. Allison shows that the United States and Soviet Union are not monoliths but rather large bureaucracies, organizations through which information is developed, interpreted, disseminated, and translated. Further, there was no hotline between the White House and the Kremlin at this time, so information had to pass through various channels, each translating it slightly as it passed. Information going through the State Department would look different from the same information passing through Department of Defense or another country. The analysis from this model suggests that the chances of war were much greater. Organizational dynamics alter rational expectations such that "nuclear crises between machines as large as the United States and Soviet governments are inherently chancy. The information and estimates available to leaders about the situation will reflect organizational goals and routines as well as facts. . . . In the crisis, the overwhelming problem will be that of control and coordination of large organizations."[42]

Not ending here, Allison applies a third, "bureaucratic politics model," to reveal conclusions even more ominous. The responsive actions advocated by leaders of the US government ranged from doing nothing to inflicting a full air strike. The ultimate decision of the blockade emerged from many uncertain political factors. Had President Kennedy proved his mettle in the earlier Bay of Pigs confrontation, the diplomatic track might have prevailed with limited debate. Had earlier events regarding Cuba not brought the tempering voices of Robert Kennedy and Theodore Sorensen into the discussions, an air strike would probably have emerged. At the same time, Nikita Khrushchev was under pressure from the Politburo to stand firm regarding similar US missiles in Turkey. In the end, "the interaction of internal games," and "the mix of personality, expertise, influence and temperament that allows a group to clarify alternatives even while it pulls and hauls for separate preferences" could indeed have yielded nuclear war as an outcome.[43]

In each case, the analytical model Allison applies tells something different about the same history. His point is not that one model is right while the others are wrong, but rather that each tells a different part of the whole. Similarly, economics is one lens on the nature and purpose of the firm; it is not the only one. Just as the Cuban Missile Crisis demanded multiple analyses to be fully understood, the corporation is complex and must be looked at through multiple lenses to be fully comprehended. Overreliance on shareholder primacy neglects the legal, social, and internal factors crucial for long-term success, stability, and purpose. Nonetheless, economics continues to assert disproportionate influence in political and social debates. Why? I believe there are at least four reasons.

First, economics is highly quantitative, and we instinctively trust numbers, even when they try to describe complex, protean phenomena like human behavior. Economists attempt to treat human behavior as if it was a quantifiable natural phenomenon, just like heat, light, and energy.[44] This is intellectually alluring but it is clearly an insufficient approach. Mid-century Federal Reserve chair William McChesney Martin, a stockbroker rather than an economist by profession, kept the economists in the basement of the Fed, in part because, as he put it, "They don't know their limitations and have a far greater sense of confidence in their analyses than I have found to be warranted."[45] For example, the concept of utility is central in economics, describing the benefits gained or satisfaction experienced with the consumption of goods or services. But while economists try, it's impossible to accurately measure utility, certainly not with a simple number focused on money.[46] Can you put a precise value on your own happiness? Despite the concept's shaky foundation, it's used in many economic models. In reality, research shows that human behavior often defies the neat calculations of economists.[47]

Similarly, the idea that business performance can be measured through the single metric of share price is both seductive in its simplicity and, again, deeply flawed. It has fueled numerous academic studies seeking the magic formula for "good governance." Researchers chase correlations between stock prices and everything from board structure to company mergers, to even in which US state a company is incorporated. Yet this narrow focus yields a distorted picture. In the real world, high shareholder returns don't guarantee a healthy company. Just look at corporate America in recent decades. Despite healthy stock returns, US companies have faced mounting problems: financial instability, declining investment, stagnant wages, widening inequality, and environmental risk.[48]

Even more dangerously, however, the seductively elegant models of mainstream economics frequently offer simplistic, preordained solutions that tend to fit into neat existing categories, reinforcing inequality and the status quo. Harvard economist Dani Rodrik argues that "mainstream economics shades too easily into ideology, constraining the choices that we appear to have and providing cookie-cutter solutions," which "debases and sacrifices other important values such as equality, social inclusion, democratic deliberation and justice."[49] In their book *Rethinking Capitalism*, economists Michael Jacobs and Mariana Mazzucato argue that the "orthodox model provides an attractively simple framework for thinking about economics and policy. . . . The fact that many policy prescriptions which follow from it favour those in positions of incumbent economic power has given it a powerful grip in public discourse."[50] European Central Bank president Christine Lagarde criticized the field of economics profession for having "blind faith" in their models, calling them a "tribal clique" who live in an insular world that often bears little connection to reality.[51]

For economist Angus Deaton, the problem with the neoclassical view of the firm's purpose goes much deeper. In his 2023 book *Economics in America*, he offers a biting critique of the present state of economics, chiding economists for moving away from their roots in moral philosophy set out in its earliest days by Adam Smith, John Locke, and others who came to economics via philosophy and other fields, rather than commerce.[52] He writes that "the discipline has become unmoored from its proper basis, which is the study of human welfare."[53] To Deaton, modern economics has become too focused on markets, efficiency, globalization, and the movement of goods, capital, and jobs.[54] Deaton challenges the idea that an unfettered free market will deliver greater economic equality and individual liberty, a misconception which, he argues, leads to the predatory brand of capitalism that is presently dominant in the United States, one that enriches corporations and the wealthy at the expense of working people, deepens inequality of wealth and opportunity, and is fueling the rise of a class system.[55] He writes, "You can't think about trade policy and think about money entirely, it's people's souls and their communities and their churches, and their lives that are at stake when jobs are dislocated . . . most economists measure human well-being in monetary terms. And that misses all the other things that matter, from the confidence and meaning people derive from jobs to the dignity of living in a functioning community in a democratic society."[56] To return to their true purpose, he argues, economists "need to abandon our sole fixation on money as a measure of human well-being."[57]

A second factor in elevating the status of economics is the "Nobel Prize in Economics," which is actually not a Nobel Prize at all, at least not one of the original Nobel Prizes established in 1901 through the estate of Alfred Nobel to honor men and women for outstanding achievements. The prize in economics was established in 1968, almost seventy years after the Nobel Prizes in physics, chemistry, physiology or medicine, literature, and peace to celebrate the three-hundredth anniversary of the founding of Sveriges Riksbank (Sweden's central bank), which continues to fund the prize today. In fact, it is not officially called the Nobel Prize in Economics but rather the "The Sveriges Riksbank Prize in Economic Sciences in Memory of Alfred Nobel." But it has become entrenched as a Nobel Prize, being awarded every year together with the other Nobel Prizes.

Oxford professor Avner Offer and Uppsala University professor Gabriel Söderberg argue in their book *The Nobel Factor* that the aim of establishing the economics prize is to "use the halo of the Nobel brand to enhance central bank authority and the prestige of market-friendly economics, in order to influence the future of Sweden and the rest of the developed world." This helps one school of economic thought—neoclassical economics—dominate the rest with ideas that favor the rich and powerful and help to weaken democratic control of money.[58] Descendants of Alfred Nobel have also questioned the legitimacy of the economics prize and demanded that the Nobel name be dropped from the award in favor of the "Riksbank Prize," claiming that their great-grandfather Alfred Nobel was highly skeptical of economics and that the discipline was never in his "will and is not in the spirit of his prizes."[59]

Economist Friedrich von Hayek, who won the prize in 1974, used his acceptance speech to argue that such a prize was dangerous, stating that he would
have advised against it because it "confers on an individual an authority which
in economics no man ought to possess." He warned that the award would
grant such an individual "an influence over laymen: politicians, journalists,
civil servants and the public generally" and that "there is no reason why a
man who has made a distinctive contribution to economic science should be
omnicompetent on all problems of society—as the press tends to treat him till
in the end he may himself be persuaded to believe."[60]

Indeed, economist Milton Friedman won the prize in 1976 for his work in
the realm of monetary economics, a domain in which he is highly regarded.
But his claims about the connections between capitalism and freedom, the
purpose of the firm, and optimal policy interventions did not emerge from his
core research expertise and yet are treated as academically supported truth.
Economist Joseph Stiglitz states that the Friedman Doctrine "was not based
on any economic theory,"[61] and Harvard professor Naomi Oreskes and historian Eric Conway write that Friedman's book *Capitalism and Freedom* is
based not on matters of what is true or false within economic science, but on
a set of values that railed against the Keynesian orthodoxy and elevated the
neoliberal ideas of a deregulated market, leading to "so many claims that are
immune to empirical confirmation or refutation."[62]

In 1977, economist Gunnar Myrdal, who won the prize alongside Hayek
in 1974, called for its abolition on the grounds that economics is a "soft" and
inexact science in which the political and social values of the scholar can influence their work. He contrasted the field with what he called the "hard" sciences, such as physics and chemistry, in which the politics of the recipient are
irrelevant. His statement was provoked by the awarding of the prize to Milton
Friedman and his right-wing politics, particularly his work with the authoritarian Pinochet regime in Chile.[63]

A third factor elevating the status of economics was the concerted effort,
often taking the form of an active public relations campaign, to build an American orthodoxy around *laissez faire* market policies and limited government.
These campaigns built upon an ideology promoted since the early twentieth
century, notably by groups like the National Association of Manufacturers. In
its early years, this ideology opposed protections that we now take for granted,

such as child labor laws, workers' compensation, the federal income tax, and elements of the New Deal. By the 1970s, it had shifted its public relations efforts to promoting an extreme form of *laissez faire* capitalism that argued that any government action in the marketplace, however well-intentioned, threatened individual freedoms and was a path towards totalitarianism.[64]

The Powell Memorandum of 1971 (discussed in Chapter 4) motivated the Chamber of Commerce and other groups to modernize their efforts to lobby the federal government and maintain, as the memorandum instructs, "constant surveillance" of television and radio content. It also spurred conservatives to undertake an aggressive media-outreach program to mold society's thinking about business, government, politics, and law, including funding neoliberal scholars and publishing books, papers, popular magazines, and scholarly journals that promoted a free-market ideology.[65] This lobbying included campaigns to rewrite textbooks, combat unions, and elevate economists like Friedrich von Hayek and Milton Friedman as household names.[66] Indeed Friedman's definitive and most widely read statement on the purpose of the firm was not published in a peer-reviewed academic journal but in the *New York Times Magazine*. The piece, in conjunction with his columns for *Newsweek* and his 1980 television series called "Free to Choose," was meant as a campaign to shift the public's ideas of how the market should be structured and how both corporations and government should operate within it.[67] This strategy aimed to shift the Overton Window—the range of ideas considered politically acceptable by the mainstream—towards a more *laissez-faire* economic climate.[68] The campaign was undeniably successful. The results can be seen, among other places, in a sharp rise in numbers of conservative think tanks and newspaper mentions between the 1980s and 2000s.[69]

In thwarting governmental efforts to regulate the economy, the Powell Memo encouraged corporate interests to also focus on the judiciary. The courts, it said, are possibly "the most important instrument for social, economic, and political change" in American government. Weeks after Powell wrote that memo, President Richard Nixon appointed him to the Supreme Court. The conservative focus on influencing the courts has only intensified since then, driven not just by a free-market agenda but other issues such as reproductive rights and gun control.

The fourth and final factor explaining the persistent intellectual dominance of neoclassical economics is fairly simple; the American business community of the 1970s had been searching for answers to the threats of rising global competition and desperately wanted to believe that the ideas of market fundamentalism were true.[70] Shareholder primacy provided a way for executives to increase profits by minimizing the concerns of employees, customers, or society.[71]

A Toxic Intellectual Legacy

Even among the supposed beneficiaries of the neoclassical worldview—corporations and shareholders—Friedman's model of neoliberalism has had a corrosive effect. By elevating the goal of maximizing shareholder value, this perspective inadvertently favors a specific kind of shareholder that can actually be detrimental to the long-term health of corporations. For example, the focus on maximizing shareholder value leads to a focus on only one type of shareholder that is, according to the legal scholar Lynn Stout, typically "shortsighted, opportunistic, willing to impose external costs, and indifferent to ethics and others' welfare."[72] While one may divide shareholders into three categories—dedicated, transient, and quasi-indexers—it is the transients that are the least desirable, trading more on technical factors like market momentum and not on company fundamentals.[73] And yet, it's this destructive shareholder type that shareholder primacy obsessively serves.

A second problem is that the focus on share price demanded by shareholder primacy has the unintended consequence of warping success metrics and incentivizing potentially harmful CEO behavior. This is starkly illustrated by the fact that stock performance constituted up to 85 percent of CEO compensation in 2020 as a means to align principal and agent interests.[74] But instead it created "an incentive to manipulate stock prices by using company money to buy back shares in order to drive prices higher"[75] and increase performance metrics like earnings per share. Indeed, between 2003 and 2013 companies in the S&P 500 index used more than half of their earnings to buy back shares to boost stock prices—purchases that turbocharged corporate CEOs' compensation but, in many cases, would have been better reinvested in the company to fund further research and development or operational improvements.

For example, Pfizer spent $139 billion on share buybacks. Apple—a company known for its R&D and innovation, and which never authorized share buybacks under its legendary CEO Steve Jobs—started buybacks in 2012 and spent $573 billion dollars on the practice between 2013 and 2023.[76] S&P 500 buybacks in 2022 set an annual record of $922.7 billion, up from 2021's $881.7 billion.[77] No surprise, then, that compensation packages for CEOs grew at a rate much faster than the stock market and the pay of typical workers, fueling harmful levels of inequality. This can have real and damaging effects on the fundamentals of a firm and its ability to perform well. For example, from 2014 to 2018, Boeing diverted 92 percent of its operating cash flow into dividends and share buybacks to benefit investors.[78] This reflected a shift in the culture of the company from one focused on quality, productivity, safety, and innovation to one focused on cost-cutting and shareholder value, with an obsession on share price. The result has been problems with the 787, the 747-8, and, most seriously, the 737 MAX, which have cost the company billions of dollars, cost airline customers their lives,[79] and tarnished decades of accumulated goodwill and brand loyalty for the company.[80] As an indictment against the trust placed in traditionally trained business managers and their obsession with share price, Tim Clark, president of Emirates Airlines, a major Boeing customer, argued that the only way to fix the company was to put engineers in charge.[81]

Last, shareholder primacy creates a focus on short-termism (aka, quarterly capitalism), which can lead to excessively short time horizons for investment planning and measures of success. One study found that 86 percent of executives believed that using a longer time horizon would positively affect performance, strengthening financial returns and increasing innovation.[82] But an equal percentage of corporate executives reported that the pressure to generate strong financial results over just two years was growing.[83] The focus on the short term has broader impacts, ultimately leading to a lagging response to long-term issues like climate change, inequality, and poverty.

Redefining the Purpose of the Firm

In his book *For Profit: A History of Corporations*, Texas A&M Law School professor William Magnuson writes,

> Corporations are public entities with a public purpose, given special rights and privileges precisely because governments believe they will contribute to the greatness of their nations. While they sometimes—perhaps even

often—stray from this purpose, their original and abiding justification has always been their ability to promote the good of all. . . . In the last century, we have lost sight of the true spirit of corporate enterprise. We have elevated profit seeking from a means to an end to an end in itself. . . . What happens in the next chapter of the global economy depends on whether we can return to the original intent of the corporation or we have sunk irrevocably into the swamp of profit maximization at all costs.[84]

There is still hope for realizing Magnuson's vision. Fueled by growing resentment from the general public, the purpose of the corporation has become the subject of considerable debate in recent years. The financial crisis, the housing bubble, staggering CEO pay, stagnating worker pay, and widening inequality with the super-affluent living conspicuously luxurious lives have all triggered a growing resentment towards corporations as they are currently managed, and the effects are obvious: a 2022 survey found that 71 percent of Americans believe that large corporations have a negative effect on the way things are going in the country.[85] Public support for shareholder primacy is eroding. A 2021 survey by Edelman found that most people rank employees and customers as the most important group for a company's long-term success (see Figure 7.1).[86] A 2022 follow-up survey by Edelman found that 73 percent of

FIGURE 7.1

Employees Now Most Important Stakeholder

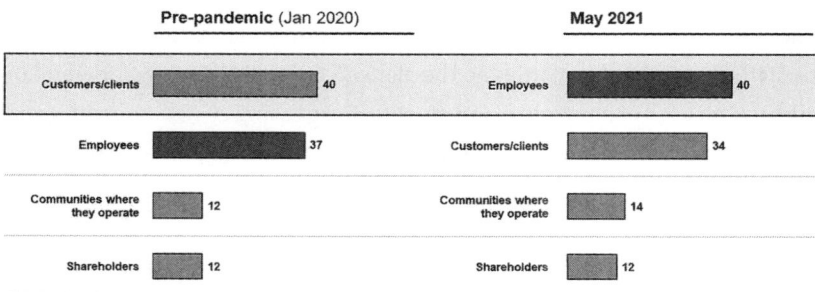

Note: Percent who ranked each group as most important to a company achieving long-term success.

Source: Edelman Trust Institute, *2021 Edelman Trust Barometer Spring Update: A World in Trauma,* 2021, https://www.edelman.com/trust/2021-trust-barometer/spring-update (accessed June 20, 2024). Courtesy of the Edelman Trust Institute—© 2024 Daniel J. Edelman, Inc.

people agree that the primary responsibility of a corporation is to benefit all its stakeholders to the fullest extent possible rather than focus on shareholders and owners; on average, 85 percent said that economic responsibilities, such as creating jobs and driving innovation, are the responsibilities of business. On average, 77 percent say that societal responsibilities, such as supporting local communities, are the responsibility of business.[87]

Many influential voices in the corporate and investment communities seem to be following suit and advocating for a more holistic approach to corporate purpose. In 2018, Larry Fink, the CEO of BlackRock, the world's largest asset manager, sent a letter to the CEOs of the companies in which it has a stake telling them that they have a responsibility not only to deliver profits but also to make "a positive contribution to society."[88] In 2019, two hundred chief executives from the Business Roundtable, including the leaders of Apple, American Airlines, Accenture, AT&T, Bank of America, Boeing, and BlackRock, issued a statement that redefined "the purpose of a corporation" beyond simply advancing the interests of shareholders to include investing in employees, delivering value to customers, and dealing fairly and ethically with suppliers.[89] In 2020, the World Economic Forum published the "Davos Manifesto" after its annual conference that redefined "the universal purpose of a company" as one that "serves society at large . . . supports communities . . . pays its fair share of taxes . . . acts as a steward of the environmental and material universe for future generations."[90]

Since those actions were taken, BlackRock has been attacked from both sides. One side says that the company is not doing enough, pointing out that BlackRock continues to invest in, and profit from, some of the most environmentally damaging companies on the planet.[91] On the other side, the company has been accused of practicing "woke politics" and using environmental, social, and governance (ESG) investment criteria as a Trojan Horse for promoting a liberal agenda. This has led some states (like Texas and Florida) to withdraw public pension and investment funds from the BlackRock portfolio and other asset managers who promote ESG investing. BlackRock has defended its policies, arguing that companies that take the broader view on ESG record higher performance and receive higher credit ratings because they have lower risk profiles, decreased market volatility, shallower drawdowns, and greater profitability.[92] In his 2022 letter to CEOs, Fink writes, "Stakeholder capitalism is not about politics. It is not a social or ideological agenda. It is not 'woke.' *It is capitalism*, driven by mutually beneficial relationships between you and the employees, customers, suppliers, and communities your company relies on to *prosper*. This is the power of capitalism."[93]

The Business Roundtable statement has also stirred some criticism. On the one side, the Council of Institutional Investors warned that action on broader social issues is not the role of corporations but that of the government, noting that "accountability to everyone means accountability to no one. It is government, not companies, that should shoulder the responsibility of defining and addressing societal objectives with limited or no connection to long-term shareholder value."[94] On the other side, some see the statement as more performative than substantive. A series of essays from the Harvard Law School Forum on Corporate Governance argue that the corporations that signed the statement did not seek approval from the board of directors,[95] and that the authors detected no major change in corporate governance guidelines, policies, or principles since the statement was drafted.[96]

Despite such criticism, it's clear that the conversation over corporate purpose has shifted. The challenge now lies in defining and implementing a more socially responsible and sustainable form of capitalism. Business schools and their graduates can be at the forefront of this change, researching and advocating for a better variant of capitalism to amend shareholder capitalism. What will that form be?

Stakeholder Capitalism

There is an increasing array of terms emerging to describe a new approach to capitalism and the purpose of the firm, such as conscious capitalism, positive capitalism, purpose-driven capitalism, and more. Michael Jensen, one of the foundational thinkers behind agency theory, has even softened his principal-agent model of shareholder primacy, arguing for "enlightened value maximization," in which corporations should still maximize total market value but also recognize that nonshareholder constituencies are essential to accomplishing this objective, such as satisfied customers, a motivated workforce, and trusting investors.[97] His thinking, as well as that embedded within these other terms and definitions, is circling around the idea of stakeholder capitalism, an idea first proposed by Darden Business School professor Ed Freeman in his 1984 book *Strategic Management: A Stakeholder Approach.*[98]

Stakeholder theory is a view of capitalism that stresses the interconnected relationships between a business and its customers, suppliers, employees, investors, communities, and others who have a stake in the organization. The theory argues that a firm should pursue multiple objectives, creating value for all stakeholders, not just shareholders. In serving these stakeholders, the idea of "corporate purpose" enters the corporate lexicon. Larry Fink at BlackRock seemingly endorsed this view in 2018: "Purpose is not a mere tagline or market campaign; it is a company's fundamental reason for being what it does every day to create value for its shareholders. Purpose is not the sole pursuit of profits but the animating force for achieving them."[99]

Two executives from the World Economic Forum, Klaus Schwab, founder and chair, and Peter Vanham, former deputy head of media, use their 2021 book *Stakeholder Capitalism: A Global Economy That Works for Progress, People and Planet* to articulate more of the Davos Manifesto and usher in more stakeholder thinking.[100] In it they contrast the two prevailing economic systems of shareholder and state capitalism, and compare them with stakeholder capitalism in which "the interests of all stakeholders in the economy and society are taken on board, companies optimize for more than just short-term profits, and governments are the guardians of equality of opportunity, a level playing field in competition, and a fair contribution of and distribution to all stakeholders with regards to the sustainability and inclusivity of the system" (see Figure 7.2).[101] Stakeholder capitalism employs a system of checks and balances "so that no one stakeholder can become or remain overly dominant. Both government and companies, the main players in any capitalist system, thus optimize for a broader objective than profits: the health and wealth of societies overall, as well as that of the planet and that of future generations."[102]

For corporations, stakeholder capitalism will require an important tactical and operational shift for both widening and lengthening their strategic view. A report from McKinsey & Company notes that stakeholder capitalism requires business leaders to define their mission as creating long-term value for customers, suppliers, employees, communities, and others, including shareholders. Profits and returns are still important, but stakeholder capitalism defines "value" in broader terms. For example, "creating a safe and healthy

FIGURE 7.2

Stakeholder Capitalism Versus Shareholder and State Capitalism

Types of Capitalism	State Capitalism	Shareholder Capitalism	Stakeholder Capitalism
Key Stakeholder	**Government**	**Company Shareholders**	**All stakeholders** matter equally
Key Characteristics	**Government** steers the economy, can intervene where necessary	The social responsibility of **business** is to increase its profits	**Society's** goal is increase the well-being of people and the planet
Implications for Companies	Business interests are **subsidiary** to state interests	**Short-term profit maximization** as highest good	Focus on **long-term value creation** and ESG measures
Advocated by		**Milton Friedman ('70)** "Shareholder Theory"	**Klaus Schwab ('71)** "Davos Manifesto" ('73)

Source: K. Schwab and P. Vanham, "What is the difference between stakeholder capitalism, shareholder capitalism and state capitalism?" *World Economic Forum,* June 21, 2021.

work environment above and beyond the minimum might save money in the form of reduced workers' compensation payments. But it may also create more subtle benefits, such as greater employee security, well-being, and loyalty."[103] The McKinsey Global Institute found that companies with a long-term view— something that is essential to stakeholder capitalism—outperformed the rest in earnings, revenue, investment, and job growth.[104]

This model fits the views of many in the general public. A 2022 report from Edelman titled *The Changing Role of the Corporation in Society* found that 71 percent of respondents globally believe that a company should take specific actions that both increase profits and improve conditions in communities where it operates.[105] And it fits even more tightly with the views of young people, who increasingly want companies to think about more than just profits. In increasing numbers, they are using their desire for social and environmental responsibility to choose an employer and are willing to quit if their expectations are not met. One survey found that 35 percent of a sample of office workers and 53 percent of Gen-Z employees in the United Kingdom said they were willing to quit their jobs if they perceived weak climate action from their employers.[106] Indeed, if a company chose to advertise that it only cares about profits (something many companies still communicate "privately" to shareholders), it would find it more difficult to recruit young talent. In one study, 64 percent of Millennials consider a company's social and environmental commitments when deciding where to work; 64 percent won't take a job if a company doesn't have strong corporate social responsibility values; and 83 percent would be more loyal to a company that helps them contribute to social and environmental issues.[107] This has caused a great number of companies to appeal to younger employees through sustainability plans and purpose-driven strategies; some are authentic, some are less so. But it's increasingly clear that talent is voting with its feet—choosing companies based in part on their commitment to more than just shareholder value creation.

The Tyranny of Shareholder Primacy

Today, many corporate executives and directors dislike a strong adherence to shareholder capitalism because it takes away their freedom and discretion to balance competing interests of the corporation's many stakeholders. As Steven Pearlstein puts it in his book *Can American Capitalism Survive?* they chafe at "being dictated to by number-crunching stock analysts and cocky hedge fund managers who understand little of what it takes to produce great products and services, manage a large organization and still feel good about what you do at the end of the day."[108]

For the business student of today and the business leader of tomorrow, the overriding imperative of shareholder primacy creates a tyranny in business management. It takes away their agency to set a vision, exercise their judgment and, importantly, live by a set of values that they hold dear. It shackles them to a notion that money is all that matters, and more specifically short-term money for selfish short-term shareholders who care about nothing other than money. The environment doesn't matter, nor does a company's employees, its community, the democracy, or even the world in which it operates. Just money. Should companies only take action if there is a profit incentive?

For example, women typically earn 82 cents for every dollar earned by men in the United States.[109] Should companies only fix this gender pay gap if they see an opportunity to make more money? And if they undertake an effort to equalize pay, should they end or reverse such efforts if they do not yield increased profits? Of course not. And yet, the overriding tyranny of shareholder primacy will limit a business school student's vocabulary for justifying what is the right thing to do and cripple their ability to do it.

On the one hand, the shackles of shareholder primacy may make one feel compelled to be narrow and selfish in one's thinking and one's actions—after all, at times it seems to be the only way to win a rigged game. It can demand behavior that business students and leaders may find abhorrent. On the other hand, it may give license to those who *wish* to be selfish. Unfortunately, as NYU professor Alison Taylor points out, there is often a business case for antisocial corporate behavior such as "tax avoidance, deregulation and even [activities that lead to] higher death rates."[110] But does that mean that business schools should create graduates who lack the moral compass to see beyond these obviously flawed "business cases"? When I hear a student precede a statement with the line "Speaking as a businessperson . . ." I stop and ask them to reflect on all that is excluded with that one simple statement, and the extent to which it grants license to narrow one's focus. Do you focus on the shareholder, or do you focus on your customers and providing the best value, or do you focus on your employees and providing a secure and enriching work environment? Ultimately, it is up to businesspeople and their best judgment on how to run an effective organization. As we have seen, this is both a legal and a moral truth. Lynn Stout captures it nicely: "Shareholder primacy is a managerial choice—not a legal requirement."[111] At the very least, business schools need to make sure they are graduating students who understand this simple truth.

Part III

THE CRUCIAL ROLE OF GOVERNMENT IN THE MARKETPLACE

Corporate Political Responsibility, Constructive Lobbying, and a New Role for Government

EIGHT

How Money Corrupts Healthy Government and Democracy

Why the Corporation Is Not a "Natural Person"

> "While American democracy is imperfect, few outside the majority of this Court would have thought its flaws included a dearth of corporate money in politics."
>
> —JOHN PAUL STEVENS, SUPREME COURT JUSTICE, DISSENTING OPINION ON THE CITIZENS UNITED CASE

Citizens United. The mere mention of this 2010 Supreme Court decision tends to get my students, and indeed many people, agitated. Numerous surveys conducted two,[1] six,[2] eight,[3] and ten[4] years after the decision find that the majority of both Republicans and Democrats oppose it, leading a *Bloomberg* writer to note that "Americans may be sharply divided on other issues, but they are united in their view of the 2010 Supreme Court ruling that unleashed a torrent of political spending: They hate it."[5] Where Karl Polanyi, the twentieth-century economic historian we met in Chapter 5, described capitalism as being embedded within democracy and given shape by law and governments,[6] democracy in the wake of *Citizens United* seems to be embedded within capitalism. Where Polanyi saw the market economy as a means to more fundamental ends, it is now becoming an end unto itself.[7]

This section of the book explores the proper relationship between business and government, taking the topic in two parts. First, it examines the proper role of business in policymaking, and second, it looks at the proper role of government in the market. But before we tackle either topic, we start with the topic of the personhood of the corporation. This topic, and the Supreme Court decision that thrust it into the democratic process and therefore into the national debate, is too important to leave as a side note in business education. Students of business must be taught how capitalism has been altered and shaped by the *Citizens United* ruling, not just through a surface understanding of the contemporary politics that influenced the decision but with a deeper understanding of the history and basis for the court's ruling. It did not emerge out of thin air. It was the product of over a century of US court decisions and precedent related to the constitutional rights of corporations. Forming an opinion on *Citizens United* requires an understanding of the notion of corporate "personhood," the idea that for-profit corporations possess a legal identity of their own—separate and distinct from their executives and shareholders—which grants them certain legal rights enjoyed by "natural persons" (legalese for real humans).

Numerous court cases since the late nineteenth century have recognized that corporations are entitled to some of the same legal protections enjoyed by natural persons. Importantly, such status also means that individual shareholders as well as individual employees are not legally liable for the corporation's actions. For example, in the 1809 case *The Bank of the United States v. Deveaux et al.*, the court ruled that businesses have the right to sue.[8] Later, in the 1819 case *Trustees of Dartmouth College v. Woodward*, the Supreme Court formally recognized corporations as having the right to enter and enforce contracts.[9] Despite the oddness of equating a company with a person, these seem like reasonable rights to be granted to corporations.

However, given that as a starting point, how far should the rights of corporate personhood go? Should corporations be entitled to the legal protections of equal protection under the Fourteenth Amendment and safeguards against unreasonable searches, seizures, and the expropriation of property without due process, as stipulated by the Fourth Amendment? Should corporations have protection against self-incrimination (Fifth Amendment)? Are they guaranteed the right to free speech (First Amendment)? Are they entitled to the right to freedom of religion (First Amendment)? All of these rights have been debated and decided by courts for more than a hundred years, with the

First and Fourteenth Amendments gaining the most attention. And this has brought us to the notion of corporate personhood that we have today. How did we get here? And what are the implications? What would the founders of the country think if they saw what we have become?

A Brief History of Corporate Personhood

The first mention of the fundamental constitutional rights of corporations in a court decision came in the 1886 Supreme Court case *Santa Clara County v. Southern Pacific Railroad Co.*. The state of California taxed fences owned by the Southern Pacific Railroad, but Southern Pacific asserted that the state constitution allowed only taxes on specific assets, namely the franchise, roadway roadbed, rails, and rolling stock. The court never specifically took up the question of the rights of the corporation. Instead, Supreme Court Chief Justice Morrison Waite asserted those rights as given, instructing the attorneys that "[t]he court does not wish to hear argument on the question whether the provision in the 14th Amendment to the Constitution, which forbids a State to deny to any person within its jurisdiction the equal protection of the laws, applies to these corporations. We are all of the opinion that it does."[10] In the final judgment, the court ruled that the state tax board had no right to levy a tax that included the value of the fences. No decision was debated or decided regarding constitutional rights. Nevertheless, the court reporter, Bancroft Davis, added a sentence in the headnote that the equal protection clause of the Fourteenth Amendment applied to corporations.

Headnotes do not form a part of the judgment and are not binding precedents. But this instance was the first time that the Supreme Court reportedly granted constitutional protections to corporations in a way similar as to natural persons. Some suspect an ulterior motive in the headnote.[11] The question of corporate personhood under the constitution had been litigated unsuccessfully for twenty years prior to this decision, and some have suggested that the court reporter—himself a former president of the Newburgh and New York Railway company—inserted the headnote to, as Northern Arizona State University professor Richard Behan writes, "achieve by deceit what corporations had so far failed to achieve in litigation."[12]

Two years later, in the 1888 *Pembina Consolidated Silver Min. & Milling*

Co. v. Commonwealth of Pennsylvania case, the court was clearer in its affirmation and supporting argument: "Under the designation of 'person' there is no doubt that a private corporation is included [in the Fourteenth Amendment]. Such corporations are merely associations of individuals united for a special purpose and permitted to do business under a particular name and have a succession of members without dissolution."[13] In 1890, Title 1, section 1 of the US Code known as the "Dictionary Act" stated that "the word 'person', or 'persons', wherever used in sections 1 to 7 of this title shall be deemed to include corporations and associations existing under or authorized by the laws of either the United States, the laws of any of the Territories, the laws of any State, or the laws of any foreign country."[14]

In its continuing quest to clarify corporate rights, courts later added some additions and limitations to its constitutional interpretation. In the 1906 case *Hale v. Henkel*, the court determined that corporations are afforded certain protections under the Fourth Amendment against unreasonable searches and seizures and are entitled to equal protection under the law. However, it clarified that a corporation does not qualify as a "person" in terms of the Fifth Amendment's safeguard against self-incrimination.[15]

This was by no means the end of the debate, with the First Amendment rights to free speech for corporations being contested in the area of political influence. For example, after it was revealed that major corporations had made donations to the Republican presidential campaigns of 1896, 1900, and 1904, the Tillman Act of 1907 was passed as the first campaign finance law in the United States. Though it was fairly weak on enforcement, it prohibited monetary contributions to federal candidates by corporations and nationally chartered banks. In 1947, the Taft-Hartley Act extended the prohibitions on monetary donations to federal political campaigns by labor unions. For a large portion of the twentieth century, it was against the law for corporations, banks, and unions to donate money to political campaigns. But the rules were still vague, and enforcement was lax.

In the wake of the Watergate scandals in 1971, the Federal Election Campaign Act (FECA) was amended in 1974 to clarify the matter, limiting the amount of political donations to candidates for federal office and requiring disclosure of contributions. More important, it created the Federal Election Commission (FEC) to enforce the law. This law became the touchstone that opened an extended series of court cases regarding the First Amendment rights of corporations to free speech and the question of whether political spending was a rightful exercise of that free speech.

In the 1976 *Buckley v. Valeo* case, some provisions of the FECA were upheld, but the Supreme Court invalidated restrictions on candidate and associated committee expenditures, constraints on independent spending by individuals separate from campaign contributions, and caps on the funds that candidates could contribute to their own campaign. The ruling differentiated between "electioneering" and "issue advocacy," stipulating that public statements are exempt from campaign finance regulations as long as they avoided using the "eight magic words" or any similar expressions that explicitly urge voters to support or oppose a specific candidate. Those words were "vote for," "elect," "support," "cast your ballot for," "____ for Congress," "vote against," "defeat," "reject," or any variations thereof. The majority opinion wrote that "expenditure limitations operate in an area of the most fundamental First Amendment activities. Discussion of public issues and debate on the qualifications of candidates are integral to the operation of the system of government established by our Constitution. The First Amendment affords the broadest protection to such political expression in order 'to assure (the) unfettered interchange of ideas for the bringing about of political and social changes desired by the people.'"[16]

In the 1978 *First National Bank v. Bellotti* case, the court struck down a Massachusetts law that prohibited corporate donations in ballot initiatives when the corporation's interests were not directly involved. The court decided that corporations had a First Amendment right to make contributions to any ballot initiative campaign they desired, arguing that "the inherent worth of the speech in terms of its capacity for informing the public does not depend upon the identity of its source, whether corporation, association, union, or individual."[17] In the 5 to 4 ruling, the dissenting opinion wrote that, "although the Court has never explicitly recognized a corporation's right of commercial speech, such a right might be considered necessarily incidental to the business of a commercial corporation. It cannot be so readily concluded that the right of political expression is equally necessary to carry out the functions of a corporation organized for commercial purposes."[18]

In a setback for advocates of corporate personhood, the court held in the 1990 *Austin v. Michigan Chamber of Commerce* case that the Michigan Campaign Finance Act, which prohibited corporations from using treasury money to make independent expenditures to support or oppose candidates in elections, did not violate the First and Fourteenth Amendments. In the 6 to 3 decision, the majority opinion decided that, while the First Amendment protected corporate expression, restrictions on independent expenditure were justified on the compelling grounds of eliminating corruption and, importantly, the appearance of corruption in political campaigns. The majority opinion warned that its goal was to combat a "different type of corruption in the political arena," the corrosive and distorting effects of immense aggregations of corporate wealth that can unfairly influence elections.[19] The dissenting opinion argued that, just because corporations are sometimes given "special advantages" by state laws and can have large treasuries, they should not be required "to forfeit their First Amendment rights" and that the statute constituted a "censorship of speech" and "discriminates on the basis of the speaker's identity."[20]

This all led up to the 2002 Bipartisan Campaign Reform Act, also known as the McCain-Feingold Act, which marked another setback for corporate First Amendment rights and set the foundation for the Citizens United case. This act banned "electioneering communications" within thirty days of a primary election and sixty days of a general election. It also prohibited the use of "soft money" in federal elections, which refers to funds raised beyond the constraints of federal campaign finance laws, intended for parties and committees rather than candidates. Further, it restricted corporations and labor unions from financing issue advertisements. This decision was reinforced by the 2003 *McConnell v. FEC* case, which upheld the two major provisions of the McCain-Feingold Act and struck down elements of the *First National Bank v. Bellotti* decision by allowing restrictions on corporate donations. These decisions set in motion the landmark *Citizens United* decision on campaign finance laws and the First Amendment rights of corporations to free speech.

The *Citizens United* Decision

In 2008, the nonprofit organization Citizens United wanted to show a film that was critical of Democratic presidential candidate Hillary Clinton—*Hillary: The Movie*—during television broadcasts within thirty days of the 2008 Democratic primaries, but the Bipartisan Campaign Reform Act (the McCain-Feingold Act) prohibited such "electioneering communications." The group sued, arguing that its right to free speech was being restricted. In the 2010 *Citizens United v. the Federal Election Committee* case, the Supreme Court ruled in favor of expanded corporate rights to free speech. It reversed the *Austin v. Michigan Chamber of Commerce* decision and parts of the *McConnell v. FEC* decision, striking down limits on corporate and union spending, limits on financing electioneering communications, and limits on soft money contributions, all on the grounds that these activities constitute a form of free speech protected by the First Amendment. In the 5 to 4 ruling, the majority opinion argued that "if the First Amendment has any force, it prohibits Congress from fining or jailing citizens, or associations of citizens, for simply engaging in political speech."[21]

President Barack Obama condemned the decision during his 2010 State of the Union Address, arguing, "Last week, the Supreme Court reversed a century of law to open the floodgates for special interests—including foreign corporations—to spend without limit in our elections. Well, I don't think American elections should be bankrolled by America's most powerful interests, or worse, by foreign entities." On television, the camera shifted to the Supreme Court judges in the front row and showed Justice Samuel Alito frowning, shaking his head, and breaking from the tradition of not reacting to State of the Union addresses to avoid appearing political as he mouthed the words, "Not true."[22]

Following the *Citizens United* decision, subsequent cases have expanded upon its precedent. In 2010, SpeechNow, an organization that aggregates funds from individual donors for collective independent expenditures, contested the constitutionality of several aspects of the FECA. These included the limits on contributions, the necessity for political committee registration, and the disclosure mandates for independent expenditures. In the 2010 *SpeechNow.org v. FEC* decision, the United States Court of Appeals for the District of Columbia Circuit ruled that FECA's limits on what individuals could contribute to SpeechNow, and what SpeechNow could accept, violated the First Amendment.[23] The unanimous nine-judge decision opened the door for the growth of SuperPACs, independent political action committees that raise unlimited sums of money from corporations, unions, and individuals with the proviso that they are not permitted to contribute to or coordinate directly with parties or candidates. In the 2014 *McCutcheon v. FEC* case, the Supreme Court ruled by a 5 to 4 vote that FECA's limit on contributions an individual can make over a two-year period to national party and federal candidate committees was unconstitutional. The majority opinion stated that "[a] contribution serves as a general expression of support for the candidate and his views but does not communicate the underlying basis for the support" since "this Court has never required a speaker to explain the reasons for his position in order to obtain full First Amendment protection."[24]

The Basis for *Citizens United*

The logic for the granting of constitutional rights to corporations is that corporations are associations of individuals, and these people should not be deprived of their constitutional rights when they act collectively. It would be an act of discrimination to restrict the free discussion of politics depending, the argument goes, "upon the identity of its source, whether corporation, association, union, or individual."[25] In addition, the courts decided that the only legitimate concern identified with money in politics is actual corruption, not the appearance of corruption. Last, the courts have ruled that spending money constitutes an act of free speech, determining that "commercial speech" and "political speech" are equivalent and protected by the First Amendment and that a corporation may participate in political speech unrelated to its commercial interests. But do these considerations reflect a fair description of the corporation, its role in political debate, and what it may mean for the integrity of elections?

To begin, is the corporation merely an association of individuals? The dissenting opinion in the 1978 *First National Bank v. Bellotti* case actually turned this logic on its head, asserting that corporate political activity was a violation of the First Amendment right to free speech, not for the corporation but for the corporation's investors. The opinion argued that "the state had a First Amendment interest in 'assuring that shareholders are not compelled to support and financially further beliefs with which they disagree.' The only purpose uniting all shareholders is to make a profit. Any issue not related to business interests could diverge from the interests of individual shareholders."[26] The dissenting opinion in the 2010 *Citizens United v. Federal Election Committee* case argued similarly that the decision ignored the rights of employees as well as shareholders who could be compelled to support political speech.[27] In the end, shareholders and employees are not often consulted about corporate political donations, and it is therefore debatable that they represent part of the collective that is making them.

Going further, how should we consider the corrupting influence of money in politics? The majority opinion in *Citizens United* argued that "independent expenditures, including those made by corporations, do not give rise to corruption or the appearance of corruption." It further stated, "The absence of prearrangement and coordination of an expenditure with the candidate or his agent not only undermines the value of the expenditure to the candidate, but also alleviates the danger that expenditures will be given as a quid pro quo for improper commitments from the candidate. . . . The fact that a corporation, or any other speaker, is willing to spend money to try to persuade voters presupposes that the people have the ultimate influence over elected officials." This position was reinforced later in the majority opinion in the 2014 *McCutcheon v. FEC* case, which stated, "Ingratiation and access . . . are not corruption. . . . [W]hile preventing corruption or its appearance is a legitimate objective, Congress may target only a specific type of corruption—'quid pro quo' corruption," which it defined as a "direct exchange of an official act for money."

But the dissenting opinion in the 1976 *Buckley v. Valeo* decision warned that "the act of giving money to political candidates . . . may have illegal or other undesirable consequences: it may be used to secure the express or tacit understanding that the giver will enjoy political favor if the candidate is elected. Both Congress and this Court's cases have recognized this as a mortal danger against which effective preventive and curative steps must be taken."[28] The dissent in *Citizens United* went further in articulating that the state's interest in limiting independent expenditures should be aimed at eradicating not just actual corruption but also its appearance in political campaigns.

Writing for the minority, Supreme Court Justice John Paul Stevens expressed concern that if the public perceives corporations as controlling elections, this could lead voters to withdraw from participation in elections.

This brings us to the question of whether the act of making a political donation is the equivalent of exercising free speech? Is this true for a corporation as much as it is for an individual? Public opinion on these questions is mixed. A survey immediately after *Citizens United* by Gallup found that 57 percent of Americans consider campaign donations to be a protected form of free speech, and 55 percent say corporate and union donations should be treated the same way under the law as donations from individuals. But at the same time, a majority think it is more important to limit campaign donations than to protect this free speech right.[29]

To that end, Justice Stevens also warned in his *Citizens United* dissent that the unique qualities of corporations made them dangerous to democratic elections. "One fundamental concern of the First Amendment is to protect the individual's interest in self-expression," Justice Stevens wrote. But corporations are, in fact, different from people in that they have the ability to amass large sums of money and when they use that money in political campaigns, it is the "furthest from the core of political expression" protected by the Constitution as it is "more transactional than ideological," designed for no purpose other than profit-making.[30] In sum, he wrote,

> The court's opinion is a rejection of the common sense of the American people, who have recognized a need to prevent corporations from undermining self-government since the founding, and who have fought against the distinctive corrupting potential of corporate electioneering since the days of Theodore Roosevelt. It is a strange time to repudiate that common sense. While American democracy is imperfect, few outside the majority of this Court would have thought its flaws included a dearth of corporate money in politics.

Arguing that the majority did not place enough emphasis on the need to prevent the "appearance of corruption" in elections, Justice Stevens warned that "the Court's ruling threatens to undermine the integrity of elected institutions across the Nation. The path it has taken to reach its outcome will, I fear, do damage to this institution. . . . A democracy cannot function effectively when its constituent members believe laws are being bought and sold.[31]

The Effects of *Citizens United*

The effects of the Supreme Court's ruling in *Citizens United* (as well as in *SpeechNow* and *McCutcheon*) have been the source of a great deal of debate over the level of influence of corporations and money in the political process, and the basis for that influence, the personhood of the corporation.

Some political experts have lauded the *Citizens United* decision for introducing what they argue to be more democratic sources of funding and breaking away from traditional politics, noting an increase in small-money donations since the ruling and that election outcomes since the decision have not always aligned with the preferences of large-money donors. For example, Capital University of Law professor Bradley Smith writes, "Far from handing power to the 1 percent, Citizens United unleashed rapid political diversification. . . . Small-dollar donors are more coveted than ever. Donald Trump raised more money from donors who gave less than $200 than any candidate in history. . . . Since Citizens United, party outsiders such as Mr. Trump and Bernie Sanders have risen to national prominence. And money hasn't been able to buy elections as predicted. . . . Citizens United deserves a share of credit for all these trends. The decision made it easier to promote (or criticize) a candidate without help from party leaders or media elites."[32] Scott Blackburn, research director at the Institute for Free Speech, argues that *Citizens United* "has allowed new, often very important, voices to be heard. The decision not only protects the right to speak, but it protects the right of Americans to hear those voices. Citizens, rather than the government, decide what arguments are worthwhile. Citizens United is one of the most important decisions of the century for protecting, fostering, and benefiting American democracy."[33]

But other legal commentators have condemned the decision, arguing that it opened opportunities for more concentrated and often hidden sources of money to influence elections though SuperPACs and "dark money" groups. OpenSecrets, a nonprofit organization based in Washington, DC, that tracks and publishes data on campaign finance and lobbying, argues that "[i]n the election cycles following Citizens United, the balance of power has shifted more and more towards outside spending groups such as SuperPACs and 'dark money' political nonprofits, unleashing unprecedented amounts of money towards political advertisements meant to influence voters."[34] Daniel Weiner, director of the elections and government program at the Brennan Center for

Justice, writes that "thanks to the Supreme Court's jurisprudence, a tiny sliver of Americans now wield more power than at any time since Watergate, while many of the rest seem to be disengaging from politics. This is perhaps the most troubling result of *Citizens United*: in a time of historic wealth inequality, the decision has helped reinforce the growing sense that our democracy primarily serves the interests of the wealthy few, and that democratic participation for the vast majority of citizens is of relatively little value."[35]

A report from the Niskanen Center, a Washington, DC–based think tank, argued that "[b]ig money groups and donors have long played a role in our elections, but court decisions have opened the floodgates to more unlimited and anonymous contributions through new funding vehicles. How much is that changing our politics? . . . Networks of dark money groups like those funded by the Koch brothers are helping move our political parties to the extremes in primary elections."[36] Furthermore, Norman Ornstein, senior emeritus fellow at the center-right think tank American Enterprise Institute, writes, "Much of the money for these entities is coming from corporations, unleashed because of the *Citizens United v. Federal Election Commission* case. In some instances, the corporations are shells designed, when their contributions are ultimately disclosed, to hide the identities of the real donors."[37]

Following the *Citizens United* (and *SpeechNow*) decisions, the landscape of political financing experienced a dramatic transformation. In the first presidential election after the *Citizens United* decision, outside group spending was more than three times greater than in the previous presidential cycle ($1 billion in 2012 versus $340 million in 2008).[38] In the first congressional elections after the *Citizens United* decision, spending by outside groups was more than four times greater than in the previous congressional cycle ($310 million in 2010 versus $70 million in 2008).

While the 2000 presidential race incurred expenses of $1.4 billion, the cost of the 2020 race escalated to $6.3 billion. This surge in spending was supported by a significant rise in outside money from groups or individuals operating independently of candidates' committees.[39] In the decade following the *Citizens United* decision, election-related expenditures by these entities soared to $4.5 billion, a stark contrast to the $750 million spent in the two decades before the ruling.[40] All outside groups, including SuperPACs, 501(c)(4) "dark money" groups, labor unions, trade associations, corporations, and others, spent a combined \$5.6 billion in federal elections between 2010 and 2018. That's just over 21 percent of all spending in federal elections over the same period.[41]

Some of the biggest political players were a small number of wealthy individual donors. Twenty-five ultra-wealthy donors made up 47 percent of all individual contributions to SuperPACs since 2010, giving \$1.4 billion of a total of \$3 billion in individual SuperPAC contributions.[42] This small group of major donors accounted for 7 percent of total election-related giving in 2018, up from less than 1 percent a decade prior.[43] Casino magnate Sheldon Adelson gave over \$100 million to political candidates in 2018, and California businessman Tom Steyer gave \$8 million to elect Terry McAuliffe governor of Virginia in 2015, funding TV spots, online ads, and door-to-door canvassing.[44]

The number of SuperPACs soared from eighty-three in the 2010 election cycle, with a collective expenditure of \$63 million, to over twenty-three hundred in the 2016 campaign, when they spent a staggering \$1.1 billion (see Table 8.1). This amounted to nearly 17 percent of the amount spent by all parties involved in the 2016 election cycle at all levels. Most of that money came from just a hundred donors. As a share of all outside money, SuperPACs spent 47 percent of outside money in 2012, increasing to 64 percent in 2016.[45]

This does not mean that individual corporate giving was not significant. According to Alex He, editor for *The Northwestern Business Review*, the money given to outside groups is "a combination of donations from corporate

TABLE 8.1

SuperPAC Spending, 2010–2018

Year	Races	PAC Spending
2010	Congressional	\$63 Million
2012	Presidential and Congressional	\$610 Million
2014	Congressional	\$345 Million
2016	Presidential and Congressional	\$1.1 Billion
2018	Congressional	\$822 Million
Total		**\$2.9 Billion**

Source: Table created by author using data from D. Dwyer, "10 years after landmark Citizens United Supreme Court decision, record cash flooding US elections," ABC News, January 20, 2020.

PACs, which are directly connected to their namesake company and can give up to $5,000 to candidates, and affiliates of companies within those interest groups, usually CEO's and upper-management types, who can give directly up to $2,700 to candidates or spend millions of dollars indirectly supporting candidates through the use of SuperPACs, which have no limitation on how much money they can take or spend on elections."[46] The top twenty corporate donors accounted for $118 million of the corporate donations to SuperPACs that were reported to the Federal Election Commission, and almost entirely backed Republicans. Only four of these twenty corporate donors were publicly traded: three were energy corporations—Chevron, NextEra Energy, and Pinnacle West Capital—and the fourth was a subsidiary of British American Tobacco. The US Chamber of Commerce was the largest corporate trade group, spending $143 million—nearly two-thirds of the total election-related spending by corporate trade associations.[47] The finance, insurance, and real estate industry gave a combined $970 million in the 2018 election cycle.[48] That sector's giving rose to $2 billion in the 2020 presidential cycle, with 52 percent of that total going directly to parties and candidates, and 48 percent going indirectly to outside groups.[49]

It would be hard to argue that this money does not have an impact on political outcomes. Mark Hanna, a Republican financier, once said, "There are two things that are important in politics. The first is money and I can't remember what the second one is."[50] Former politics writer for *The Atlantic* Philip Bump points out that "[m]ore money means more television ads or mailings, which likely means more support on Election Day. But there are a ton of variables at play, so it can be hard to differentiate between the role of money (did more TV ads spur more votes) and the communications themselves (were some ads better than others)? There are turnout issues, questions of candidate viability, scandals. So many things go into campaigns, but few are as trackable as contributions."[51]

Another important point regarding any distortions this money creates is that donations from corporations and corporate executives are not in balance with the demographics of the country. In February 2024, 42 percent of the public identified as independent, 30 percent Democrat, and 28 percent Republican according to Gallup.[52] Yet a study by Public Citizen found that between 2010 and 2020, corporations gave $282 million to Republican candidates, versus $38 million to Democratic candidates.[53] A study in the National Bureau of Economic Research found that nearly 60 percent of CEOs donated to Republican congressional and presidential candidates between 2000 and 2017.[54]

An even more alarming development is the surge in "dark money" groups. Contributions from 501(c)(4) social welfare organizations, which maintain donor anonymity, exceeded $963 million in political spending in the decade following 2010, a significant increase from the $129 million spent in the decade prior.[55] According to OpenSecrets, "Dark money groups have reported nearly $1 billion in direct spending on US elections to the FEC since Citizens United with just 10 groups bankrolled by secret donors spending more than $610 million of that. For every dollar in grey or dark money spending by groups that do not fully disclose their donors reported to the FEC during the decade before Citizens United, at least $10 were spent in the decade after."[56]

Though the *Citizens United* and *SpeechNow* rulings did not reverse the ban on foreign money in elections, they did provide opportunities for foreign actors to quietly funnel money to elections through dark money groups, nonprofits, and shell companies.[57] In the 2012 election, the Malaysian financier Jho Low was accused of giving over $1 million via an American LLC to a SuperPAC that supported Barack Obama's candidacy. During the 2016 election, a California corporation wholly owned by Chinese citizens reportedly gave $1.3 million to a SuperPAC supporting Jeb Bush's presidential candidacy. And in 2018, an Illinois corporation largely controlled by a Canadian billionaire reportedly gave $1.75 million to a SuperPAC that supported Donald Trump's campaign.[58]

Money affects not just candidate elections; even public referendums have been flooded with money, resulting in battles of large and competing pocketbooks rather than battles of ideas and public interest. In 2018, more than $1.1 billion was spent in support of and opposition to statewide ballot measures across the United States.[59] That year, California's Proposition 8— which would limit dialysis clinic profits to 15 percent above service costs—set a record for campaign spending, with opponents (mostly dialysis centers and their trade associations) putting $111.4 million into the fight while proponents could muster only $18 million. The proposition failed, as would be expected by simply looking at the size of the competing expenditures.[60]

Where does this leave us? The costs of campaigns keep rising and politicians become stuck in a "perpetual campaign" to raise money. In 2020, the US presidential and congressional races broke records with total political spending reaching $14.4 billion, more than double the total cost of the record-breaking 2016 election cycle.[61] It's estimated that the 2024 cycle will cost as much as 30 percent more.[62] While many issues divide people along political lines, concern over money in politics unites them. A 2015 survey found that an equal percentage of Democrats and Republicans (76 percent) think that money has a greater influence on politics today than before, and 68 percent of Democrats and 62 percent of Republicans think that the high cost of presidential campaigns discourages good candidates.[63] "With near unanimity," reports the *New York Times*, "the public thinks the country's campaign finance system needs significant changes." Americans are roughly split between whether the system needs "fundamental change" (39 percent) or should be "completely rebuil[t]" (46 percent), and only a negligible number believes no changes are needed.[64] Among liberals and conservatives, large majorities favor limits on campaign spending,[65] with one 2018 survey finding that 75 percent of the public supports a constitutional amendment to overturn *Citizens United.*[66] Twenty-two states and more than eight hundred cities and towns have passed resolutions or ballot initiatives calling for a constitutional amendment to overturn the decision.[67] Campaign financing seems to be diminishing public trust in the fragile democratic process, and corporations have found themselves in the center of this problem.

Our Founders' Fear: Artificial Legal Entities with Perpetual Life

In 2014, the Supreme Court offered a decision that added one more provocative dimension to the personhood of the corporation. In the *Burwell v. Hobby Lobby Stores, Inc.* case, the court found that a requirement embedded in the 2010 Patient Protection and Affordable Care Act that companies provide coverage for certain kinds of contraception was unconstitutional as it violated companies' right to religious freedom under the First Amendment. The majority opinion wrote that "[b]ecause the contraception requirement forces religious corporations to fund what they consider abortion, which goes against their stated religious principles . . . the government had not met its burden to show that there was a meaningful difference between non-profit religious institutions and for-profit religious corporations under the RFRA."[68] For many critics of the ruling, it seemed to defy logic that a retail corporation could be construed as a "for-profit religious organization," having religious beliefs beyond those of its owner or senior executives.

Reflecting on the increased power this gives to corporations, it's worth considering how the views of the United States's founding fathers, particularly Thomas Jefferson and James Madison, might align with such contemporary legal interpretations of corporate rights. Their documented concerns about the influence of "moneyed corporations" and their potential interference in public affairs suggest that they might be aghast at the extent to which corporations have been granted rights under the Constitution. Indeed, the Bill of Rights these two men drafted contains the first ten Constitutional Amendments that survive, and two more that did not: one was to control corporate expansion and dominance.[69] Author Thomas Hartmann writes that because of recent court rulings such as *Citizens United*, "America has lost the legal structures that allowed for people to control corporate behavior."[70]

Today, there have been several calls for a Constitutional amendment to abolish corporate personhood. But the core of the issue is not so absolute. To be sure, some corporate rights are essential to the proper functioning of the market. Corporations must have the right to sue, to enter and enforce contracts, and to make decisions that do not hold their employees, executives, and shareholders at legal risk. It could also be reasonably argued that corporations should be guaranteed equal protection under the law, protected from unreasonable searches and seizures or from having property taken without due process. These are all necessary rights for the effective functioning of the corporate form.

However, a critical point of contention arises regarding the distinction between the rights of individuals and those applicable to corporations, given their inherent differences. Companies are collectives of individuals (employees, investors, managers, and so on) with senior leaders who represent them for the objective of serving a customer. Their common interest in association does not necessarily include politics, nor are all members of that association consulted on the political positions of that association. But beyond these legalistic arguments, there is a commonsense one that sees individuals and corporations as inherently different. In the words of essayist Wendell Berry, "Unlike a person, a corporation does not age. It does not arrive, as most persons finally do, at a realization of the shortness and smallness of human lives; it does not come to see the future as the lifetime of the children and grandchildren of anybody in particular. It can experience no personal hope or remorse, no change of heart. It cannot humble itself. It goes about its business as if it were immortal, with the single purpose of becoming a bigger pile of money."[71] And yet, corporations are increasingly seen as "natural persons" and as a result are having an increasingly profound influence on our political institutions and therefore our social institutions.

Ironically, this outcome is at variance with the purpose of the firm as discussed in Chapter 7. It is inconsistent to argue that a firm has rights like a "natural person" while simultaneously claiming that it is merely a nexus of contracts, which is the foundation of our present conception of corporate purpose. In that foundation, Milton Friedman, Michael Jensen, and William Meckling argue that "a corporation is an artificial person"[72] and "not an individual."[73] But if that is true, one would fairly ask how can it have rights under the US Constitution? In a form of jujitsu, the proposed Accountable Capitalism Act was meant to co-opt the rationale behind *Citizens United* and apply it to alternative ends. The act argued that companies that "claim the legal rights of personhood should be legally required to accept the moral obligations of personhood,"[74] and if corporations are really just associations of individuals, it would prohibit companies from making any political expenditures without the approval of those individuals, requiring the consent of 75 percent of its directors and shareholders.[75]

In the end, the idea that political spending is an act of free speech ignores the point that corporations possess large sums of money that, if equated with speech, allow them far more influence than the individual voter who has only one vote and one voice with which to articulate political ideas. Since the nation's founding, there have been persistent fears that these "artificial entities" with "perpetual life" called corporations might grow in power and threaten democracy, leading us to question whether we have a "government of the people or a government of the corporations, by the corporations and for the corporations."[76] In the pursuit of a truly representative democracy, it is imperative that the chorus of diverse human voices is not drowned out by the resounding echo of corporate entities.

NINE

The Necessary and Constructive Role of Business in Policymaking

. . . and the Need for Guardrails

"If companies are serious about acting more responsibly, then they need to reexamine their relationship to government as well as improve their own practices. And those who want corporations to be more virtuous should expect firms to act more responsibly on both dimensions."

—DAVID VOGEL, HAAS SCHOOL OF BUSINESS

In 2020, I offered a new course at the University of Michigan called "Business in Democracy: Advocacy, Lobbying and the Public Interest," which drew students from both the schools of business and public policy into an examination of lobbying, its proper role in policymaking, and ways in which it can be done responsibly. Halfway through the semester, I asked the students what their classmates thought of them taking this course. Their answers surprised me. The business students reported that some peers asked why they would take a course on government. "What does this have to do with business?" The public policy students said that some of their peers were aghast. "You actually went into the business school? You actually took a course there? Business is the enemy!" Both groups of students expressed a viewpoint that was not only naïve, but also problematic for considering the proper balance between business and government in creating a functioning market. Far too many business students believe that government regulation is an unwarranted intrusion into the market. Far too few policy students appreciate how markets, when operating within a framework of ethical and legal parameters, are essential for achieving a society in which everyone has the opportunity to flourish.

Correcting these misperceptions is challenging; Americans' views on both government and the corporate sector are full of contradictions and entrenched partisan views, making productive debate difficult. For example, surveys show that the public both sees tremendous value in the corporate sector and is distrustful that companies will act in the public interest. That same public sees government as ineffective but wants it to protect society against corporate excess. And nearly half of Americans have hardly any confidence in either the government *or* the corporate sector.[1]

On the one side, a large majority (77 percent) of Americans believe that bankers would harm consumers if they thought they could get away with it, and 49 percent think that corruption in the industry is "widespread." At the same time, the same survey found that 64 percent believe that finance is "essential" because it provides the money businesses need to create jobs and develop new products. On the other side, 80 percent think regulators allow political biases to have an impact on their judgment, and 74 percent of Americans believe regulations often fail to have their intended effect. But at the same time, 59 percent believe regulations, at least in the past, have produced positive benefits, and 56 percent say regulations can help make businesses more responsive to people's needs.[2]

In the United States, there is a thirteen-point gap between trust in business (55 percent) and trust in government (42 percent),[3] reflecting a common lean around the world (see Figure 9.1). But many also feel that the lines between the two are becoming increasingly blurred, leading to an erosion of their faith in both democracy and capitalism. The University of Cambridge's Centre for the Future of Democracy reports that dissatisfaction with democracy has risen to an all-time global high, driven by recent events like the start of the refugee crisis in Europe, Brexit, and the elections of Donald Trump in the United States and Jair Bolsonaro in Brazil.[4] At the same time, surveys by Edelman report that "a majority of people around the world believe capitalism in its current form is doing more harm than good," driven by a rising sense of inequality in the system.[5] To counter these distressing trends and respond to concerns of society, business leaders must be taught to consider the opti-

FIGURE 9.1

Government Less Trusted Than Business

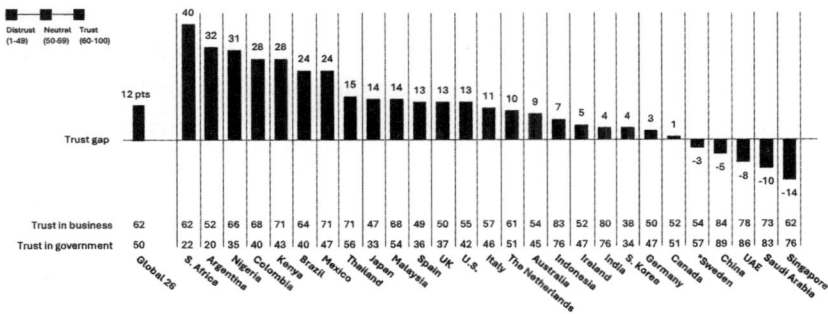

	Distrust (1–49)	Neutral (50–69)	Trust (60–100)

	Global 26	S. Africa	Argentina	Nigeria	Colombia	Kenya	Brazil	Mexico	Thailand	Japan	Malaysia	Spain	UK	U.S.	Italy	The Netherlands	Australia	Indonesia	Ireland	India	S. Korea	Germany	Canada	Sweden	China	UAE	Saudi Arabia	Singapore
Trust gap	12 pts	40	32	31	28	28	24	24	15	14	14	13	13	13	11	10	9	7	5	4	4	3	1	-3	-5	-8	-10	-14
Trust in business	62	62	52	66	68	71	64	71	71	47	68	49	50	55	57	61	54	83	52	80	38	50	52	54	84	78	73	62
Trust in government	50	22	20	35	40	43	40	47	56	33	54	36	37	42	46	51	45	76	47	76	34	47	51	57	89	86	83	76

Notes: Percent trust, and the percentage-point difference between trust in business versus government. Sweden was omitted from the global average as Edelman requires two years of data before inclusion into the final results.

Source: Edelman Trust Institute, 2023 *Edelman Trust Barometer: Global Report*, 2023, https://www.edelman.com/trust/2023/trust-barometer (accessed November 23, 2023). Courtesy of the Edelman Trust Institute—© 2024 Daniel J. Edelman, Inc.

mal balance between the respective roles of government and business in the twenty-first-century economy.

While there is a great deal of effort directed at companies to address climate change by reducing their individual carbon footprints, or inequality by raising their internal minimum wage, one of the most important steps they can take on either front is to turn their lobbying and government influence efforts towards helping government steer the entire market towards addressing those problems. This chapter will examine the extent to which business influences—at times distorts—government policy through advocacy, lobbying, and funding, and consider some remedies for a more constructive form of lobbying that serves the public interest and a functioning market. The next chapter will examine the relationship in the opposite direction by considering the proper role of government in the market and how the two can work in a more collaborative fashion.

Lobbying: The Fifth Estate

Business leaders shape the future of capitalism through government engagement—which is to say, lobbying is not inherently bad for society. Often governments seek guidance on how to set the rules of the market, ushering reforms as needed, and leaders of corporations are well placed to offer their expertise and point of view. Indeed, many call lobbying a branch of government all its own. Where the first estate is the executive, the second estate is the legislative, the third estate is the judicial, and the fourth estate is the media, some call lobbying and advising the fifth estate. In this definition, the fifth estate refers to direct influence from business and business groups, but also think tanks and foundations.[6]

And yet, lobbying is a blind spot in business education, with few business schools offering courses on "legislative affairs" or "government engagement" (more formal terms for lobbying).[7] One analysis of the top twenty business schools found that only four require courses in corporate political activity. Most other schools offer the topic as an elective, or not at all.[8] George Washington University Graduate School of Political Management offers a masters program in international lobbying, while American University offers two-week intensive lobbying workshops through its Public Affairs and Advocacy Institute, formerly known as the Lobbying Institute. Some outside observers view them in a mocking tone. One commentator asked in an online column, "Why the hell would someone go to school to become a lobbyist?"[9]

Much of the public, and many students, see lobbying as negative, envisioning the caricature of cigar-smoking operators working in dark rooms, plying lawmakers with gifts in exchange for legislative favors. But the reality of lobbying is often far more banal and focused on careful patience in relationship building with politicians and staffers and the tedious work of mastering arcane policy and legislative details.[10] For the lobbyist, building trust and instincts about how to best manage political relationships become critical, leading to the belief among many lobbyists that this craft cannot be taught. In the words of thirty-year lobbyist Thomas Susman, "Lobbying is salesmanship on a very personal level." Another lobbyist, Mike House, says, "It's all about good instincts. And instincts can never be taught."[11]

Regardless of whether the skills of lobbying can be explicitly taught, educators have a responsibility to demystify the process and explore its place within the broader economic landscape. Business students need to be taught about the constructive role of government in the market, and public policy students need to be taught about the constructive role of business in policy-making; both need to be taught about constructive ways that government and business can work together and how to promote business-government engagement as a public service, focused on the broader good and maintaining a functioning economic system rather than individual companies trying to snatch advantage by whatever means is available.

Constructive and responsible lobbying exists, and it can play a positive role in our society. Nonprofits often promote social issues through government engagement (though, of course, not all nonprofits behave saintly in Washington, DC, and state capitals), and many companies have used their lobbying power for the public good on issues such as stopping domestic violence (Mary Kay), addressing childhood obesity (The Cartoon Network), strengthening labor laws in developing countries (Levi's), promoting welfare to career programs (Cascade Engineering),[12] addressing the use of conflict-minerals in the technology sector (Intel)[13] and exposing slavery and coerced labor in the supply chain (Nestlé).[14] But these are exceptions that prove the rule; a rule that business schools should seek to change.

A Short History of Lobbying

The practice of interested parties meeting with public officials to influence legislation and public policy was established as early as the Magna Carta in England in 1215. In the United States, the practice dates to the country's founding and was supported in the Continental Congress by the belief that lobbying interests should be considered to find and promote the public good. "Special pleaders," as they were originally called, practiced their trade by waiting in the hallways outside the legislative chambers, and by frequenting the same boarding houses and taverns where government officials had their meals and drinks. The practice grew and matured on both sides of the Atlantic. Many of these special pleaders relied solely on fees from their clients—a compensation arrangement that is perhaps the origin of the concern about nefarious influence from corporate interests. The term "lobbyist" was first used in the United States in 1808 in the annals of the 10th Congress and is thought to have its antecedent in the late seventeenth-century British Parliament and the large public waiting room, known as the "lobby," just off the Chamber of the House of Commons, where members could meet with special pleaders.[15]

By and large, however, America's founding fathers had a benign view of lobbying. James Madison, for example, was concerned about special interests, or "factions," but did not see them as an evil to be eradicated, but rather as a natural element of liberty. He defined a faction as a group of citizens "united and actuated by some common impulse of passion, or of interest, adverse to the rights of other citizens, or to the permanent and aggregate interests of the community."[16] The danger, as he saw it, was not in the mere existence of factions, but in the prospect that one faction could become too powerful and trample on the rights of the minority.

The First Amendment of the Constitution guarantees the right "to petition the Government for a redress of grievances," language that means that, to this day, hiring a lobbyist is considered constitutionally protected. But while early legal thought had no problem with individuals hiring a lawyer to write reports and present them to congressional committees, "it viewed hiring lobbyists to argue someone else's views (especially in contexts outside of formal government settings), and to use their personal influence on someone else's behalf, as a betrayal of civic virtue."[17] In 1832, one judge wrote that a lobbyist is "induced to use his influence for the money he is to obtain; when, as a patriot and a citizen, he should only act for the good of his country."[18] Walt Whitman lumped "Lobbyers" in with "bribers," "sponges," and "monte-dealers . . . men, scarred inside with the vile disorder, gaudy outside with gold chains made from the people's money and harlot's money twisted together; crawling, serpentine men, the lousy combings and born freedom sellers of the earth."[19] The 1888 *Dictionary of American Politics* defined "the lobby" as "a term applied collectively to men that make a business of corruptly influencing legislators."[20]

So, while everyone was seen as having the right to petition the government, such petitioning was seen in the same light as the right to vote, something that should not be sold. Lobbying still happened, but for the first century of the country, it was viewed as incompatible with the rights and responsibilities of citizenship, therefore not serving the public interest, and something that the courts refused to sanction by enforcing lobbying contracts.[21] In 1852, Congress passed a law banning anyone from attending legislative sessions who was "employed as an agent to prosecute any claim pending before Congress." In 1877, Georgia made lobbying a crime in their state constitution after it was discovered that lawmakers had sold thirty-five million acres of land for a scandalously low price to a business conglomerate in which almost all of them were given shares. Several other states followed suit.

But America's views of lobbying steadily shifted—emphasizing the need for both robust advocacy and clear disclosure practices. In 1876, the US House of Representatives approved a resolution requiring lobbyists to register with the House Clerk, thereby conferring some legal legitimacy. Massachusetts did the same in 1890. Over time the courts began to honor and protect lobbying contracts; the idea that lobbying was a legitimate enterprise and protected by the First Amendment was slowly cemented into legal doctrine through the twentieth century. In 1946, Congress enacted the Federal Regulation of Lobbying Act, which required anyone whose "principal purpose" was to influence the passage or rejection of legislation in Congress to register and file quarterly financial reports. Violation of those reporting requirements was punishable by a fine of up to $5,000 or one year in prison and a three-year ban on lobbying. This first attempt to legislatively address lobbying at the federal level did not cover Congressional staff, the executive branch, or a large amount of grassroots lobbying.[22]

However, further controls also followed. In 1995, Congress passed the Lobbying Disclosure Act (LDA) which reformed the way lobbying activity was regulated. Driven in part by lobbying and corruption scandals, the LDA expanded the definition of lobbyists to include both in-house lobbyists (employees lobbying on behalf of their employer's interests) and outside lobbyists (persons lobbying on behalf of a third-party client), while also expanding the scope of covered officials to include not just members of Congress but also Congressional staff and political appointees in the executive branch. In 2007, the LDA was amended by the Honest Leadership and Open Government Act,[23] which strengthened disclosure requirements for anyone who spent at least 20 percent of their time lobbying in a three-month period (in-house lobbyists) or 20 percent of their time lobbying for one client (outside lobbyists), increased penalties for violations, and banned gifts and entertainment of Congressional officials.[24] In the late twentieth century, the Supreme Court sanctioned any lobbying that was not explicit, quid pro quo bribery, consistent with the ruling in the 2010 *Citizens United* decision that "Ingratiation and access . . . are not corruption."[25]

Today's Complex Battleground for Influence

In today's lobbying arena, diverse interests compete to shape public policy, often fueled by money and self-interest. Individual lobbyists, of course ply their craft, providing valuable support for under-resourced politicians, including offering expertise on specific issues, conducting research on voter attitudes and policy proposals, analyzing political landscapes, offering advice about media strategy, and organizing get-out-the-vote strategies.[26] But the complex web of influence also involves influential foundations and think tanks, which shape the state, national, and international policy conversation.

Lobbyists. The negative impression that many hold of lobbyists would seem to be supported by the amount of money and effort that is expended to influence government each year. According to journalist Ezra Klein, businesses have spent more money lobbying Congress than taxpayers have spent funding Congress since 2014.[27] In 2022, at least 13,784 organizations deployed 12,609 federal lobbyists with total lobbying expenditures reaching a record $4.1 billion, up from $3.4 billion in 2018.[28] The National Association of Realtors and the US Chamber of Commerce top the list as clients at just over $80 million each, while the pharmaceutical industry spent more than $350 million overall on federal lobbying. For the lobbyists, this can be a very lucrative business, with the top ten lobbying firms earning more than 9 percent of that $4.1 billion spent and the highest-grossing federal lobbying firm, Brownstein Hyatt Farber Schreck, reporting revenues of $61.2 million in 2022.[29]

Foundations and Think Tanks. A subtle form of lobbying exists in which ersatz academic institutions provide policy guidance to politicians in the form of whitepapers on issues and even drafts of laws their funders would like to see passed. These foundations and think tanks bring to the process research (of varying degrees of bias and quality) as well as ideological support on different priorities and outcomes. Because of this, they have often been likened to America's shadow government.[30] They range from the right to the left in their political leanings and focus on different issues, different problems, and different solutions. They can be ranked by budget (see Table 9.1), by media influence, by social media presence, and by other measures.

Some, like the Federalist Society, exert influence by placing its members into positions of power. The organization often signs off on Republican judicial nominees and was so powerful during the Donald Trump administration that Republican commentators boasted it had been "in-sourced" to the White House to help pick its nominees to the Supreme Court. Of the nine members

TABLE 9.1

Annual Budget for Notable Think Tanks in the United States

Liberal or Progressive
Brookings Institution, $105 million
World Resources Institute, $90 million
Urban Institute, $88 million
Human Rights Watch, $59 million
Center for American Progress, $41 million
Center for Budget and Policy Priorities, $37 million

Independent
RAND Corporation, $327 million
Aspen Institute, $97 million
Bipartisan Policy Center, $22 million
New America Foundation, $17 million
Earth Institute, $5 million
Worldwatch Institute, $3 million
National Bureau of Economic Research, not available

Conservative or Libertarian
Heritage Foundation, $81 million
American Enterprise Institute, $64 million
Hoover Institution, $56 million
The Cato Institute, $29 million
Federalist Society, $20 million
Acton Institute, $13 million
Competitive Enterprise Institute, $6 million

Source: Table created by author using data from "The 50 most influential think tanks in the United States," 2021, https://www.coursehero.com/file/82275430/The-50-Most-Influential-Think-Tanks-in-the-United-Statesdocx/ (accessed November 23, 2023).

of the current Supreme Court, at least five are current or former members of the society—Brett Kavanaugh, Neil Gorsuch, Clarence Thomas, Samuel Alito, and Amy Coney Barrett. Chief Justice John Roberts previously served as a member of the steering committee of the Washington, D.C., chapter, but denies ever being a member. The Federalist Society claims to be nonpartisan but tends to endorse candidates for judicial appointments who take conservative stances on abortion rights and other social issues and, as a group, opposes the regulation of private property and private businesses.

Alternatively, the Center for American Progress was created as a Democratic alternative to such influential conservative think tanks. The first president and CEO was John Podesta, former White House chief of staff to President Bill Clinton and chairman of the 2016 presidential campaign of Hillary Clinton. The Center funneled more than sixty officials into the administration of President Joe Biden, many in critical roles, and helped shape some of the legislative initiatives and executive actions that the president pursued on topics ranging from immigration to inclusivity in government agencies.[31]

Cynicism and Disenchantment

Today, with the level of moneyed interest in our political system, there is widespread cynicism and disenchantment with our democratic institutions. Not just in the United States: the OECD reports that "trust in the public decision-making process and in governments in general is waning in the vast majority of OECD countries. Citizens express doubts about their governments' ability to make the right decisions. There is a widespread view that governments are not able to effectively regulate markets, that business exerts undue influence over public policy, and that the distribution of burdens and rewards across society is unfair."[32]

Beyond outright corruption, such as Watergate in the 1970s, Iran-Contra in the 1980s, and US Senator Bob Menendez facing three federal indictments on bribery in 2024,[33] a key source of public suspicion is the "revolving door" between government and lobbying firms. Certainly, both government and business experience can be valuable assets for a lobbying career. Understanding how each sector operates—their needs, decision-making processes, and goals—can facilitate the search for mutually beneficial solutions. However, the revolving door can also be exploited for private advantage, undermining its potential benefits.

Nearly half of all members of Congress now take lobbying jobs when they leave office. Given how highly compensated lobbying jobs can be compared to the pay of elected officials, it's not hard to imagine that some elected officials come to see their time on congressional committees as an extended job interview for lobbying positions, strategically positioning themselves for future employment on Washington's K Street, where most blue-chip lobbying firms have offices just a stone's throw from the Capitol building. In all, OpenSecrets reports that 468 former members of Congress are paid lobbyists or "senior advisors" for corporations and special interests whose job it is to influence the federal government that they used to serve.

Similarly, there are hundreds of staffers who either left a member's staff for a lobbying position or, showing that the revolving door goes both ways, came to Capitol Hill after representing private interests. According to OpenSecrets, "a current or former staffer may have developed a lawmaker's political strategy as chief of staff, managed his or her contact with reporters as press secretary or worked in any number of official capacities in his or her office. . . . Capitalizing on their Capitol Hill connections to represent private interests has a powerful incentive."[34] To be sure, some lawmakers and bureaucrats join lobbying firms out of genuine passion for a cause, viewing their efforts as a form of public service. However, for many, financial gain is a powerful driver, and that fuels widespread public cynicism and distrust, tarnishing the reputation of both government and the corporate sector.

In one egregious example, the largest US accounting firms were discovered to have perfected a behind-the-scenes system to promote their interests in Washington by encouraging their tax lawyers to take senior jobs at the Treasury Department, where they could write policies that are frequently favorable to their former corporate clients before returning to their old employers where, according to Eric Sloan, co-chairman of the tax practice at the law firm Gibson, Dunn & Crutcher, the government experiences "allow them to command higher compensation upon their return."[35] From their government posts, some have approved loopholes that are exploited by their former firms, gave tax breaks to former clients, and rolled back efforts to rein in tax shelters.

The public has become weary and inured to such stories of legal corruption, but many foreign students express surprise and dismay at the extent to which money shapes America's political system They find it shocking that Americans track the fund-raising of political candidates as a sort of race before the race, predicting who will win by how much they raise and believing that these donations do not come with unspoken expectations of access or influence. (It's worth repeating, as an aside, that the Supreme Court defines corruption as, simply, "a quid pro quo deal"). We seem to have traded an era in which bribery happened but provoked outrage and consequences for an age in which corruption is abhorred but seen as inevitable.[36]

The result is the cynical political culture that nineteenth-century judges worried about when they refused to legitimize lobbying. In fact, the concern that money has a greater—and mostly negative—influence on politics unites people across the political spectrum.[37] A vast majority of Americans (90 percent) are concerned with the level of money in politics,[38] and two-thirds say that "all or most of the people who currently serve as elected officials ran for office to make a lot of money." Large majorities of both Republicans and Democrats say that "campaign donors, lobbyists and special interest groups have too much influence," and 70 percent of Americans say that they as individuals "have too little influence over the decisions their representatives make."[39] Proposed solutions to this deteriorating state of affairs fall into both voluntary and mandatory responses.

A Voluntary Solution: Corporate Political Responsibility

Similar rates of Republicans (87 percent) and Democrats (80 percent) agree with the statement, "There is a leadership crisis in the US government today."[40] This view is also prevalent among business leaders who have lamented the extent to which government is not functioning properly. But as University of Michigan professor Tom Lyon argues, they "naively ignore the role business leaders play in creating" that dysfunction.[41] As a response, numerous organizations have developed standards and guidelines to help corporations act more responsibly in their political activities; what is called Corporate Political Responsibility (CPR). Each takes a slightly different approach to addressing one piece of the overall political engagement landscape. For example, the OECD Recommendation on Principles for Transparency and Integrity helps member countries develop regulations that increase transparency, accountability, and guardrails in the practice of lobbying that can support a level playing field in public decision making.[42] The Zicklin Center for Business Ethics Research has developed a twelve-point model code of conduct specifically for corporate political spending.[43] Transparency International has developed a set of guidelines for political donations and indirect political expenditure specifically to counter issues of bribery.[44]

Other standards, such as The Responsible Lobbying Framework[45] and the Erb Principles for Corporate Responsibility[46] (at the University of Michigan where I am on the faculty) seek to provide a model for what responsible lobbying would look like, based on a series of related principles:

1. *Legitimacy.* Political activities should reflect the company's views and interests, not those of the individual manager or officer, and they will not pressure or coerce employees, shareholders, or other stakeholders to support such activities.

2. *Accountability.* Companies will create and monitor alignment between their political activities; those of third-party member organizations (such as trade associations) of which they are a part; their own purpose, values, and stated goals; and the interests of their key stakeholders.

3. *Responsibility.* Companies will champion healthy market "rules of the game" that foster competition on the basis of quality, price, and long-term value, minimizing costs externalized to other stakeholders and aligning private interests with the broader public good; support and protect America's constitutional democracy; and rely on independent, peer-reviewed science when taking stands on issues.

4. *Transparency.* Companies will report all direct political spending, spending through trade associations or other third parties influencing on their behalf, and communicate openly about their political influence approaches, outlining criteria, issues, positions, goals, stakeholder consultation processes, and affiliations.

5. *Opportunity.* Companies will coordinate and align their activities with others when they further the public good.

Limitations of Corporate Political Responsibility in an Era of Corporate Activism

Widespread adoption of CPR principles would be an important step towards rebalancing the political power of corporations towards serving the public good. That is, of course, if you take as a given that corporate interests can and should have a strong role in influencing the policy process. But some worry that such efforts further allow companies to encroach on areas where only democratically elected officials should have influence, legitimizing that role and strengthening "the link between democracy and capitalism at a time when we should instead disentangle one from the other."[47] David Vogel, professor at Berkeley's Haas School of Business, points out that such voluntary efforts should not and cannot replace public policy, noting that "[i]f companies are serious about acting more responsibly, then they need to reexamine their relationship to government as well as improve their own practices. And those who want corporations to be more virtuous should expect firms to act more responsibly on both dimensions. Civil and government regulation both have a legitimate role to play in improving public welfare. The former reflects the potential of the market for virtue; the latter recognizes its limits."[48]

Regardless of theoretical debates about the proper role of corporations, the reality is that executives increasingly find themselves compelled to take public stands on social issues—a phenomenon that has been dubbed "CEO activism."[49] Corporate leaders have been pulled or pushed into issues as diverse as anti-gay-marriage legislation in Indiana, Georgia, and North Carolina; gun rights in Georgia; the murder of the journalist Jamal Khashoggi by agents of the Saudi Arabian government; and other issues not strictly tied to their direct business interests. Often, executives are finding themselves compelled by employee pressure; Microsoft employees, for example, launched their "We Won't Build It" campaign to demand that the company cancel its contract with the Immigration and Customs Enforcement agency in protest over the Trump administration's zero tolerance policy on immigration. Companies can also be pushed by activism; when the Susan G. Komen Foundation cut off funds to Planned Parenthood, a pop-up social movement arose, forcing the policy to be walked back. Or companies can be pushed by straight business self-interests: Sanofi was forced to make a public statement on its product Ambien after actress Roseanne Barr blamed the product for a series of racist tweets she posted that caused her ABC sitcom to be canceled. The company issued a press release stating that "racism is not a known side effect of Ambien."

It seems that consumers and the general public are comfortable with such corporate presence in social debates. A 2018 survey by global public relations firm Weber Shandwick found that 77 percent of consumers agree that CEOs need to speak out when their company's values are violated or threatened; 48 percent believe CEO activism influences the decisions and actions of government; 46 percent of consumers would be more likely to buy from a company led by a CEO who speaks out on an issue they agree with. Only 10 percent would be less likely to buy, and the rate of positive purchasing behavior has risen significantly from 38 percent in 2017 to 46 percent in 2018.[50] There are at least two problems with this growing acceptance.

First, by stepping into the activism ring, business leaders find themselves with a conflict of interest between activist ethics and the corporate profit motive. Marc Benioff, CEO of Salesforce, for example, defended his stance on LGBTQ rights in Indiana by citing the data from Weber Shandwick that customers will pay more for products and services from companies that drive positive social and environmental change.[51] But if corporate forays into political, social, and environmental issues are defended on the extent to which they increase the bottom line, then any alignment between such actions and the public interest will be coincidental and often temporary.

Blackrock and JP Morgan instituted de facto sanctions on Saudi Arabia after the Jamal Khashoggi murder by canceling participation in important meetings in that country, but then resumed their participation the following year, presumably under financial pressure to regain lucrative Saudi business. Chic-fil-A took a strong stand on LGBTQ issues, arguing that gay marriage was "inviting God's judgement on our nation," only to receive word from Boston's then-mayor Thomas Menino that he was blocking the franchise in the city; the fast-food chain ultimately backed off its stand. As these engagements increase, companies become more political, and we see the risk of creating "red" and "blue" companies, causing real economic consequences for the company, and fueling further divisions in society. When the Hallmark Channel ran an advertisement featuring a gay couple, it canceled its showing after the conservative group One Million Moms protested, but then faced the counter backlash from the liberal GLAAD (Gay & Lesbian Alliance Against

Defamation) and reinstated it. When Delta challenged the National Rifle Association in the wake of mass shootings by curtailing flight discounts to its members, the State of Georgia revoked lucrative fuel subsidies. In 2019, automakers found themselves in an unenviable position of having to side with either the Trump administration in relaxing automobile emission standards or the State of California in maintaining them.[52] The ramifications for these kinds of decisions stretch the boundaries of what is within the realm of corporate strategic expertise.

The second problem is that every step that business takes into the public sphere displaces the role and responsibility of government and public institutions, reinforcing Americans' distrust of government. Benioff once admonished a group of executives to "adopt a public school." But corporate appropriation of schools is not the answer; better government-administered and tax-supported education is. No social problem can be solved by corporate largess—more than anything else, that largess is simply not sustainable (few companies survive more than a few decades at most). What's more, despite their good intentions, corporate leaders are not best placed to become de facto politicians. CEOs are not elected, they are not held accountable to voters, and they are not trained or skilled in social policy. Society makes a Faustian bargain when it displaces politicians with corporate executives.

Two examples show the pitfalls of corporate activism and meddling run amok. In 2022, Barre Seid donated his company Tripp Lite to a nonprofit organization called Marble Freedom Trust, which then sold the business for $1.65 billion, sparing Seid from paying capital gains taxes on the transaction and allowing him to make a political contribution to a conservative organization that, among other things, opposes climate change legislation.[53] That same year, Yvon Chouinard transferred his ownership of Patagonia, valued at about $3 billion, to a nonprofit organization called Holdfast Collective that will use the future profits in "fighting the environmental crisis and defending nature."[54] In each of these examples, Stanford political theorist Rob Reich (not the former labor secretary) warns, "The citizens of the United States are collectively subsidizing, through foregone tax collection, the giving preferences of the wealthy."[55]

No democratic citizen should want to live in a society where policy addressing vital social issues is decided in battles between dueling piles of money in the pursuit of more money. The true irony is that, if corporations genuinely aim to improve society, they should work to reduce their own influence in politics. This means insulating policymaking from the undue influence of moneyed interests, including their own, taking the brave step of unilateral political demobilization.[56] Where complete insulation isn't possible, strong guardrails are necessary to prevent corporations from wielding excessive influence.

A Mandatory Solution: Insulating Government from Corporate Power

Lobbying has a role to play in good government. In a vast, technologically advanced country such as the United States, lawmakers must pass legislation on a diverse array of subjects, and lobbying can provide a valuable service by offering expertise, insight, and data to lawmakers and their staff. It can also facilitate stakeholders' access to the development and implementation of public policies—in theory strengthening democratic participation.[57]

That said, over the past forty years, many democracies around the world have adopted stricter campaign spending limits to create guardrails for the amount of money that can distort democratic processes,[58] usually focusing on limits on either spending, donations, or both.[59] One country that has made notable strides in this area is France. By law, major presidential candidates in France may not spend more than 15.5 million euros on their campaigns, while the two candidates who advance to the second round are able to spend 20.7 million euros.[60] The government reimburses 20 percent of campaign costs to all parties, and if the parties gain more than 5 percent of the total vote, they are rebated 50 percent of their costs. That means only half of election funding comes from private donors. Businesses and trade unions are forbidden by law from making campaign donations,[61] and candidates cannot buy TV or radio time for advertisements; stations are required to provide equal time according to the relevance of each candidate (as measured by popularity in opinion polls). These policies are set under what is called the Principle of Equity and the Principle of Equality.[62]

The United States has moved in the opposite direction, with decisions like *Citizens United* increasing the amount of money on which candidates depend. Joe Biden spent $1.6 billion to win the 2020 presidential election, more than three times what Hillary Clinton spent in 2016.[63] Money is now essential to any political career, and many corporate executives feel that there is no choice but to provide that money. A 2013 report from the Committee for Economic Development found that 75 percent of business executives surveyed believed that "the U.S. campaign finance system is pay-to-play," 94 percent believed that "politicians cast votes to please special interests rather than voters," and 87 percent said the system "needs major reforms or a complete overhaul" as pressure on them to "contribute to political campaigns and judicial races results in a 'shake down' effect."[64] In short, lobbying has a corrosive effect on democracy when it becomes about exchanging money for access to lawmakers and their staff.[65] The result is undue influence, unfair competition, and regulatory capture to the detriment of the public interest and effective public policies. So, the challenge is to establish guardrails that will create sufficient barriers between special interests and government officials—understanding that voluntary measures (such as lobbying codes of conduct) are unlikely to filter out all bad actors intent on abusing the system. Interviews with lawmakers, congressional staff members, lobbyists, and members of the Executive Branch Career Service reveal "red flags," places to focus on for ensuring our political system is not corrupted.[66]

The Revolving Door. The most cited solution to the problem of lawmakers, staffers, and industry lobbyists swapping roles is a "cooling off" period between when a government official leaves office and begins work as a lobbyist. The Honest Leadership and Open Government Act increased the cooling off period for senators from one to two years. In 2017, President Donald Trump issued an executive order that banned executive branch employees from becoming a lobbyist for five years. In 2023, the PURE Executive Act was introduced to establish a five-year ban on lobbying by former senior executive branch personnel and to prohibit such personnel from lobbying at any time on behalf of foreign governments or entities controlled by foreign governments, and for other purposes.[67] Some have suggested outright bans on passing through the revolving door.

The Covert Nature of Lobbying. Whether they be in restaurants, bars, social clubs, or gyms, lobbyists and special interests find lawmakers where they live and work. But these seemingly casual social contacts create suspicion.[68] The response has been to strengthen disclosure requirements (including public reporting and public disclosure of lobbying activities); prohibit campaign contributions from or arranged by lobbyists; prohibit lobbyists from serving on lawmaker's fundraising committees; prohibit lobbyists from paying for, organizing, participating in, or using corporate jets to provide trips with lawmakers; and strict penalties for violation. Some have suggested that there should be prohibitions on lobbyists from access to the congressional floor, cafes, and gyms. One unusual proposal has been for the public financing of lobbying by creating an online forum for lobbyists, constituents, and other interested parties to publicly and transparently debate legislation. In the process, this would provide congressional staff, journalists, and the public access to the arguments, information, and ideas about public policy in a way that is easily searchable and sortable. Similar to online forums such as Wikipedia, Yelp, and Reddit, one could think of this as a modern variation on notice-and-comment rulemaking (in which government agencies post a proposal for new rule and then provide an opportunity for public comment) for the legislative process.[69] Some lobbyists protest that this approach will slow down the process of learning exactly what kind of information a lawmaker needs and providing it in a timely fashion. Another concern is that it may drive some lobbying activities underground.

The Use of "Marquee" Lobbyists and the Dominance of Well-Resourced Lobby Firms. The lobbying profession is driven by results—specifically, the ability to gain quick and effective access to key government officials to plead one's case. This leads to a pecking order and an inequality of access in the lobbying field. Unsurprisingly, wealthy clients get access to the best (and most) lobbyists, which can lead to more successful lobbying efforts.[70] Indeed, there are sixteen lobbyists representing business for every one representing a union or public interest group, with the public often left out.

As a corrective, Russell Berman at *The Atlantic* writes that we must begin by accepting that in today's politics, the wealthy and corporations will always be able to use their money and their "hired guns" to influence elections, one way or another. To blunt this advantage, he proposes that we focus on empowering average people by reinvigorating and expanding the public-financing system for campaigns, on both the federal and local levels,[71] as France has done. One of the key features of a public-financing system is a matching requirement. This means that for every dollar a candidate raises from small, individual donations, the public financing system would contribute a certain amount as well. By doing this, the impact of large, private donations can be balanced.

The first public financing programs in the US were enacted following the Watergate scandal of the 1970s. Since then, more than thirty jurisdictions have adopted some form of public financing, including states such as Arizona, Connecticut, Maine, and Michigan, and local governments such as New York City; Seattle; Albuquerque; Washington, DC; and Montgomery County, Maryland, among many others.[72] Seattle's Democracy Vouchers program, established in a 2015 citywide referendum, allocates four $25 vouchers to each registered voter, which can be donated to qualifying candidates for city offices. This approach aims not only to create a more equitable environment for candidates who may not have substantial financial backing from wealthy donors but also to alleviate the pressure of constant fundraising. The hope is that elected officials can devote more time to legislative duties and addressing the needs of their constituents.

At the national level, some presidential campaigns are funded in part by taxpayers who choose to direct $3 to the Presidential Election Campaign Fund when they file their tax returns. In 1977, about 29 percent of taxpayers ticked the box to contribute $3 of their taxes towards the fund. Participation dropped to 19 percent by 1992 and to 3.6 percent by 2020. Two possible reasons for the decline are the mistaken belief that donations increase tax liability, and a general apathy towards the two-party political system. That said, to be eligible for these funds, candidates must agree to spending and fundraising restrictions. Through 2004, all candidates in the general presidential election opted for public funding and reimbursement of their campaign expenses. But in 2008, Barack Obama became the first to give up this public funding, so that he could spend more than the prescribed limit. His opponent, John McCain, stuck to the limit. Since 2012 all candidates in the general presidential election have rejected public funding to avoid any constraints on the total amount they can spend.[73]

Other proposals at the federal level include the Government by the People Act, which, had it received enough votes to pass, would have instructed the government to match small-dollar donations at a six-to-one rate (or higher under certain conditions) while also giving people a $25 refundable tax credit to encourage political donations. Similarly, the Fair Elections Now Act (which also did not get enough votes) had similar provisions but would have also allowed candidates to raise unlimited donations if they did not individually exceed $150.

Political Skills Needed for Twenty-First-Century Business

Winston Churchill once said, "Some . . . regard private enterprise as a predatory tiger to be shot. Others look on it as a cow they can milk. Only a handful see it for what it really is—the strong and willing horse that pulls the whole cart along."[74] If business is the horse and cart that provides the products and services that our society needs, a functioning government builds the infrastructure and sets the rules of the road.

Many of today's business school students will become tomorrow's corporate leaders; some will even become lobbyists, and a few will have a career in politics. These future leaders should be taught the complex positives and negatives of corporate influence as an important component of a properly functioning economy. Harvard Business School professor Rebecca Henderson points out, "We must remember that free markets must be balanced by democratically accountable, transparent governments and strong civil societies, if we are to build a just and sustainable future. Business must step up to make this possible. Our economies, and with it our firms, will suffer enormously if we don't address the problems that we face."[75]

That seems to be the challenge, as business appears ill-prepared for the social and political engagements that it will be increasingly called to embrace. A Public Affairs Council survey found that 91 percent of government affairs executives reported that pressure to get involved in social issues has somewhat or significantly increased between 2016 and 2021 and they expect that pressure to continue to grow.[76] While corporate leaders might not be ideal political actors, equipping them with tools for navigating complex social issues is crucial to their success. It is naive to assume that corporate influence on lawmakers is inherently benign, as corporate interests often diverge from those of broader society. However, it's also cynical to believe that corporations cannot play a constructive role in lawmaking and public policy.

All the efforts to instill Corporate Political Responsibility or create guardrails between business and government are important. But business schools should be teaching the skills necessary to navigate complicated political terrain and then to turn those skills towards helping shift the entire market towards serving society's needs. For example, despite a widespread scientific consensus that climate change is an urgent issue, the largest five stock-market-listed oil and gas companies spend nearly $200 million per year lobbying to delay, control, or block policies to tackle climate change.[77] While CPR is a helpful step for controlling this activity, the next step is to consider how these political resources can be turned *towards* supporting policies to address climate change, not just to stop getting in the way. This would be a shift akin to Paul Polman and Andrew Winston's call for businesses to be "net positive," discussed in Chapter 7.[78]

While corporate executives have an obligation to their shareholders, employees, suppliers, and more, they are also human beings who have an obligation to the next generations of children and grandchildren to have a healthy and stable environment in which to live and a fair economy in which to thrive. Though there are constraints on their degrees of managerial freedom, they can support a stronger government that can compel them, and all their competitors, to find a new variant of capitalism that will address the needs of the twenty-first century. Teaching students that this is possible, and then giving the foundational tools to do it, is a critical role for business schools.

TEN

The Necessary and Constructive Role of the Government in the Market

Not More or Less Government, the Right Level of Government

"Wherever we look around the world, when we see inconsequential governments with limited power, as libertarians would prefer, we see 'failed states.' How much liberty and human dignity can be found there? Very little."

—JERRY TAYLOR, CO-FOUNDER, NISKANEN CENTER

Six weeks into the Great Recession of 2008,[1] Queen Elizabeth II visited the London School of Economics and asked a very straightforward question: "Why didn't anyone see the financial crisis coming?" The academics fumbled an answer. But on a return visit four years later, the Bank of England's Sujit Kapadia finally gave her one that was clearer. He said that as the global economy boomed in the precrisis years, people had grown complacent.[2] "People thought markets were efficient, people thought regulation wasn't necessary. . . . People didn't realise just how interconnected the system had become."[3] Richard Posner, a respected conservative judge and senior lecturer at the University of Chicago Law School, offers more insights in his book *A Failure of Capitalism*, arguing that "we need a more active and intelligent government to keep our model of a capitalist economy from running off the rails."[4] He accuses economists of being "asleep at the switch" and turns to John Maynard Keynes's 1936 book *The General Theory of Employment, Interest, and Money* for answers, arguing that "despite its antiquity . . . [it] is the best guide we have to the crisis."[5]

Where the prior chapter examined the role of business in policymaking, this chapter explores the role of government in the market—a historically divisive topic. For several decades beginning in the 1970s, many policymakers, scholars, and practitioners have emphasized the risks of government intervention, highlighting potential market distortions and opportunities for crony capitalism. However, rather than viewing government intervention as a necessary evil at best, recent scholarship has investigated productive avenues for collaboration between government and business. This approach builds upon the idea that, as Harvard professor John Ruggie points out, "the state by itself cannot do all the heavy lifting required to meet most pressing societal challenges and . . . it therefore needs to engage other actors to leverage its capacity."[6] This collaborative approach has brought "industrial policy"—a concept both provocative and enduring in our economy—back into the spotlight.

Early Views of the Role of Government in the Market

To begin our discussion of the role of government in the market, we return to two early figures in the establishment of our principles of capitalism and democracy: Adam Smith, the founder of economics, and James Madison, the fourth president of the United States and collaborator on the US Constitution and the Bill of Rights.

For Adam Smith, the rules of the market were not self-legislating or naturally obvious. Despite his belief in the power of self-interest to guide markets, he was not an advocate of *laissez faire* capitalism. He believed that government had three key tasks in an economy: "First, the duty of protecting the society from violence and invasion of other independent societies; secondly, the duty of protecting, as far as possible, every member of society from the injustice or oppression of every other member of it, or the duty of establishing an exact administration of justice; and, thirdly, the duty of erecting and maintaining certain publick works and certain publick institutions, which it can never be for the interest of any individual."[7]

To be sure, Smith viewed government bureaucrats with suspicion. He questioned whether any government planner could be wise enough to manage a system as complex as a market, writing that such a government official "seems to imagine that he can arrange the different members of a great society with as much ease as the hand arranges the different pieces upon a chess-board. He does not consider that the pieces upon a chess-board have no other principle of motion besides that which the hand impresses upon them; but that, in the great chess-board of human society, every single piece has a principle of motion of its own, altogether different from that which the legislature might choose to impress upon it."[8]

But Smith was also equally suspicious of businesspeople, writing that "the proposal of any new law or regulation of commerce which comes from [the business community] ought always to be listened to with great precaution, and ought never to be adopted till after having been long and carefully examined, not only with the most scrupulous, but with the most suspicious attention. It comes from an order of men, whose interest is never exactly the same with that of the public, who have generally an interest to deceive and even oppress the public, and who accordingly have, upon many occasions, both deceived and oppressed it."[9]

For James Madison, the United States was not a pure or direct democracy, but a Republic, or representative democracy, where government is elected by citizens to represent their interests.[10] The "public good" was not whatever the majority decided but was the product of a deliberative process in which people, reasoning together, undertook a genuine and open exploration of the nature of a problem and options for solving it. In this conception, the role of the government was to "refine and enlarge the public views, by passing them through the medium of a chosen body of citizens, whose wisdom may best discern the true interest of their country, and whose patriotism and love of justice will be least likely to sacrifice it to temporary or partial considerations."[11] Like Smith, James Madison believed in a central government with "few and defined" powers. His priorities for these powers included, above all, the protection of private property rights—the right to acquire, possess, and freely use property—as well as upholding contracts and eliminating artificial trade barriers.

Echoing Smith, Madison was critical of government planners. He felt that it would be unrealistic to think that "enlightened statesmen will be able to adjust . . . clashing interests and render them all subservient to the public good. Enlightened statesmen will not always be at the helm: Nor, in many cases, can such an adjustment be made at all, without taking into view indirect and remote considerations, which will rarely prevail over the immediate interest which one party may find in disregarding the rights of another, or the good of the whole."[12]

Also like Smith, Madison held a dim view of corporations, writing that "[i]ncorporated companies with proper limitations and guards may, in particular cases, be useful; but they are at best a necessary evil only."[13] He was worried about "factions" or special interests that would subvert democracy by adversely affecting the rights of minorities, property, and the public interest and saw their control as another of the government's responsibilities. "The regulation of these various and interfering interests forms the principal task of modern legislation and involves the spirit of party and faction in the necessary and ordinary operations of government."[14] He opposed Alexander Hamilton, the first US Secretary of the Treasury, over the Bank of the United States because he worried about the unchecked power of accumulations of capital that come with creating a class of bankers and moneyed interests, which could wield political power and act as de facto governments. "Where a majority are united by a common sentiment, and have an opportunity, the rights of the minor party become insecure."[15] These views set the foundation for understanding the role of government in our economy and society.

The Public's Negative View of Government's Role in the Market

The debate over the government's role in the market dates back to America's founding, and it remains a dynamic and unresolved issue today. As former labor secretary Robert Reich suggests, the concept of a "free market" depends, in fact, on government-established rules and regulations, and these rules inevitably reflect a society's evolving norms and values.[16] Agreeing on those norms and values can be challenging when partisan views diverge widely, which is the predicament America now finds herself in.

Partisan Divisions

For many conservatives, government should have a very limited role to play within the market; that the political and the economic domains are mutually exclusive and, at its most extreme, that government can do nothing right. For many liberals, government is a necessary constraint on a corporate system that would trample on individual rights and freedom to pursue profits. In 2017, only 31 percent of Republicans said government regulation was necessary, compared to 66 percent of Democrats, and 68 percent of Republicans said there was too much regulation, compared to only 20 percent of Democrats.[17] A majority (63 percent) of Republicans and Republican-leaning independents say that financial regulations have gone too far while only 31 percent say they have not gone far enough. The balance of opinion among Democrats is completely reversed with 62 percent of Democrats and Democrat-leaning independents saying the government has not gone far enough and 29 percent as say it has gone too far.[18] By 2024, the landscape had begun to shift, as far-right-leaning Republicans have supported more controls on the market, particularly around the topics of trade barriers, tariffs, protection of national industries, and blocks on immigration.[19] But overall, the issue of government's role in the market has been reduced to a simplistic debate between binary choices, such as between liberal versus conservative values, Keynesian versus neoclassical models, socialism versus capitalism, or simply more versus less government.

Trust Is Low

Beyond partisan differences on its role, trust in the government is also very low irrespective of party affiliation, as measured by numerous surveys. According to Frank Newport at Gallup News in 2015, government received "the lowest [trust] rating for any . . . sector we tested," adding that "Americans think that Congress is corrupt and not focused on the interests of the people."[20] A 2023 survey by the Pew Research Center found that "public trust in the federal government, which has been low for decades, had returned to near record lows following a modest uptick in 2020 and 2021 with fewer than two-in-ten Americans saying they trust the government in Washington to do what is right 'just about always' (1 percent) or 'most of the time' (15 percent). This is among the lowest trust measures in nearly seven decades of polling" (see Figure 10.1). Democrats had slightly more trust in government in 2023, with 25 percent saying "they trust the federal government just about always or most of the time" compared to only 8 percent of Republicans. But polling shows that this trust tends to increase among members of the party that controls the White House and reverses when that control shifts. That said, Republicans tend to

FIGURE 10.1

Public Trust in Government Near Historic Lows

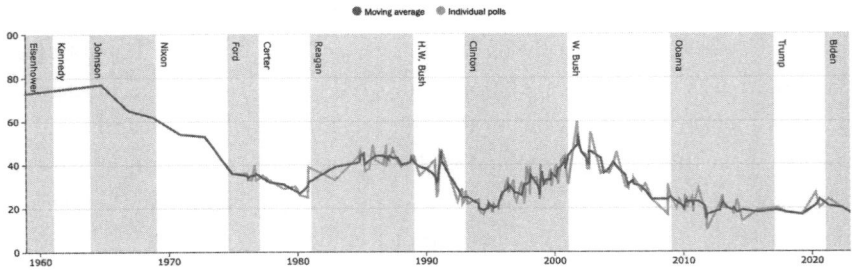

Note: Percent who say they trust the government to do what is right just about always or most of the time.

Source: "Public trust in government: 1958–2023," Pew Research Center, September 19, 2023.

express "much lower levels of trust during Democratic presidencies" while Democrats "have tended to be somewhat more consistent, regardless of which party controls the White House."[21]

Overall, just 20 percent of US adults say they trust the government in Washington to "do the right thing," a percentage that has not changed much since 2010. Americans are particularly critical of how the government manages the immigration system (just 34 percent say it does a good job), its ability to help people get out of poverty (36 percent), and effectively handle threats to public health (42 percent). Roughly two-thirds of Americans believe that the government does too little on issues affecting middle-income, lower–income, and retired people, while an equal percentage says the government does too much for high-income people. Republicans and Democrats generally agree on this point with slight majorities of both parties (52 percent of Republicans and 56 percent of Democrats) saying that it does too little on issues affecting "people like [me]."[22]

Yet Americans' unhappiness with government has long coexisted with their continued support for government stepping into the market, particularly during the pandemic, periods of economic recession, and on certain issue domains. Majorities say the government does a very good or somewhat good job responding to natural disasters (70 percent) and keeping the country safe from terrorism (68 percent). The share giving the government a positive rating for strengthening the economy declined from 54 percent to 37 percent between 2020 and 2022. Yet at the same time, 78 percent believed that the government should play a major role in the economy (and 68 percent felt the government should play a major role in protecting the environment).[23]

Looking at the conflicted and contradictory polling data, Karlyn Bowman at *Forbes* concludes, "Contradiction is a key property of public opinion, and we see it here. We want to get government off the back of business, but at the same time, we want to be protected . . . the public seems to want regulation as a hedge against bad developments or bad actors, but they have doubts about whether it will be very effective."[24]

Division by Design

There is strong evidence to suggest that this division is driven in part by the corporate influences discussed in the last chapter and a concerted messaging effort. Naomi Oreskes and Erik Conway argue in their book *The Big Myth* that market proponents in the era of shareholder capitalism "didn't simply deify the marketplace; they also demonized government and this second half of their framework is arguably the more important." The book outlines decades of effort by American business to manufacture the belief that government "cannot improve the functioning of markets; it can only interfere. Governments therefore need to stay out of the way, lest they 'distort' the market and prevent it from doing its 'magic' . . . when left unfettered and unregulated, undisturbed and unperturbed."[25] This attitude can be seen in the statements of US presidents from Ronald Reagan ("Government is not the solution to our problem, government is the problem") to Bill Clinton ("The era of big government is over") to Donald Trump ("It is time to drain the swamp in Washington, D.C.")—all statements that demean the role and underestimate the abilities of the government. The question for the next era of capitalism is, how can government move to a more constructive, collaborative, and trusted role in the market?

Towards a More Collaborative (and Realistic) Partnership

Over the past century, the role of government in the economy shifted from Keynesian economics, which promoted a strong government role in managing the market, to neoclassical economics, which favored minimal government intervention and believed in the self-correcting nature of the economy. However, the neoclassical model is now showing signs of strain as it struggles to address widening income inequality and increasing climate change. A new model for the role of government is emerging, calling for a more active role in guiding the market and creating opportunities for businesses to thrive while serving society's needs.

This is not as much of a departure as some may think. The American economy has long had government intervention, including but not limited to support for the military-industrial complex, regulations to secure competition (antitrust and prohibitions on cartels), and government-supported financing of mass consumption through relatively easy credit.[26] The bailout of financial firms in 2008 under the guise of "too big to fail" and the transfer of private debt to public debt to finance the rescues makes it clear that the government plays a significant role in the economy, even in a system that claims to embrace neoliberal principles and the self-regulating capacity of markets. Indeed, in reality, no American business creates wealth by itself. It is part of a broader society and relies on the state for certain support, such as from schools and higher education; health and social services; policing and defense; research support; and infrastructures of transport, energy, water, and waste systems. Economic output has always been coproduced with interaction between the public and the private sectors.[27]

As we consider the role of government in an economy that will follow shareholder capitalism, economist Joseph Stiglitz points out that "[w]e have moved, by and large, to a more balanced position, one that recognizes both the power and the limitations of markets, and the necessity that government play a large role in the economy, though the bounds of that role remain in dispute."[28] This shift presupposes an ability of people in government to help manage the economy, an ability for which both Adam Smith and James Madison were skeptical. Certainly, economic experts were admittedly unable to predict the Great Recession of 2008. And the government has made missteps in market forays like its investment in Solyndra, a manufacturer of thin film solar cells that the Obama administration supported with a $535 million loan in 2009, hailing it as a leader in the sustainable energy sector. But the company could not compete with conventional solar panel manufacturers and filed for bankruptcy in 2011.[29]

But that is just one failed intervention among countless others that paid off. Whether it was the creation of land-grant colleges that educated the public starting in the 1860s; Social Security, CCC, or other New Deal programs that dug us out of the Great Depression in the 1930s; the GI Bill that helped train a generation of the workforce after World War II; or the Defense Advanced Research Projects Agency (DARPA) that gave us the internet, GPS, and countless other technologies used in nondefense sectors today, the government has always been present in the economy. Author Michael Lewis, in his book *The Fifth Risk*, details many of the important yet little-noticed functions that government agencies handle better than private industry, such as the protection of food safety or the oversight of spent nuclear resources. Further, he shows how a functioning economy depends on civil servants using the best data and science available to provide vital services to all Americans.[30]

The government also plays a crucial role in innovation, particularly in early-stage R&D. Economist Mariana Mazzucato points out that many of the technologies we enjoy today would not have been possible without the government. Google's search algorithm was supported by a grant from the National Science Foundation. Three companies founded by Elon Musk—Tesla, Solar-City, and SpaceX—jointly benefited from nearly $4.9 billion in public support of various kinds. Tracing the provenance of every component in the iPhone, she notes that the HTTP protocol was developed by British scientist at CERN in Geneva; the internet began as a network of computers called Arpanet, funded by the US Department of Defense, which was also behind the development of GPS, the hard disk drive, microprocessors, memory chips, and LCD display; Siri was the outcome of a Stanford Research Institute project commissioned by DARPA; the touchscreen was the result of graduate research at the University of Delaware, funded by the National Science Foundation and the CIA. "The more I looked," she says, "the more I realized: state investment is everywhere."[31] She has also noted, "From the internet to nanotechnology, most of the fundamental technological advances of the past half century—in both basic research and downstream commercialization—were funded by government agencies, with private businesses moving into the game only once the returns were in clear sight. . . . Entrepreneurs like Bill Gates and Steve Jobs were able to create great products because they surfed the waves of government-funded technologies."[32]

In offering an expanded set of tasks for the government (in addition to traditional checks and guardrails), the philanthropic investment firm Omidyar Network lays out four essential roles. First, government must drive innovation, growth, and investment via R&D, critical infrastructure, and other key activities. Second, government must deliver critical public goods and protect communities from bad actors, harmful side effects, and unexpected shocks. Third, government must be funded with appropriate revenue and the capabilities to execute on these mandates. And fourth, government must set policies that reflect our collective values, uniting common causes behind common purposes.[33]

Three government initiatives provide concrete examples of successful market interventions that reflect some of Omidyar's recommendations.

- The US Covid-19 vaccine effort was enabled by decades of long-term investments by the federal government in every aspect of the basic science, preclinical development, and clinical trials for the vaccines. Then, when the pandemic hit, the US government executed procurement contracts that greatly reduced market risks for pharmaceutical firms—a critical step to creating successful vaccines at speed and ensuring they were available to the US public.

- In 2022, the Inflation Reduction Act earmarked $369 billion for action to reduce greenhouse gas emissions, support clean energy, and encourage electrification. In its first year, the private sector announced more than $110 billion in new clean energy manufacturing investments, including more than $70 billion for electric vehicles. One analysis by a team of energy and sustainability researchers estimates that by 2035, the IRA's acceleration of green energy has the potential to reduce emissions across the US economy by 43–48 percent compared with 2005 levels through a combination of government and industry initiatives.[34]

- The 2022 Creating Helpful Incentives to Produce Semiconductors (CHIPS) and Science Act committed billions of dollars to bolster the economy in critical sectors (such as the semiconductor capacity), catalyze R&D, and create regional high-tech hubs with a bigger, more inclusive STEM workforce. The CHIPS and Science Act includes two notable provisions. First, any semiconductor manufacturer requesting over $150 million in direct funding under the act must submit plans for providing affordable, accessible, reliable, and high-quality child care for the workers who build and facilitate their plants.[35] Second, the act directs funding towards accelerating the growth of zero-carbon industries and conducting climate-relevant research. Combined with other recent legislation, federal government annual climate spending could triple this decade, reaching more than $521 billion by the end of the decade to accelerate the development and deployment of zero-carbon energy and to prepare for the impacts of climate change (see Figure 10.2).[36]

These examples highlight an emerging model for the role of government in the market. Alternatively called "supply-side progressivism," the "abundance agenda," or "industrial policy," the core idea is to use the power of government to modify the economy and foster growth in strategically important sectors.

FIGURE 10.2

Federal Spending on Climate Change, 1990–2029

The federal government's average annual climate spending is poised to triple this decade.

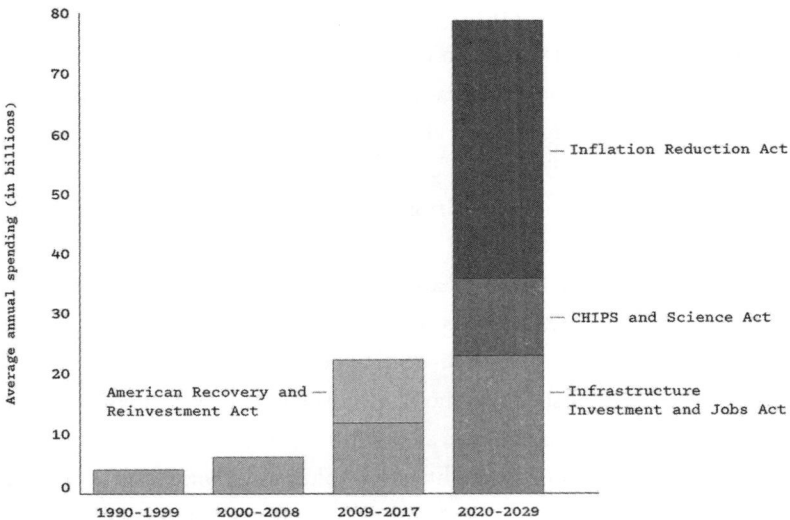

Source: L. Carey and J. Shepard, "Congress's climate triple whammy: Innovation, investment, and industrial policy," *RMI*, August 22, 2022, https://rmi.org/climate-innovation-investment-and-industrial-policy/ (accessed June 6, 2024). This image was originally published on the website TheAtlantic.com and is republished here with The Atlantic's and RMI's permission.

This elevated role for government has been anathema to both neoliberal and neoclassical thinking, both of which hold that the less government intervention in the economy, the better. But as the market increasingly shows itself unable to ensure widely shared prosperity, the desire for a stronger and collaborative government hand in the market is experiencing a resurgence in the United States and around the world, which many believe is a welcome development.[37] Rather than having continued debates over more money versus less money for government programs, the conversation can shift to spending more of the right kind of money that stimulates positive market outcomes.

What will this new arrangement look like? A first major change will be an increase in what has been called *supply-side progressivism*. Where traditional demand-side social policies focus on giving people money or vouchers to buy something they need (such as food stamps, Pell grants, housing vouchers, social security, child tax credits, and universal basic income), supply-side progressivism seeks to use government spending to more directly solve problems. For example, instead of simply lowering the cost of health insurance, the government could invest in promoting healthier lifestyles through exercise, diet, and other preventive measures. In addition, the government could combine price controls with new policies to encourage drug development, rather than solely focusing on lowering the costs of prescription drugs. While such interventions may face resistance from industries like insurance and pharmaceuticals, which currently profit from an inefficient system, they create incentives for these industries to adopt new profit-making structures. In the case of the drug industry, proper incentives could include increased funding for basic research, prizes for discovering drugs that treat specific conditions, or more public funding for drug trials.[38]

Another change will be politicians becoming more comfortable promoting market interventions because this new approach—what some commentators have called the *abundance agenda*—can appeal to people across the political spectrum. The journalist Derek Thompson explains in *The Atlantic* that if the problems we face are characterized as scarcity—not enough houses, doctors, or drugs—a mainstream liberal might seek a solution in which the government spends more money to help people out. Conversely, the typical conservative might think that the government is spending too much money and inflating the cost of these services, so we need to cut taxes and spending. Instead, Thompson writes that politicians need to target their messaging at how such interventions are focused on increasing the abundance of essential goods and allowing the market to solve the problem through innovation. This approach would appeal to liberals by providing for human welfare, and to libertarians by remedying places where bad rules are getting in the way of the common good. Thompson writes, "Altogether, America has too much venting and not enough inventing." If you want to solve the housing crisis, for example, make the regulations easier and more streamlined to build new houses, apartment complexes, and infrastructure. If you want better health care, pass laws to increase the number of US physicians by raising funding for federal residency programs, making it easier for foreign-born doctors to practice here and reducing regulatory barriers to increase access to telemedicine. Such efforts would appeal to a liberal's goal of addressing social needs and a conservative's goal of promoting national greatness, because, as Thompson writes, it would "grow the things that actually make a nation great—such as clean and safe spaces, excellent government services, fantastic living conditions, and broadly shared wealth."[39]

Whatever politicians, economists, and social commentators decide to call it, the "new" role of government in society will in fact be a return an old idea: *industrial policy*. Harvard Kennedy School of Government professor Dani Rodrik writes that "[i]ndustrial policy has been ubiquitous, and its prevalence predates the recent rise in its use and prominence in public discussions." But rather than viewing industrial policy as protectionism, trade barriers, and tariffs, whose purpose is to raise government revenues, play special interest politics, and favor certain industries, a recent shift has moved towards seeing it as "a way of promoting infant industries (such as textiles, ship building, heavy industry or most recently, chip manufacturing), large scale public research and development efforts (such as the space race or Project Warp Speed) and selective policies targeting specific industries at specific times of need (such as US manufacturing during World War II)."[40] Some categories of such policies can include supply-push policies, such as production and investment tax credits; demand-pull policies, such as federal procurement policies and made-in-America rules; RD&D policies, such as industry pilot projects (such as by the DOE) and regional innovation hubs; and market-balancing policies, such as carbon border adjustment mechanisms.

In her book *The Value of Everything: Making and Taking in the Global*

Economy, Mariana Mazzucato points out that the economy needs businesses who take risks. But private investment can be volatile and procyclical, reinforcing its own tendencies to both boom and bust. The government can stabilize demand when spending is low and stimulate the business sector when it becomes risk averse. It can do this through well-funded public R&D institutions and strong industrial policies, tilting the playing field towards socially desirable outcomes. In the end, she writes, creating economic value is a collective process. Innovation in the future's green technologies, for instance, requires both corporate investment and strong industrial policies that support all stages of the production process, from raw material sourcing to R&D and eventually the final product.[41]

This shift takes on new emphasis in an era in which geopolitics is ranked as the top risk to the global economy in 2024 by institutional investors. From wars in Ukraine and the Middle East to the threats of war in the Taiwan Strait, corporations have become both "the objects and instruments of foreign policy" as governments turn to sanctions, economic restrictions, and industrial policies to achieve geopolitical ends. This reoriented landscape requires government to work in partnership with the private sector if it hopes its efforts will succeed.[42]

One argument against industrial policy is that it often involves initial deficit spending, which some consider to be fiscally irresponsible. However, the role of deficits in economic health is a matter of debate among some experts. Some neoclassical and neoliberal economists view deficits as inherently problematic, contending that they can lead to economic instability and hinder long-term growth. On the other hand, proponents of alternative economic theories maintain that deficits are not necessarily the boogeyman they are often portrayed to be and that they can be a useful tool for stimulating economic growth and recovery, particularly during recessions. Economist Stephanie Kelton argues that it is not that high deficits cause recessions, but rather it is recessions that cause deficits to explode. Turning conventional government policies on their head, she asserts instead that austerity programs only make things worse. By withdrawing government spending to lower debt, the solution actually removes demand from the economy, which delays or even prevents recovery.[43] She endorses modern monetary theory (MMT), which holds that targeted government spending and debt can stimulate growth and create wealth for future generations. Kelton emphasizes that governments issuing their own currency cannot run out of money like households can. "Households are users of money; governments are issuers of money. . . . Government debt is nothing like personal debt." Nonetheless, it is not the imbalance between taxes collected and federal monies spent that matters. Rather, what matters is the balance of real resources to solve national challenges.[44]

Critics call MMT the "Magic Money Tree" and warn about inflation concerns. But in her book *The Deficit Myth: Modern Monetary Theory and the Birth of the People's Economy*, Kelton rebuts that she is not proposing unlimited deficit spending. Rather, she is challenging government officials to be strategic and focused in their spending to create the right kind of business activity and economic growth that is needed.[45] With no inflation and no bottlenecks, the government can address what she considers the true deficits, such as the good jobs deficit, the health care deficit, the education deficit, the infrastructure deficit, the green climate deficit, and the democracy deficit, with no fiscal constraint. MMT supports building an economy that is geared towards people over profits and people over balanced budgets. Just as the country grew its way out of World War II debt, she argues, spending for climate change is a way to boost the economy in a certain direction and moderate the costs later. And, just as was promoted by the New Deal in the 1930s, the government should become the employer of last resort, ensuring the unemployment rate remains continuously low.[46]

Dimitri Zenghelis at the London School of Economics views MMT as a framework that brings together Keynes's call for the "socialization of investment" to stabilize growth and Schumpeter's focus on punctuated equilibrium to drive mission-oriented innovation policy.[47] In his view, regulation should go beyond merely leveling the playing field; instead, it should actively tilt the playing field in favor of achieving publicly determined objectives. Just as welfare programs like the GI Bill in the postwar period and the information technology revolution at the turn of the twenty-first century ushered in economic growth and prosperity, new social missions must do the same today. "Foremost among them must be the transformative challenge of reducing and eventually eliminating greenhouse gas emissions to limit dangerous climate change, and of constraining the economy's wider environmental impacts within biophysical boundaries."[48]

A New Role for Government in a Twenty-First-Century World

As mentioned, Adam Smith outlined three essential tasks for government: "administration of justice," "maintaining certain publick institutions," and "protecting citizens." However, these responsibilities, while still crucial, are no longer sufficient to address the intricacies and challenges of a modern, globalized economy as vast and complex as that of the twenty-first century. As we move towards an economic system that prioritizes stakeholder value over shareholder primacy, redefining and expanding the scope of government intervention becomes a critical point of discussion and a catalyst for change. Consequently, government must extend far beyond Smith's three basic tasks; it should assume responsibility for supporting the market in other crucial ways:[49]

Policies That Elevate the Interests of the Future. In his book *Long Problems*, Oxford University professor Thomas Hale proposes that governments should develop something akin to sci-fi writer Kim Stanley Robinson's idea of a "ministry for the future,"[50] an organization that is mandated to consider long-term interests insulated from short-term pressures. This organization can help governments adopt informational tools to better understand the future and make it salient in the present for shifting society's preferences over time, yielding policies that must remain fluid for the long term, maintaining robust goals based on forward-planning processes while also subject to constant updating.[51]

Policies to Elevate the Role of Science in Business and Society. We now live in an age of misinformation and disinformation when public trust in academic institutions, governmental agencies, and other sources of scientific information is both critically important and rapidly eroding.[52] Many members of the public and even government leaders dangerously portray science as mere opinion. But in an era of environmental and social system upheaval, society cannot solve its greatest challenges if it does not have a common set of facts upon which to base its decisions. James Madison warned that "[a] popular government without popular information or the means of acquiring it is but a prologue to farce or tragedy or perhaps both. Knowledge will forever govern ignorance. And a people who mean to be their own Governors must arm themselves with the power knowledge gives."[53] Government needs to play a role in identifying, and where possible countering, misinformation and disinformation, while offering credible content on what scientific research has concluded and, importantly, how those conclusions were reached.

Policies That Reduce Consumption. Efforts are under way to reduce consumption of goods and resources and strive towards new models of "sustainable consumption."[54] Governments can support these efforts with policies that promote a circular economy (an economic system aimed at making the most of resources through reuse, repair, refurbishment, and recycling) and decoupling (the ability of an economy to grow without corresponding increases in environmental pressure, such as carbon emissions). What would this look like in practice? Urban design can cut the use of materials by shifting from "car habitats" to planning, zoning, and development policies that prioritize livability and new urbanism. Incentives could encourage corporations to eliminate planned obsolescence and decrease the use of more material and energy use to provide for our needs. For the consumer, policies could promote change in three areas: (1) improve consumption by encouraging more environmentally efficient or socially sustainable goods and services such as eco-labeled, organic, energy-efficient, ethical, or locally produced goods; (2) change consumption by encouraging a shift to other means of consumption, such as offering quality public transportation to replace the use of private automobiles, increasing access to plant-based proteins rather than meat, and increasing the use of shared products (such as cars) rather than buying your own; and (3) reduce the volume of consumption of goods and services such as reducing municipal waste by providing a viable compost stream, reducing food waste, changing fashion habits, offering mobility options to encourage less flying and driving, and creating incentives for living in smaller homes.[55]

Policies That Extend Planning Time Horizons. Policymakers tend to think in terms of election cycles. Business leaders tend to focus on quarterly or annual time frames. Everyday citizens struggle to sacrifice now for the sake of future generations. But such short-term thinking leads us to delay our response to critical issues, limiting the effectiveness of future responses.[56] To extend our horizons, regulators could encourage a reassessment of economic metrics such as discounted cash flows and gross domestic product and develop public and energy policies that facilitate long-term planning—for example, by implementing tax credits with forty- to sixty-year horizons. Such measures better align with the extended time scales of challenges like climate change, sea level rise, and carbon cycles, which unfold over decades, centuries, and even millennia.

Policies That Make Society More Adaptable and Resilient. The environment has entered a "new normal" that is less stable and prone to extreme weather events. Shifting the economy to prepare for this kind of uncertainty is falling to insurance companies to try to change underwriting policies to reflect climate and weather instability.[57] The government can play a role, too. The Federal Emergency Management Agency (FEMA) could revise its flood coverage and response away from rebuilding homes in perilous locations to relocating destroyed homes to more stable areas. Planning, zoning, and building standards could be redeveloped to plan for more frequent storm disasters. These kinds of policies can help us to recognize that the past is not always prologue for the future and that the environment that our children and grandchildren will grow up in is far different from the environment we grew up in.

Policies to Ensure Transparency and Accountability. Crony capitalism is always a threat when the government plays a stronger role in the market. Sometimes it is hard to tell the difference between legitimate regulatory processes and crony capitalism, as they often represent competing priorities. For example, the United Nations notes that global fishing subsidies are estimated to be as high as $35 billion. This industry support is understandable, at least politically and socially: fisheries are a key source of protein and livelihoods for millions in coastal communities. But at least $20 billion of that subsidy is directly contributing to overfishing, which in turn threatens the livelihoods of those very same coastal communities.[58]

In another example, explicit global fossil-fuel subsidies reached a record $1.7 trillion in 2022 (combined explicit and implicit subsidies were measured at $7 trillion);[59] the increase was in part an understandable effort to offset the global spike in energy prices caused by Russia's invasion of Ukraine and the economic recovery from the pandemic. However, these subsidies may have crossed the line into crony capitalism when they resulted in large multinational oil companies recording a record profit of $219 billion in the same year,[60] a particularly egregious market distortion given that 2023 was the hottest year on record due to climate change.

Similarly, between 2008 and 2010, a total of $222.7 billion in tax breaks and subsidies were given out in the United States while the nation faced the steepest recession in more than fifty years, with 56 percent of these benefits going to just four industries—finance; utilities; telecommunications; and oil, gas, and pipeline.[61] This concentration of benefits among a handful of industries during a time of widespread economic hardship raises questions about the fairness and legitimacy of these subsidies.

To prevent crony capitalism, governments often seek to implement robust transparency and accountability measures by disclosing the recipients and amounts of subsidies, conducting regular audits and impact assessments, and ensuring that subsidies are tied to specific, measurable outcomes that align with the public interest. By shining a light on these practices and holding decision makers accountable, the goal is to ensure that government interventions in the market serve the greater good rather than the narrow interests of a privileged few. But determining when economic support crosses the line into crony capitalism can be challenging.

Some on the right argue that financial support going to those who don't need it is a clear indicator, while also holding that economic inequality is justified by property rights and free markets' ability to raise overall living standards. Of course, these two beliefs are incompatible, leading to what Brink Lindsey and Steven Teles call the "conservative inequality paradox" in their book *The Captured Economy*.[62] "If our economy really is riddled with cronyism, then the beneficiaries must have pocketed large amounts of ill-gotten loot. . . . Either conservatives have overstated the amount of crony capitalism, or their dismissal of the concept of inequality as envy is misplaced."[63] Lindsey and Teles argue for a reevaluation of the knee-jerk defense of business interests and the automatic rejection of redistribution policies. Instead, they advocate for finding the right balance of market-oriented policies that simultaneously promote economic growth and address inequality.

To some on the left, however, crony capitalism can be measured in consolidation, when economic power is increasingly gathered in the hands of a savvy few, adept in using government power to attain private advantage.[64] This view seems more aligned with popular sentiment. Americans generally agree that lobbyists, major corporations, and banks have too much power, while state and local governments, the legal system, organized religion, and the military each have the right amount or too little power.[65] Only one-fifth of adults believe democracy is working "very well" in the United States, and two-thirds say "significant changes" are needed to governmental "design and structure."[66] A hands-off approach leads to extreme corporate power and extreme government control leads to crony capitalism. A more balanced approach is what is needed.

Markets Do Not Work Without the Government . . . and Effective Policies Work Best in Concert with the Private Sector

Rigid neoliberal ideologues might be surprised to find that they have more in common with advocates of government intervention than they initially thought, especially when such intervention is targeted and well-designed. Jerry Taylor, the former president and co-founder of the libertarian leaning Niskanen Center and long-time libertarian at think tanks like the Cato Institute, had an epiphany when he realized that "ideology encourages dodgy reasoning due to what psychologists call 'motivated cognition,' which is the act of deciding what you want to believe and using your reasoning power, with all its might, to get you there. Worse, it encourages fanaticism, disregard for social outcomes, and invites irresolvable philosophical disputes. It also threatens social pluralism—which is to say, it threatens freedom."[67] Taylor wrote this essay as a sort of catharsis as he made a transition in his thinking away from such ideological extremes and sought to find more balanced approaches. There were two issues in particular that moved Taylor. The first was climate change.

> The first pangs of doubt about my old ideological attachments arose from my loss of faith in the case against climate action. As I began to express doubts about the narratives offered by climate skeptics, I found it impossible to offer an argument that resonated with my libertarian colleagues. But just how, exactly, does an ideological commitment to limited government, free markets, and individual dignity inform an understanding of atmospheric physics or paleoclimate records? And what does libertarianism have to contribute regarding the case for hedging against incredibly dangerous risks stemming from the misuse of a common pool resource, such as the atmosphere? Libertarians have nothing at all to contribute to

the conversation about the science of climate change as *libertarians*. They could, however, marshal ideological insights to suggest the best means of addressing global warming if it indeed turns out to warrant a policy response (as I believe it does). For libertarians, that could mean a carbon tax, but for other, more hardline libertarians, it could mean that greenhouse gas emitters should be held liable for climate-related damages via common-law legal proceedings.[68]

The second issue for Taylor's conversion was the size and scale of the government.

Libertarians will argue passionately against the state but marshal little evidence about what sort of society might actually arise in the modern world were the state to largely disappear. Perhaps the most impressive intellectual ever to take up the libertarian cause—Robert Nozick—had absolutely nothing to say about that in *Anarchy, State, and Utopia* (my bible for most of my adult life). There is a good reason for this omission. Wherever we look around the world, when we see inconsequential governments with limited power, as libertarians would prefer, we see "failed states." How much liberty and human dignity can be found there? Very little.[69]

Indeed, Naomi Oreskes and Erik Conway argue that "the evidence suggests that higher levels of taxation and stronger degrees of regulation work better on certain metrics, notably the Human Development Index. . . . The US state that conservatives most love to hate for its high taxes and nanny-state mentality—Massachusetts—ranks number one on the HDI, closely followed by Connecticut, Minnesota, and New Jersey. In contrast, the bottom eight are all states whose voters tend to lean against government: Mississippi, West Virginia, Alabama, Arkansas, Kentucky, Louisiana, South Carolina and Tennessee."[70]

In fact, overall, "blue" states have HDIs similar to the Netherlands while "red" states are closer to Russia,[71] and they are quickly devolving from near parity on prosperity and income measures in 2008 to stark divergence ten years later (see Figure 10.3). Democratic districts in the US have seen their median household income increase from $54,000 in 2008 to $61,000 in 2018, while the income level in Republican districts declined from $55,000 to $53,000. At

FIGURE 10.3

Republican and Democratic Districts Are Rapidly Diverging

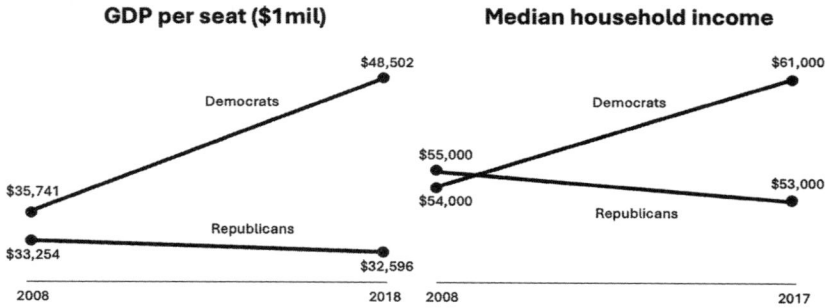

GDP per seat ($1mil)

$48,502

Democrats

$35,741

Republicans

$33,254

$32,596

2008   2018

Median household income

$61,000

Democrats

$55,000

$54,000

$53,000

Republicans

2008   2017

Source: M. Muro and J. Whiton, "America has two economies—and they're diverging fast," *Brookings* (blog), September 19, 2019.

the same time, GDP per seat in Democratic-voting districts grew from $35.7 billion in 2008 to $48.5 billion, while Republican districts saw their output decline slightly from $33.2 billion to $32.6 billion. "Blue" territories have seen their productivity climb from $118,000 per worker in 2008 to $139,000 in 2018, while Republican-district productivity stayed the same at about $110,000.[72] As one commentator writes, "They may as well be two distinct countries within the United States."[73]

While "blue" states score more highly on a range of HDI metrics, one significant additional consideration is oil. Most major producers of oil and natural gas are "red" states, with Texas and North Dakota ranking first and second and Alaska and Wyoming ranking sixth and eighth. This is important for how the inevitable switch to renewable energy will affect American politics[74] and calls attention to the need for a government role that helps to manage the just and orderly transitions needed on climate change, inequality, and a host of other issues facing this country. A revitalized government, working in partnership with the private sector through a comprehensive industrial policy framework, is essential to navigate these challenges and chart a course towards a more sustainable, equitable, and prosperous future for all Americans.

Part IV

BUSINESS SCHOOL BUILT ON A BALANCED CURRICULUM

ELEVEN

Outdated Business School Principles and Concepts

Efficiency, Value, Prosperity, and Metrics

"Bad management theories are destroying good management practices."
—SUMANTRA GHOSHAL, LONDON BUSINESS SCHOOL

Why grow? I asked this question to a class of MBA students after we had thoroughly dissected a case study on Walmart's global growth strategy. For some students, the question was ridiculous. Some thought it just odd. But for others, a lightbulb went off in their heads. They had never been encouraged to question growth. It was just taken for granted that it was necessary. Richard Reeves at the Brookings Institution writes that "capitalism is intrinsically growth-oriented. Markets don't work well in a stationary state; they are like sharks, either moving or dead."[1] But is that always true?

In my classes, I have witnessed the transformative power of prompting students to challenge the long-held assumptions that underpin their business education. Often, they come away more certain of these beliefs—but not always. As the Indian scholar Sumantra Ghoshal argues, "Bad management theories are destroying good management practices." Ghoshal believed that business schools need to teach new models and metrics, but also "stop a lot they currently do."[2] First, we need to rethink the goals of business, delving into our understanding of efficiency, value, prosperity, and the metrics used to measure performance. Second, it's essential to reimagine the ways businesses produce benefits through the market, examining our views on competition and trade. Third, we should reexamine market limits, scrutinizing our approaches to growth and consumption.

It is important to note that these examinations cannot be comprehensive at this time. We are in the midst of a discontinuity in the market, a shift from shareholder capitalism to some other form. In the interregnum, we are witnessing a confusing period when a cacophony of ideas is competing for attention on how to adapt the global economy to address our systemic challenges. Eventually a dominant model will emerge, and the chaos will settle out.[3] Until then, business schools must recognize that we do not possess all the answers; all we can do is ask the right questions and use our teaching and our research to help find their answers. That will be made easier by a redesign of our siloed curriculum, both as it exists within the business school and as it relates to disciplines around the university. To begin, we must question a few fundamental assumptions.

Technology Alone Will Not Solve Society's Challenges

The first received wisdom that business schools must question is the overriding belief that technological change alone will solve all society's problems. For example, innovations such as electric cars and rooftop solar—or likely even large innovations such as artificial intelligence or geo-engineering—will not offer a sufficient solution to climate change. It is tempting to believe that we only need to create better gadgets, and we will decarbonize the global economy. But unfortunately, we will need to be far more creative and imaginative than that.

To be sure, technology will play an important role. Business, for example, is developing the next generation of renewable energy, which has become the fastest-growing energy source in the United States. Innovations in solar photovoltaic power have led to a dramatic 99 percent decrease in price between 1980 and 2012,[4] and an increase of 90 percent installed capacity from 2000 to 2020—on course to climb to 35 percent of total US renewable generation by 2050.[5] Similarly, the cost of installed wind power has dropped from 7 cents per kWh in 2009 to below 2 cents in 2019.[6] Wind power contributed 10.3 percent of total US utility-scale electricity generation in 2022, up from basically zero twenty years before.[7] These are encouraging developments; without them our chances of addressing climate change would be nearly impossible.

But such technological advancements likely won't be the answer on their own. We cannot assume that humanity can continue its present trajectory of seeking endless economic growth and consumption. A popular equation for evaluating humanity's impact on the environment is called IPAT. Our environmental impact (I) is the product of population (P) multiplied by affluence (A) multiplied by technology (T). Global population continues to increase but may peak in the late twenty-first century. Affluence will likely continue to rise because active reductions in global wealth are contrary to the promise of a market economy (more on this later). So that leaves us with technology to reduce our impact on the natural world. But is this equation incomplete? It seems unlikely that current market forces and their resulting technologies will be sufficient to solve climate change. Do we have to also change our beliefs, values, culture, and actions?

One study finds that if European countries rely solely on technological advances, they won't be able to limit global heating to 1.5°. Without changing our lifestyles, the study finds that by 2050, there will be a yearly "overshoot" of 3.1 metric tons of CO_2-equivalent for every EU citizen.[8] Another study calculates the technological solutions discussed at the 2021 UN Conference of the Parties meetings in Glasgow (COP26) depend primarily on three resources— non-emitting electricity generated by hydropower, renewables, or nuclear fission; carbon capture and storage (CCS); and biomass—and finds that there is "no possibility" that these technologies could scale to anywhere near the levels required by the plans discussed at COP26 by 2050.[9] The danger of relying entirely on technology is that we can become complacent, changing little to face up to our challenges while gambling that technology will eventually solve them for us. Sometimes that technology will come; sometimes it doesn't come.

And sometimes that technology creates other problems, what MIT emeritus professor John Ehrenfeld calls "fixes that fail."[10] History is replete with examples of technological "solutions" that yielded unintended consequences. PCBs (polychlorinated biphenyls), introduced as coolants and insulating fluids, led to widespread environmental contamination and health hazards. CFCs (chlorofluorocarbons), once hailed for their use in refrigeration and aerosol sprays, contributed significantly to ozone layer depletion. Single-use plastics, initially celebrated for their convenience and hygiene benefits, have resulted in pervasive pollution and long-term ecological damage. What's more, new technologies are often designed to perpetuate the status quo without considering their broader impacts. For example, the move to electrify the automobile fleet is a noble effort in so far as it goes. But while the EV is a great invention, it is still another car. As we invest heavily in the transition of the automobile as well as the charging network, is the answer really another car? Or is the answer a transition to more sustainable forms of mobility, such as intermodal public transportation that is more efficient and convenient for people's travel needs? In short, we need to temper our faith in the market and technology. Perhaps environmental writer Bill McKibben put it best when he wrote that

> the environmental optimists are wrong: there is no market-oriented technological fix. Simply and radically, people have to change their lives. . . . More money makes reducing smog easier, because you can afford to build better cars; more money makes dealing with the greenhouse effect harder, because you can afford to buy more cars. So, the dream that we will grow rich enough to turn green is simply that—a dream, and one that will turn into a nightmare if we try to follow it. We face tough choices. The most pragmatic realism, rooted in the molecular structure of CO_2, demands electric cars. It also demands nothing less than heresy: an all-out drive for deep thrift, for self-restraint, for smaller families. Brute objectivity requires new ideas about what constitutes sufficiency: smaller homes, more food grown locally, repair instead of replacement.[11]

Marine biologist and influential environmental writer Rachel Carson argued as early as the 1960s that the assumption that technology can heal and preserve the natural world is founded on a belief in humanity's ability to dominate natural systems, something she says epitomizes the "arrogance of man." While she did not oppose technological development, Carson felt strongly for a sense of humility and limits in its use.[12] She advocated for a mindful approach towards nature, emphasizing the need for a balance between human requirements and ecosystem health. She states, "We are not being truly civilized if we concern ourselves only with the relation of man to man. What is important is the relation of man to all life. This has never been so tragically overlooked as in our age, when through our technology we are waging war against the natural world. It is a valid question whether any civilization can do this and retain the right to be called civilized."[13]

The existing business curriculum has much to teach about how to bring new technology into the world, drawing from a wide range of disciplines including entrepreneurship, organizational transformation, performance measurement, operations, marketing, leadership, and governance. However, it often overlooks more fundamental questions raised by thinkers like McKibben and Carson. This omission can lead to an overemphasis on innovation in business schools, inadvertently simplifying the resolution of climate issues. In the long term, as McKibbon argues, we will have to change the way we live, think, and act.

Business schools have an obligation to make students aware of a harsh truth: if we continue to desire perpetual economic expansion, endless population growth, and more stuff to buy and throw away, then we will remain stuck in the convenient and lazy mindset that technology will fix the problem for us. However, if we implement systemic changes to the structure and goals of our economy, we stand a chance of diverting from this destructive trajectory.[14]

Rethinking What Business Strives For: Efficiency, Value, Prosperity, and Metrics

To ensure they play a crucial role in this shift, business schools must rethink a series of explicit and implicit assumptions that underpin orthodox business education. For instance, nature is valued purely in terms of its use for humans. Efficiency is a key emphasis across most modules, which often means reducing costs and increasing production, without fully considering broader consequences. Approaches like discounted cash flow analysis, which emphasizes short-term financial performance, and traditional national measures of economic success like gross domestic product (GDP), are taught while more holistic approaches to measuring societal and corporate value are ignored. It's important for business schools to critically assess the limitations of these models and metrics and to redefine the objectives of business decision making to be more comprehensive and sustainable.

A Better Way to Value Nature

Business education tends to treat nature primarily as a limitless source of materials for our production systems and a limitless sink for wastes that come from those systems. But nature also has value that traditional business models cannot see. For example, viewing a forest only in terms of its timber value can lead to overlooking its other benefits, like helping to control climate change by absorbing carbon dioxide, reducing flood risks by absorbing rain, supporting diverse wildlife, and maintaining complex and interconnected ecosystems. This approach also fails to recognize any deeper significance or purpose that the existing forest might hold. So, the simple act of cutting down a forest and replanting it with acres of corn, wheat, barley, or even more trees is not equivalent; it destroys the ecosystem and its many known and unknown values.

Suzanne Simard, a Canadian scientist at the University of British Columbia, explores how the underground networks of forests characterized by fungi and roots facilitate communication and interaction between trees and plants within an ecosystem. Her work identified something called a hub tree, or "mother tree," which acts as central hub for vast underground networks that provide carbon and nutrients to support seedlings and baby trees.[15] This work challenged traditional views of the complexity of forests and served as the primary inspiration for a central character in Richard Powers's 2018 Pulitzer Prize–winning novel *The Overstory*.[16] Simard's work is prompting us to reconsider how we extract natural resources and to fully appreciate the comprehensive value these ecosystems offer.

To come to terms with the value that nature provides to us, thirteen economists, ecologists, and geographers analyzed seventeen ecosystem services in 1997 and determined the economic value for nature to the human economy as being between $16 and $54 trillion per year, with a likely figure of at least $33 trillion.[17] Many bristled at the idea of placing an economic value on nature, but the researchers used the conclusion to highlight an important point. If one compares the figure to the $18 trillion gross national product (GNP) of the world (at the time of the study), it becomes clear that the services provided by nature exceed the services provided by the human economy. Protecting nature, they argue, should therefore be given greater importance in relation to our own economic considerations.

A Better Way to Think About Sustainability

Business education will be blind to the value nature provides until it integrates natural science, ecology, and business strategy in a way that helps students understand the impact and benefits of business decisions on the natural environment. In addition, incorporating social and political science is crucial to comprehend how business activities influence society. This awareness is key to differentiating between two prevailing economic approaches to valuing nature: "weak sustainability" and "strong sustainability."

Weak sustainability assumes that natural capital (an economic term for the world's stock of natural resources) and manufactured capital (human-made assets like machinery, buildings, and technology, used to produce goods and services) are essentially substitutable and there are no essential differences between the kinds of well-being they generate. The only thing that matters is the total value, which should be at least maintained or ideally increased for the sake of future generations. So, for example, it does not matter whether the current generation uses up nonrenewable resources or emits greenhouse gases into the atmosphere as long as there is a greater source of wealth and technology left to the next generation, such as machines, roads, ports and capital, to fix their problems. The Environmental Kuznets Curve (see Figure 11.1) supports the weak sustainability model, in which an economy must initially tolerate increased levels of pollution to attain a corresponding level of eco-

FIGURE 11.1

Environmental Kuznets Curve

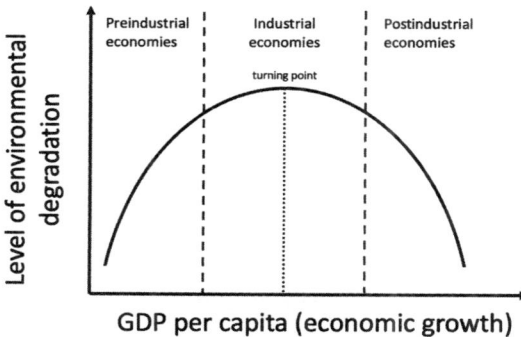

GDP per capita (economic growth)

Source: Figure created by author.

nomic growth. But it eventually reaches a turning point at which pollution decreases because the economy has reached a level at which people have the desire and the economic means to address it.

The school of so-called strong sustainability counters that nature is not a mere stock of resources but rather a network of ever-changing living and nonliving elements that interact in ways that determine the ecosystem's capacity to provide for human society. Arguing that natural and manufactured capital are not substitutable, they point out that the Environmental Kuznets Curve may work for some natural resources (local air and water) but not for others (notably transboundary ones such as the global climate). What's more, some environmental damages are irreversible. We can go too far with levels of pollution (such as greenhouse gas emissions or fisheries collapse) and doom a future generation to a problem that they cannot fix. This view was first articulated in the 1972 report *The Limits to Growth*, which argued that our limited understanding of the hazards of certain types of pollution, the location or level of critical thresholds, and the joint effects of combinations of pollutants can lead us to underestimate the true harmfulness of our economic growth.[18]

One final argument against weak sustainability and the Kuznets Curve is called the Jevons paradox, which holds that people consume more when products are made more efficient.[19] For instance, more energy-efficient LCD screens has led to screens being placed in restaurants, in elevators, and on billboards. So, while pollution may decline with rising affluence, other variables such as energy, land, and resource use (sometimes called the "ecological footprint") may not. Regrettably, conventional business education tends to overlook the crucial principles of strong sustainability and the notable shortcomings inherent in the widely accepted weak sustainability perspective.

A Better Way to Measure Efficiency

In business education, the pursuit of efficiency is universally accepted as beneficial. Certainly, if we reduce prices, it's efficient for the consumer; if we increase profits, it's efficient for the investor. But is this always a good thing? We tend to optimize efficiency on one metric, leaving us blind to impacts elsewhere in the system. What if reducing prices involves moving production overseas, leaving entire communities devastated by the closure of local businesses? What if aggregate efficiency improvements are not evenly distributed, making some constituents better off while impoverishing others?

Unfortunately, such questions are overlooked in business education. And the results can be seen in the behavior of business students after they graduate. A 2022 study in the National Bureau of Economic Research examined businesses in the United States and Denmark and found that managers with a business degree reduced their employees' wages by 6 percent over a five-year period with no improvement in output, investment, or employment growth, while nonbusiness managers shared profits with their workers. The study concludes that these outcomes are the product of "practices and values acquired in business education."[20] Texas A&M Law School professor William Magnuson writes that business school graduates often emerge with a mindset shaped by an overly narrow focus: "Market morality has given way to market efficiency. If a company is profitable, it must be efficient, and efficiency is the good we are after. . . . We have abandoned the founding purpose of the corporation as a tool for crafting a flourishing society."[21]

Guiding this short-sighted approach to management is a key concept in economic theory, known as Pareto efficiency (or Pareto optimality). An outcome is called Pareto efficient if resources have been allocated in such a way that it is impossible to redistribute them so that at least one person is better off, and nobody is worse off. In 1954, economists Kenneth Arrow and Gerard Debreu published a general equilibrium model that argued that perfectly competitive free markets eventually result in a Pareto efficient outcome in which prices will balance aggregate supply with aggregate demand for every commodity in the economy.[22] The model is used as a general reference for other microeconomic models of competitive economy and is a crucial part of general equilibrium theory in business and economics. But Pareto efficiency does not always lead to desirable outcomes. Economist Amartya Sen pointed this out, arguing Pareto efficiency makes no allowance for freedom and equity. He writes, "There is a danger in being exclusively concerned with Pareto-optimality. An economy can be optimal in this sense even when some people are rolling in luxury and others are near starvation as long as the starvers cannot be made better off without cutting into the pleasures of the rich. . . . In short, a society or an economy can be Pareto-optimal and still be perfectly disgusting."[23] Within business schools, we have focused too much attention on Pareto efficiency and not enough on distribution and fairness. This narrow focus can be seen in metrics we use and values these metrics profess, notably discounted cash flows and GDP.

Better Metrics for Corporate and National Performance

A dollar today is worth more than a dollar tomorrow. This is true in many cases and is a staple in business education. But it can also be overdone. In a challenge to the orthodoxy of discounted cash flow analysis, economist Nicholas Stern stirred a healthy debate in 2007 when he questioned the use of discount rates when calculating the future costs and benefits of climate change mitigation and adaptation.[24] Using an unusually low rate of 1.4 percent, he argued that it is inherently unethical to use standard discount rates on certain issues. For example, most large multinational corporations use a discount rate between 10 percent and 15 percent in business valuations. But a discount rate of 10 percent has the implicit assumption that anything ten years out and longer is worthless. Is that true? Arturo Cifuentes and David Espinoza argue that valuation techniques like the discounted cash flow method are "anchored in arcane ideas" that "favor short term gains at the expense of future generations."[25] That is the future of humanity's children and grandchildren, and the environment that they will depend upon has value far beyond what discounted cash flow, or indeed any economic analysis, can fully provide.

It is interesting to note that flaws in discounted cash flow analysis have been observed for decades. In 1928, Cambridge economist Frank Ramsey called discount rates "a practice which is ethically indefensible and arises merely from the weakness of the imagination."[26] In 1948, economist Roy Harrod argued that discounting future utility "is a weakness" and pure time preference is "a polite expression for rapacity and the conquest of reason by passion."[27] In 2019, economist Robert Solow argued that "no generation 'should' be favored over any other. . . . We can think of intergenerational discounting as a concession to human weakness or as a technical assumption of convenience (which it is)."[28] Yet in most business school courses, the metric is often used without any of this context. While an introductory accounting class might briefly touch upon these criticisms, they are typically set aside as students regularly apply discounted cash flow analysis in their subsequent courses, reinforcing its unchallenged acceptance.

GDP is another dominant metric with major flaws. It is calculated as the sum of the value of goods and services produced over a given time period and is used as a measure of national economic health. But, as the journalist Justin Fox points out, GDP is problematic for at least three reasons. "First, it is flawed even on its own terms: It misses lots of economic activity (unpaid household work, for example) and, as a single-number representation of vast, complex systems, is inevitably skewed. Second, it fails to account for economic and environmental sustainability. And third, readily available alternative measures may reflect well-being far better, by considering factors such as educational achievement, health, and life expectancy."[29] Even economist Simon Kuznets, who developed the first version of GDP in 1937, warned that we should not confuse the economy's total output with economic well-being.[30] And yet, that is what we do in business school, in business, in politics, and in society.

GDP measures national health only in terms of the movement of money. But some money movements are good, and others are bad. I, for example, may choose to eat all my meals at Krispy Kreme Donuts and McDonalds, and GDP will go up. Then I have a heart attack and go to the hospital, and GDP goes up. Then I die and my family pays for a funeral and burial, and GDP goes up again. Are all these of equal value? Of course not.[31] Does this kind of example play out in real life?[32] Yes. The country of Madagascar sought to increase GDP by increasing its production and export of wood. But the country deforested at such an alarming rate that it hampered future opportunities from this renewable resource. The goal of GDP growth sent them in the wrong direction.[33] No wonder the World Health Organization called GDP "an inappropriate measure of progress that perversely rewards profit-generating activities which harm people and destroy ecosystems."[34]

What are we really trying to measure? The US economy, for example, grew at a rate of about 5 percent in 2023, as measured by real gross domestic product. But while the country ranks number one in the world for GDP at $27 trillion, it ranks number twenty-five in the Social Progress Index, where it scores poorly on environmental performance, access to quality education, and health care. GDP is also skewed towards the wealthy.[35] Indeed, it is mathematically possible for a GDP growth rate of 3 percent to equate to a 10 percent growth rate for the rich, no growth for the middle class, and a loss for the poor. This has played out in real life, as the pursuit of economic growth since the beginning of the shareholder capitalism era has contributed to a rise in inequality, mortality rates, and political polarization.[36] In the United States, only the top 1 percent have gained from GDP growth since 1980.[37] "You can churn out all the GDP you want," says Harvard Business School professor Rebecca Henderson, "but if the suicide rates go up, and the depression rates go up, and the rate of children dying before they're four goes up, it's not the kind of society you want to build."[38] Martin Kirk, head of strategy for The Rules, a global network of activists, writers, artists, and others who work to challenge the root causes of global poverty and inequality, points out that

> [g]lobally, the trends are clear. Since 1990, global gross domestic product . . . has increased 271 per cent, and yet both the number of people living on less than $5 a day, and the number of people going hungry have also increased, by 10% and 9% respectively. Add to that the wage stagnation across the developed world and increasing inequality both within and between countries pretty much everywhere, and the shakiness of this basic logic becomes evident. . . . As we grow, so we destroy. . . . This is the logic of the cancer cell, but at least in medicine we recognise it as the definition of a disease; in politics and economics we call it progress.[39]

Various alternatives to GDP are under development, though they often get no more than a passing mention at business schools, if at all. These include the Genuine Progress Indicator, UN Human Development Index, UN Inclusive Wealth Report, Happy Planet Index (New Economic Forum), Food Sustainability Index (Barilla Center for Food and Nutrition), Ecological Footprint (Global Footprint Network), and Gross National Happiness (Bhutan), just to name a few. Former French president Nicolas Sarkozy formed a commission in 2010 to look at how GDP might be reformed. Led by economists Amartya Sen and Joseph Stiglitz, the report recommended new metrics that shift economic emphasis from simply the production of goods to a broader measure of overall well-being.[40] These metrics included addressing how GDP fails to account for wealth passed to future generations, economic inequality (noting that average income increases can still leave most people worse off), and the environmental impacts of economic decisions.

At the heart of these efforts to reform economic measurement is a deeper reality: to meet our current challenges, we need to rethink our approach to consumption itself. We need to look beyond money as the only measure of value, and rethink how business creates that value.

Reimagining How Business Provides Benefit: Competition and Trade

The prevailing competition models in business education often rely on aggressive metaphors of warfare, conquest, and dominance. Likewise, the standard models of trade prioritize overall efficiency, often overlooking the fact that this pursuit benefits some while disadvantaging others. While these models may appear straightforward and manageable in an academic setting, they fail to accurately reflect the complexities and needs of real-world dynamics, especially in addressing our collective challenges.

Market Competition Is Not (Always) War

It is common for business school students to be told to "capture market share," "steal customers," "defend position," "rally the troops," "establish a beachhead," and "counterattack."[41] In their book *Hardball*, George Stalk and Rob Lachenauer, two directors of The Boston Consulting Group, offer their "hardball manifesto," in which "hardball competitors" can "unleash massive and overwhelming force, exploit anomalies, devastate profit sanctuaries, raise competitors' costs, and break compromises" to "gain extreme competitive advantage—neutralizing, marginalizing, or even destroying competitors." Firms should be willing to "hurt their rivals," be "ruthless" and "mean," and "enjoy watching their competitors squirm."[42] In their accompanying *Harvard Business Review* article, "Hardball: Five Killer Strategies for Trouncing the Competition," they contrast "winners in business" who "play rough and don't apologize for it" with "softball players," who by contrast "aren't intensely serious about winning." They go on to state that the recent focus of management science "around soft issues such as leadership, corporate culture, knowledge management, talent management, and employee empowerment has encouraged the making of softball players."[43]

What are the unintended consequences of such bellicose metaphors? As Mark Chussil writes in the *Harvard Business Review*, such language makes "an implicit statement about the nature of competing businesses." Other firms are seen as "enemies who see us as enemies."[44] This is not the only way to run a business, nor is it often the best way if you hope to stay in business for the long term. And this is not the posture it takes to creatively address our collective and systemic challenges like climate change and income inequality. Instead, there exist opportunities for companies to work together in a collaborative fashion, something that is not possible if the mindset and reputation of the company is to be "ruthless" and "mean." Sometimes business strategy involves looking to novel and collaborative partnerships with competitors, as well as nonprofits, government, and seemingly unrelated companies to create new types of business models.

In one example, the Ford Motor Company experimented with an unusual partnership between Whirlpool, Sunpower, Eaton, Infineon, KB Homes, and Georgia Tech in the MyEnergi Lifestyle initiative to envision how future American homes would be integrated and optimized in a holistic and efficient way. The core motivation behind this effort is that home solar panels use the photons produced by sunlight to generate direct current (DC) electricity which is turned into alternating current (AC) before being fed into the home's wiring system. But appliances, like computers, use a transformer to turn that AC power back to DC power. This is wasteful, and the partnership examined the feasibility of an entirely DC home. This would require DC-powered appliances, like dishwashers and driers, which could then be further optimized by employing grid-monitoring technologies that inform the clothes washer when to run or the refrigerator when to go into the defrost cycle based on when demand is lowest (or in the event of real-time energy pricing, when energy is cheapest). All these coordinated efforts would make the home and the grid more energy efficient at a systemic level and not just on an individual component basis.

Other times businesses can engage in both competition and cooperation with suppliers, customers, and other firms at the same time, producing complementary or related products. Called "coopetition," this is a frequent strategy in the technology industry, where cooperation between competitors allows them to share unique complementary assets to achieve common gains. Despite being fierce competitors in the smartphone market, for example, Samsung supplies key components such as screens and memory chips for Apple's iPhones. This partnership allows them to leverage each other's strengths for mutual benefit, despite their rivalry in selling finished products.

A related model, "pre-competitive collaboration," involves two or more companies coming together to address a shared problem that doesn't have an impact on direct business competition or contribute to unfair advantage.

This model differs from other forms of private-sector collaboration in that it takes place before differentiation in the marketplace occurs. So, for example, a group of companies could develop common metrics and strategies around issues like offering a living wage, creating gender salary parity, reducing carbon emissions, eliminating the destructive effects of palm oil production, increasing sustainable yields of fisheries, and other issues for the long-term benefit of society.[45] IMAGINE is a nonprofit organization that is trying to put this idea into practice, convening coalitions of "Hero CEOs" working together in a pre-competitive fashion with other corporate leaders across industries to make positive impactful changes and raise the bar together.

Limitations of Neoliberal Free Trade

The dominant Ricardian model of comparative advantage is built on the idea of exploiting country-level differences in labor, capital, and resources in trade relations so that countries can benefit by reaching agreement that allows each to do what it does comparatively well and achieve economies of scale in production. That is, if each country produces a limited range of goods, it can produce each of these goods at a larger and more efficient scale than if it tried to produce everything on its own.

But if comparative advantage exploits the advantages a country possesses in providing cheaper goods and services, we must also consider how free trade creates unfair distributional consequences for people who lack power.[46] While trade may lead to growth for some within the economy (namely those with capital invested), they can leave others (namely labor) devastated. The 1992 North American Free Trade Agreement (NAFTA), for example, increased trade overall between the United States, Canada, and Mexico. But it also moved production capacity from the United States to neighboring countries with cheaper labor, leaving entire local communities devastated by the closure of local businesses. In the wake of NAFTA, the US auto sector lost roughly 350,000 jobs between 1994 and 2000, while Mexican auto sector employment increased from 120,000 to 550,000 workers.[47]

On a more global level, trade has caused tensions between developed and developing nations. Some have even argued that it has fueled the rise of terrorism: when developed nations exploit resources in developing countries without fair economic returns to the local populace, it can lead to social unrest and support for extremist groups.[48] Indeed, free trade has increased global power imbalances dramatically. Financier, philanthropist, and political activist George Soros emphasizes the moral dimensions of global financial markets, noting their immense size and power. According to Soros, these markets can destabilize a country's economy by freely moving vast sums of capital across the world. He contrasts this with domestic trade, such as within the United States, where various social and political institutions provide checks and balances, curbing certain market behaviors. However, Soros points out that these regulatory forces are absent in international markets. So, a trader in New York can press a switch and move large amounts of capital out of Asia and unwittingly (or indifferently) cause the Asian financial crisis.[49]

Beyond labor, should a country with the resources to dispose of toxic pollution exploit this comparative advantage in the world marketplace? This very notion was suggested in an internal memo from Lawrence Summers, then chief economist for the World Bank, to some colleagues in December 1992.[50] He argued that dirty industries should be moved to less developed countries since poor countries will lose less money because they have less to begin with, and the demand for a clean environment for aesthetic and health reasons is likely to have very high income-elasticity (think the Kuznets Curve). The ensuing controversy forced Mr. Summers to clarify that it "is not my view, the World Bank's view, or that of any sane person that pollution should be encouraged anywhere, or that dumping of untreated toxic wastes near the homes of poor people is morally or economically defensible. My memo tried to sharpen the debate on important issues by taking as narrow-minded an economic perspective as possible."[51] Perhaps—but in revealing the absurdity of narrow economic arguments (intentionally or not), Summers presented a critical challenge to those who support both free trade and a clean environment.

Now is an essential time for business schools to raise questions about international trade. The global economic system stands at a crossroads, with growing nationalism in the United States and China, Russia's invasion of Ukraine, and supply-chain vulnerabilities exposed during the Covid-19 pandemic all indicating that the status quo may be under threat. Countries have begun recognizing the challenges and dangers that come with interdependence.[52] In the wake of the Russian invasion of Ukraine, for example, western European nations have taken steps to decouple from Russian natural gas. Similarly, in the US, there's growing debate about reducing economic ties with China, particularly as China adopts a more assertive global stance and shows signs of being an unreliable trade partner. To be sure, the economies of China and the United States may be too deeply entwined to be separated without causing chaos. But the point stands: business schools must avoid treating global trade as an unchangeable certainty. It's also essential not only to consider who benefits from global trade but also to understand the human costs involved.

Reexamining Limits on the Market: Growth and Consumption

Karl Johan Perrson, the CEO of H&M,[53] once asked, "What would it mean if we all consumed 20% less? I believe it would be catastrophic. It would mean 20% less jobs, 20% less taxes, 20% less money for schools, doctors, roads. The global economy would collapse. I'm firmly convinced that growth has made the world a better place today than it was 20 years ago. And it will be better in 20 years than it is today."[54] Is this true? If it is, we face what Author J. B. Mackinnon calls the "consumer's dilemma." In his book *The Day the World Stops Shopping*, he writes that "the planet says we consume too much: in North America, we burn the earth's resources at a rate five times faster than they can regenerate. And despite our efforts to 'green' our consumption—by recycling, increasing energy efficiency, or using solar power—we have yet to see a decline in global carbon emissions. The economy says we must always consume more [but] . . . the 21st century has brought a critical dilemma into sharp relief: we must stop shopping."[55] To examine this dilemma, he asks the question, What would really happen if we simply stopped shopping? And he asked it just as the pandemic began a natural experiment. What he found was not economic collapse but rather an economic and social adjustment as some people invested more in their physical and emotional wellness, the pleasure of caring for their possessions, and closer relationships with the natural world and one another. Unfortunately, the pandemic also hampered such social connection, leaving many isolated and anxious, limiting the extent of the social change possible. Regardless, his book questions the premise that the economy must always grow, particularly in the form of impulse buying, vanity, and the desire to keep up with others.

The rub is that business education is predicated on a belief that the economy can and must continue to grow. The problem is that perpetual economic growth is not possible, and the shibboleth that growth is essential for human flourishing creates a trap that many see no way out of. Paul Farrell writes in the *Wall Street Journal* that "we are addicted to the myth of perpetual economic growth" and it is "killing America."[56] We must begin to teach about limits to growth and different kinds of growth.

Limits to Growth

In 1798, Thomas Robert Malthus wrote his famous "Essay on the Principles of Population,"[57] in which he argued for the first time that there may be limits to the carrying capacity of the Earth. He reasoned that the rate of growth of the population exceeded the rate of growth of food production and, eventually, humanity would face starvation. While his premise may have been sound, some of his underlying assumptions and his conclusions were not. He failed to anticipate technological advancements in pesticides, fertilizers, and commercial farming techniques. Yet his central argument has remained in many forms, with many supporters and detractors. In 1968, Stanford University ecologist Paul Ehrlich wrote the best-selling book *The Population Bomb*,[58] in which he predicted worldwide famine and other major societal upheavals if we did not limit population growth. That prophesy also did not come true.

In 1992, Donella Meadows, Dennis Meadows, and Jorgen Randers wrote *Beyond the Limits* (a follow-up to the 1972 book *The Limits to Growth*) in which they used systems dynamics models to come to a similar conclusion that "human use of essential resources and generation of pollutants has surpassed sustainable rates. . . . Unless there are significant reductions in material and energy flows, the world faces an uncontrolled decline in per capita food output, energy use and industrial production. . . . In order to avoid this decline, growth in material consumption and population must be eased down at the same time as there is a rapid and drastic increase in the efficiency of materials and energy use."[59] The critical factor they identified as driving resource depletion to unsustainable levels is "overshoot," whereby humanity doesn't know the damage that it is doing until well after it is done, and the environmental and human value is lost.

Examples to support the thesis behind *The Limits to Growth* are plentiful. As mentioned earlier, there is a litany of chemicals that were once thought to be beneficial, only to be found after their application to be a lingering danger to humans, animals, or the environment: chlorofluorocarbons (CFCs), polychlorinated biphenyl (PCB), and dichlorodiphenyltrichloroethane (DDT), just to name a few. Countless dams and developments have decimated fragile ecosystems that were later deemed critical for a stable ecosystem. For example, Houston recognized after Hurricane Harvey that it needs wetlands and floodplains to absorb the surge of tropical storms, but many of those essential areas had been lost to development. Fisheries have been extracted well beyond levels necessary to maintain them, greenhouse gases are being emitted now that will remain in the atmosphere for between a few years to thousands of years, and many species were driven to extinction before we even knew our actions were putting them at risk. To avoid this fate, Meadows, Meadows, and Randers argue for an altered market system that incorporates "concerns for carefully balancing our long- and short-term goals and emphasizing equity and quality of life."[60]

Existing within the limits imposed by natural systems seems like a rather self-evident necessity. Yet business education rarely incorporates insights from natural sciences for perspectives on the biosphere or addresses the environmental impact of business decisions. Few students will have encountered Herman Daly's famous argument that the economy is a subsystem of the environment, "which is finite, non-growing, and materially closed, although open to a continual, but non-growing, throughput of solar energy. When the economy grows in physical dimensions, it incorporates matter and energy from the rest of the ecosystem into itself. It must, by the law of conservation of matter and energy (First Law of Thermodynamics), encroach on the ecosystem, diverting matter from previous natural uses. More human economy (more people and commodities) means less natural ecosystem."[61]

To feed our growing economy, humans consume more than a hundred billion tons of natural resources per year,[62] or roughly eleven tons of natural resources for every person on Earth. That includes over forty-two billion tons of non-metallic minerals, twenty-three billion tons of biomass, fifteen billion tons of fossil fuels, and ten billion tons of metal ores. We also produce over two billion tons of solid waste each year, over ten million tons of toxic chemicals, thirty-six billion tons of carbon dioxide,[63] and four hundred and sixty million tons of plastic waste,[64] which are buried in landfills, burned for fuel, or released into terrestrial or aquatic environments.

These numbers have been increasing for decades to meet our rapidly growing demands for food, fresh water, timber, fiber, and fuel, such that we are changing ecosystems more rapidly and extensively than in any comparable period in human history. This has resulted in a substantial and largely irreversible loss in the diversity of life on Earth.[65] On our current trajectory, 90 percent of the Earth's precious topsoil may be at risk by 2050[66]; oceans may carry more plastic than fish (by weight) by 2050[67]; an estimated 57 percent to 70 percent of the world's species could go extinct by 2070[68]; and global mean temperatures could reach 2.7°C above preindustrial levels by 2100.[69] While the impact of these changes would be felt differently around the world, nowhere would be immune to prolonged heatwaves, droughts, and extreme weather events that become increasingly common and severe.[70] Tim Jackson, a professor of sustainable development at the University of Surrey, warns that if these trends continue, "by the end of the century our children and grandchildren will face a hostile climate, depleted resources, the destruction of habitats, the decimation of species, food scarcities, mass migrations and, almost inevitably, war."[71]

Scientists think that the Earth has a maximum carrying capacity of between nine and ten billion people, on the basis of nature's limited availability of freshwater, capacity to produce food, and ability to absorb pollution.[72] But this number assumes the technology we have today, that everyone consumes what they need, and that consumption levels are similar around the world. Meanwhile, the arithmetic grows increasingly daunting each year. As of the early 2000s, the average middle-class American consumes 3.3 times the subsistence level of food and almost 250 times the subsistence level of clean water needed for a single person. If everyone on Earth lived like a middle-class American, then the planet might have a carrying capacity of around two billion.[73] As a result, if global population reaches 9.6 billion by 2050, the equivalent of almost three planets could be required to provide the natural resources needed to sustain current lifestyles. To avoid this impossibility, we can hope for technological miracles that not only address climate change but make food production, biodiversity conservation, waste removal, and more all suddenly feasible. But hope is always a gamble—and usually a longshot at that. It would be irresponsible to not also rethink the kind of growth we actually seek.

Different Kinds of Growth

This chapter opened with the question, Why grow? Implicit in this question is the assumption that there is only one type of growth: more! We need a more sophisticated notion of the kind of growth we seek. And for that, we can consider alternative models of growth, ranging from the more moderate to the more extreme views of economic progress and the technological advancement that makes it possible.

Slow Growth. Dietrich Vollrath, an economist at the University of Houston and the author of *Fully Grown: Why a Stagnant Economy Is a Sign of Success,* argues that constantly higher growth rates are neither possible nor desirable.[74] In fact, he argues, slower rates of economic growth are "the optimal response to massive economic success" and the result of personal choices of individual consumers. He points out that as countries like the United States have become wealthier, their inhabitants have chosen to spend less time at work and to have smaller families. Vollrath estimates that about two-thirds of the recent slowdown in GDP growth can be accounted for by the decline in the growth of labor inputs. But rather than seeing this as any sort of failure, it reflects "the advance of women's rights and economic success." He cites a switch in spending patterns from tangible goods—such as clothes and furniture—to services, such as child and health care, which have risen from 40 percent of GDP in 1950 to more than 70 percent in 2023. And service industries, which tend to be labor-intensive, exhibit lower rates of productivity growth since their output is intangible. In the manufacturing sector, on the other hand, outputs are tangible and can be counted easily in economic calculations of productivity. Since rising productivity is a key component of GDP growth, the expansion of the service sector will constrain it. But again, he writes, "That reallocation of economic activity away from goods and into services comes down to our success. We've gotten so productive at making goods that this has freed up our money to spend on services." Vollrath's analysis implies that all the major economies are likely to see slower growth rates as their populations become more affluent and, importantly, age—a pattern established in Japan in the 1990s.

Green Growth and Decoupling. While Vollrath challenges the growth imperative, other thinkers and economists have proposed different kinds of growth that we should pursue. Economist Joseph Stiglitz argues for what many call "green growth," which seeks to grow the economy while "decoupling" its impact on the environment.[75] In short, the idea is predicated on the belief that we innovate products that are less resource-intensive and, coupled with behavior change, use less energy and generate less waste. Many European governments, the World Bank, and the Organization for Economic Cooperation and Development have taken positions that, given the right policy measures, we can enjoy a different form of growth and prosperity while reducing carbon emissions and our consumption of natural resources. A 2018 report by the Global Commission on the Economy and Climate declares, "We are on the cusp of a new economic era: one where growth is driven by the interaction between rapid technological innovation, sustainable infrastructure investment, and increased resource productivity. This is the only growth story of the 21st century. It will result in efficient, livable cities; low-carbon, smart and resilient infrastructure; and the restoration of degraded lands while protecting valuable forests. We can have growth that is strong, sustainable, balanced, and inclusive."[76]

While many warn that this approach relies too much on technology alone, there are some indications this prediction is already playing out. The United States watched national greenhouse emissions fall by 15–18 percent between 2005 and 2019, while GDP increased by around 29 percent. Further, forty-one US states plus the District of Columbia reduced their CO_2 emissions while increasing GDP between 2005 and 2017.[77] Globally, at least twenty-five countries have reduced greenhouse gas emissions while increasing GDP between 2005 and 2019 (see Figure 11.2). These results were possible though renewable energy generation, reductions in electricity use, reductions in industrial and residential energy use, and changes in behavior.[78] To continue such trends, green-growth advocates argue, governments should fund scientific research into green technology and pass taxes on fossil fuels, all while maintaining the pursuit of continued economic growth. Not all agree.

Post-Growth. Some contend that green growth is misguided, unrealistic, and not sustainable, calling instead for a "post-growth economy." Pointing out that continued economic growth is projected to drive a significant increase in energy demand over the coming decades, post-growth advocates argue that decarbonizing the economy in its present form will be impossible. They take umbrage with the concept of "relative decoupling," where the growth rate of

FIGURE 11.2

Countries That Achieved Economic Growth While Reducing CO_2 Emissions, 2005–2020

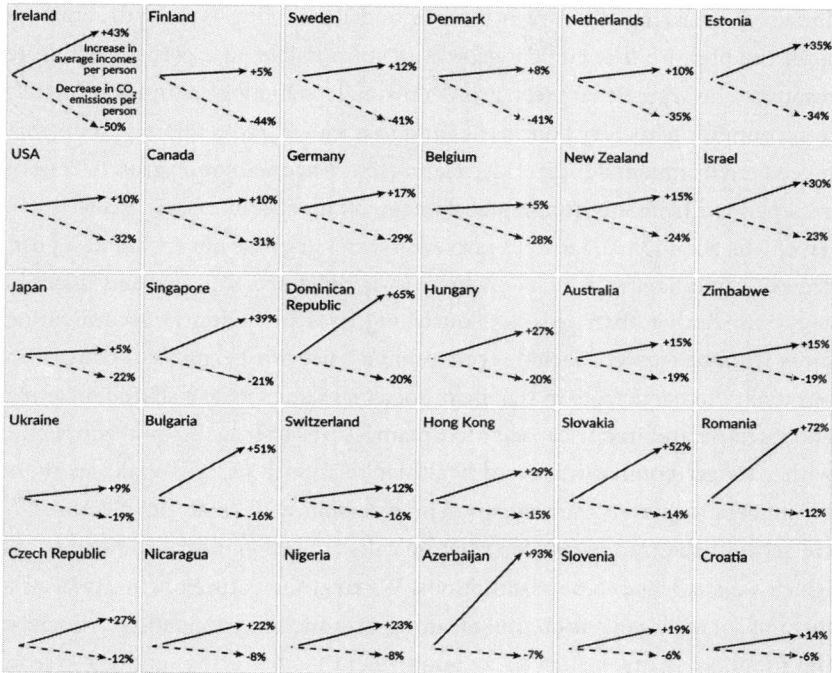

Notes: Solid lines show the increase in average incomes per person; dotted lines show the decrease in CO_2 emissions per person. Emissions are adjusted for trade. Data sources are from Global Carbon Project & World Bank. There are more countries that achieved the same, but only those countries for which data are available and for which each change exceeded 5% are shown.

Source: R. Hannah, "Many countries have decoupled economic growth from CO_2 emissions, even if we take offshored production into account," *Our World In Data*, 2021, https://ourworldindata .org/co2-gdp-decoupling (accessed December 4, 2023). CC BY 4.0 author Max Roser.

environmental damage is less than the growth rate for the economy but still positive (that is, carbon emissions decrease as a percentage of GDP but still increase). Instead, they argue, there should be "absolute decoupling," wherein the environmental damage decreases irrespective of economic growth.[79] And many post-growth advocates resist the idea of gambling on dramatic technological change to drive absolute decoupling because so many technological advancements in the past have resulted in profoundly negative unintended consequences.[80]

Tim Jackson takes this extreme view in his book *Prosperity Without Growth*,[81] declaring that green growth and decoupling is a myth. Starting from the premise that endless growth is not possible on a planet with finite resources, he argues that green growth through technological innovation fails to account for planetary boundaries and that we will cross tipping points that exceed environmental limits.[82] He claims that since economic growth cannot be separated from environmental damage on an absolute basis, growth will have to be abandoned. He does not see this as a negative but envisions a post-growth capitalism in which "prosperity" is redefined to transcend material concerns. Rather than seeking flourishing lives by endlessly accumulating more stuff, he reasons, societies can attain a truer prosperity that "consists in our ability to participate in the life of society, in our sense of shared meaning and purpose and in our capacity to dream." Lives of frugality and simplicity, with stronger communities and healthier relationships, will make us more genuinely prosperous than our present obsession with "material pleasures."[83] He sets out the framework for what he calls "the economy of tomorrow" in which we challenge some assumptions. We treat the nature of enterprise as a form of social organization, the meaning of work as participation in society, the function of investment as a commitment to the future, and the role of money as a social good, offering a view of the economy that is transformed in ways that protect employment, promote and facilitate social investment, reduce inequality, and support both ecological and financial stability.[84]

Degrowth. For some, even that is not far enough, and they advocate for a push towards "degrowth," under which the only real solution is to produce and consume less by shrinking our economies to cope with the carrying capacity of the planet. First proposed in the 1970s by a group of French intellectuals and widely dismissed as too radical for its time, degrowth has been reinvigorated by the present challenge of the climate crisis. It is based on the idea of shifting from a GDP-driven economy to an economy driven by concerns for the well-being of humans and the ecosystem, using metrics like life expectancy, health, education, housing, and ecologically sustainable initiatives and work.[85] The goal is to make the economy work for people, not people working for the economy. People such as Noam Chomsky, Yanis Varoufakis, and Sir Anthony

Giddens have expressed some degree of support for the idea, which has found its greatest support at a grassroots level.[86] In a 2018 poll in France, 54 percent of respondents supported degrowth, while 46 percent supported green growth.[87] According to Julia Steinberger, a professor of ecological economics at the University of Lausanne, the amount of stuff people need in order to be satisfied in their lives is going down. "The empirical evidence is very, very strong and it shows that human development indicators, life satisfaction indicators, all of these things do saturate at a moderate level of income, at a moderate level of energy use, and not only that, but those income and energy levels are actually dropping over time."[88] The degrowth movement calls on advanced countries to embrace zero or even negative GDP growth. "The faster we produce and consume goods, the more we damage the environment. . . . There is no way to both have your cake and eat it. . . . If humanity is not to destroy the planet's life support systems, the global economy should slow down."[89]

This exploration of different growth models—from Vollrath's vision of slow growth to the aspirations of green growth, post-growth ideologies, and even the radical notion of degrowth—offers unique insights. Yet it's clear there is no definitive answer on which path is best. What binds them together, however, is the implication that a fundamental reevaluation of consumption is essential. We need to reconsider not just how we grow, but also how and what we consume. This necessity to redefine consumption paves the way for our next focus: understanding how excessive consumption is at the heart of the challenges we face.

Excessive Consumption Is a Root Problem

We now come to the Gordian knot at the heart of our discussion about how best to reform the global economy. We cannot have an economy that remains within the limits of the biosphere if it is based on the consumption of unlimited amounts of materials and energy. At the root of the issue lies the questions that Milton Friedman raised about freedom and the market. Do we, particularly in the affluent West, have a right to anything, anytime, from anywhere? Is this even possible on a planet with finite resources? Unfortunately, the business curriculum either answers both questions in the affirmative or doesn't bother to ask them at all. The curriculum is based on endless, and often mindless, consumption.[90] More is always better. J. B. Mackinnon writes,

Consumer research consistently shows that exposure to what can easily add up to thousands of advertisements a day, most of them telling us that money, possessions, and the right image are a path to happiness, success, and self-worth, does in fact tend to make us feel worse about ourselves. In cities, especially (where most people now live), the crowds of other consumers and glut of advertising constantly cause us to doubt our social status. In the words of Tim Jackson, we are persuaded to spend money we don't have on things we don't need to create impressions that won't last on people we don't care about.[91]

But is a reduced, more sustainable level of consumption even possible? Or is the term an oxymoron? Business education and research needs to explore this question in more depth. That exploration begins with the question of whether the desire to consume is innate or learned? Environmentalist Paul Kingsnorth points an accusatory finger at slick marketing strategies that stimulate the senses, feed our pleasure centers, and compel us to pursue instant pleasure through an unquenchable material appetite. This system, to Kingsnorth, stands in direct contradiction to every spiritual tradition in history by glorifying wealth and accumulation, building a fabricated platform of want, and ultimately colonizing the mind.[92] The antidote, Kingsnorth argues, is to reconnect with the idea of limits as an opportunity to free ourselves from our present system of mindless consumption for its own sake.

One proposed solution is a form of consuming preferences, called LOHAS (Lifestyles of Health and Sustainability). Hailing from different walks of life, LOHAS consumers share a set of values: concern for the planet, authenticity, personal fulfillment, holistic health, and social conscience. LOHAS consumers are vigilant researchers, reading labels, webpages, reviews, and corporate social responsibility reports to make informed decisions, on not just the attributes of products but also how they are made. Their preferences go far beyond organic food and recycled content. They want to buy from brands that care about the planet, pay living wages, establish sustainable supply chains, and take positions on social and political issues that they care about.[93] I am married to a LOHAS consumer and have seen this behavior in action. The total addressable market for LOHAS in the United States was estimated at $473 billion in 2022, up from $290 billion in 2008 and is predicted to grow at 10 percent per year.[94]

The burgeoning LOHAS movement raises an interesting question: Can companies help accelerate a change in consumption patterns? The World Business Council for Sustainable Development suggests that companies can use three tools for driving this shift: (1) innovation of new products that offer the same service or satisfy the same need but reduce the impact on the environment; (2) choice editing, when companies limit offerings to only include sustainable options; and (3) choice influencing, which involves guiding consumer desires towards sustainable products through marketing, behavioral nudges, and education, making sustainable offerings more appealing.[95] Research has shown that people can be quite malleable to such efforts. An executive at Walmart once told me that shifting consumers from incandescent lightbulbs to LEDs is as simple as putting the former on the bottom shelf and the latter at eye level. A research study found that to convince conservative consumers to purchase an energy-efficient lightbulb, they would simply label it as saving money rather than protecting the environment (liberals would buy either labeling).[96] Indeed, if consumers were not so malleable, corporations would not be spending the vast amounts of money that they do on advertising. But that does not mean that this is easy. Many surveys show that consumers say they want sustainable products but are less likely to follow through while shopping. To overcome this "intention-action gap," marketers have developed new and targeted strategies such as using social influence, shaping good habits, leveraging the domino effect of multiple efforts, talking to the heart and not just the brain, and favoring experiences over ownership.[97]

Can companies make a profit by convincing consumers to consume less? Patagonia is exploring these strategies with its Common Threads, Worn Wear, and Repair is a Radical Act initiatives, which encourage people to buy used clothing or repair damaged clothing in order to make it last.[98] Dell, Adidas, Method, and others have taken steps to address the critical issue of ocean plastics by developing programs to stop plastics from entering the environment, making new products with recycled ocean plastics, and developing alternatives to plastics such as biomaterials.[99] Some LOHAS consumers are wary of the motives behind such actions, seeing green marketing as merely a public relations ploy to increase market share and convince people to spend more money on products. Some of the skepticism is undoubtedly warranted. But it's also true that the climate crisis has prompted some within the advertising industry to undertake a self-examination. For instance, the Advertising Association, a trade association representing advertisers, agencies, media, and research services in the UK advertising industry, says its industry has a role to play in enabling and encouraging the sort of behavior change necessary to create a decarbonized society.[100] This is an aspirational goal that will test the ability of corporations to use their power to lead society towards a decarbonized economy. But this goal cannot be achieved unless we begin to think differently in business, moving from simply the dyadic relationship between producer and consumer with the goal of increasing sales, to thinking more systemically about the many aspects of a purchasing decision, its unintended and ancillary consequences, and the many individuals, organizations, and ecosystems that are involved. This brings us to an appreciation of systems.

Bringing Systems Thinking into Business Education

Business education often focuses sequentially on management aspects like strategy, marketing, finance, and operations—as if they were discrete tools rather than part of the integrated challenge of operating a business. As a result, business schools are training managers to optimize for one element of the system while being blind to impacts on others. Emphasizing systems thinking and integrating knowledge across different business areas and their social, economic, political, and environmental contexts will better equip students to tackle the complex problems of the twenty-first century.

For example, our food supply systems are far more complex than most business school students understand. In our present economy, 92.2 percent of food in United States is purchased indirectly from producers, requiring that it travel long distances (on average about fifteen hundred miles) and consume high levels of fossil fuels. Only 7.8 percent is bought directly from producers through farmers markets, farm stands, and Community Supported Agriculture.[101] At the large chain grocery store, the farmer receives only 14.5 cents on the dollar, while intermediaries take the rest: processors, packagers, transporters, wholesalers, retailers, and food service providers.[102] Most obviously, this makes it very hard for small-scale farmers to stay in business. But more systemically, this means that local areas become less able to support themselves with local food, and more dependent on global supply chains, heightening their vulnerability. What's more, money earned in local communities

tends to stay in local communities, resulting in a virtuous cycle of higher profits, which results in better jobs, and more community-based loans from local
banks, which supports local businesses, and more taxes to local municipalities.

As food supply systems have become more industrial and concentrated
since the 1950s, the number of farms dropped by two-thirds while the average
size more than doubled. Today, industrial farms account for only 5 percent of
farms, but 63.8 percent of production, while small-scale family farms represent 89 percent of US farms but only 17.8 percent of production.[103] Larger-scale
industrial farms tend to turn large areas into monoculture; rely heavily on
chemical pesticides, herbicides, and fertilizers; destroy habitat for local species
(notably pollinators); produce lower-quality mass-produced food; and wreak
economic damage on local communities by paying lower wages. For instance,
nearly three-quarters of chicken growers who contract with large corporations like Tyson and Perdue live below the poverty line, ironically relying on
food stamps to survive while producing our food.[104] Without an appreciation
for systemic thinking, business students focusing solely on profit fail to see
these broader implications of seemingly straightforward business decisions.

At the end of the day, real solutions to issues like climate change lie at
the level of the system.[105] They cannot be measured by one company or one
product but must include the entire system of which it is a part. Even if one
or two major energy companies made a transition to net zero in an aggressive
timeline (which seems unlikely), it would be insufficient. A sustainable energy
system requires a revolution of the whole grid, encompassing generation,
transmission, distribution, use, and mobility. To be fair to business schools, a
failure to instill systems thinking is a shortfall of all contemporary education.
As the twentieth century American architect and philosopher Buckminster
Fuller warned, American education's "ever-increasing specialization [threat-
ens] our ability to appreciate how systems work. Moreover, in school we learn
to break problems down into parts, which enables focus and progress in many
fields of knowledge but blinds us to larger patterns and relationships. Traditional management systems similarly break down into parts, inhibiting collaboration and innovation in favor of reliability and efficiency."[106]

Systems thinking means looking at the big picture to solve problems, not
just focusing on tiny details. Instead of taking things apart to understand
them, you try to see how all the pieces work together.[107] It's a way of thinking,

not just a set of rules. You consider all the connected parts of the problem—the technical stuff, the people involved, and how any change might affect everyone.[108]

To hone our integration skills, Peter Senge's book *The Fifth Discipline* describes the five disciplines for creating a learning organization.[109] The first four are personal mastery for deepening our personal vision; understanding our mental models; building shared vision; and team learning. The fifth discipline is systems thinking, which is necessary for integrating the other four. But business education suffers from a lack of fifth discipline systems thinking when, instead of treating the company as one big system and understanding how every part of the business will influence every other part, we teach students to view the firm and our skill sets as many individual units, with each person or group only paying attention to their own tasks. As a result, the different parts of the organization may interfere with each other without realizing it. And this is before even considering how the business as a whole interacts with the wider world.

The value of systems thinking will eventually manifest at the firm level as well as at the societal and global levels. That is to say, it is becoming simply good business and good for society.[110] In her book *Right Kind of Wrong: The Science of Failing Well*, Harvard Business School professor Amy Edmondson sees systems thinking as a critical skill for business leaders to avoid complex failures. Once you start seeing systems—seeing connections between parts—you begin to see ways to alter the most important elements in the system to reduce unwanted failures and to promote greater innovation, safety, or other valued outcomes. She argues that we often reach for the quick fix and tempting shortcuts, yielding solutions that Senge warns offer a short-term change that "ends up exacerbating the problem it was intended to fix." But systems thinking involves analyzing relationships and interactions between parts rather than looking at parts in isolation.[111] Teaching systems thinking in business schools will thus be beneficial for students' careers. But it also has the added benefit essential for addressing larger, complex challenges: it will be a crucial tool for solving the "wicked" problems we face, notably climate change and inequality. One potential model for solving these twin problems is a systems-based approach termed "regenerative capitalism."

Regenerative Capitalism

Regenerative capitalism offers a transformative, systems-based approach for aligning economic systems with the sustainable and holistic principles found in nature. Its founding belief, as described by John Fullerton, founder and president of the Capital Institute think tank, is that "[t]he universal patterns and principles the cosmos uses to build stable, healthy, and sustainable systems throughout the real world can and must be used as a model for economic-system design."[112] According to this theory, everything in the universe—be it bacteria, hurricanes, or even human societies—is organized into systems whose interlinked parts work together in some larger process or pattern. Thus, living systems, nonliving systems, and societal systems can be integrated into a network of balanced, vibrant, and regenerative economies. For example, a regenerative agricultural system that supports both the local economy and ecosystem health could serve as a microcosm of this approach, reflecting a balance between human activity and natural processes.

According to Jack Stephens, writer and co-founder of Soul Self Living, regenerative capitalism "differs most from current approaches to sustainability in that, instead of focusing on social and environmental health using traditional reductionist logic to 'solve problems,' it aims directly at building healthy human networks as the objective, drawing on universal principles and patterns, with 'sustainability' becoming an outcome, a natural byproduct of systemic health. It is like (holistic) healthcare in contrast to (reductionist) disease care."[113] Fullerton argues that regenerative capitalism pulls from both liberal and conservative political philosophies and, instead of jettisoning capitalism wholesale, it intends to "preserve and build on the many strengths of our free enterprise system, while addressing its failings head on."[114] He describes what is needed as "something akin to humanity's economic Copernican moment," bringing our economy and practice into alignment with how systems in nature actually work.[115] This is certainly a lofty goal but without setting such an ambitious objective, we will never know which way to go.

A New Kind of Business Curriculum

I earned my undergraduate degree in chemical engineering in 1983. One of our classes focused on designing process plants, for which we sketched out how chemicals flowed through various units in the plant. In these diagrams, we often added a simple arrow pointing to the edge of the page, marking it "to waste," to indicate where the chemical leftovers would go. We did not consider ways to reuse, recycle, or reduce those waste streams. We just sent them "away." That would be irresponsible today, and the engineering curriculum is being redesigned to train engineers not only to know how to develop new technologies, but also to understand (at least a little bit) about the social and natural environment in which those technologies will be deployed.

Indeed, engineering education seems to be in the midst of the sort of reckoning that I believe business schools need to face. In recent years, the National Science Foundation and others have argued that engineering education needs to address teamwork and communication skills, shift from a "sit-and-listen" to an engaged and hands-on experience, and address the profession's gender gap. In response, the Olin College of Engineering was created to "go beyond a disciplinary perspective of engineering, and beyond the definition of engineering as 'using science to solve technical problems.' Engineers need to work across disciplinary boundaries to ask not only 'How might we build it?' but also 'Who is it for?' 'Why are we building it?' 'Who else is impacted?' and 'Should we build it at all?'—and to develop the disciplinary humility necessary to recognize the limits of engineering and to collaborate with experts in other fields." The overall message was simple but profound: "Engineering education must not only focus on producing good workers, but also on developing good people and good citizens."[116]

Business schools must follow this lead. We need to own up to the role we play in creating the problems that society now faces through the courses we teach, the theories we espouse, and the values we profess. In some cases, we must stop doing what we are doing; in other cases, we need to do things differently. The opportunities to correct outdated business models can be found throughout the business curriculum. Accounting and finance teaching could be revised to incorporate social and environmental metrics in conjunction with economic metrics to inform management decisions that fully consider the corporation and society. Human resource teaching could help by eliminating the term "human resources," which tends to objectify people in the same way we tend to objectify nature—focusing instead on the inherent dignity and meaning of work and on fostering new forms of employee engagement that help employees thrive and flourish.[117] Organizational teaching could explore forms of governance other than the presently excessive attention paid to private-equity-owned and publicly traded corporations and instead teach corporate forms such as employee- or community-owned businesses and other models that come from indigenous traditions around the world. Courses in operations can move away from linear production models and supply chains in which raw materials are extracted, turned into products, sold to consumers, and disposed of at the end of their life. Instead, new models can be taught that reduce the need for raw materials and the creation of waste, such as life cycle analysis, which examines the total environmental and economic costs of product from "cradle to grave"; industrial ecology, which seeks to link waste streams from one company that may be used as a feedstock in another; and the circular economy, a model focused on minimizing waste by designing products for easy recycling right from the start and ensuring that materials are recycled in a way that retains their highest value, rather than just being used for low-value purposes like fuel.

The key is to break down the current model of business education, which is based on teaching distinct and disconnected disciplines—strategy, operations, finance, accounting, marketing, organizational behavior, and marketing— and teach instead a more balanced, systemic approach. This new method would weave connections among these areas of study while also incorporating insights from other crucial fields. In particular, business education must be enriched in several key areas:

- Natural science, to understand the biosphere and the impact of business decisions on the environment, including aspects like resource extraction, supply chains, manufacturing, consumption, and disposal

- Social sciences, for a deeper insight into the human implications of corporate actions

- Political science, to grasp how business activities affect society through factors like tax policy, wage requirements, and health care

- Government courses, enabling constructive engagement with governments in promoting an effective and dynamic economy

- Engineering, to both comprehend and contribute to the emerging innovations and technologies entering the market

When business logic becomes the only logic for evaluating decisions, something is lost, and our approach becomes incomplete. Does this mean we jettison the key tenets of traditional business education? No, but it does require educators to approach them differently. "Going forward," write The-LifeIWant.com co-founder Christine Bader and Emory University professor Wesley Longhofer in a sensible op-ed, "we will continue to include [Milton] Friedman in our syllabi. But we will teach it as a relic for what people used to believe, rather than the model of capitalism that we need today."[118] This approach allows for a critical assessment of past theories while paving the way for the more relevant models needed today.

Throughout modern history, business education has encountered demands for change—be it post the 1929 stock market crash, the 2001 Enron Scandal, the 2008 Great Recession, or the 2020 Covid crisis. Yet each time, the response has been incremental, barely scratching the surface of deeply ingrained managerial values and assumptions. In the face of today's profound systemic challenges, mere elective additions to an otherwise unchanged curriculum will be ineffective. To genuinely embed the significance of people and the planet in business education, a radical shift is needed, in both the curriculum's structure and its underlying philosophy. Business education doesn't just need an update, it requires a complete transformation, one that will help future leaders to create a sustainable, equitable future for both people and the planet.

TWELVE

The Noble Calling of Business and Business Education

"Man's [sic] search for meaning is the primary motivation of his life and not a 'secondary rationalization' of instinctual drives. This meaning is unique and specific in that it must and can be fulfilled by him alone; only then does it achieve a significance which will satisfy his own will to meaning."

—VICTOR FRANKL, *MAN'S SEARCH FOR MEANING*

David Foster Wallace opened his 2005 commencement speech at Kenyon College with a story. "There are these two young fish swimming along and they happen to meet an older fish swimming the other way, who nods at them and says 'Morning, boys. How's the water?' And the two young fish swim on for a bit, and then eventually one of them looks over at the other and goes 'What the hell is water?'" What he draws from the story is that the realities in which we live are often the "hardest to see and talk about."[1]

The cultural environment of business school, like water, is hard to see if you swim in it every day and know no other environments, such as what is found in engineering, public policy, or environmental science. And if students don't know what that reality is, they will blindly succumb and conform, becoming something other than what they were meant to be—often without even being aware of the narrow path they were channeled through. Organizational behavioralist Herbert Shepard warns students not to be a "cormorant," a bird that is so good at catching fish that a fisherman ties a rope to its foot, puts a band around its neck so it cannot swallow and takes each fish the bird catches for himself. His admonishment is not to be someone who is good at a particular skill but uses that skill to serve someone else's purpose.[2]

Unfortunately, a good number of our students fall into this trap, as Yale professor William Deresiewicz observes in his book *Excellent Sheep: The Miseducation of the American Elite and the Way to a Meaningful Life*. Today's students are very able, he writes, but they also act like sheep, pursuing external affirmation that follows the crowd.[3] I see this playing out earlier and earlier in people's lives. I sit on high-school scholarship committees and see students building their resumes from the seventh or eighth grade. Teaching this practice so early risks implanting the lesson that the measure of one's worth comes from outside oneself. For business school students, the worth of their education is increasingly measured by status of the school or job and its "return on investment." As a result, students continue on their narrow path by seeking out high-paying jobs in consulting or finance. But "return" here is measured through only "vaguely understood objectives—status, wealth, success—which usually translates into money."[4] A university education is, all too often, more attuned to creating dutiful employees than it is at creating individual leaders or entrepreneurs who seek to forge their own path. This does not lead to the kind of business leadership we need.

Instead, business schools need to bring a sense of meaning and purpose more centrally into the curriculum, and help students determine how to direct that purpose towards both leading businesses and serving society. Where prior generations may have seen these two objectives as separate, solving today's challenges requires that they be linked. More to the point, helping our students live meaningful and fulfilling lives requires that they be linked. Psychologist Victor Frankl writes that "man's search for meaning is the primary motivation in his life and not a 'secondary rationalization' of instinctual drives. This meaning is unique and specific in that it must and can be fulfilled by him alone; only then does it achieve a significance which will satisfy his own *will* to meaning."[5] Or, as the thirteenth-century Islamic scholar and poet Jalāl al-Dīn Muḥammad Rūmī (or simply Rumi) writes, in the pursuit of purpose, "It's your road, and yours alone. Others may walk it with you, no one can walk it for you."

Business education needs to bring the whole person into the education process, inspiring their hearts as much as engaging their heads, appealing not just to their rational intellect and analytic side, but also to their emotional and aspirational side. Unfortunately, business education focuses more on knowledge that is delivered in a stock form that varies little among students. We need to help students find their own purpose and their own calling in management for themselves. To do this, the curriculum itself must be overhauled, with renewed scrutiny on how it shapes students' thinking. Everything must be focused not just on providing skills and a lucrative professional network, but also on helping them develop their own set of aspirational values. This is a challenge, not just for students but also for faculty, as purpose cannot be taught in the standard classroom format. Professors must become guides, not just experts.

The Values in Today's Business Schools

Many students approach business school with a mindset that matches the "greed is good" ideology of Gordon Gekko in Oliver Stone's movie *Wall Street*. In the movie, Gekko (played by Michael Douglas) delivers a now famous speech that articulates that ideology: "The point is, ladies and gentlemen, that greed, for lack of a better word, is good. Greed is right, greed works. Greed clarifies, cuts through, and captures the essence of the evolutionary spirit. Greed in all its forms: greed—for life, for money, for love, for knowledge—has marked the upward surge of mankind." Oliver Stone crafted *Wall Street* as a cautionary tale, reflecting on the business world's value system that prioritizes profit and wealth above all else. Based on corporate raiders Carl Icahn and Ivan Boesky, who gutted companies and extracted wealth for themselves, Gekko's character was meant to serve a purpose similar to that of John Milton's Lucifer in *Paradise Lost*. Just as Milton's devil tempts with his charismatic rhetoric, Gekko's persuasive conviction in greed's virtue is designed to challenge and probe our beliefs. He twists familiar concepts like ambition and drive, perverting them into a justification for unchecked self-interest. However, much like the deceptive allure of Milton's antagonist, Gekko's philosophy is a corrupt force, intended by Stone to be a critical commentary on the dangerous allure of unchecked greed in the corporate world. Unfortunately, the performance was so powerful that people misunderstood its message. Douglas reported that this was "the biggest surprise of my career; that people say this seductive villain has motivated [them] to go into business." Oliver Stone echoed the same experience: "I can't tell you how many young people who have come up to me and said, 'I went to Wall Street because of that movie.'"[6]

Research supports Douglas and Stone's experiences. Business school has indeed become a training ground for many aspiring Gordon Gekkos. One study found that students who apply to business (and economics) score higher on the "dark triad" traits of narcissism, psychopathy, and Machiavellianism than their peers in schools such as psychology and political science. These students also score consistently lower on the personality trait of agreeableness and instead tend to be more competitive, skeptical, and tough-minded.[7] These traits were present at enrollment, and the business school environment amplifies those preexisting tendencies.

Studies have found that business (and law) school education promotes a view of human nature and a behavioral pattern that heavily emphasizes self-interest.[8] One study reveals that management education notably enhances the prioritization of "self-oriented values" among students. Through their business education, students increasingly focus on what others think of them and place greater importance on personal ambitions such as achieving a comfortable and exciting life, seeking pleasure, gaining social recognition, acquiring social power, and maintaining a public image. Conversely, the emphasis on "others-oriented values"—including aspirations for a peaceful world, appreciation of beauty, inner harmony, true friendship, wisdom, helpfulness, love, politeness, and loyalty—tends to diminish over the course of a two-year degree program.[9] Compared to their peers in other fields, business students are often found to adopt a more instrumentally rational approach to management ethics. This mindset leads to increased dishonesty in academic pursuits, stemming from a rise in egocentric behavior—and, one assumes, that increased dishonesty likely continues into their professional life.[10]

One factor contributing to students' weakened ethical reasoning is the extent to which they are taught to boil all decisions down to numbers. At the encouragement of their teachers and peers, "crunch the numbers" becomes the standard angle of attack for almost all problems. As business school professors Long Wang, Chen-Bo Zhong, and Keith Murnighan explain, this mindset is characterized by the simplification of complex, diverse features and components into a single value or utility metric, facilitating comparison across different qualitative and quantitative aspects. However, studies indicate that such a "calculative mindset" may inadvertently predispose individuals to apply quantitative analysis to nonquantitative problems. This emphasis on cognitive processing can subsequently lead to unintended social and moral consequences, including increasingly selfish, unethical, and immoral behavior.[11]

Why have greed and selfishness become so entrenched in business schools? To some, the dominance of economics-related courses in the MBA curricula leads to more positive attitudes towards greed and greed's moral acceptability.[12] Neoclassical economists tend to portray their field as an "objective science" that is divorced from morality, likening themselves to physicists who study empirical facts to address questions of "what is" and not "what ought to be." But the reality is otherwise.[13] And importantly, the values embedded within economics, like the water that David Foster Wallace talked about, are implicit, blinding not only some of its practitioners to their presence, but also the students who are taught it.

At the center of economics education is the idea of *homo economicus*—that we, as humans, seek to maximize our utility function. That utility function is limited to measuring things that have a price and we can buy, and our motivations are assumed to be that we try to consume the most we can within our income (and sometimes beyond our income). Wants (versus needs) are seen as unbounded and subjective, and the good of the person becomes synonymous with subjective material preferences. This model endorses egoism, elevates material pursuits, and ignores ethical formation.[14] It supports a belief that individuals act solely for their self-interest and will, by the laws of the market, produce positive outcomes for society at large. Those laws of the market support the idea that the economy can be analyzed as a system of self-regulating free markets, operating by their own laws in isolation from the rest of society.[15]

Economist Stephen Marglin offers a critique of such economic assumptions in his book *The Dismal Science: How Thinking Like an Economist Undermines Community*, arguing that modern economics is built on a set of half-truths: "that individuals are autonomous, self-interested, and rational calculators with unlimited wants and that the only community that matters is the nation-state." In the process, he writes, "market relationships erode community," justifying "a world in which individuals are isolated from one another and social connections are impoverished as people define themselves in terms of how much they can afford to consume."[16] Business education, informed by economics, is based on the assumption that humans are selfish and thus untrustworthy. London Business School professor Sumantra Ghoshal points out that business courses grounded in economics and agency theory, for example, teach students that

> managers cannot be trusted to do their jobs—which, of course, is to maximize shareholder value—and that to overcome "agency problems" managers' interests and incentives must be aligned with those of the shareholders by, for example, making stock options a significant part of their pay. In courses on organizational design, grounded in transaction cost economics, we have preached the need for tight monitoring and control of people to prevent "opportunistic behavior."[17]

This education not only relies on generalizations about individual behavior, but also shapes the behavior of those who apply its principles and are guided by its values. Research has found that exposure to this pedagogy leads people to behave in more self-interested ways, such as being more willing to free-ride.[18] This led Luigi Zingales at the University of Chicago Booth School of Business to ask in *Bloomberg*, "Do business schools incubate criminals?" arguing that experimental evidence suggests that the teaching of economics makes students more selfish and less concerned about the common good. This is not intentional, and many teachers are not aware of what they are doing. But, he warned, when "teachers pretend to be agnostic, they subtly encourage amoral behavior without taking any responsibility."[19]

According to Craig Smith, professor of ethics and social responsibility at INSEAD, "Students come in with a more rounded view of what managers are supposed to do but when they go out, they think it's all about maximizing shareholder value."[20] And, according to some close observers of business schools, the educational diet has a significant impact. Sumantra Ghoshal argues that business research and education "has had some very significant and negative influences on the practice of management. These influences have been less at the level of adoption of a particular theory and more at the incorporation, within the worldview of managers, of a set of ideas and assumptions that have come to dominate much of management research."[21]

In the worldview propagated at business schools, moral responsibility to the common good is subsumed by the overriding objective of efficiency.[22] Economist E. F. Schumacher writes in his classic book *Small Is Beautiful: A Study of Economics as If People Mattered* that economics leads us to believe that if something is uneconomic, it is illegitimate because it doesn't maximize profit for an individual. Schumacher writes that economics looks at the value of goods and services only through the view of humans and considers no value to goods like a clean, safe, and healthy environment or social relations in a healthy and flourishing community because their monetary value cannot be calculated. As a result, the market takes the sacredness out of life because there can be nothing sacred in something that has a price and can be sold. He concludes that this leads to a view of the market as "the institutionalization of individualism and non-responsibility."[23] This is not the kind of environment that can create the best leaders for business who are sometimes required to pass on short-term efficiency and profits in order to better serve its customers (and society). And more than that, in many ways the values in this environment are misconceived.

Where These Values Lead Us Astray

Is *homo economicus* an accurate reflection of human nature? Not always, according to research from both evolutionary biology and psychology. Harvard biologist Edward O. Wilson, for example, argues that evolutionary research shows that humans have relied on cooperation and group work for productivity through history. In his research, he finds that team players who sublimate selfish desires for the good of the group outcompete noncooperators, thereby ensuring their genes are passed on to future generations.[24] Alternatively, the pursuit of self-interest by individuals in a group setting tends to result in suboptimal collective outcomes.[25]

The work of political economist Elinor Ostrom supports this notion, challenging the notion of the "tragedy of the commons," which posits that individuals, acting in their own rational economic interest, will inevitably overuse and degrade common resources. Instead, her work showed that, while a selfish farmer might have an advantage over other farmers in his village, a village that solved the tragedy of the commons would have a decisive advantage over other villages.[26] In other words, communities based on self-interested competition may yield some successful individuals, but the community overall will not do as well as one that is based on collaboration.

Even Charles Darwin, on whom Herbert Spencer based his idea of "survival of the fittest," believed that instincts for cooperation and altruism enhanced the ability of humans not only to survive, but to become the dominant species. "There can be no doubt that a tribe including many members who, from possessing a high degree of the spirit of patriotism, fidelity, obedience, courage and sympathy [and who] were always ready to give aid to each other and to sacrifice themselves for the common good, would be victorious over most other tribes; and this would be natural selection."[27] In a commonly shared story, the anthropologist Margaret Mead was asked what she considered to be the first sign of civilization in a culture. Mead's answer was a fifteen-thousand-year-old fractured femur found in an archaeological site that had healed.[28] Without the benefits of modern medicine, it takes about six weeks of rest for a fractured femur to heal. During that time, you cannot run from danger or hunt for food, and you will die. But with the aid of others, you can survive.[29]

Research in psychology suggests that human beings are social creatures who are inclined to bond in communities,[30] and our instinct and intuition is to cooperate with others.[31] By studying snap decisions, for example, researchers have found that selfish behavior comes from thinking too much, not too little. According David Rand of Yale University, "Most people think we are intuitively selfish," but "our lab experiments show that making people rely more on intuition increases cooperation."[32] Much contemporary evidence suggests that selfishness is actually learned.[33] One field study in twelve countries determined that our preferences in economic choices are shaped by the interactions of everyday life.[34] Research also shows that altruism, like self-control, can be learned and maintained over an individual's lifetime.[35] In short, most of us are genuinely prosocial. And if we're not, selflessness can be learned just like selfishness.[36]

The field of economics, on the other hand, is predicated on an opposing and often incorrect view of human behavior, one that can be neatly summarized by the seventeenth-century English philosopher Thomas Hobbes, who famously described life as "solitary, poor, nasty, brutish and short." Hobbes viewed human nature as self-serving, power-hungry, and driven by fear of others and death[37] and argued that society needs structures to rein in these dark impulses.[38] This Hobbesian view has influenced centuries of economic thought, promoting selfish behavior as the norm, and it's a perspective vividly reflected in many US corporations. Journalist Joris Luyendijk notably described the London financial services sector in the aftermath of the 2008 credit crisis as "a Hobbesian universe of all-against-all, with relationships that are characteristically nasty, brutish and short."[39] Even outside times of crisis, practices like the "rank and yank" talent-management approach (in which the lowest-performing workers in companies are routinely dismissed) perpetuate this cutthroat competition, setting employees against each other in a manner reminiscent of Hobbes's bleak view of human nature.

The pervasive belief in *homo economicus*, the self-interested economic man, seeps into our everyday perceptions, leading us to doubt the existence of true altruism. This skepticism turns into a self-fulfilling prophecy: when we view most people as inherently selfish, we tend to portray genuine acts of kindness as having a selfish motive. Psychologists have found that when people (mostly in Western cultures) do something out of the goodness of their hearts, they even portray their own motives as selfish. One American psychologist noted, "People seem loathe to acknowledge that their behavior may have been motivated by genuine compassion and kindness."[40] Echoing this observation over a century earlier, nineteenth-century French philosopher Alexis de Tocqueville remarked that "Americans . . . enjoy explaining almost every act of their lives on the principle of self-interest." De Tocqueville saw this as a disservice. "Americans are hardly prepared to admit that they do give way to emotions of this sort."[41]

What is the effect of this pervasive pessimism about human nature? Historian Rutger Bregman writes in his book *Humankind: A Hopeful History* that "[i]f we believe most people can't be trusted, that's how we will treat each other, to everyone's detriment." But "if we want to tackle the greatest challenges of our times—from the climate crisis to our growing distrust of one another—than I think the place we need to start is our view of human nature. . . . If we believe most people are decent and kind, everything changes. We can completely rethink how we organize our schools and prisons, our businesses, and democracies. And how we live our lives."[42] Unfortunately, business schools as presently structured can stand in the way of that goal.

Today's Business Students Are Changing the Face of Business Education

One of my students told me that she felt that her values were under attack every time she walked into the business school building. She is not alone. Many students report a desire to go into business but a sense that maintaining their values is a constant challenge. And this leads to a hopeful observation that the "dark triad" inclinations of incoming business students may be phasing out of date. I see a shift in student attitudes in my recent years of teaching, as more and more students are turning to schools of business with a sense of purpose to serve society. A 2019 Gallup poll found that 97 percent of young business professionals want a career with "purpose."[43] That same year, nearly 25 percent of incoming students stated that they wanted a job focused on social impact after graduating, nearly 50 percent wanting to do so later in their careers.[44] These students arrive with a fresh perspective, keen to explore and redefine the economic, social, and environmental roles of corporations, as well as their own potential as future leaders. This is an important and healthy shift, both for society and for our graduates' individual careers.

Journalist Charles Duhigg writes about returning to Harvard Business School for his graduating class's fifteenth reunion in 2019 and finding a set of peers who were both hugely successful and deeply unhappy. When he was accepted to Harvard in 2001, he felt like he had won the "lottery ticket, a gilded highway to world-changing influence, fantastic wealth and—if those self-satisfied portraits that lined the hallways were any indication—a lifetime of deeply meaningful work." At the reunion, however, he found his "former classmates weren't overjoyed by their professional lives—in fact, they were miserable." As he looked deeper, he found that a large portion of American workers shared this misery. He writes, "In the mid-1980s, roughly 61 percent of workers told pollsters they were satisfied with their jobs. Since then, that number has declined substantially, hovering around half; the low point was in 2010, when only 43 percent of workers were satisfied. . . . The rest said they were unhappy, or at best neutral, about how they spent the bulk of their days."[45] Citing studies showing that increases above subsistence income provide diminishing returns to worker satisfaction, Duhigg writes that the more important factors to professional contentment are control of one's time, the authority to act on one's own expertise, and a sense that one's work is meaningful. It is on this last point that business schools must focus more of their attention.

Envisioning a New Set of Values to Guide Business Education

What alternative values might underpin business education moving forward? To answer this question, we must broaden our perspective to consider diverse value systems and how they might influence our present capitalist economy. The following three examples illustrate how such an expanded perspective might play out.

A System of Commerce Guided by Buddhism

E. F. Schumacher offered an interesting exercise in his book *Small Is Beautiful,* when he proposed a system of commerce that revolves around Buddhist values. Though such a system does not exist, he imagined a Buddhist economy in which work is meant to be meaningful and creative, not a source of stress and distaste; machines are used to improve a person's work, not to replace it or make it boring; recreation is found more in spending time with friends and in nature than in the consumption of resources; the economy is measured by the health and creativity of its members as much as by the amount of things it produces and consumes.

In a Buddhist economy the goals of simplicity and balance with nature lead to using more local and ecologically sensitive materials and sources of energy. This kind of economy doesn't necessarily use what is cheapest on the market, but instead uses what best serves its aims of simplicity and nonviolence. The goal in such an economy is to produce and consume only as much as is necessary and leave the rest of your time for artistic creativity and self-improvement. "The keynote of Buddhist economics is simplicity and non-violence," writes Schumacher, but "for the modern economist this is very difficult to understand. He is used to measuring the 'standard of living' by the amount of annual consumption, assuming all the time that a man who consumes more is 'better off' than a man who consumes less. A Buddhist economist would consider this approach excessively irrational: since consumption is merely a means to human well-being, the aim should be to obtain the maximum of well-being with the minimum of consumption."[46] This may sound like an idealistic vision, but it is not so far from the values embedded within many religious traditions.

A System of Commerce Guided by Catholic Social Teaching

In his book *Cathonomics: How Catholic Social Teaching Can Create a More Just Economy*, Fordham University Gabelli Fellow Anthony Annett offers another moral and ethical reframing of commerce that answers big questions that, he asserts, neoclassical economics fails to adequately address. What is the nature of the human being, the purpose and goal of life, and the right course of action in certain circumstances?[47] Table 12.1 shows how he compares the underlying assumptions behind neoclassical economics and its view of *homo economicus* with a Catholic view that humans are inherently communal and relational beings, emphasizing cooperation over transactional independence. As you can see, this comparison reveals a fundamental divergence in worldviews and approaches to addressing global issues. Might Annett's imagined economy more accurately reflect the values and beliefs of the world's 1.4 billion Catholics as well as non-Catholics who seek a more humane market experience? This is an important question as the world's markets increasingly globalize.

It Is Time to Globalize the Curriculum

As capitalism spreads throughout the world and more countries grow their economies to provide for their people, it is morphing and evolving to reflect the needs of each specific context. Unfortunately, the knowledge produced by management researchers at Western business schools and the education that it produces are not always applicable to other parts of the world. A neoclassical, shareholder-primacy worldview may have limited value for running a small family business in Tunisia or a co-op in northeast Brazil.[48] This is important because the world is changing and the economic dominance that the United States has enjoyed since World War II is now being rivaled by other countries. In the second half of the twentieth century, the success of American-based multinational corporations led to the dominance of North American management and business schools. However, new economic centers in India, China, and elsewhere are emerging that conceive of business and business school ed-

TABLE 12.1

Assumptions of Neoclassical Economics Versus Catholic Social Teaching

	Neoclassical Economics	Catholic Social Teaching
Understanding of the person	Autonomous individuals	Beings-in-relation
Motivations of the person	Self-interest	Solidarity, reciprocity/gratuitousness
Good of the person	Satisfaction of subjective material preferences	Integral human development
Good of society	Aggregation of subjective material preference satisfaction	The common good
Market functioning	Competition	Competition, solidarity, reciprocity/gratuitousness
Standard of judgement	Pareto efficiency, economic growth	Universal destination of goods, preferential option for the poor
Understanding of rights	Property rights	Economic rights
Norms of justice	Commutative	Commutative, distributive, contributive
Role of government	Neutral referee, correct market failures	Solidarity, subsidiarity
Treatment of nature	Extractive (in service of GDP)	Integral ecology

Source: A. Annett, *Cathonomics: How Catholic Tradition Can Create a More Just Economy,* (Washington, DC: Georgetown University Press, 2022): 72. © 2022 by Georgetown University Press. Reprinted with permission. www.press.georgetown.edu.

ucation through a different set of economic, institutional, and cultural perspectives. To prepare students for this growing reality, business schools need to globalize their curriculum.[49]

Some critics believe they must go even further in making way for new points of view. Pressures are mounting to "decolonize the business curriculum," undertaking a more radical questioning of the Western model itself.[50] Just as E. F. Schumacher warned that Buddhist economics would be difficult for the modern economist to understand, much less accept, a truly global and decolonized curriculum poses a similar challenge. To be frank, most faculty are too steeped in the Western model to speak with authority on alternative views. This leads to frustration. Students want their professors to "be the grown-ups" and take a lead, rather than simply respond to student demands.[51] But the truth is that we may not know the right way to approach these challenges yet. The kinds of values that will replace those that support shareholder capitalism have not yet materialized. But rather than allowing that ambiguity to make us shy away from these topics, we need to include the students in the process of discovery.

Helping Business Students Find Their Purpose and Calling

In her book *The Top 5 Regrets of the Dying*, palliative care nurse Bronnie Ware finds that the top regret she heard from those who knew they were going to die was "I wish I'd had the courage to live a life true to myself, not the life others expected of me."[52] Hospice nurse Grace Bluerock found the same with her patients, many having regrets about sticking to a job they never enjoyed and wishing instead that they had chosen "work that was in line with their purpose and passions—work that they were excited about and gave them a sense of fulfillment."[53] I see a drive to avoid this fate among students today, and business schools need to help them on their quest to live a life true to themselves.

Practical Reasons for Adding the Pursuit of a Calling to Business Education. It may sound obvious, but research has shown that the attainment of intrinsic aspirations is positively related to psychological health, while the pursuit of extrinsic aspirations is related positively to indicators of ill-being.[54] Other studies have found that individuals who pursue intrinsic goals—such as personal growth, close relationships, and community involvement—score higher in various positive indicators including vitality, positive affect, and self-actualization than individuals who pursue extrinsic goals (identified as money and fame). Extrinsically motivated people score higher in various negative indicators including depression, anxiety, and physical symptoms. Similar results have been found in diverse countries and with working adults as well as college students.[55] Another study found that those who strongly valued financial success relative to personal growth, close relationships, and community involvement report poorer psychological health, suggesting a dark side to the pursuit of the traditional "American dream."[56] In considering the pursuit of purpose and meaning in life, author and educator Parker Palmer turns to an old Quaker saying, "Let your life speak," in which a vocation comes not from willfulness, but from listening.

> I must listen to my life and try to understand what it is truly about—quite apart from what I would like it to be about—or my life will never represent anything real in the world, no matter how earnest my intentions. That insight is hidden in the word vocation itself, which is rooted in the Latin for "voice." Vocation does not mean a goal that I pursue. It means a calling that I hear. Before I can tell my life what I want to do with it, I must listen to my life telling me who I am. I must listen for the truths and values at the heart of my own identity, not the standards by which I must live—but the standards by which I cannot help but live if I am living my own life.[57]

This sounds like the opposite kind of experience from what our students have within business school, where they have little opportunity for such reflection. Classes, clubs, social activities, and the hunt for the first summer internship or job at graduation dominate their attention from the moment they arrive on campus.

But herein lies a teacher's most sacred calling: guiding not just the technical but the moral and, yes, spiritual development of their students. Author David Brooks draws a distinction between two sets of virtues, what he calls the résumé virtues and the eulogy virtues: "The résumé virtues are the skills you bring to the marketplace. The eulogy virtues are the ones that are talked about at your funeral—whether you were kind, brave, honest or faithful. Were you capable of deep love? We all know that the eulogy virtues are more important than the résumé ones. But our culture and our educational systems spend more time teaching the skills and strategies you need for career success than the qualities you need to radiate that sort of inner light. Many of us are clearer on how to build an external career than on how to build inner character." In trying to understand those that focused more on the eulogy virtues, Brooks writes, "I came to the conclusion that wonderful people are made, not born—that the people I admired had achieved an unfakeable inner virtue, built slowly from specific moral and spiritual accomplishments."[58]

So, helping students find their calling and purpose can be accomplished, and indeed must be accomplished. But Brooks also points out a challenge. While some of this quest for purpose and meaning can be taught as academic subjects with books and lectures, "we learn most virtues the way we learn crafts, through the repetition of many small habits and practices, all within a coherent moral culture—a community of common values, whose members aspire to earn one another's respect."[59] By the 1960s, he laments, "moral education was in full scale retreat" as educators focused more on metrics of learning rather than the deeper spirit. Indiana University professor of education B. Edward McClellan adds that the research ideal replaced the humanistic ideal of cultivating the whole student in higher education. As a result, the big questions—How do you live a good life? What is the meaning of life?—got lost.[60]

The work of neuroscientist Iain McGilchrist suggests that some of this shift may also lie in our teaching emphasis from left to right brain thinking. "The right hemisphere pays attention to the Other, whatever it is that exists apart from ourselves, with which it sees itself in profound relation. . . . the left hemisphere pays attention to the virtual world that it has created, which is self-consistent, but self-contained, ultimately disconnected from the Other, making it powerful, but ultimately only able to operate on, and to know, itself."[61] MIT professor emeritus John Ehrenfeld sees our great social and environmental challenges as the product of too much left brain thinking that has led to dangerous consequences. "The ills and failings of modernity spring from an excess of left-brain domination and to put the planet back on track toward flourishing, the brain must be re-balanced to restore the right hemisphere to its proper role as master, yielding actions that care for the immediate external world."[62] Writing about the same shift but in more numinous terms, chairman of IMC Pan Asia Alliance Group and founder of the culture consultancy company Octave Frederick Tsao writes,

The greatest point of leverage for us all is a transformation in consciousness. It is not simply a matter of changing what we do, we must also change who we are. Without such deep-rooted change, we cannot address the challenges of the new era effectively. Having a consciousness of connectedness changes how we think and act. We become more empathetic and compassionate. When we see ourselves as an integral part of the natural world rather than separate from it, we become more attuned to how our actions affect not only humanity but life itself.[63]

Reforming the Curriculum to Aid Students in the Pursuit of a Calling. This book is about reforming business schools, and in reality, aiding a student's exploration of their calling requires a new approach to teaching, one that allows time and space for discernment where students are encouraged to explore it. It requires professors to abandon the current didactic model of teaching,[64] in which they pour their knowledge into students' brains. Instead, they must aim to touch students' hearts—inspire them, not just inform them. I admit, such an approach poses a great challenge to who we are as professors. Whereas we have traditionally seen the classroom as a place where we impart knowledge, now we must see it as a place where we guide students in developing character, wisdom, judgment, and purpose. For some, this will be an unfamiliar role, and they might be unprepared and even unwilling to take it on. But we must become less academic in our approach and more developmental; less hierarchical and top-down and more facilitative and collaborative; less Cartesian and more humanistic.

To be sure, we must teach students the basics of business management. But we must also teach them to seriously consider the vast power that they may someday possess to shape and guide society and how they can most responsibly wield that power. We must spend less time on the "how" of business through the tools of management such as strategy, accounting, finance, and operations and more time on the "why"—the purpose in support of which they will deploy these tools. Rather than teaching management as a precise science, we need to infuse the curriculum with more of the liberal arts and humanities.[65] Rather than simply imparting knowledge, we need to help students develop wisdom.

A wise business leader does not make decisions based solely on knowledge such as patterned information, regression analyses, and p values. Instead, she or he assesses that knowledge and makes a decision based on wisdom, vision, character, judgment, integrity, and purpose. Many of the problems we face in today's world are caused by applying knowledge without wisdom; "We act but we do not act wisely."[66] We apply economic or technocratic solutions to problems that require a broader understanding of spillover effects and unintended consequences in the social and physical contexts in which they are applied. The business curriculum should be reoriented to add the emphasis that there is much more to business than the bottom line and much more to business leadership than chasing it.

Students should be taught to look deep inside themselves to consider management as a calling, in a spirit similar to that with which we train doctors—a move away from the simple pursuit of a career for private personal gain towards a vocation that is based on a higher professional and moral purpose.[67] Students must discover how to connect their career with their conscience. As corporate attorney James Gamble writes, "Power needs to be constrained by conscience" if students wish to learn and practice a craft with integrity.[68] This integrity will, in turn, counter the drive for status, which is predominantly measured by monetary reward (and for which business schools are ranked).

Guided by an inner moral compass, students must decide what kind of a manager they are meant to be, what kind of career they aspire to have, and what kind of legacy they hope to leave. We should not be afraid to ask them to consider more than their own personal success and consider how they can also serve society. Rather than only asking, "How much money will I make?" we must help them to also ask, "How do I want to leave the world better than I found it?" Instead of only asking, "What career track gives me the most opportunity for professional development?" help them to also ask, "What pursuits will bring me closer to making a meaningful contribution to others in my business, my community, and society?" These are the questions that lead to a meaningful career—and to the sort of leaders who can step up to face the challenges facing society in the decades ahead.

Today, students are often discouraged from even trying to find their calling. A college education is increasingly valued simply for the skills it provides to earn a salary and then achieve happiness by purchasing the goods that salary affords. Some have little choice but to adopt this mercenary approach.

College simply costs too much money, and they amass such large debts that they find themselves accepting jobs that they may not really want in order to pay down that debt. But this approach to educational value crowds out the less measurable but more important journey of discovering how to live a meaningful and productive life. Our commercial society suggests to students that happiness derives from consuming more stuff. Its central message is that a person's value is measured by what we accumulate and what others see, rather than by what they believe or how they act. But contrary to many messages in our society, individuality is not measured by our outward appearance—clothes, tattoos, posture—it is measured by how we think and what we do. College degrees, fancy cars, big houses, and happy Facebook posts: these have all become ways of proving to people around us that we have worth. But they are projections and are often false.

Developing a Program to Help Students Find Their Purpose and Calling. The Merriam-Webster dictionary defines purpose as "something set up as an object or end to be attained," a calling as "a strong inner impulse toward a particular course of action especially when accompanied by conviction of divine influence; the vocation or profession in which one customarily engages," and a vocation similarly as "a summons or strong inclination to a particular state or course of action." Therefore, we can think of a purpose as the central motivating aims of one's life—the reasons you get up in the morning and the motivating force that guides your life decisions, influences behavior, shapes goals, offers a sense of direction, and creates meaning. We can think of a calling or vocation as the way you carry that purpose out, a unique contribution or service that you can undertake to make your purpose real and actionable. One's purpose is much more stable and enduring; one's calling or vocation can be more fluid. My own purpose in life is to foster a healthier environment by changing how we appreciate and understand it. My calling or vocation for carrying out that purpose is teaching and writing as a professor. One day I will retire, and my calling or vocation will change, though my purpose will likely endure. It is who I am, and it is the reason I get up in the morning, even when the headwinds are strong.

The truth is that we all have a purpose and calling. It's just that some are more thoughtfully arrived at and more altruistic, while others may be blindly accepted and self-orientated. A theologian once told me that he can tell you what you worship by how you spend your time because a calling is the active manifestation of what you value. In the words of David Foster Wallace, "In the day-to-day trenches of adult life, there is actually no such thing as atheism. There is no such thing as not worshipping. Everybody worships. The only choice we get is what to worship."[69] Similarly, David Brooks warns us to "be watchful over what you love, because you become what you desire."[70] That desire, love, or activity is your life's work and satisfaction will come from knowing who you are and what you are called to do. Or, as the Hindu scriptures the Upanishads point out, "You are what your deep driving desire is; As your deep driving desire is, so is your will; As your will is, so is your deed; As your deed is, so is your destiny." Satisfaction in your life's work comes from knowing who you are and what you are called to do, and then sticking with your idea of how a life well lived is measured as you see where that spirit takes you.

A process of guided discernment from learned faculty in a culturally rich and intellectually diverse learning environment—this is the recipe for rescuing students from becoming cormorants. It will lead to more focused, balanced, and mature students who will be thoughtful about why they are pursuing their education and how they might choose to direct it towards a career that is personally, professionally, and socially meaningful. There are several methods that are available, and there is plenty of space for innovation to improve upon them. I offer one model for such a program, "Management as a Calling," that I have developed at the Ross School of Business (go to http://andrewhoffman.net/, click on "Teaching," and then click on "MO635: Management as a Calling"). I offer it as but one model, and there are many other ways to do this that fit each professor's, student's, and school's culture.

The Positive Outcomes of Finding a Calling in Management

There's pure joy when you take control of your life, defy the "rules" around you, and take the risk to find work that you deeply connect with. As organizational development scholar Herbert Shepard writes,

> We have been brought up to live by rules that mostly have nothing to do with making our lives worth living. . . . Work is something you have to

be compensated for, because it robs you of living. Play is something you usually have to pay for, because your play is often someone else's work. . . . [But] a master in the art of living draws no sharp distinction between his work and his play, his labor and his leisure, his mind and his body, his education and his recreation. He scarcely knows which is which. He simply pursues his vision of excellence through whatever he is doing and leaves others to determine whether he is working or playing. To himself he always seems to be doing both.[71]

Beyond the sheer joy of taking your own oath of purpose, the benefits of a calling are multiple. A deepened awareness of purpose can help students become more resilient as they advance in their career and face setbacks. This is particularly important for students who take jobs in consulting, a field whose business model is to churn through people and one in which students may find themselves let go for reasons beyond their control. Even if purpose-driven students enter consulting, they will be more likely to find a path within it that brings them joy, and if they are expelled in the brutal "rank and yank" promotion system, they will be more likely to be able to pick themselves up, dust themselves off, and continue on their path.

Jim March, an emeritus professor at Stanford University, taught a course called "Management Through the Classics" before he passed away in 2018. To him, the most important book that business students should read is *Don Quixote*, explaining that Quixote "offers a basis for thinking about what justifies great action. Why do we do what we do? Our standard answer is that we do what we do because we expect it to lead to good consequences. Quixote reminds us that there is another possible answer: We do what we do because it fulfills our identity, our sense of self. Identity-based actions protect us from the discouragement of disappointing feedback. We live in a world that emphasizes realistic expectations and clear successes. Quixote had neither. But through failure after failure, he persists in his vision and his commitment. He persists because he knows who he is."[72] This is the essence of a calling. Have a vision, see a reality, make it so, even when those around you (like those around Don Quixote) think it is foolish or crazy. Having a clear internal compass can help students to be more like Don Quixote.

This can be beneficial in other, more immediate, ways. In his book *Life on*

Purpose: How Living for What Matters Most Changes Everything, University of Michigan public health professor Victor Strecher finds that a strong transcending purpose is good for your health and well-being and reduces defensiveness to change.[73] Overall, someone with a purpose will be more focused, more determined, more successful in their endeavors. As Friedrich Nietzsche pointed out, "[One] who has a *why* to live for can bear with almost any *how.*" Here are some ideas for how students who find their purpose choose a career and decide to stay within it, and what they can do once they've found it.

Good Goods. When a student has a clear sense of their calling, they will be more thoughtful about the kind of work they do. I have always been puzzled by students who express an ambivalence to what kind of career they pursue, being equally interested in a job with a consumer goods company as a job at a hospital or a nonprofit organization. Can students really be so flexible? Anthony Annett writes about the pursuit of "good goods," where the purpose of business is oriented towards the common good, "to meet human needs through the creation and development of goods and services."[74] This leads towards work that has a noble purpose and gives priority to creating good jobs, valuable products, and stable services. It is moving beyond "rentier capitalism," in which companies seek to occupy a position in the market where they can extract more profits than is proportional to their work. In the words of economist Joseph Stiglitz, good work is a move away from "wealth grabbing or rent seeking, trying to steal a larger fraction of the economic pie" and towards a recognition of "the true sources of wealth of a country and . . . the ability to get wealthy by creating wealth and contributing to society."[75]

Conscious Quitting. Once they take jobs, people with a calling will be more discerning about staying with that firm. This is happening with increasing frequency with young people in the post-Covid world. In 2023, a survey in the United States and the United Kingdom found that nearly 50 percent of employees said that they would consider resigning from their job if the values of the company did not align with their own, with climate change and economic inequality at the top of their list. Roughly 33 percent said that they have already resigned a position for this reason, and among Gen-Z and Millennial employees that number goes up to almost 50 percent.[76] Another survey with ten thousand energy professionals found that just over 60 percent consider the way that a company acts on environmental and social issues to be a major factor in their decision to join or leave a company.[77] These surveys show that students are increasingly searching for ways to live out their values through their work.

Public Citizenship. When they are successful, people with a calling to serve society will be more attentive to their role as citizen and not just as wealthy businessperson. The median starting salary for an MBA graduate in 2022 was $115,000, with some top-ranked graduates starting much higher,[78] while the top consulting firms offered base salaries as high as $190,000 with $30,000 signing bonuses and $60,000 performance bonuses.[79] In 2021, the median CEO compensation at one of the top three hundred and fifty US firms was $27.8 million.[80] Graduates with a calling will dedicate their wealth and energy to their purpose, involving themselves in the world around them and not just locking themselves and their fortunes behind the walls of gated communities and private country clubs. To assist this, business education should do more to teach future business leaders about serving on the boards of organizations in the nonprofit, health care, or other service-oriented fields; running for elected office or playing a role in local administration; and becoming philanthropists (to causes other than donations to their alma mater). These roles for the corporate executive are never covered in business education, and too many business students see their future impact only in the economic sphere and not the civic sphere. But guided reflection can yield business leaders who are more civic-minded, both in terms of their individual actions and in terms of stewarding the institutions of the market, government, and philanthropy to be truer to the spirit of democracy and an equal voice for all, not just the wealthy elite.[81]

Make the Pursuit of a Calling and Purpose the Norm

Rutger Bregman warns that "to stand up for human goodness means weathering a storm of ridicule. You'll be called naïve. Obtuse. Any weakness in your reasoning will be mercilessly exposed. Basically, it's easier to be a cynic," which he calls "just another word for laziness. It's an excuse not to take responsibility."[82] To overcome this cynicism, Stanford professor of education Bill Damon in his book *Noble Purpose: Joy of Living a Meaningful Life* challenges people to look for "purpose exemplars," people who represent models of noble behavior in service of good causes. He also points out that finding a calling is a gift that should be both celebrated and passed on to others.[83] So by highlighting exemplars and being one yourself, we can model careers that defy the typical wealth extraction and opportunism that Joseph Stiglitz warns against. Rather than seeing this path as an odd outlier, it becomes the road *more* traveled.

Consider, for example, that in 1923, Frederick Banting, James Collip, and Charles Best were awarded US patents for the discovery of insulin and the method used to make it. They then sold these patents to the University of Toronto for $1, with Banting famously stating, "Insulin does not belong to me, it belongs to the world." He wanted everyone who needed it to have access to it.[84] Similarly in 1955, Jonas Salk was asked who owned the patent to the polio vaccine he had developed and made available for free, and he answered, "Well, the people, I would say. There is no patent. Could you patent the sun?"[85] Some may hear these stories and think they are heroic outliers, not applicable to the corporate sector. But they are not.

In 1995, when a fire destroyed three of Malden Mills' four buildings in Massachusetts, CEO Aaron Feuerstein handed out holiday bonuses and announced that he would keep all 3,000 employees on the payroll with full benefits for ninety days and spend hundreds of millions of dollars to replace the lost buildings. He stated, "The basic idea that you can't serve the interest of the shareholder and the worker simultaneously is foreign to me. Their interests go together. I have a responsibility to the worker, both blue-collar and white-collar. It would have been unconscionable to put 3,000 people on the streets and deliver a deathblow to the cities of Lawrence and Methuen. Maybe on paper our company is worthless to Wall Street, but I can tell you it's worth more."[86]

According to Patagonia founder Yvon Chouinard, "The capitalist ideal is you grow a company and focus on making it as profitable as possible. Then, when you cash out, you become a philanthropist. We believe a company has a responsibility to do that all along—for the sake of the employees, for the sake of the planet."[87] In response to President Trump's Tax Cuts and Jobs Act, which would have reaped the company a $10 million windfall, Patagonia CEO Rose Marcario called it "irresponsible" and pledged that the company would be giving the entire rebate to different nonprofit environmental groups "committed to protecting air, land and water and finding solutions to the climate crisis."[88] Some may hear these stories and think they are privately held companies, not applicable to the publicly traded corporate sector. But that's not the case either.[89]

After the January 6, 2021, assault on the US Capitol, Charles Schwab shut down its PAC "in light of a divided political climate and an increase in attacks on those participating in the political process." After receiving criticism for its involvement in the Minnesota governor's election in 2010, Target established a board-level committee to oversee political donations.[90] In 2009, Paul Polman eliminated quarterly earnings reports the first day he took over as CEO of Unilever because "[w]e needed to remove the temptation to work only towards the next set of numbers."[91] All these examples challenge our standard notions of "rational" self-interested business behavior and elevate the possibilities of economic engagement that is more humane. In many ways, we might see such behavior as bizarre because it is uneconomic. But we need to bring such thinking back to the world of business, to consider the needs of society at least on a similar plane as that of business's economic needs.

A New Kind of Business School

Corporations play an increasingly outsized role in our modern world. The market—comprising business, government, civil society, and others—is the most powerful set of organizing institutions on Earth, and business is the most powerful entity within it. While government is critical to addressing our challenges, business must evolve to become a willing partner, turning its unmatched powers of ideation, production, and distribution to bear on what society needs. People are demanding it: a 2016 survey by the Global Strategy Group found that "84% of Americans believe that businesses have a responsibility to bring social change on important issues, just behind the President (89%) and Congress (92%)." The study also found that "81% of Americans believe corporations should take action to address important issues facing society; and 88% believe corporations have the power to influence social change."[92] It is business and the market that can provide solutions at the scale we need them. But for this to happen, we need to cultivate leaders who see their career as a calling to lead businesses *and* serve society. Business schools must help those future leaders along that path, guiding them in a discernment process that takes seriously the power that they will one day wield.

But this presents a challenge to business schools: a business school cannot instill a sense of purpose and calling in its students if it does not have one of its own. Rather than merely crafting a "value statement" for the purpose of differentiating in a crowded market, schools must truly live by their principles. As a community, business schools must clarify the aspirational principles that guide all aspects of their structure, including

- How students are selected and socialized
- The structuring of the curriculum, co-curriculum, and pedagogy that shape these students
- The recruiters who are invited to campus to place these students in leadership positions
- The selection of role models who exemplify the principles these students are meant to emulate
- The acceptance of donations that impact the physical and cultural facilities in which these students will learn
- How faculty are trained, selected, socialized, and rewarded to better serve students

Some of my colleagues express unease at the idea of bringing values so deeply into the curriculum and culture and express even more unease at the idea of teaching values in the classroom. But the point is that we already are. Values permeate our curriculum in ways both visible and invisible, and we are already professing a set of values whether we acknowledge them or not: that continuous economic growth is possible; that government has a limited role in the market; that the environment is an unlimited source of materials and a limitless sink for waste; that people are largely selfish, driven by avarice and greed; that efficiency is always good; that work is merely a supply chain input and the worker is merely a human resource. This has to change.

The time has come to rejuvenate the intellectual and moral training of future business leaders and shift to a new set of aspirational principles that requires we take a normative stand on what kind of world we want and what kind of leaders we want to take us there. We should present a positive vision of a future to be embraced and not just train students to accept the world as it is (or as we may perceive it to be). To do this, business schools should recommit to training students in a spirit similar to that which we use to train doctors, moving away from teaching simply the mechanics of running a business and towards instilling a vocation in business that is based on a higher professional and moral purpose. The curriculum should reach the whole student, engaging their rational side, but also inspiring their emotional and empathetic side; returning to the aspirations that Adam Smith held for the market. It should help students move away from becoming driven by external image and status and more towards their own intrinsic motivations for pursuing a career and a life. In this way, graduates will become more self-directed, resilient, open to change, and focused on the people and society that will depend upon them. The "dark triad" will recede as the motivations of greed and self-interest will be replaced by the virtues of sufficiency, love, and moderation, leading its students (and faculty and staff) to measure self-worth by character and not by material goods or in comparison to others.

If we are successful in shepherding in such a curriculum change, we will have helped future business leaders develop the wisdom and character they will need to see the broader connections and interdependencies of the social and natural worlds around us.[93] This is our challenge. It is up to us to choose to accept or reject it. In the end, business schools will either be part of the solution and a force for constructive and aspirational change or a part of the problem by maintaining the status quo.

Acknowledgments

First and foremost, I want to thank the Institute for Business in Global Society (BiGS) at the Harvard Business School for granting me a fellowship for the 2023–2024 academic year. I have not had such an opportunity to dive so deeply into a full-length project like this since I wrote my dissertation thirty years ago. I am grateful for all the people that made this such a rich experience: the Institute staff: Olivia Barba, Barbara DeLollis, Sarah Gazzaniga, Drew Keller, and Amram Migdal; the other climate fellows: Omar Asensio, Gunther Glenk, Conor Hickey, Jonas Meckling and Robyn Meeks; and the faculty: Joe Aldy, Julie Battilana, Ranjay Gulati, Rebecca Henderson, Hubert Joly, Bob Kaplan, John Macomber, Naomi Oreskes, Forest Reinhardt, Dan Schrag, Deb Spar, Rob Stavins, Jim Stock, Mike Toffel, Peter Tufano, and Mike Tushman.

I want to acknowledge two professors in particular. I want to thank Max Bazerman for being such a steady and solid mentor and guide through my career, even calling the BiGS fellowship to my attention and recommending I apply. I also want to thank my advisor John Ehrenfeld for continuing to engage with me and the wider world on the topic of sustainability, influencing and guiding my thinking and evolution. Being in Cambridge afforded me the gift of spending more time with both Max and Marla, and John and Ruth.

I want to extend special thanks to my editor Eben Harrell, who helped clarify my argument and tighten my prose, and my two research assistants: Charlie Richards, for helping with the sections on national capitalist models and human selfishness, and Kanika Rana, for helping with citations.

I want to thank the team at Stanford University Press: Richard Narramore, for his guidance on the framing and titles of the book and chapters; David Horne, for his attention to detail in style editing; and Tiffany Mok for guiding all the parts of the production process.I want to thank Richard Hall and Congressman Sandy Levin for their help in developing my course "Business in Democracy," Rosie Sharp for her help in developing my course "Reexamining Capitalism," and all the University of Michigan students who took both courses. A lot of the thinking that went into these courses, coupled with my thirty years of researching, writing, and teaching about business and sustainability, went into the structure and content for this book.

I want to thank the Arthur Vining Davis Foundations and John Churchill for funding my "Management as a Calling" program, and all the people who graciously helped me devise the program's details, including Jerry Canavaugh, Bill Damon, A. R. Elangovan, Marshall Ganz, Tom McClain, Ron Nahser, Carla Ogunrinde, Bob Quinn, Lance Sandelands, Jeff Seabright, and Monica Worline. And again, I want to thank the University of Michigan students who signed up to take the program as well as those who helped as teaching assistants in 2022–2023: Tom Kraeutler, Alli Lesovoy, Michael O'Gorman, Caroline Suttlehan, and Allison Winstel; and in 2023–2024: Akbar Arsiwala, Jill Dannis, Ash Martinez, Michael O'Gorman, and Maddie Parrish. This program also informed my thinking in this book.

Last, I want to thank my wife, Joanne, for being willing to uproot our life in Ann Arbor to experience a year in my home state of Massachusetts.

About the Author

ANDREW J. HOFFMAN is the Holcim (US) Professor of Sustainable Enterprise at the University of Michigan, a position that holds joint appointments in the Stephen M. Ross School of Business and the School for Environment and Sustainability. For the 2023–2024 academic year, he was a visiting climate fellow at the Institute for Business in Global Society at the Harvard Business School. He researches, writes, and teaches about the processes by which environmental and social issues both emerge and evolve as social, political, and managerial considerations. He has published over one hundred articles and book chapters, as well as eighteen books, which have been translated into six languages. He earned his PhD in both Management and Civil & Environmental Engineering at MIT and lives with his wife, journalist and writer Joanne Will, in Ann Arbor, Michigan. For more information go to http://www.andrewhoffman.net. His books include

*The Engaged Scholar: Expanding the Impact of
Academic Research in Today's World*

Management as a Calling: Leading Business, Serving Society

*Re-engaging with Sustainability in the Anthropocene Era:
An Institutional Approach* (with Dev Jennings)

*Business and the Natural Environment: A Research
Overview* (with Susse Georg)

Finding Purpose: Environmental Stewardship as a Personal Calling

How Culture Shapes the Climate Change Debate

*Constructing Green: The Social Structures of
Sustainability* (editor, with Rebecca Henn)

Flourishing: A Frank Conversation About Sustainability (with John Ehrenfeld)

*Business and the Environment: Critical Perspectives in Business
and Management,* Volumes I-IV, (editor, with Susse Georg)

*The Oxford Handbook on Business and the Natural
Environment* (editor, with Tima Bansal)

Builder's Apprentice: A Memoir

*Memo to the CEO: Climate Change, What's Your
Business Strategy?* (with John Woody)

*Carbon Strategies: How Leading Companies Are
Reducing Their Climate Change Footprint*

*Organizations, Policy and the Natural Environment: Institutional
and Strategic Perspectives* (editor, with Marc Ventresca)

*From Heresy to Dogma: An Institutional History
of Corporate Environmentalism*

*Competitive Environmental Strategy: A Guide
to the Changing Business Landscape*

*Global Climate Change: A Senior Level Dialogue at the
Intersection of Economics, Strategy, Technology, Science,
Politics and International Negotiation* (editor)

Notes

Preface

1. As quoted in K. Tippett, "Anand Giridharadas: When the market is our only language," *On Being*, November 15, 2018.

2. D. Elgin, "Global warming and carbon dioxide ethics," *Huffington Post*, October 23, 2012.

3. R. W. Emerson, *Commencement Address to the Harvard Divinity School*, July 15, 1838.

Chapter 1

1. M. Roser, "Extreme poverty: How far have we come, and how far do we still have to go?" *Our World in Data*, 2021, https://ourworldindata.org/extreme-poverty-in-brief (accessed October 8, 2023).

2. W. R. Scott and G. Davis, *Organizations and Organizing: Rational, Natural and Open Systems Perspectives* (Oxfordshire, UK: Routledge, 2000).

3. H. Joly, *The Heart of Business: Leadership Principles for the Next Era of Capitalism* (Boston: Harvard Business Review Press, 2021).

4. IPCC, in "Climate change 2014: Impacts, adaptation, and vulnerability: Summary for policymakers," 2014, https://www.ipcc.ch/site/assets/uploads/2018/02/ar5_wgII_spm_en.pdf (accessed February 26, 2022).

5. J. Watts, "We have 12 years to limit climate change catastrophe, warns UN," *The Guardian*, October 8, 2018.

6. IPCC, "Climate change 2014."

7. The World Bank, "New report examines risks of 4 degree hotter world by end of century," November 18, 2012, https://www.worldbank.org/en/news/press-release/2012/11/18/new-report-examines-risks-of-degree-hotter-world-by-end-of-century (accessed October 6, 2023).

8. R. Mogul, E. Mitra, M. Suri, and S. Saifi, "India and Pakistan heatwave is 'testing the limits of human survivability,' expert says," CNN, May 2, 2022.

9. S. Fidler, "Environmental risks loom large among World Economic Forum members," *Wall Street Journal*, January 15, 2020.

10. J. Ewing, "Climate change could cause the next financial meltdown," *New York Times*, January 23, 2020.

11. UNICEF, "Children displaced in a changing climate," 2023, https://www.unicef.org/reports/children-displaced-changing-climate (accessed October 6, 2023).

12. P. Dizikes, "The productive career of Robert Solow," *MIT News*, January/February, 2020: 12.

13. N. Kirsch, "The 3 richest Americans hold more wealth than bottom 50% of the country, study finds," *Forbes*, November 9, 2017.

14. N. Hanauer, "The top 1% of Americans have taken $50 trillion from the bottom 90%—and that's made the U.S. less secure," *Time*, September 14, 2020.

15. J. Gans, "These billionaires have more money than the US Treasury right now," *The Hill*, May 26, 2023.

16. C. McGreal, "Angus Deaton on inequality: 'The war on poverty has become a war on the poor'," *The Guardian*, October 7, 2023.

17. J. Horowitz, R. Igielnik, and R. Kochhar, "Trends in income and wealth inequality," Pew Research Center, January 9, 2020.

18. H. Zaidy, "The American Dream is much easier to achieve in Canada," CNN Business, January 20, 2020.

19. Oxfam, "World's billionaires have more wealth than 4.6 billion people," 2020, https://www.oxfam.org/en/press-releases/worlds-billionaires-have-more-wealth-46-billion-people (accessed September 21, 2023).

20. R. Riddell, N. Ahmed, A. Maitland, M. Lawson, and A. Taneja, "Inequality Inc. How corporate power divides our world and the need for a new era of public action," *Oxfam International Briefing Paper*, January 15, 2024.

21. A. Thériault, "Richest 1% bag nearly twice as much wealth as the rest of the world put together over the past two years," *Oxfam International*, January 16, 2023.

22. R. Kleinfeld, *Polarization, Democracy, and Political Violence in the United States: What the Research Says* (Washington, DC: Carnegie Endowment for International Peace, 2023).

23. P. Farrell, "Myth of perpetual growth is killing America," *Wall Street Journal*, June 12, 2012.

24. J. Stiglitz, "Progressive capitalism is not an oxymoron," *New York Times*, April 19, 2019.

25. G. Zucman, "It's time to tax the billionaires," *New York Times*, May 3, 2024.

26. "Do the rich pay their fair share?" *Oxfam*, January 14, 2024.

27. G. White, "Stiglitz: Here's how to fix inequality," *The Atlantic*, November 2, 2015.

28. A. Hoffman, "Why management research needs a radical rethink," *Financial Times*, July 5, 2023.

29. R. Henderson and K. Ramanna, *Do Managers Have a Role to Play in Sustaining the Institutions of Capitalism?* (Washington, DC: Brookings Institution, 2015).

30. As quoted in C. Riback, "Joseph Stiglitz: Saving capitalism from itself," *Chris Riback's Conversations*, June 21. 2019, https://chrisriback.com/joseph-stiglitz-saving-capitalism-from-itself/.

31. NYU Stern Center for Sustainable Business, https://www.stern.nyu.edu/experi ence-stern/about/departments-centers-initiatives/centers-of-research/center-sustain able-business (accessed October 8, 2023).

32. HEC Paris, "Leading European business schools unite to accelerate business response to climate crisis," 2021, https://www.hec.edu/en/news-room/leading-europe an-business-schools-unite-accelerate-business-response-climate-crisis (accessed October 8, 2023).

33. C. Galdón et al., "Business schools must do more to address the climate crisis," *Harvard Business Review*, February 1, 2022: 1.

34. J. Ehrenfeld and A. Hoffman, *Flourishing: A Frank Conversation on Sustainability* (Stanford, CA: Stanford University Press, 2013).

35. J. Will, "The last harvest: My stepfather and the demise of the family farm," *The Globe and Mail*, December 8, 2018.

36. P. Tufano, "A bolder vision for business schools," *Harvard Business Review*, March 11, 2020.

37. A. Hoffman and D. Ely, "Time to put the fossil-fuel industry into hospice," *Stanford Social Innovation Review*, Fall 2022: 28–37.

38. "The global backlash against climate policies has begun," *The Economist*, October 11, 2023.

39. M. Friedman, "The social responsibility of business is to increase its profits," *New York Times Magazine*, September 13, 1970.

40. K. Polowy, " 'Greed is good': Oliver Stone explains origin and relevance of classic 'Wall Street' line 30 years later," *Yahoo! News*, September 22, 2017.

41. S. M. Gardiner, "Climate justice," in *The Oxford Handbook of Climate Change and Society*, ed. J. S. Dryzek, R. B. Norgaard, and D. Schlosberg, 309–322 (Oxford, UK: Oxford University Press, 2011)..

42. A. Ross Sorkin, "Ex-corporate lawyer's idea: Rein in 'sociopaths' in the boardroom," *New York Times*, July 29, 2019.

43. D. Noor, "US oil lobby launches eight-figure ad blitz amid record fossil fuel extraction," *The Guardian*, January 10, 2024.

44. S. Hall, "Exxon knew about climate change almost 40 years ago," *Scientific American*, October 26, 2015.

45. A. Gale, "Sacklers sacked but Purdue still caused opioid epidemic," *Journal of the Missouri State Medical Association* 119, no. 2 (2022): 109.

46. M. Forsythe and W. Bogdanich, "McKinsey settles for nearly $600 million over role in opioid crisis," *New York Times*, November 5, 2021.

47. W. Bogdanich and M. Forsythe, "How McKinsey has helped raise the stature of authoritarian governments," *New York Times*, December 15, 2018.

48. A. LaFrance, "The despots of Silicon Valley," *The Atlantic*, March 2024.

49. A. Pollack, "Drug goes from $13.50 a tablet to $750, overnight," *New York Times*, September 20, 2015.

50. D. McDonald, "When you get that wealthy, you start to buy your own bullshit: The miseducation of Sheryl Sandberg," *Vanity Fair*, November 27, 2018.

51. Baker Library Historical Collections, https://www.library.hbs.edu/hc/buildinghbs/core-body-of-knowledge.html (accessed May 10, 2024).

52. S. Long, "The financialization of the American elite," *American Affairs*, Fall 2019.

53. R. Khurana, *From Higher Aims to Hired Hands: The Social Transformation of American Business Schools and the Unfulfilled Promise of Management as a Profession* (Princeton, NJ: Princeton University Press, 2010): jacket.

54. R. A. Gordon and J. E. Howell, *Higher Education for Business.* (New York: Columbia University Press, 1959).

55. J. L. Zimmerman, "Can American business schools survive?" *SSRN*, September 11, 2001.

56. H. A. Simon, *Models of My Life* (Boston: MIT Press, 1991): 138.

57. R. Khurana, K. Kimura, and M. Fourcade, *How Foundations Think: The Ford Foundation as a Dominating Institution in the Field of American Business Schools* (Cambridge, MA: Harvard Business School, 2011), Working Paper 11–070.

58. W. Bennis and J. O'Toole, "How business schools lost their way," *Harvard Business Review* 83, no. 5 (2005): 96–104.

59. P. Carlile, S. Davidson, K. Freeman, and N. Venkatraman (eds.), *Reimagining Business Education: Insights and Actions from the Business Education Jam* (Bingley, UK: Emerald Group, 2016): 1.

60. J. Pfeffer, "Ensuring relevance, reach and respect," in *Reimaging Business Education: Insights and Actions from the Business Education Jam*, ed. P. Carlile et al., 97–99 (Bingley, UK: Emerald Group, 2016).

61. J. Pfeffer and C. Fong, "The end of business schools? Less success than meets the eye," *Academy of Management Learning and Education* 1, no. 1 (2002): 78–85.

62. S. Datar, D. Garvin, and P. Cullen (eds.), *Rethinking the MBA: Business Education at a Crossroads.* (Cambridge, MA: Harvard Business Press, 2010).

63. Pfeffer, "Ensuring relevance, reach and respect."

64. Pfeffer and Fong, "The end of business schools?"

65. S. Datar, D. Garvin, and P. Cullen, "Rethinking the MBA: Business education at a crossroads," *Journal of Management Development* 30, no. 5 (2011): 451–462.

66. Bennis and O'Toole, "How business schools have lost their way."

67. R. Jacoby, *The Last Intellectuals: American Culture in the Age of Academe* (New York: Basic Books, 2000): 154.

68. Carlile, Davidson, Freeman, and Venkatraman, *Reimagining Business Education*, 82.

69. A. Hoffman, *The Engaged Scholar: Expanding the Impact of Academic Research in Today's World* (Stanford, CA: Stanford University Press, 2021).

70. S. Martinez-Conde, "Has contemporary academia outgrown the Carl Sagan effect?" *The Journal of Neuroscience*, February 17, 2016.

71. N. Kristof, "Professors, we need you!" *New York Times*, February 15, 2014.

72. R. Webster, "Superstar prof asks: Are B-schools a scam?" *Poets & Quants*, February 16, 2022.

73. S. Shinn, "What's wrong with business schools today," *AACSB*, February 14, 2022.

74. D. Bachrach et al., "On academic rankings, unacceptable methods, and the social obligations of business schools," *Decision Sciences* 48, no. 3 (2017): 561–585.

75. Department of Justice, "Former Temple Business School dean sentenced to over one year in prison for rankings fraud scheme," US Attorney's Office, Eastern District of Pennsylvania, 2022, https://www.justice.gov/usao-edpa/pr/former-temple -business-school-dean-sentenced-over-one-year-prison-rankings-fraud-scheme (accessed September 21, 2023).

76. Khurana, *From Higher Aims to Hired Hands*, jacket.

77. Stiglitz, "Progressive capitalism is not an oxymoron."

78. D. Yaffe-Bellany, "Shareholder value is no longer everything, Top CEOs say," *New York Times*, August 19, 2019.

79. K. Schwab, *Davos Manifesto 2020: The Universal Purpose of a Company in the Fourth Industrial Revolution* (Davos, Switzerland: World Economic Forum, 2020).

80. P. Polman, and A. Winston, "The net positive manifesto," *Harvard Business Review*, September-October 2021.

81. L. Fink, "The power of capitalism," *BlackRock*, https://www.blackrock.com/ corporate/investor-relations/larry-fink-ceo-letter (accessed February 4, 2024).

82. A. Hoffman, *The Engaged Scholar: Expanding the Impact of Academic Research in Today's World*, (Stanford, CA: Stanford University Press, 2021).

83. The Aspen Institute, "These business professors have ideas worth teaching," May 12, 2018, https://www.aspeninstitute.org/blog-posts/business-professors-ideas -worth-teaching/ (accessed February 4, 2024).

84. T. Hart, C. Fox, K. Ede, and J. Korstad, "Do, but don't tell. The search for social responsibility and sustainability in the websites of the top-100 US MBA programs," *International Journal of Sustainability in Higher Education* 16, no. 5 (2015): 706–728.

Chapter 2

1. M. Ballew et al., *Global Warming's Six Americas Across Age, Race/Ethnicity, and Gender* (New Haven, CT: Yale Program on Climate Change Communication, 2023).

2. I. Wylie, "What Generation Z wants from a business masters," *Financial Times*, September 4, 2022.

3. Yale University/WBCSD, *Rising Leaders on Environmental Sustainability and Climate Change: A Global Survey of Business Students* (New Haven, CT: Yale University Center for Business and the Environment, 2015).

4. Net Impact, *Business as Unusual: The Social and Environmental Impact Guide to Graduate Programs—For Students by Students* (San Francisco: Net Impact, 2014).

5. A. Jack, "The rise of the 'sustainable' MBA," *Financial Times*, January 21, 2020; J. Moules, "MBA students seek higher 'purpose' than mere money," *Financial Times*, October 20, 2019.

6. A. Hoffman, *Finding Purpose: Environmental Stewardship as a Personal Calling*, (Leeds, UK: Greenleaf, 2016).

7. T. S. Eliot, *Four Quartets* (San Diego: Harcourt, 1943).

8. M. Shellenberger and T. Nordhaus, *The Death of Environmentalism: Global Warming in a Post-Environmental World* (Oakland, CA: The Breakthrough Institute, 2004).

9. R. Williams, *Resources of Hope: Culture, Democracy, Socialism* (Brooklyn, NY: Verso, 1989).

10. Hoffman, *Finding Purpose.*

Chapter 3

1. S. Datar, D. Garvin, and P. Cullen (eds.), *Rethinking the MBA: Business Education at a Crossroads.* (Cambridge, MA: Harvard Business Press, 2010): 5–6.

2. S. Dameron and T. Durand (eds.), *Redesigning Management Education and Research: Challenging Proposals from European Scholars.* (Northampton, MA: Edward Elgar, 2011): 10.

3. P. Carlile, S. Davidson, K. Freeman, and N. Venkatraman (eds.), *Reimagining Business Education: Insights and Actions from the Business Education Jam.* (Bingley, UK: Emerald Group, 2016): 1.

4. F. Phillips, C. Hsieh, C. Ingene, and L. Golden, "Business schools in crisis," *Journal of Open Innovation: Technology, Market, and Complexity* 2, no. 3 (2016): 10.

5. S. Ghoshal, "Bad management theories are destroying good management practices," *Academy of Management Learning & Education* 4, no. 1 (2005): 75–91.

6. A. Hoffman, *The Engaged Scholar: Expanding the Impact of Academic Research in Today's World* (Stanford, CA: Stanford University Press, 2021).

7. L. Ormans, "50 journals used in FT research rank," *Financial Times*, September 12, 2016.

8. D. Meyerson, *Tempered Radicals: How People Use Difference to Inspire Change at Work* (Boston: Harvard Business School Press, 2001).

9. A. R. Elangovan and A. Hoffman, "The pursuit of success in academia: Plato's ghost asks 'What then?'" *Journal of Management Inquiry*, 2019, doi.org/10.1177/10564 92619836729.

10. As quoted in A. Hoffman, K. Ashworth, C. Dwelle, P. Goldberg, A. Henderson, L. Merlin, Y. Muzyrya, N. Simon, V. Taylor, C. Weisheit, and S. Wilson, *Academic Engagement in Public and Political Discourse: Proceedings of the Michigan Meeting* (Ann Arbor, MI: Michigan Publishing, 2015): 46.

11. M. Heidegger, *What Is Called Thinking?* trans. J. G. Gray (New York: Harper and Row, 1968).

12. C. Reincke, A. Bredenoord, and M. van Mil, "From deficit to dialogue in science communication: The dialogue communication model requires additional roles from scientists," *EMBO reports* 21, no. 9 (2020): e51278.

13. D. Brooks, *The Second Mountain: The Quest for a Moral Life* (New York: Random House, 2019).

14. A. Hoffman, "Academic 'elders' wanted: Inquire within," *AACSB*, January 2, 2024.

15. S. Kerr, "On the folly of rewarding A, while hoping for B," *Academy of Management Journal* 18, no. 4 (1975): 769–783.

16. Responsible Research for Business and Management, https://www.rrbm. network/ (accessed May 4, 2024).

17. I. Wylie, "What Generation Z wants from a business masters," *Financial Times*, September 4, 2022.

18. J. Benjamin, "Business class: The bankrupt ideology of business school," *The New Republic*, May 14, 2018.

19. S. Long, "The financialization of the American elite," *American Affairs*, Fall 2019.

20. Wylie, "What Generation Z wants from a business masters."

Chapter 4

1. F. Jameson, "Future city," *New Left Review*, May/June 2003.

2. N. Oreskes and E. Conway, *The Big Myth: How American Business Taught Us to Loathe Government and Love the Free Market* (New York: Bloomsbury, 2023).

3. E. Beinhocker and N. Hanauer, "Redefining capitalism." *McKinsey Quarterly*, 2014 (3rd quarter): 160–169.

4. R. Gomory and R. Sylla, "The American corporation," *Daedalus* 142, no. 2 (2013): 102–118.

5. It is interesting to note that, while the first corporations in the United States emerged in the seventeenth and eighteenth centuries, the oldest business in the world is a construction company in Japan called Kongō Gumi, which has been in operation since 578 and specializes in shrines and temples. In 2006, corporate debt hit it hard, and it lost its independent status. It is now a subsidiary of Takamatsu Construction Group.

6. R. Khurana, A. Klaber, and E. Baldwin, *Technical Note: An Abridged History of the American Corporation*, Harvard Business School, 2010, Technical Note 411–069.

7. T. Guinnane, R. Harris, N. Lamoreaux, and J. Rosenthal, "Putting the corporation in its place," *Enterprise & Society* 8, no. 3 (2007), 687–729.

8. "The Potomac Company," The George Washington Presidential Library, https://www.mountvernon.org/library/digitalhistory/digital-encyclopedia/article/the-potomac-company/ (accessed October 30, 2023).

9. Khurana, Klaber, and Baldwin, *Technical Note.*

10. J. Williamson and P. Lindert, "America's revolution: Economic disaster, development, and equality," *The Centre for Economic Policy Research*, https://cepr.org/voxeu/columns/americas-revolution-economic-disaster-development-and-equality (accessed October 30, 2023).

11. S. Smith, "The American economy of 1776," *NPR*, July 5, 2019.

12. "Ten facts about the American economy in the 18th century," *The George Washington Museum*, https://www.mountvernon.org/george-washington/colonial-life-today/early-american-economics-facts (accessed October 30, 2023).

13. P. Hebert, "Frederick Douglass' economic critique of racism in *My Bondage,*

My Freedom," *Readings in American Literature,* 2020, https://2020hebert152w.com mons.gc.cuny.edu/2020/06/24/frederick-douglass-economic-critique-of-racism-in -my-bondage-my-freedom/ (accessed January 28, 2024).

14. F. Douglass, "The accumulation of wealth," *Frederick Douglass's Paper,* November 28, 1856, https://jacobin.com/2020/02/frederick-douglass-railed-against-economic -inequality (accessed January 28, 2024).

15. S. Mintz, "Historical context: Was slavery the engine of American economic growth?" *The Gilder Lehrman Institute of American History,* https://www. gilderlehrman.org/history-resources/teaching-resource/historical-context-was -slavery-engine-american-economic-growth (accessed October 30, 2023).

16. L. Cunningham, *Corporations and Other Business Organizations: Cases and Materials* (Durham, NC: Carolina Academic Press, 2020).

17. R. Ransom, *The Economics of the Civil War,* University of California, Riverside, https://web.mnstate.edu/stutes/Econ411/Readings/civil.htm (accessed, October 30, 2023).

18. S. Zickuhr, "New research shows slavery's central role in U.S. economic growth leading up to the Civil War," *The Washington Center for Equitable Growth,* June 24, 2021.

19. J. Hummel, "U.S. slavery and economic thought," *Econlib,* https://www.econlib .org/library/enc/usslaveryandeconomicthought.html (accessed October 30, 2023).

20. Ransom, *Economics of the Civil War.*

21. US Department of State, *The U.S. Economy: A Brief History,* https://usa. usembassy.de/etexts/oecon/chap3.htm (accessed October 30, 2023).

22. D. Gans and D. Kendall, "A capitalist joker: The strange origins, disturbing past, and uncertain future of corporate personhood in American law," *John Marshall Law Review* 44 (2010): 643–699.

23. Khurana, Klaber, and Baldwin, *Technical Note*

24. R. Sylla, "How the American corporation evolved over two centuries," *Proceedings of the American Philosophical Society* 158, no. 4 (2014): 354–363.

25. Gomory and Sylla, "The American corporation.

26. L. Rothman, "How American inequality in the Gilded Age compares to today," *Time,* February 5, 2018.

27. H. Spencer, *The Principles of Biology* (Forest Grove, OR: University Press of the Pacific, 1865/2002): 444.

28. H. Spencer, *Social Statics* (Princeton, NJ: Robert Schalkenbach Foundation, 1851/1995).

29. As quoted in J. Mickelthwait and A. Woolridge, *The Company: A Short History of a Revolutionary Idea* (New York: The Modern Library, 2003): 71.

30. C. F. Adams, "A chapter of Erie," *North American Review,* July 1869.

31. T. Roosevelt, "First annual message," December 3, 1901, The American Presidency Project, https://www.presidency.ucsb.edu/documents/first-annual-message-16 (accessed October 26, 2023).

32. Oreskes and Conway, *The Big Myth.* 417.

33. Mickelthwait and Woodridge, *The Company*, 59.

34. "Great Depression facts," *Franklin D. Roosevelt Presidential Library and Museum*, https://www.fdrlibrary.org/great-depression-facts (accessed October 13, 2023).

35. J. M. Keynes, *The General Theory of Employment, Interest and Money*, (Camden, UK: Palgrave Macmillan, 1936).

36. R. Martin, "The age of customer capitalism," *Harvard Business Review*, January-February 2010.

37. Mickelthwait and Woodridge, *The Company*, 84.

38. A. Chandler, *The Visible Hand: The Managerial Revolution in American Business* (Cambridge, MA: Belknap Press of Harvard University Press, 1977): 1.

39. J. K. Galbraith, *The New Industrial State* (New York: Houghton Mifflin, 1967).

40. J. K. Galbraith, *American Capitalism: The Concept of Countervailing Power* (New York: Houghton Mifflin, 1952).

41. A. Ross Sorkin, "How shareholder democracy failed the people," *New York Times*, August 20, 2019.

42. As quoted in Mickelthwait and Woodridge, *The Company*, 118.

43. As quoted in D. Strohl, "Fact Check: Did a GM president really tell Congress 'What's good for GM is good for America?'" *Hemmings*, September 5, 2019.

44. D. Riesman, N. Glazer, and R. Denney, *The Lonely Crowd: A Study of the Changing American Character* (New Haven, CT: Yale University Press, 1950).

45. W. Whyte, *The Organization Man* (New York: Simon & Schuster, 1956).

46. L. Prieto and S. Phipps, "How 20th-century black business leaders envisioned a more just capitalism," *Harvard Business Review*, April 7, 2021.

47. Ross Sorkin, "How shareholder democracy failed the people."

48. R. Nader, *Unsafe at Any Speed: The Designed-In Dangers of the American Automobile* (New York: Grossman, 1965).

49. J. Burns, *Milton Friedman: The Last Conservative* (New York: Farrar, Straus and Giroux, 2023).

50. L. Powell, *Powell Memorandum: Attack on American Free Enterprise System*, Washington & Lee University School of Law Scholarly Commons, 1971, https://scholarlycommons.law.wlu.edu/powellmemo/ (accessed October 24, 2023).

51. M. Jensen and W. Meckling, "Theory of the firm: Managerial behavior, agency costs and ownership structure," *Journal of Financial Economics* 3, no. 4 (1976): 305–360.

52. Jensen and Meckling, "Theory of the firm."

53. As quoted in C. Riback, "Joseph Stiglitz: Saving capitalism from itself," *Chris Riback's Conversations*, June 21, 2019.

54. Millennium Ecosystem Assessment, *Ecosystems and Human Well-Being: Synthesis Report* (Washington DC: Island Press, 2005): 1.

55. Stockholm Resilience Center, "Planetary boundaries," 2023, https://www.stockholmresilience.org/research/planetary-boundaries.html (accessed October 8, 2023).

56. P. Crutzen, "The 'Anthropocene'," in *Earth System Science in the Anthropocene*, ed. E. Ehlers and T. Krafft (Berlin, Heidelberg: Springer, 2006).

57. In 2024, the international Subcommission on Quaternary Stratigraphy (SQS)

voted against the proposal to create an Anthropocene epoch. Some argued that the Anthropocene should instead be defined as an "event in geological history," similar to the rise of atmospheric oxygen just over two billion years ago, known as the Great Oxidation Event. Regardless, the term has become a broad cultural concept already used by many to describe the era of accelerating human impacts, such as climate change and biodiversity loss. A. Witze, "Geologists reject the Anthropocene as Earth's new epoch—after 15 years of debate," *Nature*, March 6, 2024.

58. E. Altvater et al. (eds.), *Anthropocene or Capitalocene? Nature, History, and the Crisis of Capitalism* (New York: PM Press, 2016).

59. Stockholm Resilience Center, "Planetary Boundaries."

60. Offering hope that we can address these trends, one planetary boundary is on the mend: ozone depletion has been reversed after the Montreal Protocol was enacted in 1987, leading to an expected recovery of the ozone layer near the middle of the twenty-first century.

61. As quoted in G. Wearden, "David Attenborough tells Davos: 'The Garden of Eden is no more'," *The Guardian*, January 21, 2019.

62. A. Shah, "Consumption and consumerism," *Global Issues*, January 5, 2014.

63. L. Chancel, T. Piketty, E. Saez, and G. Zucman, "World inequality report," 2022, https://wir2022.wid.world/ (accessed February 13, 2024).

64. D. Kennedy, "The climate divide," *Science* 299, no. 5614 (2003): 1813.

65. R. Kochhar and A. Cilluffo, "How wealth inequality has changed in the U.S. since the Great Recession, by race, ethnicity and income," Pew Research Center, November 1, 2017.

66. S. Lund, J. Manyika, L. Hilton Segel, A. Dua, B. Hancock, S. Rutherford, and B. Macon, *The Future of Work in America: People and Places, Today and Tomorrow* (Washington, DC: McKinsey Global Institute, 2019).

67. B. Lindsey and S. Teles, *The Captured Economy: How the Powerful Enrich Themselves, Slow Down Growth, and Increase Inequality* (Oxford, UK: Oxford University Press, 2017).

68. T. Prado and J. Bauer, "Big Tech platform acquisitions of start-ups and venture capital funding for innovation. Information," *Economics and Policy* 59 (2022): 100973.

69. M. Gilens and B. Page, "Testing theories of American politics: Elites, interest groups, and average citizens." *Perspectives on Politics* 12, no. 3 (2014): 564–581.

70. D. Matthews (2016) "Remember that study saying America is an oligarchy? 3 rebuttals say it's wrong." *Vox*, May 9, 2016.

71. Martin, "The age of customer capitalism."

72. A. Annett, *Cathonomics: How Catholic Tradition Can Create a More Just Economy* (Washington, DC: Georgetown University Press, 2022): 117.

73. C. Atkins, O. White, A. Padhi, K. Ellingrud, A. Madgavkar, and M. Neary, *Rekindling US Productivity for a New Era* (Washington, DC: McKinsey Global Institute, 2023).

74. S. Denning, "The origin of 'the world's dumbest idea': Milton Friedman," *Forbes*, June 26, 2013.

75. J. Manyika, G. Pinkus, and M. Tuin, *Rethinking the Future of American Capitalism* (Washington, DC: McKinsey Global Institute, 2020).

76. B. Hall, "Six challenges in designing equity-based pay," *National Bureau of Economic Research*, August 2003.

77. L. Mishal and J. Kandra, "CEO pay has skyrocketed 1,322% since 1978," *Economic Policy Institute*, April 10, 2021.

78. M. Jensen and K. Murphy, "Performance pay and top-management incentives," *The Journal of Political Economy* 98, no. 2 (1990): 225–264.

79. J. Bivens and J. Kandra, "CEO pay has skyrocketed 1,460% since 1978," *Economic Policy Institute*, October 4, 2022.

80. Bivens and Kandra, "CEO pay has skyrocketed 1,460% since 1978."

81. Mishal and Kandra, "CEO pay has skyrocketed 1,322% since 1978."

82. R. Neate, "World's five richest men double their money as poorest get poorer," *The Guardian*, January 15, 2024.

83. R. Foroohar, "American capitalism's great crisis," *Time*, May 12, 2016.

84. M. Jacobs and M. Mazzucato (eds.), *Rethinking Capitalism: Economics and Policy for Sustainable and Inclusive Growth* (Hoboken, NJ: Wiley-Blackwell, 2016).

85. BPC Staff, "GE to sell most of its finance arm, once one of largest in the country," *Business Record*, April 10, 2015.

86. G. Mukunda, "The price of Wall Street's power," *Harvard Business Review*, June 2014.

87. R. Foroohar, *Makers and Takers: The Rise of Finance and the Fall of American Business* (New York: Crown Business, 2016): 14.

88. B. Lindsey, "The conservative inequality paradox," *National Review*, November 7, 2017.

89. Jacobs and Mazzucato, *Rethinking Capitalism*.

90. C. Bravard, J. Pontillo, and A. Hoffman, *For Whom We Play the Game: Advice to the Next Generation of Business Leaders from Paul Polman* (Ann Arbor, MI: University of Michigan, 2021), 30, https://deepblue.lib.umich.edu/handle/2027.42/168414 (accessed February 13, 2024).

91. A. Hoffman and L. Sandelands, "Getting right with nature: Anthropocentrism, ecocentrism and theocentrism," *Organization & Environment* 18, no. 2 (2005): 141–162.

92. As quoted in D. Leonhardt, "A CEO who's scared for America," *New York Times*, March 31, 2019.

93. As quoted in F. Ryan, "There's already a class war—and it's the conservatives who are waging it," *The Guardian*, November 27, 2019.

94. J. Stiglitz, "Progressive capitalism is not an oxymoron," *New York Times*, April 19, 2019.

95. M. Parker, "Why we should bulldoze the business school," *The Guardian*, April 27, 2018.

96. S. J. Gould, "The creation myths of Cooperstown," *Natural History*, November 1989.

97. E. Warren, *Accountable Capitalism Act*, 2018, https://www.warren.senate.gov/

imo/media/doc/Accountable%20Capitalism%20Act%20One-Pager.pdf (accessed November 23, 2023).

98. S. Pearlstein, *Can American Capitalism Survive?* (New York: St. Martin's Press, 2018): 103.

99. J. Davis, "Is shareholder capitalism a suicide pact?" *Medium*, June 2023.

Chapter 5

1. G. Hubbard, "Even my business-school students have doubts about capitalism," *The Atlantic*, January 2, 2022.

2. J. Kocka, *Capitalism: A Short History,* (Princeton, NJ: Princeton University Press, 2016): 21.

3. As quoted in Spectrum Staff, "Adam Smith: Selfishness or self-interest?" *Spectrum*, January 23, 2009.

4. As quoted in E. Butler, *The Condensed Wealth of Nations and the Incredibly Condensed Theory of Moral Sentiments* (United Kingdom: Adam Smith Research Trust, 2011): 78.

5. A. Smith, *The Theory of Moral Sentiments*, 6th ed. (Cambridge, UK: Cambridge University Press, 1759/2002).

6. J. DeLoach, "When in doubt, apply Warren Buffett's newspaper test," *Corporate Compliance Insights*, June 21, 2023.

7. Y. Levin, "Recovering the case for capitalism," *National Affairs*, Spring 2010.

8. As quoted in B. Friedman, "Economic origins and aims: A role for religious thinking?" *Reflections: A Magazine of Theological and Ethical Inquiry*, Spring 2010.

9. J. Viner, "Adam Smith and laissez faire," *Journal of Political Economy* 35, no. 2 (1927): 198–232.

10. Levin, "Recovering the case for capitalism."

11. A. Smith, *An Enquiry into the Nature and Causes of the Wealth of Nations* (New York: Random House, 1776/1940), Book IV, Chap. 2.

12. Smith, *Theory of Moral Sentiments*, Part IV, Chap. 1.

13. Smith, *Enquiry into the Nature and Causes of the Wealth of Nations*, Book I, Chap. 2.

14. As quoted in C. Robin, "Empathy & the economy," *The New York Review of Books*, December 8, 2022.

15. Smith, *Enquiry into the Nature and Causes of the Wealth of Nations*, Book I, Chap. 1.

16. J. Schumpeter, *Capitalism, Socialism and Democracy* (New York: Harper & Brothers, 1942): 82–83.

17. M. Weber, *The Protestant Ethic and The Spirit of Capitalism* (New York: Scribner, 1905/1930).

18. A. McKinnon, "Elective affinities of the Protestant ethic: Weber and the chemistry of capitalism," *Sociological Theory* 28, no. 1 (2010): 108–126.

19. A. Annett, *Cathonomics: How Catholic Tradition Can Create a More Just Economy* (Washington, DC: Georgetown University Press, 2022): 103.

20. M. Mazzucato, "Innovation, the state and patient capital," in *Rethinking Capitalism: Economics and Policy for Sustainable and Inclusive Growth*, ed. M. Jacobs and M. Mazzucato (Oxford, UK: Wiley-Blackwell, 2016): 107.

21. K. Polanyi, *The Great Transformation: The Political and Economic Origins of Our Time* (Boston: Beacon Press, 2001 [1944]): 144.

22. Omidyar Network. "Our call to reimagine capitalism in America," https://omidyar.com/wp-content/uploads/2020/09/Guide-Design_V12_JTB05_interactive-1.pdf (accessed November 3, 2023): 4.

23. K. Sale, *Rebels Against the Future: The Luddites and Their War on the Industrial Revolution: Lessons for the Computer Age* (New York: Perseus Books Group, 1996).

24. K. Marx, *Das Kommunistische Manifest/The Communist Manifesto* (London: Workers' Educational Association, 1848), Chap. 1.

25. K. Marx, *The German Ideology* (London: Lawrence and Wishart, 1940), Part I.

26. Marx, *Das Kommunistische Manifest/The Communist Manifesto*, Chap. 4.

27. D. Boucoyannis, "The equalizing hand: Why Adam Smith thought the market should produce wealth without steep inequality," *Perspectives on Politics* 11, no. 4 (2013): 1051–1070.

28. Smith, *Enquiry into the Nature and Causes of the Wealth of Nations*, Book V, Chap. 1.

29. F. Taylor, *The Principles of Scientific Management* (Mineola, NY: Dover, 1911).

30. As quoted in D. Mele, "Ethics in management: Exploring the contributions of Mary Parker Follett," *International Journal of Public Administration* 30, no. 4 (2007): 405–424.

31. M. P. Follett, *Creative Experience* (New York: Longman's, Green, 1924): 122.

32. A. Mitzman, *The Iron Cage: An Historical Interpretation of Max Weber* (Piscataway, NJ: Transaction, 1971).

33. Polanyi, *Great Transformation*, 76.

34. J. M. Keynes, "Economic possibilities for our grandchildren," in *Essays in Persuasion* (New York: W.W. Norton, 1930/1963): 358–373.

35. N. Oreskes and E. Conway, *The Big Myth: How American Business Taught Us to Loathe Government and Love the Free Market* (New York: Bloomsbury, 2023).

36. M. Friedman, *Capitalism and Freedom* (Chicago: University of Chicago Press, 1962): 6.

37. L. Keyserling, "Review: Capitalism and freedom," *Annals of the American Academy of Political and Social Science* 350 (1963): 195–196.

38. As quoted in A. Moore, "Milton Friedman's pencil," *The New Inquiry*, December 17, 2012.

39. Friedman, *Capitalism and Freedom*, 2.

40. A. Rand, *Atlas Shrugged* (New York: Random House, 1957).

41. A. Rand, "Introduction to Objectivism," https://aynrand.org/ideas/overview/ (accessed October 10, 2023).

42. Oreskes and Conway, *The Big Myth*, 265.

43. Oreskes and Conway, *The Big Myth*, 279.

44. Oreskes and Conway, *The Big Myth*, 270.

45. J. Burns, *Milton Friedman: The Last Conservative* (New York: Farrar, Straus and Giroux, 2023).

46. J. Gamble, "The most important problem in the world," *Medium*, March 13, 2019.

47. As quoted in G. Schuster, *Christianity and Human Relations in Industry* (London: Epworth Press, 1951): 109. [Note: Some have questioned the authenticity of this quote by Keynes, but it was attributed by Sir George Ernest Schuster, a British barrister, financier, colonial administrator, Liberal politician, and contemporary of John Maynard Keynes.]

48. J. Davis, "Is shareholder capitalism a suicide pact?" *Medium*, July 17, 2023.

49. Davis, "Is shareholder capitalism a suicide pact?"

50. T. Piketty, *Le Capital au XXIe Siècle/ Capital in the Twenty-First Century* (Paris: Éditions du Seuil/ Cambridge, MA: Harvard University Press, 2013/2014): 1.

51. Piketty, *Le Capital au XXIe Siècle/ Capital in the Twenty-First Century*, 10.

52. J. Sachs, "Twentieth-century political economy: A brief history of global capitalism," *Oxford Review of Economic Policy* 15, no. 4 (1999): 90–101.

53. E. Gould, "Decades of rising economic inequality in the U.S.," *Economic Policy Institute*, March 27, 2019.

54. L. Zingales, *A Capitalism for the People: Recapturing the Lost Genius of American Prosperity* (New York: Basic Books, 2012): 24.

55. US Bureau of Labor Statistics, *A Profile of the Working Poor, 2021*, BLS Reports, November 2023.

56. E. Anderson, *Private Government: How Employers Rule Our Lives (and Why We Don't Talk About It)* (Princeton, NJ: Princeton University Press, 2017).

57. E. Anderson, "How bosses are (literally) like dictators," *Vox*, September 3, 2017.

58. Annett, *Cathonomics*, 110.

59. S. Lohr, "Why isn't new technology making us more productive?" *New York Times*, May 24, 2022.

60. S. Captain, "When will robots take our jobs?" *Fast Company*, April 21, 2022.

61. S. Zahidi, V. Ratcheva., G. Hingel, and S. Brown, *The Future of Jobs* (Geneva, Switzerland: World Economic Forum, 2020).

62. As quoted in R. Feloni, "50 years after the introduction of the 'Friedman Doctrine,' It's time to create a new capitalism," *JUST Capital*, September 18, 2020.

63. T. Hale, *Long Problems: Climate Change and the Challenge of Governing Across Time* (Princeton, NJ: Princeton University Press, 2024).

64. J. Schlefer, *The Assumptions Economists Make* (Cambridge, MA: Belknap Press of Harvard University Press, 2012).

65. J. Schlefer, "There is no invisible hand," *Harvard Business Review*, April 10, 2012.

66. G. Liu, *Adam Smith's America: How a Scottish Philosopher Became an Icon of American Capitalism* (Princeton, NJ: Princeton University Press, 2022).

67. As quoted in R. Feloni, "The economist Joseph Stiglitz explains why he thinks the late Milton Friedman's ideas have contributed to rising inequality in the US," *Business Insider*, March 13, 2018.

68. J. Stiglitz, "Foreword," in J. Schumpeter, *Capitalism, Socialism and Democracy* (Boston: Beacon Press, 2001): 1–2.

69. R. Reich, "To reverse inequality, we need to expose the myth of the 'free market'," *The Guardian*, December 9, 2020.

70. B. Appelbaum, "50 years of blaming Milton Friedman. Here's another idea," *New York Times*, September 18, 2020.

71. R. Posner, *A Failure of Capitalism: The Crisis of '08 and the Descent into Depression* (Cambridge, MA: Harvard University Press, 2011): 107–112.

72. As quoted in Oreskes and Conway, *The Big Myth*, 270.

73. A. Hoffman, *Management as a Calling: Leading Business, Serving Society* (Stanford, CA: Stanford University Press, 2021).

74. International Energy Agency, "World energy outlook 2021," https://www.iea.org/reports/world-energy-outlook-2021 (accessed November 1, 2023).

75. "COP28 ends with call to 'transition away' from fossil fuels; UN's Guterres says phaseout is inevitable," *United Nations News*, December 13, 2023.

76. B. Plumer, "Quitting oil income is hard, even for states that want climate action," *New York Times*, July 7, 2022.

77. X. Garcia Casals, B. Parajuli, and R. Ferroukhi, *Measuring the Socio-Economics of Transition: Focus on Jobs* (Abu Dhabi, United Arab Emirates: International Renewable Energy Agency, 2020).

78. A. Hoffman and D. Ely, "Time to put the fossil-fuel industry into hospice," *Stanford Social Innovation Review*, Fall 2022: 28–37.

79. M. Egan, "This billionaire warns that America's massive wealth gap could lead to conflict," CNN Business, December 22, 2020.

80. P. Georgescu, "Capitalists, arise: We need to deal with income inequality," *New York Times*, August 7, 2015.

81. W. Scheidel, *The Great Leveler: Violence and the History of Inequality from the Stone Age to the Twenty-First Century* (Princeton, NJ: Princeton University Press, 2017).

82. D. Chakrabarty, "Climate and capital: On conjoined histories," *Critical Inquiry* 41, no. 1 (2014): 1–23.

83. A. Mikhail, "Enlightenment Anthropocene," *Eighteenth-Century Studies* 49, no. 2 (2016): 211–231.

84. A. Hoffman, P. D. Jennings, and N. Poggioli, "Institutional policies for a healthy Anthropocene society," *Behavioral Science & Policy* 7, no. 2 (2021): 111–127.

85. K. Charman, "Ecuador first to grant nature constitutional rights," *Capitalism Nature Socialism* 19, no. 4 (2008): 131–133.

86. I. Kaminski, "Streams and lakes have rights, a US county decided. Now they're suing Florida," *The Guardian*, May 1, 2021.

87. Center for Democratic and Environmental Rights, https://www.centerforenvironmentalrights.org/rights-of-nature-law-library (accessed January 14, 2024).

88. O. Bowcott, "International lawyers draft plan to criminalise ecosystem destruction," *The Guardian*, November 30, 2020.

89. J. Schumpeter, *Capitalism, Socialism and Democracy* (New York: Harper & Brothers, 1942): 61.

90. R. Sobel, "The death of capitalism: Schumpeter's prognosis coming true," *The Fraser Institute Blog*, November 4, 2021.

91. Deloitte, *The Deloitte Global Millennial Survey 2019*, 2019, https://www2.deloit te.com/content/dam/Deloitte/global/Documents/About-Deloitte/deloitte-2019-mil lennial-survey.pdf (accessed October 10, 2023).

92. R. Cramer, "Framing the millennial wealth gap: Demographic realities and divergent trajectories," New America, 2019, https://www.newamerica.org/millennials /reports/emerging-millennial-wealth-gap/framing-the-millennial-wealth-gap-demo graphic-realities-and-divergent-trajectories/ (accessed October, 10, 2023).

93. R. Chetty, D. Grusky, M. Hell, N. Hendren, R. Manduca, and J. Narang, "The fading American dream: Trends in absolute income mobility since 1940." *Science* 356, no. 6336 (2017): 398–406.

94. Zingales, *A Capitalism for the People*, xvi.

95. L. Saad, "Socialism as popular as capitalism among young adults in U.S.," Gallup, November 25, 2019, https://news.gallup.com/poll/268766/socialism-popular -capitalism-among-young-adults.aspx (accessed October 10, 2023).

96. I. Wylie, "What Generation Z wants from a business masters," *Financial Times*, September 4, 2022.

97. Millennium Ecosystem Assessment, *Ecosystems and Human Well-Being: Synthesis Report* (Washington, DC: Island Press, 2005): 1.

98. Oreskes and Conway, *The Big Myth*, 424.

99. J. Marangos, "Social dividend versus basic income guarantee in market socialism," *International Journal of Political Economy* 34, no. 3 (2004): 20–40.

100. R. Henderson and K. Ramanna, *Do Managers Have a Role to Play in Sustaining the Institutions of Capitalism?* (Washington, DC: Brookings Institution, 2015).

101. J. Haidt, "Three stories about capitalism," *The Righteous Mind Blog*, July 20, 2014, https://righteousmind.com/three-stories-about-capitalism/ (accessed October 13, 2023).

102. Haidt, "Three stories about capitalism."

Chapter 6

1. A. Case and A. Deaton, *Deaths of Despair and the Future of Capitalism* (Princeton, NJ: Princeton University Press, 2020).

2. US Department of Health and Human Services, *New Surgeon General Advisory Raises Alarm about the Devastating Impact of the Epidemic of Loneliness and Isolation in the United States*, May 3, 2023.

3. Centers for Disease Control and Prevention, "National diabetes statistics report," https://www.cdc.gov/diabetes/data/statistics-report/index.html (accessed April 17, 2024).

4. Y. Levin, "Recovering the case for capitalism," *National Affairs*, Spring 2010.

5. D. Acemoglu and J. Robinson, *Why Nations Fail: The Origins of Power, Prosperity and Poverty* (New York: Crown Business, 2012).

6. OECD, "Social expenditure database (SOCX)," 2022, https://www.oecd.org/social/expenditure.htm (accessed October 17, 2023).

7. J. Kocka, *Capitalism: A Short History* (Princeton, NJ: Princeton University Press, 2016).

8. In practice, this is not always the case, as evidenced by the underpayment of certain professions whose societal value far exceeds their financial compensation and opportunities for economic mobility.

9. C. Rose and R. Henderson, *Note on Comparative Capitalism*, Harvard Business School, 2018, Case 9-315-077.

10. M. Feldmann, "Global varieties of capitalism," *World Politics* 71, no. 1 (2019): 162–196.

11. Kocka, *Capitalism.*

12. E. Lie, "Context and contingency: Explaining state ownership in Norway," *Enterprise & Society* 17, no. 4 (2016): 904–930.

13. Kocka, *Capitalism*, 154.

14. International Monetary Fund, "Government expenditure, percent of GDP," https://www.imf.org/external/datamapper/exp@FPP/USA/FRA/JPN/GBR/SWE/ESP/ITA/ZAF/IND (accessed October 13, 2023).

15. Our World in Data, "Military expenditure as a share of GDP, 1961 to 2016," https://ourworldindata.org/grapher/military-expenditure-as-a-share-of-gdp-long?tab=table&time=1961..latest (accessed February 29, 2024).

16. The Tax Foundation, "International tax competitiveness index 2022," 2022, https://taxfoundation.org/research/all/global/2022-international-tax-competitiveness-index/ (accessed October 17, 2023).

17. OECD, "General government spending (indicator)," 2023, https://data.oecd.org/gga/general-government-spending.htm (accessed on October 17, 2023).

18. Heritage Foundation, "2023 index of economic freedom," 2023, https://www.heritage.org/index/country/unitedstates (accessed October 18, 2023).

19. Heritage Foundation, "2023 index of economic freedom."

20. Rose and Henderson, *Note on Comparative Capitalism.*

21. Kocka, *Capitalism.*

22. S. Holmberg, "Workers on corporate boards? Germany's had them for decades," *New York Times*, January 6, 2019.

23. B. Dooley and H. Ueno, "Why Japan's jobless rate is just 2.6% while the U.S.'s has soared." *New York Times.* June 20, 2020.

24. Kocka, *Capitalism.*

25. "The 2023 crony-capitalism index," *Economist*, May 2, 2023.

26. "The 2023 crony-capitalism index."

27. M. Lavault, "Does the United States have social welfare like Canada? An interview with Professor Daniel Béland," *McGill Journal of Political Studies*, November 11, 2020.

28. As quoted in W. Reed, "Don't call Scandinavian countries 'socialist'," *FEE Stories*, April 18, 2023..

29. Heritage Foundation, "2023 Index of Economic Freedom," https://www.heritage.org/index/country/unitedstates (accessed October 18, 2023).

30. Kocka, *Capitalism.*

31. "The new model: Sweden," *Economist*, October 13. 2012.

32. Bertelsmann Stiftung, "SGI 2020: Denmark: Social policies," SGI 2020, https://www.sgi-network.org/2020/Denmark/Social_Policies (accessed October 13, 2023).

33. A. McKay, "Scandinavian 'socialism': The truth of the Nordic model," *Life in Norway*, August 3, 2020.

34. McKay, "Scandinavian 'socialism'."

35. D. Bunn, S. Bray, and J. Haddinga, "Insights into the tax systems of Scandinavian countries," *The Tax Foundation*, April 20, 2023.

36. L. Edwards, "The myth of Scandinavian socialism," *The Heritage Foundation*, April 20, 2022.

37. "Conservative vs. liberal," *Diffen*, https://www.diffen.com/difference/Conservative_vs_Liberal (accessed January 5, 2024).

38. S. Pearlstein, *Can American Capitalism Survive? Why Greed Is Not Good, Opportunity Is Not Equal, and Fairness Won't Make Us Poor* (New York: St. Martin's Press, 2018): 23.

39. Though my own political preferences tend to favor the liberal end of the spectrum, I appreciate the value in democratic disagreement and debate and will work to be evenhanded in my presentation of the right-left distinctions.

40. T. Vargish, "Why the person sitting next to you hates limits to growth," *Technological Forecasting and Social Change* 16 (1980): 179–189.

41. J. Clifton, "Many differences between liberals and conservatives may boil down to one belief," *Scientific American*, March 1, 2023.

42. A. Smith, *An Enquiry into the Nature and Causes of the Wealth of Nations* (New York: Random House, 1776/1940), Book I, Chap. 8.

43. L. Denworth, "Conservative and liberal brains might have some real differences," *Scientific American*, October 26, 2020.

44. L. Saad, "Americans decry power of lobbyists, corporations, banks, feds," *Gallup*, April 11, 2011.

45. M. Johnson, "Free markets," https://mikejohnson.house.gov/issues/issue/?IssueID=14900 (accessed December 1, 2023).

46. Denworth, "Conservative and liberal brains."

47. Congressional Progressive Caucus, "The progressive promise," https://progressives.house.gov/the-progressive-promise (accessed December 1, 2023).

48. J. Horowitz, R. Igielnik, and R. Kochhar, "Most Americans say there is too much economic inequality in the U.S., but fewer than half call it a top priority," Pew Research Center, January 9, 2020.

49. H. Schneider, and C. Kahn, "Majority of Americans favor wealth tax on very rich: Reuters/Ipsos poll," *Reuters*, January 10, 2020.

50. K. Schaeffer, "Key facts about Americans and guns," Pew Research Center, September 13, 2023.

51. Schaeffer, "Key facts about Americans and guns."

52. A. Tyson, C. Funk, and B. Kennedy, "What the data says about Americans' views of climate change," Pew Research Center, August 9, 2023.

53. N. Klein, "Capitalism vs. the climate," *The Nation*, November 28, 2011.

54. A. Hoffman, "The culture and discourse of climate skepticism," *Strategic Organization* 9, no. 1 (2011): 77–84.

55. I. Feygina, J. Jost, and R. Goldsmith, "System justification, the denial of global warming and the possibility of 'system sanctioned change'," *Personality and Social Psychology Bulletin* 36, no. 3 (2010): 326–338.

56. A. McCright, K. Dentzman, M. Charters, and T. Dietz, "The influence of political ideology on trust in science," *Environmental Research Letters* 8 (2013): 1–9.

57. S. Goldenberg, "Secret funding helped build vast network of climate denial think tanks," *The Guardian*, February 14, 2013.

58. Y. Heath and R. Gifford, "Free-market ideology and environmental degradation: The case of belief in global climate change," *Environment and Behavior* 38, no. 1 (2006): 48–71.

59. T. Vargish, "Why the person sitting next to you hates limits to growth," *Technological Forecasting and Social Change* 16 (1980): 179–189.

60. A. Hoffman, *How Culture Shapes the Climate Change Debate* (Stanford, CA: Stanford University Press, 2015).

61. D. Himmelstein, R. Lawless, D. Thorne, P. Foohey, and S. Woolhandler, "Medical bankruptcy: Still common despite the Affordable Care Act," *American Journal of Public Health* 109, no. 3 (2019): 431–433.

62. "Medical bankruptcies by country 2024," World Population Review, 2024, https://worldpopulationreview.com/country-rankings/medical-bankruptcies-by-country (accessed January 5, 2024).

63. E. Gonzalez, "Health care costs threaten the future of small businesses that survive COVID," *The Hill*, March 10, 2021.

64. "U.S. healthcare spending rises to $4.5 trillion in 2022," *Reuters*, December 13, 2023.

65. T. Johnson, "Healthcare costs and U.S. competitiveness," *Council on Foreign Relations*, March 26, 2012.

66. A. Dunn, "Democrats differ over best way to provide health coverage for all Americans," Pew Research Center, July 26, 2019.

67. The Cato Institute, "Health care," https://www.cato.org/health-care (accessed February 29, 2024).

68. J. Haskins, "Finally, a conservative plan to fix America's broken health care system," *The Hill*, July 10, 2021.

69. US Bureau of Labor Statistics, *A Profile of the Working Poor, 2021*, BLS Reports, November 2023.

70. G. Schulte, "Poll: Majority of voters now say the government should have a universal basic income program," *The Hill*, August 14, 2020.

71. H. Gilberstadt, "More Americans oppose than favor the government providing a universal basic income for all adult citizens," Pew Research Center, August 19, 2020.

72. O. Jarow, "Basic income is less radical than you think," *Vox*, October 13, 2023.

73. L. Lee, "Homeless people in Vancouver were given $5,500 cash, no strings attached. They used it to secure housing and even start saving," *Business Insider*, January 1, 2024.

74. Lee, "Homeless people in Vancouver were given $5,500 cash."

75. T. Smith-Carrier, "Implementing a basic income means overcoming myths about the 'undeserving poor'," *The Conversation*, December 4, 2023.

76. S. Jayachandran, "Social programs can sometimes turn a profit for taxpayers," *New York Times*, July 10, 2020.

77. N. Hendren and B. Sprung-Keyser. "A unified welfare analysis of government policies." *Quarterly Journal of Economics* 135, no. 3 (2020): 1209–1318.

78. M. Bolotnikova, "Welfare's payback," *Harvard Magazine*, November-December 2020.

79. A. Cole, "Details and analysis of Donald Trump's tax plan, September 2016," The Tax Foundation, September 19, 2016.

80. T. Fisher, "How past income tax rate cuts on the wealthy affected the economy," *Politico*, September 27, 2017.

81. McKay, "Scandinavian 'socialism'."

82. P. Goodman, "The Nordic model may be the best cushion against capitalism. Can it survive immigration?" *New York Times*. July 11, 2019.

83. Goodman, "The Nordic model may be the best cushion against capitalism."

84. S. Pearlstein, *Can American Capitalism Survive? Why Greed Is Not Good, Opportunity Is Not Equal, and Fairness Won't Make Us Poor* (New York: St. Martin's Press, 2018).

85. As quoted in S. Illing, "Is capitalism worth saving? A debate with economics writer Steven Pearlstein," *Vox*, February 26, 2019.

86. E. Warren, "Accountable Capitalism Act," 2018, https://www.warren.senate .gov/imo/media/doc/Accountable%20Capitalism%20Act%20One-Pager.pdf (accessed November 23, 2023).

87. As quoted in Illing, "Is capitalism worth saving?"

Chapter 7

1. L. Stout, *The Problem of Corporate Purpose* (Washington, DC: Brookings Institution, 2012).

2. N. Oreskes and E. Conway, *The Big Myth: How American Business Taught Us to Loathe Government and Love the Free Market* (New York: Bloomsbury, 2023).

3. R.Coase, "The nature of the firm," *Economica* 4, no. 16 (1937): 386–405.

4. M. Friedman, *Capitalism and Freedom* (Chicago: University of Chicago Press, 1962).

5. R. Nader, *Unsafe at Any Speed: The Designed-In Dangers of the American Automobile* (New York: Grossman, 1965).

6. M. Friedman, "The social responsibility of business is to increase its profits," *New York Times Magazine*, September 13, 1970: 32–33, 122, 124, 126.

7. M. Jensen and W. Meckling, "Theory of the firm: Managerial behavior, agency costs and ownership structure," *Journal of Financial Economics* 3, no. 4 (1976): 305–360.

8. "Theory of the firm: Jensen and Meckling on managerial behaviour, agency

costs and ownership structure," Athenarium, https://athenarium.com/theory-firm -jensen-meckling-agency-costs/ (accessed October 23, 2023).

9. W. Meckling and M. Jensen, "Reflections on the corporation as a social invention," in *Controlling the Giant Corporation: A Symposium*, ed. R. Hansen (Rochester, NY: Center for Research in Government Policy and Business, 1982): 82–95.

10. J. Harrison,. R. Phillips, and R. E. Freeman, "On the 2019 business roundtable 'statement on the purpose of a corporation'," *Journal of Management* 46, no. 7 (2020): 1223–1237.

11. L. Stout, *The Shareholder Value Myth: How Putting Shareholders First Harms Investors, Corporations, and the Public* (Oakland, CA: Berrett-Koehler, 2012).

12. L. Stout, "The problem with corporate purpose," *Brookings Institution Issues in Governance Studies* 48, no. 1 (2012).

13. *Dodge v. Ford Motor Company*, 204 Mich. 459, 170 N.W. 668, Casetext, 1919, https://casetext.com/case/dodge-v-ford-motor-co (accessed November 1, 2023).

14. J. Macey, "A close read of an excellent commentary on Dodge v. Ford," *Virginia Law & Business Review*, January 1, 2008.

15. M. T. Henderson, "Everything old is new again: Lessons from Dodge v. Ford Motor Company," Olin Working Paper No. 373, University of Chicago Law School, 2007.

16. *Principles of Corporate Governance: Analysis and Recommendations* (Philadelphia: American Law Institute, 1994), Section 4.01: "A Recommendations of Corporate Practice Concerning the Board and the Principal Oversight Committees."

17. *Principles of Corporate Governance: Analysis and Recommendations* (Philadelphia: American Law Institute, 1994), Section 2.01: "The Objective and Conduct of the Corporation."

18. M. Kelly, *The Divine Right of Capital: Dethroning the Corporate Aristocracy* (San Francisco: Berrett-Koehler, 2003): 54.

19. *Burwell v. Hobby Lobby Stores, Inc.*, Cornell Law School Legal Information Institute, 2014, https://www.law.cornell.edu/supremecourt/text/13-354#writing-13-354_ OPINION_3 (accessed October 24, 2023).

20. Stout, "The problem with corporate purpose," 6.

21. Stout, "The problem with corporate purpose," 6.

22. Stout, "The problem with corporate purpose," 6.

23. Stout, "The problem with corporate purpose," 7.

24. S. Dening, "The origin of 'the world's dumbest Idea': Milton Friedman," *Forbes*, June 26, 2013.

25. E. Durkheim, *De la Division du Travail Social* (Paris: Ancienne Libraririe Germer Baillière, 1893).

26. J. Lincoln and D. Guillot, "Durkheim and organizational culture," IRLE Working Paper No. 108–04, 2004, http://irle.berkeley.edu/workingpapers/108-04.pdf (accessed October 23, 2023).

27. P. Drucker, *The Future of Industrial Man* (New York: The John Day Company, 1942).

28. P. Drucker, *Concept of the Corporation* (New York: The John Day Company, 1946).

29. J. Mickelthwait and A. Woolridge, *The Company: A Short History of a Revolutionary Idea* (New York: The Modern Library, 2003): 114.

30. J. Dublino, "What your business can learn from Peter Drucker," Business.com, August 15, 2023.

31. P. Drucker, *Management: Tasks, Responsibilities, Practices* (London: Routledge, 19974): 56.

32. As quoted in R. Atkinson and M. Lind, "Is big business really that bad?" *The Atlantic*, April 2018.

33. As quoted in "Peter Drucker on marketing," *Forbes*, July 3, 2006.

34. Dublino, "What your business can learn from Peter Drucker."

35. As quoted in J. Makower, "Milton Friedman and the social responsibility of business," *Greenbiz*, November 24, 2006.

36. As quoted in F. Guerrera, "Welch condemns share price focus," *Financial Times*, May 12, 2009.

37. P. Polman and A. Winston, "The net positive manifesto," *Harvard Business Review*, September-October 2021.

38. A. Ignatius, "Former Unilever CEO Paul Polman says aiming for sustainability isn't good enough—The goal is much higher," *Harvard Business Review*, November 19, 2021.

39. F. Hesselbein, "How did Peter Drucker see corporate responsibility?" *Harvard Business Review*, June 9, 2010.

40. As quoted in Ignatius, "Former Unilever CEO Paul Polman says aiming for sustainability isn't good enough."

41. G. Allison, *Essence of Decision*, (New York: Harper Collins, 1971): 259.

42. Allison, *Essence of Decision*, 260.

43. Allison, *Essence of Decision*, 260.

44. R. Nadeau, "The economist has no clothes," *Scientific American*, April 1, 2008.

45. As quoted in I. Sawhill, "It's the economists, stupid," *Democracy*, Winter 2019.

46. L. Keller, "The problem with the concept of utility and its measurement," *Polish Journal of Political Science* 1, no. 4 (2015): 6–44.

47. M. Karacuka and A. Zaman, "The empirical evidence against neoclassical utility theory: A review of the literature," *International Journal of Pluralism and Economics Education* 3, no. 4 (2012): 366–414.

48. M. Jacobs and M. Mazzucato, "Introduction," in *Rethinking Capitalism: Economics and Policy for Sustainable and Inclusive Growth*, ed. M. Jacobs and M. Mazzucato (Oxford, UK: Wiley-Blackwell, 2016): 17.

49. D. Rodrik, "Rescuing economics from neoliberalism," *Boston Review*, November 6, 2017.

50. Jacobs and Mazzucato, "Introduction," 17.

51. T. Moller-Neilsen, "'A tribal clique': Lagarde denounces economists at Davos," *Euractiv*, January 17, 2024.

52. As quoted in S. Donnan, "A Nobel Laureate offers a biting critique of economics," *Bloomberg*, September 29, 2023.

53. A. Deaton, *Economics in America: An Immigrant Economist Explores the Land of Inequality* (Princeton, NJ: Princeton University Press, 2023): 233.

54. As quoted in Donnan, "A Nobel Laureate offers a biting critique of economics."

55. As quoted in C. McGreal, "Angus Deaton on inequality: 'The war on poverty has become a war on the poor'," *The Guardian*, October 7, 2023.

56. As quoted in Donnan, "A Nobel Laureate offers a biting critique of economics."

57. Deaton, *Economics in America*, 237.

58. A. Offer and G. Söderberg, *The Nobel Factor: The Prize in Economics, Social Democracy, and the Market Turn* (Princeton, NJ: Princeton University Press, 2016).

59. J. Thompson, "Take the Nobel name off economics prize, say relatives," *The Independent*, December 2, 2001.

60. F. Hayek, "Banquet speech," The Sveriges Riksbank Prize in Economic Sciences in Memory of Alfred Nobel, 1974, https://www.nobelprize.org/prizes/economic -sciences/1974/hayek/speech/ (accessed October 23, 2023).

61. As quoted in R. Feloni, "50 years after the introduction of the 'Friedman Doctrine,' it's time to create a new capitalism," *JUST Capital*, September 18, 2020.

62. Oreskes and Conway, *The Big Myth*, 275.

63. L. Silk, "Nobel award in economics: Should prize be abolished?" *New York Times*, March 31, 1977: D9.

64. Oreskes and Conway, *The Big Myth*, 5.

65. N. Pahwa, "Time to fight: How the Powell memo convinced big business it was losing American hearts and minds," *Slate*, August 30, 2021.

66. Oreskes and Conway, *The Big Myth*.

67. J. Burns, *Milton Friedman: The Last Conservative* (New York: Farrar, Straus and Giroux, 2023).

68. J. Overton, "The Overton Window," The Mackinac Center for Public Policy, https://www.mackinac.org/OvertonWindow (accessed March 1, 2024).

69. L. McDonald, "Think tanks and the media: How the conservative movement gained entry into the education policy arena," *Educational Policy*, June 18, 2013.

70. Oreskes and Conway, *The Big Myth*.

71. Dening, "The origin of 'the world's dumbest Idea'."

72. Stout, "The problem with corporate purpose."

73. R. Pozen, *Curbing Short-Termism in Corporate America: Focus on Executive Compensation* (Washington, DC: Brookings Institution, 2014).

74. L. Mishal and J. Kandra, "CEO pay has skyrocketed 1,322% since 1978," *Economic Policy Institute*, April 10, 2021.

75. R. Feloni, "The economist Joseph Stiglitz explains why he thinks the late Milton Friedman's ideas have contributed to rising inequality in the US," *Business Insider*, March 13, 2018.

76. S. Patnaik, "Wall Street wants to know whether Apple the buyback king will continue to plow $90 billion into stock buybacks—or go higher," *Bloomberg*, April 17, 2023.

77. S&P Global, "S&P 500 Q4 2022 buybacks tick up, as 2022 sets a record," *PR Newswire*, March 21, 2023.

78. S. Sorscher, "What will it be, Boeing? Great airplanes that generate cash flow or great cash flow, period?" *The Seattle Times*, July 5, 2019.

79. Two 737-MAX crashes, one in 2018 in Indonesia and the other in Ethiopia 2019, killed 346 passengers, and in 2024 a mid-cabin door fell off a flight from Portland, Oregon, to Ontario, California, at 16,000 feet, forcing an emergency landing.

80. C. Isidore, "Boeing was once known for safety and engineering. But critics say an emphasis on profits changed that," CNN, February 5, 2024.

81. M. Rains, "Boeing needs to hire an engineer as its next CEO," *Business Insider*, March 28, 2024.

82. "Long-termism versus short-termism: Time for the pendulum to shift?" *Institutional Investor*, June 13, 2016.

83. T. Koller, J. Manyika, and S. Ramaswamy, "The case against corporate short termism," *Milken Institute Review*, McKinsey Global Institute, April 4, 2017.

84. W. Magnuson, *For Profit: A History of Corporations* (New York: Basic Books, 2022): 12.

85. A. Dunn and A. Cerda, "Anti-corporate sentiment in U.S. is now widespread in both parties," Pew Research Center, November 17, 2020.

86. Edelman Trust Institute, "2021 Edelman Trust barometer spring update: A world in trauma," 2021, https://www.edelman.com/trust/2021-trust-barometer/spring-update (accessed June 20, 2024).

87. Edelman Trust Institute, "2022 Edelman Trust barometer special analysis: The changing role of the corporation in society," 2022, www.edelman.com/sites/g/files/aatuss191/files/2022-10/2022%20Edelman%20Trust%20Barometer%20Special%20Analysis%20Role%20of%20Business%20BIGs%20FINAL_10%2020PM.pdf (accessed June 20, 2024).

88. "Larry Fink's 2019 letter to CEOs: Purpose & profit," https://www.blackrock.com/corporate/investor-relations/larry-fink-ceo-letter (accessed March 1, 2024).

89. D. Yaffe-Bellany, "Shareholder value is no longer everything, Top CEOs say," *New York Times*, August 19, 2019.

90. K. Schwab, *Davos Manifesto 2020: The Universal Purpose of a Company in the Fourth Industrial Revolution* (Davos, Switzerland: World Economic Forum, 2020).

91. G. Dembicki, "Wall Street's sustainable darling is profiting from climate change," *Vice*, May 24, 2019.

92. W. Henisz, T. Koller, and R. Nuttall, "Five ways that ESG creates value," *McKinsey Quarterly*, November 14, 2019.

93. "Larry Fink's 2022 letter to CEOs: The power of capitalism," https://www.blackrock.com/corporate/investor-relations/larry-fink-ceo-letter (accessed March 1, 2024).

94. A. Ross Sorkin, "How shareholder democracy failed the people, *New York Times*, August 20, 2019.

95. L. Bebchuk, L. and R. Tallarita, "Was the business roundtable statement on corporate purpose mostly for show?—(1) Evidence from lack of board approval," Har-

vard Law School Forum on Corporate Governance, 2020, https://corpgov.law.harvard.edu/2020/08/12/was-the-business-roundtable-statement-on-corporate-purpose-mostly-for-show-1-evidence-from-lack-of-board-approval/ (Aaccessed October 26, 2023).

96. L. Bebchuk and R. Tallarita, "Was the business roundtable statement mostly for show?—(2) evidence from corporate governance guidelines," Harvard Law School Forum on Corporate Governance, 2020, https://corpgov.law.harvard.edu/2020/08/18/was-the-business-roundtable-statement-mostly-for-show-2-evidence-from-corporate-governance-guidelines/ (accessed October 26, 2023).

97. M. Jensen, "Value maximization, stakeholder theory, and the corporate objective function," *Journal of Applied Corporate Finance* 22, no. 1 (2010): 32–42.

98. E. Freeman, *Strategic Management: A Stakeholder Approach* (Boston: Harper and Row, 1984).

99. Harrison, Phillips, and Freeman, "On the 2019 business roundtable 'statement on the purpose of a corporation'."

100. K. Schwab and P. Vanham, *Stakeholder Capitalism: A Global Economy That Works for Progress, People and Planet* (Hoboken, NJ: Wiley, 2021).

101. World Economic Forum, "What is the difference between stakeholder capitalism, shareholder capitalism and state capitalism?" *The Davos Agenda*, January 26, 2021.

102. World Economic Forum, "What is the difference between stakeholder capitalism, shareholder capitalism and state capitalism?"

103. V. Hunt, R. Nuttall, and Y. Yamada, *From Principle to Practice: Making Stakeholder Capitalism Work* (New York: McKinsey & Company, 2021): 1.

104. D. Barton, J. Manyika, T. Koller, R. Palter, J. Godsall, and J. Zoffer, "Where companies with a long-term view outperform their peers," *McKinsey Global Institute*, February 8, 2017.

105. Edelman Trust Institute, "2022 Edelman Trust barometer special analysis."

106. D. Nicholls-Lee, "The 'climate quitters' ditching corporate roles," *BBC Worklife*, October 22, 2023.

107. Cone Communications, "2016 Millennium employee engagement study," 2016, https://calisanbagliligi.files.wordpress.com/2019/10/75bb1-2016conecommunicationsmillennialemployeeengagementstudy_pressreleaseandfactsheet.pdf (accessed November 2, 2023).

108. S. Pearlstein, *Can American Capitalism Survive? Why Greed Is Not Good, Opportunity Is Not Equal, and Fairness Won't Make Us Poor* (New York: St. Martin's Press, 2018): 202.

109. R. Kochhar, "The enduring grip of the gender pay gap," Pew Research Center, March 1, 2023.

110. A. Taylor, "We shouldn't always need a 'business case' to do the right thing," *Harvard Business Review*, September 19, 2017.

111. Stout, *The Shareholder Value Myth*, 4.

Chapter 8

1. "Super PACs having negative impact, say voters aware of 'Citizens United' ruling," Pew Research Center, , January 17, 2012.

2. L. Burton, "In New York, republicans and democrats join forces to overturn Citizens United," *Yes!*, June 29, 2016.

3. A. Balcerzak, "Study: Most Americans want to kill 'Citizens United' with constitutional amendment," The Center for Public Integrity, May 10, 2018.

4. L. Field, "10 years later, Americans stand opposed to Citizens United," *The Hill*, January 17, 2020.

5. G. Stohr, "Americans want Supreme Court to turn off political spending spigot," *Bloomberg*, September 28, 2015.

6. K. Polanyi, *The Great Transformation: The Political and Economic Origins of Our Time* (Boston: Beacon Press, 2001 [1944]): 144.

7. A. Annett, *Cathonomics: How Catholic Tradition Can Create a More Just Economy* (Washington, DC: Georgetown University Press, 2022): 103.

8. *The Bank of the United States v. Deveaux et al*, 1809, Cornell Law School Legal Information Institute, https://www.law.cornell.edu/supremecourt/text/9/61 (accessed November 7, 2023).

9. *Trustees of Dartmouth College v. Woodward*, 1819, Cornell Law School Legal Information Institute, https://www.law.cornell.edu/supremecourt/text/17/518 (accessed November7, 2023).

10. *Santa Clara County v. Southern Pacific Railroad Co.*, 1886, Justia US Supreme Court, https://supreme.justia.com/cases/federal/us/118/394/ (accessed January 20, 2024).

11. A. Winkler, "'Corporations are people' is built on an incredible 19th-century lie," *The Atlantic*, March 5, 2018.

12. As quoted in T. Van Flein, "Headnotes and the course of history," *Alaska Bar Rag*, May-June 2003.

13. *Pembina Consolidated Silver Min. & Milling Co. v. Commonwealth of Pennsylvania*, 1888, Cornell Law School Legal Information Institute, https://www.law.cornell.edu/supremecourt/text/125/181 (accessed October 24, 2023).

14. *15 U.S. Code § 7—"Person" or "persons" defined*, 1890, Cornell Law School Legal Information Institute, https://www.law.cornell.edu/uscode/text/15/7 (accessed October 24, 2023).

15. "Mitt Romney was right: Corporations ARE people," Bradshaw Law Group, June 4, 2015.

16. *James L. Buckley et al., Appellants, v. Francis R. Valeo, Secretary of the United States Senate et al.*, 1976, Cornell Law School Legal Information Institute, https://www.law.cornell.edu/supremecourt/text/424/1 (accessed October 24, 2023).

17. *First National Bank of Boston et al., Appellants, v. Francis X. Bellotti etc.*, 1978, Cornell Law School Legal Information Institute, https://www.law.cornell.edu/supremecourt/text/435/765 (accessed October 24, 2023).

18. *First National Bank of Boston et al., Appellants, v. Francis X. Bellotti etc.*

19. *Richard H. Austin, Michigan Secretary of State and Frank J. Kelley, Michigan*

Attorney General, Appellants v. Michigan Chamber of Commerce, 1990, Cornell Law School Legal Information Institute, https://www.law.cornell.edu/supremecourt/text/494/652 (accessed October 24, 2023).

20. *Richard H. Austin, Michigan Secretary of State and Frank J. Kelley, Michigan Attorney General, Appellants v. Michigan Chamber of Commerce.*

21. *Citizens United v. Federal Election Commission*, 2010, Cornell Law School Legal Information Institute, https://www.law.cornell.edu/supct/html/08-205.ZS.html (accessed October 24, 2023).

22. A. Silverleib, "Gloves come off after Obama rips Supreme Court ruling," CNN, January 28, 2010.

23. *Speechnow.org v. FEC*, 2010, Federal Election Committee, https://www.fec.gov/legal-resources/court-cases/speechnoworg-v-fec/ (accessed November 7, 2023).

24. *McCutcheon v. Federal Election Commission*, 2014, Cornell Law School Legal Information Institute, https://www.law.cornell.edu/supremecourt/text/12-536 (accessed October 24, 2023).

25. *First National Bank of Boston et al., Appellants, v. Francis X. Bellotti.*

26. *First National Bank of Boston et al., Appellants, v. Francis X. Bellotti.*

27. *Citizens United v. Federal Election Commission.*

28. *James L. Buckley et al., Appellants, v. Francis R. Valeo, Secretary of the United States Senate.*

29. L. Saad, "Public agrees with court: Campaign money is 'free speech'," *Gallup*, January 22, 2010.

30. *Citizens United v. Federal Election Commission.*

31. *Citizens United v. Federal Election Commission.*

32. B. Smith, "Celebrate the Citizens United decade," *Wall Street Journal*, January 20, 2020.

33. S. Blackburn, "Citizens United after 10 Years: More speech, better democracy," *Institute for Free Speech*, January 16, 2020.

34. K. Evers-Hillstrom, R. Arke, and L. Robinson, "A look at the impact of Citizens United on its 9th anniversary," OpenSecrets, January 21, 2019.

35. D. Weiner, "Citizens United five years later," Brennan Center for Justice, January 15, 2015.

36. Niskanen Center, *How Campaign Money Has Changed Elections After Citizens United*, August 15, 2018

37. N. Ornstein, "Effect of Citizens United felt two years later," American Enterprise Institute, January 18, 2012.

38. T. Lincoln, "Ten years after Citizens United," Public Citizen, January 15, 2020.

39. D. DeSilver and P. Van Kessel, "As more money flows into campaigns, Americans worry about its influence," Pew Research Center, December 7, 2015.

40. K. Evers-Hillstrom, "More money, less transparency: A decade under Citizens United," OpenSecrets, January 14, 2020.

41. D. Dwyer, "10 years after landmark Citizens United Supreme Court decision, record cash flooding US elections," ABC News, January 20, 2020.

42. Lincoln, "Ten years after Citizens United."

43. Evers-Hillstrom, "More money, less transparency."

44. A. He, "Election 2018: How big business spent its money," *Northwestern Business Review*, November 7, 2018.

45. Dwyer, "10 years after landmark Citizens United Supreme Court decision."

46. He, "Election 2018."

47. Lincoln, "Ten years after Citizens United."

48. He, "Election 2018."

49. OpenSecrets, "Interest groups," 2020, https://www.opensecrets.org/industries ?cycle=2020 (accessed April 23, 2024).

50. As quoted in He, "Election 2018."

51. P. Bump, "Does more campaign money actually buy more votes: An investigation," *The Atlantic*, November 13, 2013.

52. "Party affiliation," *Gallup*, https://news.gallup.com/poll/15370/party-affiliation .aspx (accessed March 11, 2024).

53. Lincoln, "Ten years after Citizens United."

54. A. Cohen, M. Hazan, R. Tallarita, and D. Weiss, "The politics of CEOs," National Bureau of Economic Research, May 2019, Working Paper 25815.

55. Evers-Hillstrom, "More money, less transparency."

56. A. Massoglia, "'Dark money' in politics skyrocketed in the wake of Citizens United," OpenSecrets, January 27, 2020.

57. Evers-Hillstrom, "More money, less transparency."

58. J. Schwartz, "John Paul Stevens was right: Citizens United opened the door to foreign money in U.S. elections," *The Intercept*, July 18, 2019.

59. Ballotpedia, "2018 ballot measures," 2018, https://ballotpedia.org/2018_ballot_ measures (accessed January 6, 2024).

60. J. Woolfolk and K. Bartley, "More money spent to sway California voters on Nov. 6," *Daily Democrat*, October 31, 2018.

61. K. Evers-Hillstrom, "Most expensive ever: 2020 election cost $14.4 billion," OpenSecrets, February 11. 2021.

62. E. Helmore, "Record $15.9bn in US political ad spending expected for 2024," *The Guardian*, December 8, 2023.

63. DeSilver and Van Kessel, "As more money flows into campaigns."

64. "Americans' views on money in politics," *New York Times*, June 2, 2015.

65. DeSilver and Van Kessel, "As more money flows into campaigns."

66. S. Kull, "Americans evaluate campaign finance reform," *Voice of the People*, May 2018, https://www.documentcloud.org/documents/4455238-campaignfinancere port.html (accessed November 7, 2023).

67. "Public Citizen applauds reintroduction of democracy for all amendment," Public Citizen, January 19, 2023.

68. *Burwell v. Hobby Lobby Stores, Inc.*, Oyez, 2014, https://www.oyez.org/cases/ 2013/13-354 (accessed January 20, 2024).

69. T. Hartmann, *Unequal Protection: The Rise of Corporate Dominance and the Theft of Human Rights*, (Emmaus, PA: Rodale Books).

70. Hartmann, *Unequal Protection*, jacket.

71. W. Berry, "The idea of a local economy," *Orion*, Winter 2001.

72. M. Friedman, "The social responsibility of business is to increase its profits," *New York Times Magazine*, September 13, 1970: 33.

73. M. Jensen and W. Meckling, "Reflections on the corporation as a social invention," *Midland Corporate Finance Journal* 1, no. 3 (1983).

74. E. Warren, "Accountable Capitalism Act," 2018, https://www.warren.senate.gov/imo/media/doc/Accountable%20Capitalism%20Act%20One-Pager.pdf (accessed November 23, 2023).

75. M. Yglesias, "Elizabeth Warren has a plan to save capitalism," *Vox*, August 15, 2018.

76. R. Gomory and R. Sylla, "The American corporation," *Daedalus, the Journal of the American Academy of Arts & Sciences* 142, no. 2 (2013): 102–118.

Chapter 9

1. E. Ekins, "Wall Street vs. the regulators: Public attitudes on banks, financial regulation, consumer finance, and the Federal Reserve," The Cato Institute, September 1, 2017.

2. K. Bowman, "Where is the public on government regulation?" *Forbes*, October 23, 2017.

3. Edelman Trust Institute, 2023 Edelman Trust barometer: Global report, 2023, https://www.edelman.com/trust/2023/trust-barometer (accessed November 23, 2023).

4. R. Foa, A. Klassen, M. Slade, A. Rand, and R. Collins, *The Global Satisfaction with Democracy Report 2020*. (Cambridge, UK: Centre for the Future of Democracy, 2020).

5. M. John, "Capitalism seen doing 'more harm than good' in global survey," *Reuters*, January 20, 2020.

6. J. McGann, *The Fifth Estate: Think Tanks, Public Policy, and Governance* (Washington, DC: Brookings Institution, 2016).

7. A. Alemanno, "Business schools need to teach their graduates to lobby responsibly," *Times Higher Education*, May 1, 2021.

8. D. Schular, K. Rehbein, and C. Green, "Is it time to treat corporations' political activity as an academic field?" *Rice Business Wisdom*, January 10, 2017.

9. M. Cottle, "Earn your degree in . . . lobbying?" *The Daily Beast*, April 3, 2014.

10. L. Drutman, "A better way to fix lobbying," *Issues in Governance Studies*, Brookings Institution, June 2011.

11. T. Goldman, "Forget creativity: Can lobbying be taught?" *Washington Post*, October 22, 2012.

12. K. Peterson and M. Pfitzer, "Lobbying for good," *Stanford Social Innovation Review*, Winter 2009.

13. A. Hoffman, C. Espana, I. Robinson, H. Bukhari, and D. Hodge, "Intel: Undermining the Conflict Mineral Industry," case study #1-429-411, (Ann Arbor, MI: Erb Institute, William Davidson Institute, University of Michigan, 2015).

14. M. Mendoza, "Nestle admits slavery and coercion used in catching its seafood," CBC News, November 23, 2015.

15. D. Wolfensberger, *An Introductory Essay for the Wilson Center's Congress Project Seminar on Congress, Lobbyists. and the Public Interest*, May 18, 2001.

16. J. Madison, J. "*The Federalist* No. 10," National Archives, 1987, https://founders.archives.gov/documents/Madison/01-10-02-0178 (accessed November 30, 2023).

17. A. Mayyasi, "When lobbying was illegal," *Priceonomics*, April 15, 2016.

18. Z. Teachout, "The forgotten law of lobbying," *Election Law Journal* 13, no. 1 (2014): 4–26.

19. W. Whitman, "The eighteenth presidency," in *Walt Whitman: Poetry and Prose*, ed. J. Kaplan (New York: Library of America College Editons, 1996/1856): 1338.

20. E. Brown and A. Strauss, *A Dictionary of American Politics: Comprising Accounts of Political Parties, Measures and Men, Etc.* (New York: A.L. Burt, 1888): 315.

21. Mayyasi, "When lobbying was illegal."

22. K. Hong, T. Rosen, and A. Chugh, "Lobbying regulation: A global phenomenon," *Reuters*, November 6, 2023.

23. US Senate, "U.S. Senate passes comprehensive lobbying and ethics reform bill," 2007, https://www.rules.senate.gov/news/minority-news/u-s-senate-passes-comprehensive-lobbying-and-ethics-reform-bill (accessed November 27, 2023).

24. Hong, Rosen, and Chugh, "Lobbying regulation."

25. Z. Teachout, *Corruption in America: From Benjamin Franklin's Snuff Box to Citizens United* (Cambridge, MA: Harvard University Press, 2014): 232.

26. J. Thurber, "From campaigning to lobbying," in *Shades of Gray: Perspectives on Campaign Ethics*, ed. C. Nelson, D. Dullo, and S. Medvic, Chap. 9 (Washington, DC: Brookings Institution, 2002): 151–170.

27. E. Klein, "Corporations now spend more lobbying Congress than taxpayers spend funding Congress," *Vox*, July 15, 2015.

28. T. Giorno, "Federal lobbying spending reaches $4.1 billion in 2022—the highest since 2010," OpenSecrets, January 26, 2023.

29. Giorno, "Federal lobbying spending reaches $4.1 billion in 2022."

30. "Think tanks and policy institutes," https://www.citizensource.com/Opinion&Policy/ThinkTanks.htm (accessed November 22, 2023).

31. S. Stein and N. Lorecki, "The most influential think tank of the Biden era has a new leader," *Politico*, June 30, 2021.

32. OECD, *Lobbyists, Governments and Public Trust, Volume 3, Implementing the OECD Principles for Transparency and Integrity in Lobbying* (Paris: OECD Publishing, 2014): 11.

33. B. Drenon, "Bob Menendez: US Senator holds back tears and denies charges on Senate floor," BBC News, January 9, 2024.

34. OpenSecrets, "The revolving door," https://www.opensecrets.org/revolving/ (accessed November 30, 2023).

35. As quoted in J. Drucker and D. Hakim, "How accounting giants craft favorable tax rules from inside government," *New York Times*, September 19, 2021.

36. Mayyasi, "When lobbying was illegal."

37. D. DeSilver and P. Van Kessel, "As more money flows into campaigns, Ameri-

cans worry about its influence," Pew Research Center, December 7, 2015.

38. S. Kull, "Americans evaluate campaign finance reform," *Voice of the People*, May 2018, https://www.documentcloud.org/documents/4455238-campaignfinancere port.html (accessed November 7, 2023).

39. A. Cerda and A. Daniller, "7 facts about Americans' views of money in politics," Pew Research Center, October 23, 2023.

40. E. Davis, "Poll: Americans are down on society's leaders—Especially in politics," *US News & World Report*, December 12, 2023.

41. T. Lyon et al., "CSR needs CPR: Corporate sustainability and politics," *California Management Review* 60, no. 4 (2018): 5–24.

42. OECD, *Lobbyists, Governments and Public Trust*.

43. CPA-Wharton Zicklin Center, "Model code of conduct for corporate political spending," https://politicalaccountability.net/hifi/files/CPA-Wharton-Zicklin---model-code-of-conduct-for-corporate-political-spending---10-13-20-.pdf (accessed November 28, 2023).

44. Transparency International UK, "Global anti-bribery guidance," https://www .antibriberyguidance.org/guidance/12-political-engagement/best-practice#Body MoneyElectionsElectedOfficialsandCombatingCorruptionFINAL (accessed November 28, 2023).

45. S. Hodgson and D. Witte, "The responsible lobbying framework," 2020, https://www.responsible-lobbying.org/the-framework (accessed November 28, 2023).

46. "The erb principles for corporate political responsibility," https://erb.umich. edu/partner-with-erb/erb-principles/ (accessed January 5, 2024).

47. V. Ramaswamy, "The 'stakeholders' versus the people," *Wall Street Journal*, February 12, 2020.

48. D. Vogel, *The Market for Virtue: The Potential and Limits of Corporate Social Responsibility* (Washington, DC: Brookings Institution, 2007): 173.

49. A. Chatterji and M. Toffel, "The new CEO activists," *Harvard Business Review*, January-February 2018.

50. Weber Shandwick, "CEO activism in 2018: Half of Americans say CEO activism influences government," 2018, https://webershandwick.com/news/ceo-activism -in-2018-half-of-americans-say-ceo-activism-influences-government (accessed December 1, 2023).

51. M. Benioff and M. Langely, *Trailblazer: The Power of Business as the Greatest Platform for Change* (New York: Crown Currency, 2019).

52. "How car makers got caught between Trump and California," *Wall Street Journal*, October 31, 2019.

53. K. Vogel and S. Goldmacher, "An unusual $1.6 billion donation bolsters conservatives," *New York Times*, August 22, 2022.

54. D. Pendleton and B. Steverman, "Patagonia billionaire who gave up company skirts $700 million tax hit," *Bloomberg*, September 15, 2022.

55. As quoted in D. Matthews, "The case against billionaire philanthropy," *Vox*, December 17, 2018.

56. D. Lund and L. Strine Jr., "Corporate political spending is bad business," *Harvard Business Review*, January-February 2022.

57. OECD, *Lobbyists, Governments and Public Trust*.

58. "Political finance database," International Idea, https://www.idea.int/data-tools/data/country?country=76&database_theme=302 (accessed March 16, 2024).

59. P. Waldman, "How our campaign finance system compares to other countries," *The American Prospect*, April 4, 2014.

60. "Spending rules curb campaigning on French TV," *Reuters*, August 9, 2007.

61. "How French parties and politicians are funded," *France 24*, June 7, 2010.

62. "What are the rules for French presidential candidates appearing on TV?" *The Local France*, December 15, 2021.

63. "2020 presidential race," OpenSecrets, https://www.opensecrets.org/2020-presidential-race (accessed March 16, 2024).

64. "CED's longstanding, nonpartisan call to action on money in politics," Committee for Economic Development, November 2013.

65. R. Berman, "How can the U.S. shrink the influence of money in politics?" *The Atlantic*, March 16, 2016.

66. B. Levine, "Red flags," in *The Art of Lobbying: Building Trust and Selling Policy*, Chap. 3 (Washington, DC: CQ Press, 2008).

67. Govtrack, "H.R. 5594: PURE Executive Act, 2023, https://www.govtrack.us/congress/bills/118/hr5594 (accessed November 30, 2023).

68. L. Drutman, "A better way to fix lobbying," *Issues in Governance Studies*, Brookings Institution, June 2011.

69. Drutman, "A better way to fix lobbying."

70. Drutman, "A better way to fix lobbying."

71. R. Berman, "How can the U.S. shrink the influence of money in politics?" *The Atlantic*, March 16, 2016.

72. Campaign Legal Center, "Public financing of elections," https://campaignlegal.org/democracyu/inclusion/public-financing-elections (accessed November 30, 2023).

73. J. Cagé, "How Barack Obama spurred the end of America's public presidential election funding system," *Promarket*, April 27, 2020.

74. International Churchill Society, "Speech Woodford, Essex," 1959, https://winstonchurchill.org/publications/finest-hour/finest-hour-118/wit-and-wisdom-12/ (accessed November 30, 2023).

75. As quoted in R. Feloni, "50 years after the introduction of the 'Friedman Doctrine,' it's time to create a new capitalism," *JUST Capital*, September 18, 2020.

76. Public Affairs Council, "Taking a stand: How corporations engage on social issues," 2021, https://pac.org/publications/research/taking-stand-corporations-engage-social-issues/ (accessed January 5, 2024).

77. S. Laville, "Top oil firms spending millions lobbying to block climate change policies, says report," *The Guardian*, March 21, 2019.

78. P. Polman and A. Winston, *Net Positive: How Courageous Companies Thrive by Giving More Than They Take* (Cambridge, MA: Harvard Business Review Press, 2021).

Chapter 10

1. Beginning in 2007, US markets experienced the Great Recession, the most severe economic and financial meltdown since the Great Depression. It began with the subprime mortgage crisis and culminated with huge losses at many large investment and commercial banks in the United States and Europe, the fall of Lehman Brothers, and the creation of the Troubled Asset Relief Program, which allocated $426.4 billion to a series of financial institutions that were deemed "too big to fail." The US government later collected $441.7 billion in return from these loans, recording a profit of $15.3 billion.

2. R. Neate, "Queen finally finds out why no one saw the financial crisis coming," *The Guardian*, December 13, 2012.

3. As quoted in D. Orrell, "Why we missed the storm," *World Finance*, November 23, 2018.

4. R. Posner, *A Failure of Capitalism: The Crisis of '08 and the Descent into Depression* (Cambridge, MA: Harvard University Press, 2011).

5. As quoted in J. Cassidy, "After the blowup," *The New Yorker*, January 3, 2010.

6. J. Ruggie, "Global governance and "new governance theory": Lessons from business and human rights," *Global Governance* 20 (2014): 5–17.

7. A. Smith, *An Enquiry into the Nature and Causes of the Wealth of Nations* (New York: Random House, 1776/1940), Book V, Chap. 1.

8. A. Smith, *The Theory of Moral Sentiments*, 6th ed. (Cambridge, UK: Cambridge University Press, 1790/2002), Part VI, Chap. 2.

9. Smith, *Enquiry into the Nature and Causes of the Wealth of Nations*, Book I, Chap..

10. J. Madison, "*The Federalist* No. 10," National Archives, 1987, https://founders.archives.gov/documents/Madison/01-10-02-0178 (accessed November 30, 2023).

11. Madison, "*Federalist* No. 10."

12. Madison, "*Federalist* No. 10."

13. J. Madison, "Letter to J.K. Paulding," March 10, 1827, in *The Writings of James Madison, Volume 9 (1819–1836)*, ed. Gaillard Hunt (New York: Putnam, 1900): 35.

14. Madison, "*Federalist* No. 10."

15. J. Madison, "Speech at the Philadelphia Convention," 1787, https://archive.csac.history.wisc.edu/3._James_Madison_Speech_at_the_Philadelphia_Convention.pdf (accessed November 30, 2023).

16. R. Reich, "To reverse inequality, we need to expose the myth of the 'free market'," *The Guardian*, December 9, 2020.

17. "The partisan divide on political values grows even wider: Government, regulation and the social safety net," Pew Research Center, October 5, 2017.

18. S. Smith, "Public remains divided over role of government in financial regulation," Pew Research Center, March 2, 2017.

19. T. Tiffany, T. Alloway, and J. Weisenthal, "What Trump's 60% China tariffs would mean for the US economy," *Bloomberg*, February 12, 2024.

20. F. Newport, "Americans want more than just budget cuts," *Gallup*, June 9, 2017.

21. "Public trust in government: 1958–2023," Pew Research Center, September 19, 2023.

22. C. Doherty et al. "Americans' views of government: Decades of distrust, enduring support for its role," Pew Research Center, June 6, 2022.

23. Doherty, "Americans' views of government."

24. K. Bowman, "Where is the public on government regulation?" *Forbes*, October 23, 2017.

25. N. Oreskes and E. Conway, *The Big Myth: How American Business Taught Us to Loathe Government and Love the Free Market* (New York: Bloomsbury, 2023): 1.

26. J. Kocka, *Capitalism: A Short History* (Princeton, NJ: Princeton University Press, 2016): 153.

27. M. Jacobs and M. Mazzucato, "Introduction," in *Rethinking Capitalism: Economics and Policy for Sustainable and Inclusive Growth*, ed. M. Jacobs and M. Mazzucato (Oxford, UK: Wiley-Blackwell, 2016): 1–27.

28. J. Stiglitz, "Foreword," in J. Schumpeter, *Capitalism, Socialism and Democracy* (Boston: Beacon Press, 2001): vii.

29. M. Bathon, "Solyndra lenders ahead of government won't recover fully," *Bloomberg*, October 17, 2012.

30. M. Lewis, *The Fifth Risk: Undoing Democracy* (New York: W.W. Norton, 2019).

31. As quoted in J. Medeiros, "This economist has a plan to fix capitalism. It's time we all listened," *Wired*, August 10, 2019.

32. M. Mazzucato, "Innovation, the state and patient capital" in *Rethinking Capitalism: Economics and Policy for Sustainable and Inclusive Growth*, ed. M. Jacobs and M. Mazzucato (Oxford, UK: Wiley-Blackwell, 2016): 104.

33. Omidyar Network, "Our call to reimagine capitalism in America," https://omidyar.com/wp-content/uploads/2020/09/Guide-Design_V12_JTB05_interactive-1.pdf (accessed November 3, 2023).

34. "Nine breakthroughs for climate and nature in 2023 you may have missed." BBC News, December 14, 2023.

35. M. Boteach, "The CHIPS Act reinforces the obvious: Child-care is a public necessity," The Hill, April 3, 2023.

36. R. Meyer, "Congress just passed a big climate bill. No, not that one," *The Atlantic*, August 10, 2022.

37. "Industrial policy is back," Project Syndicate, September 28, 2023.

38. E. Klein, "The economic mistake the left is finally confronting," *New York Times*, September 19, 2021.

39. D. Thompson, "A simple plan to solve all of America's problems," *The Atlantic*, January 12, 2022.

40. D. Rodrik, R. Juhasz, and N. Lane, "Economists reconsider industrial policy," Project Syndicate, August 4, 2023.

41. M. Mazzucato, *The Value of Everything: Making and Taking in the Global Economy* (New York: PublicAffairs, 2018).

42. J. Miscik, P. Orszag, and T. Bunzel, "Geopolitics in the C-suite," *Foreign Affairs*, March 11, 2024.

43. S. Kelton, "The failure of austerity: Rethinking fiscal policy," in *Rethinking Capitalism: Economics and Policy for Sustainable and Inclusive Growth*, ed. M. Jacobs and M. Mazzucato (Oxford, UK: Wiley-Blackwell, 2016): 28–46.

44. Kelton, "The failure of austerity."

45. S. Kelton, *The Deficit Myth: Modern Monetary Theory and the Birth of the People's Economy* (New York: PublicAffairs, 2020).

46. Kelton, *The Deficit Myth.*

47. D. Zenghelis, "Decarbonization: Innovation and the economics of climate change," in *Rethinking Capitalism: Economics and Policy for Sustainable and Inclusive Growth*, ed. M. Jacobs and M. Mazzucato (Oxford, UK: Wiley-Blackwell, 2016): 172–190.

48. Jacobs and Mazzucato, "Introduction," 20.

49. A. Hoffman, P. D. Jennings, and N. Poggioli, "Institutional policies for a healthy Anthropocene society," *Behavioral Science & Policy* 7, no. 2 (2021): 111–127.

50. K. S. Robinson, *The Ministry for the Future: A Novel* (London: Orbit Books, 2020).

51. T. Hale, *Long Problems: Climate Change and the Challenge of Governing Across Time* (Princeton, NJ: Princeton University Press, 2024).

52. J. Kavanagh and M. Rich, *Truth Decay: An Initial Exploration of the Diminishing Role of Facts and Analysis in American Public Life* (Santa Monica, CA: RAND Corporation, 2018).

53. J. Madison, "Letter to W.T. Barry," August 4, 1822, in *The Writings of James Madison, Volume 9 (1819–1836)*, ed. Gaillard Hunt (New York: Putnam, 1900).

54. *A Vision for Sustainable Consumption* (Washington, DC: World Business Council for Sustainable Development, 2011).

55. O. Mont, M. Lehner, and C. Dalhammar, "Sustainable consumption through policy intervention—A review of research themes," *Frontiers in Sustainability* 3 (2022): 921477.

56. Hale, *Long Problems.*

57. B. Hope and N. Friedman, "Climate change is forcing the insurance industry to recalculate," *Wall Street Journal*, October 2, 2018.

58. "Regulating fisheries subsidies," United Nations Conference on Trade and Development, https://unctad.org/project/regulating-fisheries-subsidies (accessed January 14, 2024).

59. S. Black, I. Parry, and N. Vernon, "Fossil fuel subsidies surged to record $7 trillion," *IMF Blog*, August 24, 2023.

60. R. Bousso, "Big oil doubles profits in blockbuster 2022," Reuters, February 8, 2023.

61. M. Salter, "Crony capitalism, American style: What are we talking about here?" Harvard Business School, Working Paper 15–025, October 22.

62. B. Lindsey and S. Teles, *The Captured Economy: How the Powerful Enrich Themselves, Slow Down Growth, and Increase Inequality* (Oxford, UK: Oxford University Press, 2017).

63. B. Lindsey, "The conservative inequality paradox," *National Review,* November 7, 2017.

64. D. D'Amato, "Don't confuse the free market with crony capitalism," The Hill, March 30, 2017.

65. L. Saad, "Americans decry power of lobbyists, corporations, banks, feds," Gallup, April 11, 2011.

66. N. Gross, "Is the United States Government too big?" *The New York Times,* May 11, 2018.

67. J. Taylor, "The alternative to ideology," Niskanen Center, https://www. niskanencenter.org/the-alternative-to-ideology/ (accessed December 1, 2023).

68. Taylor, J. "The alternative to ideology."

69. Taylor, "The alternative to ideology."

70. Oreskes and Conway, *The Big Myth,* 420.

71. P. Chiariello, "8 economic indicators. Are red or blue states better?" *Applied Sentience,* July 30, 2020.

72. M. Muro and J. Whiton, "America has two economies—and they're diverging fast," *Brookings* (blog) September 19, 2019, https://www.brookings.edu/articles/america-has-two-economies-and-theyre-diverging-fast/ (accessed August 13, 2024).

73. J. Klement, "Red states, blue states: Two economies, one nation," *Enterprising Investor,* March 13, 2018.

74. Chiariello, "8 economic indicators."

Chapter 11

1. R. Reeves, "Capitalism used to promise a better future. Can it still do that?" *Brookings,* June 5, 2019, https://www.brookings.edu/articles/capitalism-used-to -promise-a-better-future-can-it-still-do-that/ (accessed August 13, 2024).

2. S. Ghoshal, "Bad management theories are destroying good management practices," *Academy of Management Learning & Education* 4, no. 1 (2005): 75–91.

3. T. Kuhn, *The Structure of Scientific Revolutions* (Chicago: University of Chicago Press, 1962).

4. G. Kavlak, J. McNerney, and J. Trancik, "Evaluating the causes of cost reduction in photovoltaic modules," *Energy Policy* 123 (2018): 700–710.

5. Center for Climate and Energy Solutions, "Renewable energy," https://www.c2es .org/content/renewable-energy/ (accessed December 9, 2023).

6. B. Lillian, "DOE report confirms wind energy costs at all-time lows," *North American Windpower,* August 15, 2019.

7. US Energy Information Administration, "Electric power monthly," March 26, 2024. https://www.eia.gov/electricity/monthly/ (accessed April 3, 2024).

8. S. Hanegreefs, "Technology alone won't save us from the climate crisis, researcher says," *Phys.org,* January 26, 2024.

9. J. Allwood, "Technology will not solve the problem of climate change," *Financial Times,* November 16, 2021.

10. J. Ehrenfeld, "Beware moral hazards, systems blindness, and shifting the

burden," *The Way to Flourish*, December 14, 2015, https://www.johnehrenfeld.com/2015/12/14/beware_moral_hazards_systems_b/.

11. B. McKibben, "Not so fast," *New York Times Magazine*, July 23, 1995: 24, 25.

12. R. Carson, *Silent Spring* (Boston: Houghton Mifflin, 1962).

13. R. Carson, "Speech in acceptance of the Schweitzer Medal of the Animal Welfare Institute," quoted in P. Brooks, *The House of Life: Rachel Carson at Work* (Boston: Houghton Mifflin, 1972): 316.

14. A. Hoffman, "Climate change and our emerging cultural shift," *Behavioral Scientist*, September 30, 2019.

15. S. Simard, *Finding the Mother Tree: Discovering the Wisdom of the Forest* (New York: Knopf, 2021).

16. R. Powers, *The Overstory* (New York: W.W. Norton, 2018).

17. R. Costanza et al., "The value of the world's ecosystem services and natural capital," *Nature* 387 (May 15, 1997): 253–260.

18. D. H. Meadows, D. L. Meadows, J. Randers, and W. Behrens, *The Limits to Growth* (Dulles, VA: Potomac Associates Books, 1972).

19. B. Alcott, "Jevons' paradox," *Ecological Economics* 54, no. 1 (2005): 9–21.

20. D. Acemoglu, A. He, and D. Le Maire, *Eclipse of Rent-Sharing: The Effects of Managers' Business Education on Wages and the Labor Share in the US and Denmark* (No. W29874). National Bureau of Economic Research, 2022.

21. W. Magnuson, *For Profit: A History of Corporations* (New York: Basic Books, 2022): 10–11.

22. K. Arrow and G. Debreu, "Existence of an equilibrium for a competitive economy," *Econometrica* 22, no. 3 (1954): 265–290.

23. A. Sen, *Collective Choice and Social Welfare* (Cambridge, MA: Harvard University Press, 2018): 68–69.

24. N. Stern, *The Economics of Climate Change: The Stern Review* (Cambridge, UK: Cambridge University Press, 2007).

25. A. Cifuentes and D. Espinoza, "Infrastructure investing and the peril of discounted cash flow," *Financial Times*, November 3, 2016.

26. F. Ramsey, "A mathematical theory of saving," *The Economic Journal* 38, no. 152 (1928): 543–559.

27. R. Harrod, *Towards a Dynamic Economics* (London: Macmillan, 1948): 40.

28. R. Solow, "An almost practical step towards sustainability," *Resources*, August 23, 2019.

29. J. Fox, "The economics of well-being," *Harvard Business Review*, January-February 2012.

30. D. Leonhardt, "Why you shouldn't believe those GDP numbers," *New York Times*, December 15, 2019.

31. Bobby Kennedy captured the flaws in GDP during a speech at University of Kansas in 1968. "Even if we act to erase poverty, there is another greater task, it is to confront the poverty of satisfaction—purpose and dignity—that afflicts us all. Too much and for too long, we seemed to have surrendered personal excellence and com-

munity values in the mere accumulation of material things. Our Gross National Product, now, is over $800 billion dollars a year, but that Gross National Product—if we judge the United States of America by that—that Gross National Product counts air pollution and cigarette advertising, and ambulances to clear our highways of carnage. It counts special locks for our doors and the jails for the people who break them. It counts the destruction of the redwood and the loss of our natural wonder in chaotic sprawl. It counts napalm and counts nuclear warheads and armored cars for the police to fight the riots in our cities. It counts Whitman's rifle and Speck's knife, and the television programs which glorify violence in order to sell toys to our children. Yet the gross national product does not allow for the health of our children, the quality of their education or the joy of their play. It does not include the beauty of our poetry or the strength of our marriages, the intelligence of our public debate or the integrity of our public officials. It measures neither our wit nor our courage, neither our wisdom nor our learning, neither our compassion nor our devotion to our country, it measures everything in short, except that which makes life worthwhile. And it can tell us everything about America except why we are proud that we are Americans." Source: R. Kennedy, "Remarks at the University of Kansas," March 18, 1968, https://www.jfkli brary.org/learn/about-jfk/the-kennedy-family/robert-f-kennedy/robert-f-kennedy -speeches/remarks-at-the-university-of-kansas-march-18-1968 (accessed December 4, 2023).

32. A. Hoffman, *Management as a Calling: Leading Business, Serving Society* (Stanford, CA: Stanford University Press, 2021).

33. K. Ehrhardt-Martinez, "Social determinants of deforestation in developing countries: A cross-national study," *Social Forces* 77, no. 2 (1998): 567–586.

34. World Health Organization, "Valuing health for all: Rethinking and building a whole of-society approach," 2022, https://cdn.who.int/media/docs/default-source/ council-on-the-economics-of-health-for-all/who_councilbrief3.pdf (accessed December 6, 2023).

35. J. Stiglitz, "It's time to retire metrics like GDP. They don't measure everything that matters," *The Guardian*, November 24, 2019.

36. A. Banerjee and E. Duflo, *Good Economics for Hard Times* (New York: PublicAffairs, 2019).

37. A. Annett, *Cathonomics: How Catholic Tradition Can Create a More Just Economy* (Washington, DC: Georgetown University Press, 2022): 126.

38. D. Rotman, "Capitalism is in crisis. To save it, we need to rethink economic growth," *Technology Review*, October 14, 2020.

39. M. Kirk, "It's time to move beyond growth for growth's sake," *Aeon Ideas*, November 27, 2015.

40. J. Stiglitz, A. Sen, and J. Fitoussi, *Mismeasuring Our Lives: Why GDP Doesn't Add Up* (New York: The New Press, 2010).

41. M. Chussil, "'Rally the troops' and other business metaphors you can do without," *Harvard Business Review*, November 24, 2016.

42. G. Stalk, R. Lachenauer, and J. Butman, *Hardball: Are You Playing to Play or Playing to Win?* (Cambridge, MA: Harvard Business Review Press, 2004).

43. G. Stalk and R. Lachenauer, "Hardball: Five killer strategies for trouncing the competition," *Harvard Business Review*, April 2004.

44. Chussil, "'Rally the troops'."

45. N. Barker, D. Ely, N. Galvin, A. Shapiro, and A. Watts, *Enacting Systems Change: Pre-Competitive Collaboration to Address Persistent Problems* (Ann Arbor, MI: University of Michigan Ross School of Business, 2021).

46. J. Stiglitz, "The overselling of globalization," Roosevelt Institute Working Paper, August 2017.

47. A. Chatzky, J. McBride, and M. Sergie, "NAFTA and the USMCA: Weighing the impact of North American trade," *Council on Foreign Relations*, July 1, 2020.

48. J. Fullerton, *Regenerative Capitalism: How Universal Principles and Patterns Will Shape Our New Economy*, The Capital Institute, April 2015.

49. G. Soros, *The Crisis of Global Capitalism: Open Society Endangered* (New York: PublicAffairs, 1998).

50. "Let them eat pollution," *The Economist*, February 8, 1992: 66.

51. L. Summers, Letters: "Polluting the poor," *The Economist*, February 15, 1992: 6.

52. H. Farrell and A. Newman, "Chained to globalization: Why it's too late to decouple," *Foreign Affairs*, January-February 2020.

53. H&M is a major player in the fast fashion industry, which the United Nations Economic Commission for Europe says has led to an "environmental and social emergency." The clothing industry is responsible for about 10 percent of global greenhouse gas emissions and consumes more energy than aviation and shipping combined.

54. As quoted in J. Lee, "H&M CEO: Reducing consumption isn't the answer," *Triple Pundit*, February 5, 2015.

55. J. B. MacKinnon, *The Day the World Stops Shopping: How Ending Consumerism Saves the Environment and Ourselves* (New York: HarperCollins, 2021).

56. P. Farrell, "Myth of perpetual growth is killing America," *Wall Street Journal*, June 12, 2012.

57. T. Malthus, "An essay on the principles of population," in *British Society and Politics*, ed. J.F.C. Harrison (New York: Harper & Row, 1965 [1798]).

58. P. Ehrlich, *The Population Bomb* (New York: Balantine, 1968).

59. D. Meadows, D. Meadows, and J. Randers, *Beyond the Limits* (Post Mills, VT: Chelsea Green, 1992): jacket.

60. Meadows, Meadows, Randers, *Beyond the Limits*.

61. H. Daly, *Economics for a Full World*, speech delivered on the occasion of the Blue Planet Prize, Tokyo, November 2014.

62. M. Hood, "Global resource consumption tops 100 bn tonnes for first time," Phys.org, January 21, 2020.

63. "Global CO_2 emissions rebounded to their highest level in history in 2021," *International Energy Agency*, March 8, 2022.

64. "Nine breakthroughs for climate and nature in 2023 you may have missed." BBC News, December 14, 2023.

65. United Nations, *Ecosystems and Human Well-Being: General Synthesis* (Washington, DC: Island Press, 2005).

66. United Nations, "FAO warns 90 per cent of Earth's topsoil at risk by 2050," Food and Agriculture Organization, July 27, 2022.

67. R. Harrington, "By 2050, the oceans could have more plastic than fish," *Business Insider*, January 26, 2017.

68. C. Román-Palacios and J. Wiens, "Recent responses to climate change reveal the drivers of species extinction and survival," *PNAS* 117, no. 8 (2020): 4211–4217.

69. E. Roston, "Climate projections again point to dangerous 2.7°C rise by 2100," *Bloomberg*, November 10, 2022.

70. "This is what 3°C of global warming looks like," *The Economist*, October 30, 2021.

71. As quoted in E. Crooks, "Prosperity without growth," *The Financial Times*, November 22, 2009.

72. N. Wolchover, "How many people can Earth support?" NBC News, October 11, 2011.

73. S. Dovers and C. Butler, "How many people can Earth actually support?" *Australian Academy of Science*, https://www.science.org.au/curious/earth-environment/how-many-people-can-earth-actually-support (accessed December 6, 2023).

74. D. Vollrath, *Fully Grown: Why a Stagnant Economy Is a Sign of Success* (Chicago: University of Chicago Press, 2019).

75. J. Stiglitz, "Is growth passé?" *Project Syndicate*, December 9, 2019.

76. The Global Commission on the Economy and Climate, *Unlocking the Inclusive Growth Story of the 21st Century: Accelerating Climate Action in Urgent Times*, The New Climate Economy, 2018.

77. D. Saha and J. Jaeger, "Ranking 41 US states decoupling emissions and GDP growth," *World Resources Institute*, July 28, 2020.

78. Z. Hausfather, *Absolute Decoupling of Economic Growth and Emissions in 32 Countries*, The Breakthrough Institute, 2021.

79. J. Hickel and G. Kallis, "Is green growth possible?" *New Political Economy* 25, no. 4 (2020): 469–486.

80. J. Hickel et al., "Urgent need for post-growth climate mitigation scenarios," *Nature Energy* 6 (2021): 766–768.

81. T. Jackson, *Prosperity Without Growth: Foundations for the Economy of Tomorrow* (Abingdon, UK: Routledge, 2017).

82. As quoted in L. Busk, "Degrowth and the future of capitalism: A critical review of recent literature," *Emancipations: A Journal of Critical Social Analysis* 2, no. 1 (2023): Article 10.

83. As quoted in E. Crooks, "Prosperity without Growth," *The Financial Times*, November 22, 2009.

84. As quoted in J. Cassidy, "Can we have prosperity without growth?" *The New Yorker*, February 3, 2020.

85. F. DeMaria, F. Schneider, F. Sekulova, and J. Martinez-Alier, "What is degrowth? From an activist slogan to a social movement," *Environmental Values* 22, no. 2 (2013): 191–215.

86. T. Roulet and J. Bothello, "Why 'de-growth' shouldn't scare businesses," *Harvard Business Review*, February 14, 2020.

87. P. Moati, "L'utopie écologique séduit les Français." *Le Monde*, November 21, 2019.

88. As quoted in A. Westervelt, "Ad industry grapples with role selling consumption in climate crisis," *The Guardian*, November 21, 2023.

89. G. Kallis, *Degrowth* (New York: Columbia University Press, 2018): 1.

90. K. Rysddal, "Unilever CEO: For sustainable business, go against 'mindless consumption,'" *Marketplace*, June 11, 2013.

91. J. B. MacKinnon, *The Day the World Stops Shopping: How Ending Consumerism Saves the Environment and Ourselves* (New York: Harper-Collins, 2021): 117.

92. P. Kingsnorth, "Want is the acid," *Substack*, September 15, 2021.

93. Ethos, "What to know about marketing to LOHAS food and beverage consumers," https://www.ethos-marketing.com/blog/reach-market-to-lohas/ (accessed December 8, 2023).

94. S. Oshione, "LOHAS market research," *Wonder*, 2022, https://askwonder.com/research/lohas-market-research-brgpmi96r (accessed December 8, 2023).

95. World Business Council for Sustainable Development, *A Vision for Sustainable Consumption* (Geneva, Switzerland: WBCSD, 2011).

96. D. Grometa, H. Kunreuthera, and R. Larrick, "Political ideology affects energy-efficiency attitudes and choices," *Proceedings of the National Academy of Sciences* 110, no. 23 (2013): 9314–9319.

97. K. White, D. Hardisty, and R. Habib, "The elusive green consumer," *Harvard Business Review*, July-August, 2019.

98. Patagonia Common Threads, https://www.patagonia.com/blog/2011/09/introducing-the-common-threads-initiative/ (accessed July 3, 2024).

99. D. Lear, "Eliminating ocean plastic pollution must be a commercial and global priority," *The National*, November 14, 2018.

100. Westervelt, "Ad industry grapples with role selling consumption in climate crisis."

101. S. Low et al., *Trends in U.S. Local and Regional Food Systems*, AP-068, U.S. Department of Agriculture, Economic Research Service, January 2015.

102. Center for Sustainable Systems, University of Michigan, *U.S. Food System Factsheet*, 2023, Pub. No. CSS01–06.

103. Center for Sustainable Systems, *U.S. Food System Factsheet*.

104. A. Lowrey, "The human cost of chicken farming," *The Atlantic*, November 11, 2019.

105. J. Ehrenfeld and A. Hoffman, *Flourishing: A Frank Conversation on Sustainability* (Stanford, CA: Stanford University Press, 2013).

106. A. Edmondson, *Right Kind of Wrong: The Science of Failing Well* (New York: Atria Books, 2023): 108.

107. J. Atwater, "Teaching systemic thinking: Educating the next generation of business leaders," *The Systems Thinker*, November 23, 2015.

108. M. Morganelli, *What Is Systems Thinking?* Southern New Hampshire University, March 18, 2020.

109. P. Senge, *The Fifth Discipline: The Art & Practice of the Learning Organization* (New York: Doubleday, 1990).

110. M. Fischoff, "Business schools can use systems thinking for sustainability," *Network for Business Sustainability*, May 19, 2023.

111. A. Edmondson, *Right Kind of Wrong*.

112. J. Fullerton, *Regenerative Capitalism: How Universal Principles and Patterns Will Shape Our New Economy*, The Capital Institute, 2015.

113. J. Stephens, "Regenerative economy," Soul Self Living, March 12, 2016.

114. J. Fullerton, "Regenerative economies for a regenerative civilization," *Kosmos*, Fall-Winter 2015.

115. Fullerton, *Regenerative Capitalism*.

116. Olin College of Engineering, "Strategic plan: Impact-centered education, 2022–2027," https://www.olin.edu/about-presidents-office/strategic-plan-2022-2027 (accessed December 9, 2023).

117. Ross School of Business, Center for Positive Organizations, https://positiveorgs.bus.umich.edu/ (accessed July 3, 2024).

118. C. Bader and W. Longhofer, "This long-standing tenet of American capitalism must change—now," *Ensia*, September 24, 2020.

Chapter 12

1. D. F. Wallace, "This is water," Commencement address at Kenyon College, https://fs.blog/david-foster-wallace-this-is-water/ (accessed December 10, 2023).

2. H. Shepard, "On realization of human potential: A path with a heart," in *Working with Careers*, ed. M. Arthur et al. (New York: Columbia University, 1984): 25–46.

3. W. Deresiewicz, *Excellent Sheep: The Miseducation of the American Elite and the Way to a Meaningful Life* (New York: Free Press, 2014): 1.

4. Deresiewicz, *Excellent Sheep*.

5. V. Frankl, *Man's Search for Meaning* (Boston: Beacon Press, 2006): 93.

6. J. Doyle, "Wall Street's Gekko, 1980s–2010," *The Pop History Dig*, February 4, 2010, https://pophistorydig.com/topics/wall-streets-gekko-1980s-2010/ (accessed December 10, 2023).

7. A. Vedel and D. Thomsen, "The dark triad across academic majors," *Personality and Individual Differences* 116 (2017): 86–91.

8. J. Elegido, "Business education and erosion of character," *African Journal of Business Ethics* 4, no. 1 (2009).

9. V. Krishnan, "Impact of MBA education on students' values: Two longitudinal studies," *Journal of Business Ethics* 83 (2008): 233–246.

10. R. Racko, "The values of economics," *Journal of Business Ethics* 154 (2019): 35–48.

11. L. Wang, C. Zhong, and K. Murnighan, "The social and ethical consequences of a calculative mindset," *Organizational Behavior and Human Decision Processes* 125, no. 1 (2014): 39–49.

12. L. Wang, D. Malhotra, and K. Murnighan, "Economics education and greed," *Academy of Management Learning & Education* 10, no. 4 (2011): 643–660.

13. R. Racko, "The values of economics," *Journal of Business Ethics* 154 (2019): 35–48.

14. A. Annett, "Restoring ethics to economics," International Monetary Fund, March 2018, https://www.imf.org/en/Publications/fandd/issues/2018/03/point2 (accessed December 10, 2023).

15. E. Anderson, *Private Government: How Employers Rule Our Lives (and Why We Don't Talk About It)* (Princeton, NJ: Princeton University Press, 2017).

16. S. Marglin, *The Dismal Science: How Thinking Like an Economist Undermines Community* (Cambridge, MA: Harvard University Press, 2010): jacket.

17. S. Ghoshal, "Bad management theories are destroying good management practices," *Academy of Management Learning & Education* 4, no. 1 (2005): 75–91.

18. R. Frank, T. Gilovich, and D. Regan, "Does studying economics inhibit cooperation?" *Journal of Economic Perspectives* 7, no. 2 (1993): 159–171.

19. L. Zingales, "Do business schools incubate criminals?" *Bloomberg*, July 16, 2012.

20. S. Murray, "MBA teaching urged to move away from focus on shareholder primacy model," *Financial Times*, July 7, 2013.

21. Ghoshal, "Bad management theories."

22. A. Annett, *Cathonomics: How Catholic Tradition Can Create a More Just Economy* (Washington, DC: Georgetown University Press, 2022).

23. E. F. Schumacher, *Small Is Beautiful: A Study of Economics as If People Mattered* (New York: HarperPerennial, 1973): 42.

24. J. Evans, "Groups are the driving force of human evolution, Edward Wilson says," Phys.Org, April 9, 2012.

25. L. Caporael, R. Dawes, J. Orbelland, and A. Van de Kragt, "Selfishness examined: Cooperation in the absence of egoistic incentives," *Behavioral and Brain Sciences* 12, no. 4 (1989): 683–699.

26. E. Ostrom, *Governing the Commons: The Evolution of Institutions for Collective Action* (Cambridge, UK: Cambridge University Press, 1990).

27. As quoted in S. Pearlstein, *Can American Capitalism Survive?* (New York: St. Martin's Press, 2018): 41.

28. Some have disputed the authenticity of this story. Regardless, it illustrates an interesting insight on human cooperation.

29. R. Blumenfeld, "How a 15,000-year-old human bone could help you through the coronacrisis," *Forbes*, March 21, 2020.

30. R. Bregman, *Humankind: A Hopeful History* (New York: Back Bay Books; Little, Brown, 2020): 69.

31. D. Rand, J. Greene, and M. Nowak, "Spontaneous giving and calculated greed," *Nature* 489 (2012): 427–430.

32. D. Rand, "Cooperation, fast and slow: Meta-analytic evidence for a theory of social heuristics and self-interested deliberation." *Psychological Science* 27, no. 9 (2016): 1192–1206.

33. M. Hutson, "Selfishness is learned," *Nautilus*, May 27, 2016.

34. J. Henrich, R. Boyd, S. Bowles, C. Camerer, E. Fehr, H. Gintis, and R. McElreath, "In search of homo economicus: Behavioral experiments in 15 small-scale societies," *American Economic Review* 91, no. 2 (2001): 73–78.

35. Annett, "Restoring ethics to economics."

36. Hutson, "Selfishness is learned."

37. Bregman, *Humankind*, 47.

38. The eighteenth-century Genevan philosopher Jean Jacques Rousseau offered a different view, arguing that moral behavior is innate and that the controlling forces that Hobbes endorsed were the problem. "Man is naturally good, and that it is from these institutions alone that men become wicked."

39. As quoted in Bregman, *Humankind*, 71.

40. D. Miller, "The norm of self-interest," *American Psychologist* 54, no. 12 (1999): 1053–1060.

41. As quoted in Miller, "The norm of self-interest."

42. Bregman, *Humankind*.

43. A. Jack, "The rise of the 'sustainable' MBA," *Financial Times*, January 21, 2020.

44. J. Moules, "MBA students seek higher 'purpose' than mere money," *Financial Times*, October 20, 2019.

45. C. Duhigg, "Wealthy, successful and miserable: The upper echelon is hoarding money and privilege to a degree not seen in decades. But that doesn't make them happy at work," *New York Times*, February 21, 2019.

46. Schumacher, *Small Is Beautiful*, 54.

47. Annett, *Cathonomics*, 72.

48. T. Durand and S. Dameron, "Where have all the business schools gone?" *British Journal of Management* 22, no. 3 (2011): 559–563.

49. S. Datar, D. Garvin, and P. Cullen, "Rethinking the MBA: Business education at a crossroads," *Journal of Management Development* 30, no. 5 (2011): 451–462.

50. S. B. Banerjee, "Decolonizing management theory: A critical perspective," *Journal of Management Studies* 59, no. 4 (2022): 1074–1087.

51. I. Wylie, "What Generation Z wants from a business masters," *Financial Times*, September 4, 2022.

52. As quoted in S. Steiner, "Top five regrets of the dying," *The Guardian*, February 1, 2012.

53. G. Bluerock, "The 9 most common regrets people have at the end of life," *mdgmindfulness*, 2023, https://www.mindbodygreen.com/articles/the-most-common-regrets-people-have-at-the-end-of-life (accessed December 10, 2023).

54. C. Niemiec, R. Ryan, and E. Deci, "The path taken: Consequences of attaining intrinsic and extrinsic aspirations in post-college life," *Journal of Research in Personality* 43, no. 3 (2009), 291–306.

55. T. Kasser and R. Ryan, "Further examining the American dream: Differential correlates of intrinsic and extrinsic goals," *Personality and Social Psychology Bulletin* 22, no. 3 (1996): 280–287.

56. T. Kasser and R. Ryan, "A dark side of the American dream: Correlates of fi-

nancial success as a central life aspiration," *Journal of Personality and Social Psychology* 65, no. 2 (1993): 410.

57. P. Palmer, "Leading from within," in *Let Your Life Speak*, Chap. 5 (San Francisco: Jossey-Bass, 2000): 4.

58. D. Brooks, "The moral bucket list," *New York Times*, April 11, 2015.

59. D. Brooks, "How America got mean," *The Atlantic*, August 14, 2023.

60. B. McClellan, *Moral Education in America: Schools and the Shaping of Character from Colonial Times to the Present* (New York: Teachers College Press, 1999).

61. I. McGilchrist, *The Master and His Emissary: The Divided Brain and the Making of the Western World* (New Haven, CT: Yale University Press, 2009): 93.

62. J. Ehrenfeld, "To reach flourishing, turn right sharply at the next corner," *Journal of Management, Spirituality and Religion*, 2023, https://doi.org/10.51327/ODQL3210.

63. F. C. Tsao, "The science of life and wellbeing: Integrating the new science of consciousness with the ancient science of consciousness," *Journal of Management, Spirituality & Religion* 18, no. 6 (2021): 7–18.

64. C. Reincke, A. Bredenoord, and M. van Mil, "From deficit to dialogue in science communication: The dialogue communication model requires additional roles from scientists," *EMBO Reports* 21, no. 9 (2020): e51278.

65. H. Mintzberg, *Managers Not MBAs: A Hard Look at the Soft Practice of Managing and Management Development* (Oakland, CA: Berrett-Koehler, 2005).

66. R. Ackoff, "From data to wisdom," *Journal of Applied Systems Analysis* 16, no. 1 (1989): 3–9.

67. A. Hoffman, "Management as a calling," *Stanford Social Innovation Review*, September 4, 2018.

68. J. Gamble, "The most important problem in the world," *Medium*, March 13, 2019.

69. Wallace, "This Is water."

70. D. Brooks, *The Second Mountain: The Quest for a Moral Life* (New York: Random House, 2019): 199.

71. H. Shepard, "On realization of human potential: A path with a heart," in *Working with Careers*, ed. M. Arthur, L. Bailyn, D. Levinson, and H. Shepard (New York: Center for Research on Careers, Graduate School of Business, Columbia University, 1984): 25.

72. As quoted in L. Mooney, "James March: What Don Quixote teaches us about leadership," *Insights by Stanford Business*, February 19, 2014, https://www.gsb.stanford .edu/insights/james-march-what-don-quixote-teaches-us-about-leadership (accessed December 10, 2023).

73. V. Strecher, *Life on Purpose: How Living for What Matters Most Changes Everything* (New York: Harper One, 2016).

74. Annett, *Cathonomics*, 153.

75. As quoted in C. Riback, "Joseph Stiglitz: Saving capitalism from itself, *Chris Riback's Conversations*, June 21, 2019, https://chrisriback.com/joseph-stiglitz-saving -capitalism-from-itself/ (accessed December 8, 2023).

76. P. Polman, "2023 net positive employee barometer: From quiet quitting to con-

scious quitting," 2023, https://www.paulpolman.com/wp-content/uploads/2023/02/MC_Paul-Polman_Net-Positive-Employee-Barometer_Final_web.pdf (accessed October 24, 2023).

77. "The Global Energy Talent Index report 2022," https://www.getireport.com/reports/2022/ (accessed January 3, 2024).

78. S. Thomas-Oxtoby, "MBA grads reliably earn a six-figure salary in these 6 industries," *Fortune Education*, May 5, 2023.

79. S. Lake, "Base salaries for MBA grads at top consulting firms are nearing $200K in 2023," *Fortune Education*, January 20, 2023.

80. J. Bivens and J. Kandra, "CEO pay has skyrocketed 1,460% since 1978," *Economic Policy Institute*, October 4, 2022.

81. R. Reich, "Philanthropy in the service of democracy," *Stanford Social Innovation Review*, Winter 2019.

82. Bregman, *Humankind*, 19.

83. W. Damon, *Noble Purpose: Joy of Living a Meaningful Life* (Conshohocken, PA: Templeton Press, 2003).

84. As quoted in M. Rozsa, "Insulin used to be affordable—and then, seemingly out of nowhere, it wasn't. Why?" *Salon*, November 16, 2022.

85. As quoted in B. Palmer, "Jonas Salk: Good at virology, bad at economics," *Slate*, April 13, 2014.

86. As quoted in C. Risen, "Aaron Feuerstein, mill owner who refused to leave, dies at 95," *New York Times*, November 5, 2021.

87. As quoted in N. Paumgarten, "Patagonia's philosopher king," *The New Yorker*, September 12, 2016.

88. As quoted in A. Folley, "Patagonia calls Trump tax cut 'irresponsible,' says it will donate $10M corporate tax cut to environmental groups," The Hill, November 28, 2018.

89. On a personal level, I was once stranded on a southern Japanese island because of an incoming typhoon. The hotel where I was staying was fully booked so the manager, who spoke no English, took me to a hotel with a vacancy. Rather than exploiting the fact that I had no options, that hotel charged a "typhoon rate" which was in fact lower, not higher than standard. My business school colleagues have trouble comprehending the logic behind such a decision. And frankly, I still marvel that they did that.

90. D. Lund and L. Strine Jr., "Corporate political spending is bad business," *Harvard Business Review*, January-February 2022.

91. As quoted in G. James, "Why Unilever stopped issuing quarterly reports," *Inc.*, January 23, 2018.

92. "Business & politics: Do they mix? GSG's fourth annual study," *Global Strategy Group*, 2016, https://globalstrategygroup.com/2016/12/06/business-politics-mix-gsgs-fourth-annual-study/ (accessed December 14, 2023).

93. A. Hoffman, "Business education as if people and the planet really matter," *Strategic Organization* 19, no. 3 (2021): 513–525.

Index

Page numbers in italics refer to figures and tables.